THE CLAY SANSKRIT LIBRARY

FOUNDED BY JOHN & JENNIFER CLAY

WWW.CLAYSANSKRITLIBRARY.COM

WWW.NYUPRESS.ORG

First Edition 2006.

The Clay Sanskrit Library is co-published by
New York University Press
and the JJC Foundation.

Further information about this volume
and the rest of the Clay Sanskrit Library
is available on the following websites:
www.claysanskritlibrary.com
www.nyupress.org.

ISBN-13: 978-0-8147-6723-8 (cloth : alk. paper)
ISBN-10: 0-8147-6723-0 (cloth : alk. paper)

Artwork by Robert Beer.
Typeset in Adobe Garamond at 10.25 : 12.3+pt.
XML-development by Stuart Brown.
Editorial input by Dániel Balogh, Tomoyuki Kono,
Eszter Somogyi & Péter Szántó.
Printed in Great Britain by St Edmundsbury Press Ltd,
Bury St Edmunds, Suffolk, on acid-free paper.
Bound by Hunter & Foulis, Edinburgh, Scotland.

MAHĀBHĀRATA
BOOK SEVEN

DROṆA
VOLUME ONE

EDITED AND TRANSLATED BY

VAUGHAN PILIKIAN

NEW YORK UNIVERSITY PRESS
JJC FOUNDATION
2006

Library of Congress Cataloging-in-Publication Data
Mahābhārata. Droṇaparvan. English & Sanskrit.
Mahabharata. Book seven, Drona /
translated by Vaughan Pilikian. – 1st ed.
p. cm. – (The Clay Sanskrit library)
Includes bibliographical references and index.
Epic poetry.
In English and Sanskrit (romanized) on facing pages;
includes translation from Sanskrit.
ISBN-13: 978-0-8147-6723-8 (cloth : alk. paper)
ISBN-10: 0-8147-6723-0 (cloth : alk. paper)
I. Title. II. Title: Drona.
BL1138.242.D76E5 2006
294.5'92304521–dc22 2006022412

CONTENTS

A *sandhi* grid is printed on the inside of the back cover

SANSKRIT ALPHABETICAL ORDER

Vowels:	*a ā i ī u ū ṛ ṝ ḷ ḹ e ai o au ṃ ḥ*
Gutturals:	*k kh g gh ṅ*
Palatals:	*c ch j jh ñ*
Retroflex:	*ṭ ṭh ḍ ḍh ṇ*
Dentals:	*t th d dh n*
Labials:	*p ph b bh m*
Semivowels:	*y r l v*
Spirants:	*ś ṣ s h*

GUIDE TO SANSKRIT PRONUNCIATION

a	b*u*t
ā, â	f*a*ther
i	s*i*t
ī, î	f*ee*
u	p*u*t
ū, û	b*oo*
ṛ	vocalic *r*, American p*ur*dy or English p*re*tty
ṝ	lengthened *ṛ*
ḷ	vocalic *l*, ab*le*
e, ê, ē	m*a*de, esp. in Welsh pronunciation
ai	b*i*te
o, ô, ō	r*o*pe, esp. Welsh pronunciation; Italian s*o*lo
au	s*ou*nd
ṃ	*anusvāra* nasalizes the preceding vowel
ḥ	*visarga*, a voiceless aspiration (resembling English *h*), or like Scottish lo*ch*, or an aspiration with a faint echoing of the preceding vowel so that *taiḥ* is pronounced *taihⁱ*
k	lu*ck*
kh	blo*ckh*ead
g	*g*o
gh	bi*gh*ead
ṅ	a*n*ger
c	*ch*ill
ch	mat*chh*ead
j	*j*og
jh	aspirated *j*, he*dgeh*og
ñ	ca*ny*on
ṭ	retroflex *t*, *t*ry (with the tip of tongue turned up to touch the hard palate)
ṭh	same as the preceding but aspirated
ḍ	retroflex *d* (with the tip of tongue turned up to touch the hard palate)
ḍh	same as the preceding but aspirated
ṇ	retroflex *n* (with the tip

	of tongue turned up to touch the hard palate)
t	French *t*out
th	ten*t h*ook
d	*d*inner
dh	guil*dh*all
n	*n*ow
p	*p*ill
ph	u*ph*eaval
b	*b*efore
bh	a*bh*orrent
m	*m*ind
y	*y*es
r	trilled, resembling the Italian pronunciation of *r*
l	*l*inger
v	*w*ord
ś	*sh*ore
ṣ	retroflex *sh* (with the tip of the tongue turned up to touch the hard palate)
s	hi*ss*
h	*h*ood

CSL PUNCTUATION OF ENGLISH

The acute accent on Sanskrit words when they occur outside of the Sanskrit text itself, marks stress, e.g. Ramáyana. It is not part of traditional Sanskrit orthography, transliteration or transcription, but we supply it here to guide readers in the pronunciation of these unfamiliar words. Since no Sanskrit word is accented on the last syllable it is not necessary to accent disyllables, e.g. Rama.

The second CSL innovation designed to assist the reader in the pronunciation of lengthy unfamiliar words is to insert an unobtrusive middle dot between semantic word breaks in compound names (provided the word break does not fall on a vowel resulting from the fusion of two vowels), e.g. Maha·bhárata, but Ramáyana (not Rama·áyana). Our dot echoes the punctuating middle dot (·) found in the oldest surviving forms of written Indic, the Ashokan inscriptions of the third century BCE.

The deep layering of Sanskrit narrative has also dictated that we use quotation marks only to announce the beginning and end of every direct speech, and not at the beginning of every paragraph.

CSL PUNCTUATION OF SANSKRIT

The Sanskrit text is also punctuated, in accordance with the punctuation of the English translation. In mid-verse, the punctuation will not alter the *sandhi* or the scansion. Proper names are capitalized. Most Sanskrit metres have four "feet" *(pāda):* where possible we print the common *śloka* metre on two lines. In the Sanskrit text, we use French *Guillemets* (e.g. *«kva saṃcicīrṣuḥ?»*) instead of English quotation marks (e.g. "Where are you off to?") to avoid confusion with the apostrophes used for vowel elision in *sandhi.*

Sanskrit presents the learner with a challenge: *sandhi* ("euphonic combination"). *Sandhi* means that when two words are joined in connected speech or writing (which in Sanskrit reflects speech), the last letter (or even letters) of the first word often changes; compare the way we pronounce "the" in "the beginning" and "the end."

In Sanskrit the first letter of the second word may also change; and if both the last letter of the first word and the first letter of the second are vowels, they may fuse. This has a parallel in English: a nasal consonant is inserted between two vowels that would otherwise coalesce: "a pear" and "an apple." Sanskrit vowel fusion may produce ambiguity. The chart at the back of each book gives the full *sandhi* system.

Fortunately it is not necessary to know these changes in order to start reading Sanskrit. For that, what is important is to know the form of the second word without *sandhi* (pre-*sandhi*), so that it can be recognized or looked up in a dictionary. Therefore we are printing Sanskrit with a system of punctuation that will indicate, unambiguously, the original form of the second word, i.e., the form without *sandhi*. Such *sandhi* mostly concerns the fusion of two vowels.

In Sanskrit, vowels may be short or long and are written differently accordingly. We follow the general convention that a vowel with no mark above it is short. Other books mark a long vowel either with a bar called a macron (*ā*) or with a circumflex (*â*). Our system uses the macron, except that for initial vowels in *sandhi* we use a circumflex to indicate that originally the vowel was short, or the shorter of two possibilities (*e* rather than *ai*, *o* rather than *au*).

When we print initial	*â*, before *sandhi* that vowel was	*a*
	î or *ê*,	*i*
	û or *ô*,	*u*
	âi,	*e*
	âu,	*o*

ā,	*ā* (i.e., the same)
ī,	*ī* (i.e., the same)
ū,	*ū* (i.e., the same)
ē,	*ī*
ō,	*ū*
āi,	*ai*
āu,	*au*

', before *sandhi* there was a vowel *a*

FURTHER HELP WITH VOWEL SANDHI

When a final short vowel (*a*, *i* or *u*) has merged into a following vowel, we print ' at the end of the word, and when a final long vowel (*ā*, *ī* or *ū*) has merged into a following vowel we print " at the end of the word. The vast majority of these cases will concern a final *a* or *ā*.

Examples:

What before *sandhi* was *atra asti* is represented as *atr' âsti*

atra āste	*atr' āste*
kanyā asti	*kany" âsti*
kanyā āste	*kany" āste*
atra iti	*atr' êti*
kanyā iti	*kany" êti*
kanyā īpsitā	*kany" ēpsitā*

Finally, three other points concerning the initial letter of the second word:

(1) A word that before *sandhi* begins with *ṛ* (vowel), after *sandhi* begins with *r* followed by a consonant: *yatha" rtu* represents pre-*sandhi* *yathā ṛtu*.

(2) When before *sandhi* the previous word ends in *t* and the following word begins with *ś*, after *sandhi* the last letter of the previous word is *c* and the following word begins with *ch*: *syāc chāstravit* represents pre-*sandhi* *syāt śāstravit*.

(3) Where a word begins with *h* and the previous word ends with a double consonant, this is our simplified spelling to show the pre-*sandhi*

form: *tad hasati* is commonly written as *tad dhasati*, but we write *tadd hasati* so that the original initial letter is obvious.

COMPOUNDS

We also punctuate the division of compounds (*samāsa*), simply by inserting a thin vertical line between words. There are words where the decision whether to regard them as compounds is arbitrary. Our principle has been to try to guide readers to the correct dictionary entries.

EXAMPLE

Where the Deva·nágari script reads:

कुम्भस्थली रक्षतु वो विकीर्णसिन्दूररेणुर्द्विरदाननस्य ।
प्रशान्तये विघ्नतमश्छटानां निष्ठ्यूतबालातपपल्लवेव ॥

Others would print:

kumbhasthalī rakṣatu vo vikīrṇasindūrareṇur dviradānanasya /
praśāntaye vighnatamaśchaṭānāṃ niṣṭhyūtabālātapapallaveva //

We print:

Kumbha|sthalī rakṣatu vo vikīrṇa|sindūra|reṇur dvirad'|ānanasya
praśāntaye vighna|tamaś|chaṭānāṃ niṣṭhyūta|bāl'|ātapa|pallav" êva.

And in English:

"May Ganésha's domed forehead protect you! Streaked with vermilion dust, it seems to be emitting the spreading rays of the rising sun to pacify the teeming darkness of obstructions."

"Nava·sáhasanka and the Serpent Princess" I.3 by Padma·gupta

INTRODUCTION

Night is falling.

M. Heidegger, 'Wozu Dichter?'

THE 'MAHA·BHÁRATA' tells the story of the decline of the descendants of King Bharata into anarchy and bloodshed. The future calamity is set in motion when the great monarch's last unsullied heir, King Shántanu, falls for Sátyavati, the daughter of the chieftain of a lowly tribe of fishermen. Only after Shántanu has persuaded his son Bhishma to abdicate all claim to the throne does the chieftain allow the king to marry his daughter. Shántanu and his new wife have two sons together, but though the younger prince marries twice, both of them die before having children of their own. However, their bereaved mother was no virgin bride: she decides to summon from the wilderness her own illegitimate child, and instructs him to father with the youthful widows an inheritor for the throne. Though they agree to the idea, the women are less than enamored of their husbands' half-brother. In fact, they are both so frightened by the strange eremite that one screws her eyes shut while they have sex, and the other turns white with fear. Both become pregnant; the first gives birth to a blind boy named Dhrita·rashtra and the second to a pale and sickly child called Pandu. Neither seems naturally suited to the role of king. In time, Pandu becomes monarch, but after a series of wars he decides to move to the forest and leaves Dhrita·rashtra to take charge of the imperial city. One day, while out hunting, Pandu shoots a deer as it mates with a doe. Little does he realize, the deer is in fact an ascetic in animal form, and as revenge the recluse curses Pandu to die the moment he tries to make love to a woman. Once again the dynasty is threatened. Taking drastic measures, Pandu's two wives decide to use mantras to invoke the gods as lovers, and Kunti gives birth to children fathered by Dharma, Vayu and Indra, and Madri to twins by the Ashvins. Despite their parentage, these children become misleadingly known as "the Pándavas" or "sons of Pandu," which biologically, at least, they are not. Pandu himself dies when at long last he finds it impossible to resist the charms of his younger wife.

By now, Dhrita·rashtra has also married and his own extraordinary spouse has borne him a hundred sons and one daughter who become known as the Káuravas, "the descendants of Kuru," Shántanu's grandfather. Dhrita·rashtra's eldest child, Duryódhana, has designs on the throne, while Yudhi·shthira, the son of Dharma, firstborn to Pandu's first wife, believes himself to be the rightful heir, and there follows a series of murder plots, broken promises and awkward compromises that culminate in the final absurdity of a dice match that will decide which of them takes the kingdom for himself. Yudhi·shthira proves to be an enthusiastic if unlucky gambler and loses everything, including the Pándavas' shared wife Dráupadi. He and his brothers are forced into a lengthy exile. Thirteen years later, the Pándavas return from the forest, determined to wrest their kingdom back from their cousins by force. Alliances are forged across the land and war is at last declared.

At the beginning of the present volume, we join the action during an uneasy hiatus after ten days of fighting. The warring cousins stand face to face on the battlefield, awestruck by the fall of Bhishma, symbolic patriarch to Káuravas and Pándavas alike. He will spend the rest of the battle a mere spectator, his life ebbing slowly as each day passes. Now it is Drona's turn to take his place as the leader of Duryódhana's armies. Though a brahmin by birth, Drona was once an instructor in the arts of war to both the Pándavas and the Káuravas, and like Bhishma he accepts his post only with a certain reluctance. The fighting begins once more. However, Duryódhana is so desperate to gain ground against the Pándavas that it is not long before he angrily accuses Drona of fighting halfheartedly against his former students. Drona replies that only if the great Pándava warrior Árjuna is removed from the battlefield can he stand any chance of defeating his opponents. The kings of Tri·garta step forward and challenge Árjuna to a duel he cannot refuse, and Drona sets about destroying the army that Árjuna leaves behind him. In response, Yudhi·shthira decides to send his nephew Abhimányu, Árjuna's son, to counter Drona's advance. Eager to please his uncle, Abhimányu sets off for the Káurava line and, breaking through it, causes havoc among Duryódhana's troops. But Abhimányu's achievements take him too far. After a sequence of battles, he finds himself cut off from the rest of the Pándavas, and despite his ferocious determination he is finally overwhelmed by a group of his enemies and killed. Yudhi·shthira realizes too late that he has sent his nephew to an inevitable doom. He is plunged into despair, and the sun sets on a scene of mourning in the Pándava camp.

The children of a blind pretender fighting the sons of a man too frail to risk the act of coition: we seem closer to picaresque than to the hallowed territory of epic. My very compressed account of the narrative from the beginning of the 'Maha·bhárata' up to the end of the present volume might vitiate its subtleties, but it certainly brings out its very modern sense of the absurd. Indeed, the epic is a highly ironic text, a fact rarely remarked upon by its exegetes. Traditionally, the battle scenes that rage without relief through the five books at the heart of the poem have been interpreted as a moral lesson in the incandescently destructive power of worldly greed and desire. This is, in fact, more or less how the dying Bhishma will explain the events of the war in the enormous discourses of Book Twelve. Yet Bhishma will declaim his verdict from a bed of arrows: his words are literally couched in an image whose simple power they cannot, in the end, overcome. Similarly, the 'Bhágavad Gita,' the epic's most famous teaching on action without desire, is recounted moments before the unleashing of a wild and delirious violence inspired by distinctly human passions, an irony further underscored by the fact that it is a figure on one side of this highly partisan conflict who delivers the sacred message of the 'Gita.'

Like all great art, the 'Maha·bhárata' fascinates for reasons we cannot explain. It does not offer simple moral lessons or comforting fables about the world. What it depicts, on a canvas broader than any before or since, is the fecundity and chaos of human life. These may be men and women of legend, but they are figments in a vision that we, as residents of a century millennia after it was first conjured, can still recognize with surprising and perhaps alarming ease. The men and women of the epic are human beings who lie and cheat, deceive one another and themselves, weep, fulminate, scorn and manipulate, and even those supposed exemplars of virtue, Yudhi·shthira and Krishna, are no less part of this human comedy than any of the characters who surround them. What obsess the protagonists in the epic above all else are their immediate worldly concerns. Once the conflict has begun in earnest, these concerns can be reduced to a singular objective: how to win the war, and Káurava and Pándava alike twist all of the resources of action and rhetoric to do so. The price each side pays is enormous. Were we to approach the epic as Aristotelians, we would identify the battle books as the tragic center of its narrative, as in their dense passages the flawed splendor of the epic's cast is displayed in all of its light and darkness. And as the war draws on, it is darkness that predominates.

Everything is fading in the world of the 'Maha·bhárata.' With the onset of war, the very structure of the cosmos, its *dharma*, is giving way. A term such as *dharma* is difficult to translate into English, for the simple reason that we do not have an equivalent everyday notion that infuses our experience of life, the inkling of a force that conserves or upholds the universe as it is and ought to be. Perhaps modernity abolished the idea from our lexicon: the ancient Egyptian *maat* has a meaning far closer to *dharma* than anything in today's English.[1] But what we see in the 'Maha·bhárata' is the dramatization of *a/dharma*, what happens when *dharma* collapses, perhaps what always happens when so vague and ideational a concept comes into contact with human reality.

In the verbal and physical conflicts of the 'Maha·bhárata,' *dharma* is demolished and rebuilt again and again. Yudhi·shthira's name Dharma·raja even shares its etymology with Dhrita·rashtra's, a typical example of the game the epic plays with similarity and difference. In this contest of royal inheritance, the very identities of the rivals seem to blur the distinctions between them, just as their birthlines fade or break in the narrative that has brought them to this point of no return, and just as the fratricide that their rivalry has triggered will now build towards the bizarre closing passages of 'Drona,' when the fighting explodes into a nocturnal massacre where it no longer seems to matter who kills whom.

It is the relentlessness of these scenes that may alienate the reader who comes to them for the first time. The great deluge of blood in the 'Maha·bhárata' is the most prodigious, sustained and devastating vision into the charnel house of human conflict in the history of world literature. The only things remotely like it are the 'Iliad,' the 'Aeneid' and the 'Inferno,' and even their horrors seem almost twee alongside the infinite ferocity of the 'Maha·bhárata'. 'Drona' is in itself a huge text. At first glance, we find scene after scene that seem to blend into one. But there is a definite sequence of events in the book, extending from Drona's accession to the post of commander of the Káurava forces, through Abhimányu's tragic death and the demise of Jayad·ratha and Ghatótkacha, to the cruel deception and beheading of Drona. Concision is not the point; the epic is as much a cultural force as a literary work, and is unencumbered by the niceties of compositional convention that we might expect of it. Yet wound about its events is the undulating texture of the epic's poetry. The reader will find that a certain synesthesia is the inevitable consequence of close association with it—the text can fruitfully be approached like a piece of music, but one in form much closer to the gathering swell of a raga than to the frozen arc of a symphony. The deeper we delve into the detail of what happens, the more is revealed to our eyes and ears. Verses are never repeated precisely but are inflected, recast or transformed, and all the time, line by line, the tale moves on, riverine and enveloping, occasionally meandering gently, at other times twisting suddenly, like the haunted streams of blood that crisscross the plain of Kuru·kshetra.

There is no question in my mind that the battle books yield the finest poetry of the epic. At its best, the language of the 'Maha·bhárata' has a sort of flinty lyricism: notches on a stick rather than the pearls on a necklace of later *kāvya*. One might even go so far as to say that the Indological tradition has suffered a measure of Freudian repression in its need to "solve" the problem of the epic's delight in such scenes by pushing its emphasis towards otherworldly concerns and away from the events within which it is steeped. Cultures across the world, particularly the more civilized, have always enjoyed the spectacle of violence, and in the materialist cosmos of the 'Maha·bhárata' it is the moment at which life is turned into death that is fetishized and that fascinates. There is nothing in the epic that demands redemption. Its action all takes place in a cosmos far from the divided world in which we readers of modern English find ourselves, a molten universe where art and science are still interfused, where gods and men mingle, and comic and cosmic destinies are played out as one. For the battle between the Káuravas and Pándavas is also a celestial war—we are told elsewhere in the epic that the gods have been incarnated in human form to save the earth from the ravages of the demons that hold it captive. Thus the cosmological imagery of the battlefield: warriors rise and set like the sun and arrows fall like monsoon rain. But to call such descriptions mere "similes" is to underplay their significance. The path traced by the warrior from youth through glory to decline is as elemental here as the track of the sun from dawn through noon to dusk. The sun rises every day until the end of time, just as the violence of the warrior's life continues until violent death brings its conclusion. And so the world as an objective realm, as something beyond the self, is driven back. There are no descriptions of the weather: we don't see the landscape, the rain or the moon, only shields, jewels and swords, mirrors for the sun. What we witness in the battle scenes is as natural as the turning of the earth. Yet at the same time, man's nature condemns itself, and the curse for the epic's actors is that to realize this is not to overcome it. This is the epic's final irony, and through it we are returned to the familiar pain of being alive and being human. Never very distant is the elegiac regret that no other way seems possible, that the relentless passage of time carries all before it, that the alternatives to this inescapable cycle can be only dimly sensed, like memories from a fading dream. Karna puts it well.

I see it now: this world is swiftly passing.

'Drona' 2.4

Note on the Text and Translation

The recension translated by the Clay Sanskrit Library is Nila·kantha's, and I have drawn on four sources to construct the text presented herein. These are the 1834–39 Calcutta Edition, Kinjawadekar's twentieth-century version of the Bombay Editon, and the two Deva·nágari *Dn* manuscripts of the Critical Edition. Some line counts are my own, but *adhyāya* divisions are all from original sources. A concordance given below should make comparision with the Critical Edition relatively straightforward.

A word on the formal structure of the epic for those who are coming to it for the first time. The narration can best be understood through theatrical conventions; the 'Maha·bhárata' is recounted as a dialogue between characters, and stories are nested within stories in an increasingly intricate fashion as the epic progresses. The prime speaker is the seer Ugra·shravas, who is retelling to a group of hermits the story he heard being narrated to the king Janam·éjaya, a descendent of the Pándavas, by Vaishampáyana, a pupil of Vyasa. The divine seer Vyasa is credited by the epic, rather fancifully, as its composer. In the battle books, it is Dhrita·rashtra's charioteer Sánjaya who takes over most of the narration, visiting the blind king at his palace back in the royal city of Hástina·pura to report on what has happened. Much is made of Vyasa granting Sánjaya some sort of magical sight that enables him to describe the battle in such vivid and telescopic detail, but it seems likely that this is principally an attempt, perhaps late in the epic's composition, to explain a structural device very much in keeping with the mode of the rest of the 'Maha·bhárata.'

Though the topic is a fascinating one, it is unfortunately not possible here to enter into a detailed discussion about how I have set about transposing the structures and shapes of Epic Sanskrit into the very different ones of modern English. If a translation needs a preamble to justify it then it is anyway unlikely to succeed. All the same, a few comments may help to explain why the English text has taken the form that it has. Despite its immensity, and its shifts in colour and tone, the epic's voice maintains a certain register throughout, one born of the strange encounter between an oral, folkloric tradition and a hieratic, literary language. I have tried to preserve the singularity of this register, and rather than naturalism I have sought an idiom in English reflective of the stark and glittering intensity of the original. Particularly in the battle scenes, verses can build into circular and almost incantatory sequences that perhaps are better suited to poetry than to prose. There is no punctuation to speak of in the Sanskrit manuscripts, and any but the sparest intervention into the text with commas and colons does a violence to its subtlety and music. Resisting unnecessary syntax also in my translation I have tried to follow these unbroken sequences as closely as possible, which can create some labyrinthine passages that twist and turn but, one hopes, never lose the reader completely. Any confusion bred in reading the Sanskrit is almost always clarified in recitation; above all I have attempted to write an English text that can be read aloud, and that matches the patterns, quirks and excitements of oral narration so uniquely captured by the Sanskrit scribes of the 'Maha·bhárata.'

Concordance of Canto Numbers with the Critical Edition

CSL	CE
1.1	1.1
6.1	5.21
7.1	5.34
7.10	6.1
8.1	7.1
49.1	48.38
50.1	48.39
51.1	49.1
52.1	—

Note that Nila·kantha's text is longer than the Critical Edition. The latter omits verses that are present in the former, and moves several substantial sections to its appendices. The concordance above only notes points where this fact disrupts equivalence between cantos. Greater care has to be taken at the level of the verse. For example, CSL.23.1 has its equivalent at CE.22.1, while CSL.23.74 has its equivalent at CE.23.60, and CSL.23.97 has no equivalent at all in the main body of CE.

Bibliography

THE 'MAHA·BHÁRATA' IN SANSKRIT

The Mahābhārata. Edited by Siromani, N. and Gopala, N. Calcutta: Baptist Mission Press, 1834–9.

The Mahābhāratam. Edited by Kinjawadekar, R. Poona: Chitraśāla Prakāśana, 1929–37.

The Mahābhārata. Critically edited by Sukthankar, V.K., Belvalkar, S.K., Vaidya, P.L. *et al*. Poona: Bhandarkar Oriental Research Institute, 1933–66.

THE 'MAHA·BHÁRATA' IN TRANSLATION

The Mahabharata of Krishna-Dwaipayana Vyasa. Ganguli, K.M. (trans.) [early editions ascribed to the publisher, P.C. Roy]. Calcutta: Bharata Press, 1884–99.

FURTHER READING AND REFERENCES

Halliwell, S. (trans.), *Aristotle's Poetics*. Cambridge: Harvard University Press, 1995.

Brodbeck, S., introduction to *The Bhagavad Gita* (trans. Mascaró, J.). Harmondsworth: Penguin, 2003.

Heidegger, M., *Holzwege*. Frankfurt am Main: Klostermann, 1950. ["Wozu Dichter" from *Holzwege* is translated as "What Are Poets For?" in *Poetry, Language, Thought*. trans. Albert Hofstadter, New York: Harper & Row, 1971.]

Hopkins, E. W., *The Great Epic of India: Its Character and Origin*. New York: C. Scribner's Sons, 1901.

JAMISON, S., *The Ravenous Hyenas and the Wounded Sun*. Ithaca: Cornell University Press, 1991.

OBERLIES, T., *A Grammar of Epic Sanskrit*. Berlin: Walter de Gruyter, 2003.

PILIKIAN, V., "Like Suns Risen at the End of Time: Metaphor and Meaning in the Mahābhārata," in the *Journal of Vaishnava Studies,* vol. 14 no. 2. Poquoson: Deepak, 2006.

SØRENSEN, S., *An Index to the Names in the Mahābhārata*. London: Williams and Norgate, 1904–25.

DRAMATIS PERSONÆ

Most of the individuals in the 'Maha·bhárata' are known by their given names and perhaps another indicative of parentage. The glossary at the end of the book will assist in making sense of the huge cast. However, some of its central figures enjoy the prestige of multiple names, patronymics and epithets. This can be confusing, but their use is crucial to the flow and rhythm of the Sanskrit. My decisions regarding which to translate and which to leave in as they are have been motivated by the aim of trying to retain their colorful effect in the text. The list below features all the main characters with more than two names, and is intended as a quick reference for the bewildered reader.

ÁRJUNA: THE MIDDLE PÁNDAVA, SON OF INDRA AND KUNTÍ also known as Dhanan·jaya, the Victor / Jishnu, the Conquering Sun / Kirítin, the Diademed Warrior / Kauntéya, son of Kuntí / Savya·sachin, the Left Handed Archer / Pándava, son of Pandu / Partha, son of Pritha / Phálguna, the Red Star Fighter / Víjaya, the Champion

ABHIMÁNYU: SON OF ÁRJUNA AND SUBHÁDRA also known as Árjuni, son of Árjuna / Karshni, the Dark One's son[2] / Phálguni, son of the Red Star Fighter / Saubhádra, son of Subhádra

BHISHMA: SON OF SHÁNTANU AND GREAT UNCLE OF THE PÁNDAVAS AND KÁURAVAS also known as Apagéya, son of Ápaga/Deva·vrata, the Paragon / Shántanava, son of Shántanu

BHIMA·SENA: THE SECOND PÁNDAVA, SON OF VAYU AND KUNTI also known as Bhima / Kauntéya, son of Kuntí / Pándava, son of Pandu / Partha, son of Pritha / Vrikódara, Dogbelly

DRONA: TEACHER OF THE PÁNDAVAS AND KÁURAVAS, AND NEWLY-

APPOINTED COMMANDER OF THE KÁURAVA ARMIES also known as Achárya, the Teacher / Bharadvája, son of Bharad·vaja / Rukma·ratha, Warrior of the Golden Chariot

DURYÓDHANA: DHRITA·RASHTRA'S ELDEST SON AND YUDHI·SHTHIRA'S RIVAL also known as Dhartaráshta son of Dhrita·rashtra / Suyódhana

INDRA: WARRIOR GOD OF THE VEDAS also known as Mághavan / Shakra / Vásava

KARNA: SON OF SURYA, THE SUN GOD, AND UNACKNOWLEDGED HALF-BROTHER TO THE OTHER PÁNDAVAS also known as / Radhéya, son of Radha / Suta·putra, the Horseman's Son / Vaikártana, born of the sun

KRISHNA: THE VRISHNI CHIEFTAIN, ÁRJUNA'S DRIVER, AND INCARNATION OF VISHNU also known as Áchyuta, the-Unfallen / Dashárha, lord of the Dashárhas / Go·vinda, the Herdsman / Hrishi·kesha, the Wild Maned / Janárdana, Stirrer of Hearts / Késhava, Longhair / Mádhava, slayer of Madhu / Pundarikáksha, the Lotus Eyed God / Shauri, grandson of Shuri / Vasudéva, son of Vasu·deva / Vishvak·sena, the Almighty.

RUDRA: FIERCE DEITY WHO COMES TO BE KNOWN AS SHIVA also known as Maha·deva, the Great God / Sharva, the God Who Kills With Arrows / Sthanu, the Still One /

Try·ámbaka, the Three Eyed God / Kapálin, the skull-bearer

YUDHI·SHTHIRA: THE ELDEST OF THE PÁNDAVAS, SON OF DHARMA AND KUNTÍ also known as Ajáta·shatru, the matchless king / Dharma·raja, the righteous king / Kauntéya, son of Kuntí / Partha, son of Pritha / Pándava, son of Pandu

NOTES

1 The term *dharma* has resurfaced in "countercultural" forms in the West, although these bear little if any relation to the idea and its significance in the world of the 'Maha·bhárata.'

2 The name "Krishna," literally "Dark," multiples through the epic, and it can be confusing to keep the different characters separate. The principal Krishna is the son of Vasu·deva and incarnation of Vishnu, and the speaker of the 'Bhágavad Gita.' His sister Dráupadi is also known as Krishná, with the feminine ending *-ā*. The third important Krishna is Krishna Dvaipáyana, mythical composer of the 'Maha·bhárata' and biological father of Pandu and Dhrita·rashtra. To make things yet more complicated, Árjuna is sometimes called Krishna, but this mostly happens when they are being referred to in the dual, as "the Krishnas," and so I have not indicated this in the Dramatis Personae. Árjuna as Krishna features most prominently in Abhimányu's patronymic Karshni, "son of the Dark One," i.e., son of Árjuna. Cf. note to 7.29.

1–15

THE ANOINTING OF DRONA

JANAMEJAYA uvāca.

1.1 TAM A|PRATIMA|sattv'|âujo|bala|vīrya|parākramam
hataṃ Deva|vrataṃ śrutvā Pāñcālyena Śikhaṇḍinā
Dhṛtarāṣṭras tadā rājā śoka|vyākula|cetanaḥ
kim aceṣṭata, vipra'|rṣe, hate pitari vīryavān?
tasya putro hi, bhagavan, Bhīṣma|Droṇa|mukhai rathaiḥ
parājitya mah"|êṣv|āsān Pāṇḍavān rājyam icchati.
tasmin hate tu, bhagavan, ketau sarva|dhanuṣmatām
yad aceṣṭata Kauravyas tan me brūhi dvi|j'|ôttama.

VAIŚAMPĀYANA uvāca.

1.5 nihataṃ pitaraṃ śrutvā Dhṛtarāṣṭro jan'|âdhipaḥ
lebhe na śāntiṃ Kauravyaś cintā|śoka|parāyaṇaḥ.
tasya cintayato duḥkham aniśaṃ pārthivasya tat
ājagāma viśuddh'|ātmā punar Gāvalgaṇis tadā.
śibirāt Saṃjayaṃ prāptaṃ niśi Nāg'|āhvayaṃ puram
Āmbikeyo mahā|rāja Dhṛtarāṣṭro 'nvapṛcchata.
śrutvā Bhīṣmasya nidhanam a|prahṛṣṭa|manā bhṛśam
putrāṇāṃ jayam ākāṅkṣan vilalāp' āturo yathā.

DHṚTARĀṢṬRA uvāca.

saṃsādhya tu mah"|ātmānaṃ
Bhīṣmaṃ bhīma|parākramam
kim akārṣuḥ paraṃ, tāta,
Kuravaḥ kāla|coditāḥ?

JANAM·ÉJAYA spoke.

So Bhishma the Paragon* lay dying. His courage and heroism, his power and splendor and soul were without equal on earth, yet somehow the Panchála Shikhándin had overcome him.* I can imagine the sorrow that engulfed Dhrita·rashtra when he heard of his uncle's fall. What did the mighty king do? His son still yearned to wrest the kingdom from the great Pándava archers and it was Drona and Bhishma whom he thought would lead his chariots to victory. But now the most brilliant of all bowmen was no more. Tell me, o sage, o great ascetic: what did the scion of Kuru* do? 1.1

VAISHAMPÁYANA spoke.

When he heard that his father was dying, Dhrita·rashtra 1.5
son of Kuru and lord of men was possessed with anxiety and grief and could find no peace. He brooded long over his sorrows. Then puresouled* Sánjaya son of Gaválgana came to see the king. Returning from the royal camp, he arrived in the night at Hástina·pura, and the son of Ámbika asked him what he knew. O great king, Dhrita·rashtra listened without cheer to Sánjaya's account of Bhishma's violent demise. Though sick at heart with grief, still he dreamt that his sons might win the war.

DHRITA·RASHTRA spoke.

Tell me my boy. What did the Kurus do as they stood beside the body of the great and fearsome Bhishma? Time has ravaged my children, plunged them into an ocean of
sorrow. Their hale and hardy champion has been brought 1.10
down. What did they do? O Sánjaya. Even the massed ranks

1.10 tasmin vinihate śūre dur|ādharṣe mah"|âujasi
kiṃ nu svit Kuravo 'kārṣur nimagnāḥ śoka|sāgare?
tad udīrṇaṃ mahat sainyaṃ trailokyasy' âpi Saṃjaya
bhayam utpādayet tīvraṃ Pāṇḍavānāṃ mah"|âtmanām.
Deva|vrate tu nihate Kurūṇām ṛṣabhe tadā
yad akārṣur nṛ|patayas tan mam' ācakṣva, Saṃjaya.

SAṂJAYA uvāca.

śṛṇu, rājann, eka|manā vacanaṃ bruvato mama
yat te putrās tad" âkārṣur hate Deva|vrate mṛdhe.
nihate tu tadā Bhīṣme, rājan, satya|parākrame
tāvakāḥ Pāṇḍaveyāś ca prādhyāyanta pṛthak pṛthak.
1.15 vismitāś ca prahṛṣṭāś ca kṣatra|dharmaṃ niśāmya te
sva|dharmaṃ nindamānāś ca praṇipatya mah"|ātmane.
śayanaṃ kalpayām āsur Bhīṣmāy' â|mita|tejase
s'|ôpadhānaṃ, nara|vyāghra, śaraiḥ saṃnata|parvabhiḥ.
vidhāya rakṣāṃ Bhīṣmāya samābhāṣya paras|param
anumānya ca Gāṅgeyaṃ kṛtvā c' âpi pradakṣiṇam
krodha|saṃrakta|nayanāḥ samavekṣya paras|param
punar yuddhāya nirjagmuḥ kṣatriyāḥ kāla|coditāḥ.
tatas tūrya|ninādaiś ca bherīṇāṃ ca mahā|svanaiḥ
tāvakānām anīkāni pareṣāṃ c' âpi niryayuḥ.

of the army of the three worlds would cower when the Pándavas raise their swords. Tell me what the Kuru chieftains* decided now that the Paragon, the bull of their herd, lay dying on the earth.

SÁNJAYA spoke.

O majesty. Listen closely to my words and I will tell you what your children did when the man sworn to the gods was struck down. O lord, brave Bhishma's fall drove all other thoughts from the minds of your sons and of the sons of Pandu. Stunned and solemn and true to the code of their kind, 1.15
they set aside their own loyalties and bowed their heads before the great man. They first arranged a resting place cushioned by arrows of knotless wood and on it o king they gently laid the body of magnificent Bhishma, muttering to one another as they did. Then they stood reverentially to the left side of Ganges' son and paid him their respects. They glanced at one another and anger burned red in their eyes. Their minds turned once more to war for they are warriors, and time drives warriors on. The armies of both sides rippled to the blare of horns and the thunder of drums.

1.20 vyāvṛtte 'hani, rāj'|êndra, patite Jāhnavī|sute
amarṣa|vaśam āpannāḥ kāl'|ôpahata|cetasaḥ
an|ādṛtya vacaḥ pathyaṃ Gāṅgeyasya mah"|ātmanaḥ
niryayur Bharata|śreṣṭhāḥ śastrāṇy ādāya sarvaśaḥ.
mohāt tava sa|putrasya vadhāc Chāṃtanavasya ca
Kauravyā mṛtyusād bhūtāḥ sahitāḥ sarva|rājabhiḥ.
aj'|âvaya iv' â|gopā vane śvā|pada|saṃkule
bhṛśam udvigna|manaso hīnā Deva|vratena te.
patite Bharata|śreṣṭhe babhūva Kuru|vāhinī
dyaur iv' âpeta|nakṣatrā, hīnaṃ kham iva vāyunā,
1.25 vipanna|sasy" êva mahī, vāk c' âiv' â|saṃskṛtā yathā,
āsur" îva yathā senā nigṛhīte purā Balau,
vidhav" êva var"|ārohā, śuṣka|toy" êva nimna|gā,
vṛkair iva vane ruddhā pṛṣatī hata|yūtha|pā,
sv|ādharṣā hata|siṃh" êva mahatī giri|kandarā.
Bhāratī Bharata|śreṣṭha patite Jāhnavī|sute
viṣvag|vāta|hatā rugṇā naur iv' āsīn mah"|ârṇave.
balibhiḥ Pāṇḍavair vīrair labdha|lakṣair bhṛś'|ârditā
sā tad" āsīd bhṛśaṃ senā vyākul'|âśva|ratha|dvi|pā.
viṣaṇṇa|bhūyiṣṭha|narā kṛpaṇā draṣṭum ābabhau
tasyāṃ trastā nṛ|patayaḥ sainikāś ca pṛthag|vidhāḥ
pātāla iva majjanto hīnā Deva|vratena te.

O king of kings, as the day of Bhishma's fall grew long 1.20
the Káuravas grew wanton. Their minds had been buckled by time. Heedless of the salutary words of the great son of Ganges,* one by one the best of the Bharatas drew their swords and stepped forth. It was first your folly and the folly of your children but now the death of Shántanu's son that delivered the Káuravas and all their allies over to death. The Paragon had been their shepherd and without him they were convulsed with panic like sheep in a forest thronged with beasts. Deprived of the very greatest of their number, the Kuru soldiers were like a starless sky, like a void without
air, like a cropless field, like broken speech, like the demon* 1.25
horde when Bali was in chains. They were pitiful as a widow in her prime, a once deep river run dry, a spotted doe with a dead mate in a wood beset by wolves. They lay open to plunder like a mountain cave when its guardian beast lies slain. O lord of the Bharatas when the son of Jáhnavi fell, the army of your Bhárata kin were like a splintered and battered ship adrift on the broad and windy ocean. The mighty Pándavas saw that their prize was within reach. Their warriors had devastated the Káurava force and its lines of elephants, horses and chariots were in disarray. Without the Paragon to lead the Káurava army even the very mightiest of its wretched number felt his heart sink, and each chieftain and soldier regardless of rank trembled as if hell itself was opening beneath his feet.

1.30 Karṇaṃ hi Kuravo 'smārṣuḥ sa hi Deva|vrat'|ôpamaḥ
sarva|śastra|bhṛtāṃ śreṣṭhaṃ rocamānam iv' âtithim.
bandhum āpad|gatasy' êva tam ev' ôpāgaman manaḥ
cukruśuḥ Karṇa Karṇ' êti tatra Bhārata pārthivāḥ
Rādheyaṃ hitam asmākaṃ Sūta|putraṃ tanu|tyajam
sa hi n' âyudhyata tadā daś'|âhāni mahā|yaśāḥ.
s'|âmātya|bandhuḥ Karṇo vai tam āhvayata mā|ciram
Bhīṣmeṇa hi mahā|bāhuḥ sarva|kṣatrasya paśyataḥ.
rathеṣu gaṇyamāneṣu bala|vikrama|śāliṣu
saṃkhyāto 'rdha|rathaḥ Karṇo dvi|guṇaḥ san nara'|rṣabhaḥ.
1.35 rath'|âtiratha|saṃkhyāyāṃ yo 'gra|ṇīḥ śūra|sammataḥ
pitṛ|vitt'|âmbu|dev'|ēśān api yo yoddhum utsahet.
sa tu ten' âiva kopena, rājan, Gāṅgeyam uktavān:
«tvayi jīvati Kauravya n' âhaṃ yotsye kathaṃ cana.
tvayā tu Pāṇḍaveyeṣu nihateṣu mahā|mṛdhe
Duryodhanam anujñāpya vanaṃ yāsyāmi Kaurava
Pāṇḍavair vā hate Bhīṣme tvayi svargam upeyuṣi
hant" âsmy eka|rathen' âiva kṛtsnān yān manyase rathān.»
evam uktvā mahā|rāja daś'|âhāni mahā|yaśāḥ
n' âyudhyata tataḥ Karṇaḥ putrasya tava sammate.

It was at that very moment that like the sudden return 1.30
of a stranger the Kurus recalled the only man who bore compare to Bhishma: Karna, best of all the swordsmen that have lived. Their thoughts o turned to him alone as one crushed by calamity reaches out for a friend. Karna, Karna, the chieftains cried. Yet although the humble son of Radha born to a horseman* had set aside his life for our cause, fabled Karna had by then not set foot on the battlefield for ten full days. It was Bhishma himself who then fetched mighty Karna and all of his ministers before us.

In the words of warriors of main and courage and even temper, Karna is reckoned a bull in the herd of men,* a
man worth twice any of his peers. Heroes celebrate him as 1.35
the greatest warrior and champion they can name, one who could meet in war the rulers of stars and and sea and sky.* Passion had driven his words to Bhishma: "While you live o son of Kuru I will not fight. Either you wipe out the Pándavas in this great war and I take my leave of Duryódhana and depart for the forest or the Pándavas will kill you Bhishma and you will ascend to heaven. Then I will mount my chariot and by my own hand destroy every and any warrior whom you can name." So it was o majesty that for ten days Karna refused to fight. Your son deferred to the decision that the fabled warrior had made.*

1.40 Bhīṣmaḥ samara|vikrāntaḥ Pāṇḍaveyasya, pārthiva,
jaghāna samare yodhān a|saṃkhyeya|parākramaḥ.
tasmiṃs tu nihate śūre satya|saṃdhe mah"|âujasi
tvat|sutāḥ Karṇam asmārṣus tartu|kāmā iva plavam.
tāvakās tava putrāś ca sahitāḥ sarva|rājabhiḥ
hā Karṇa iti c' âkrandan kālo 'yam iti c' âbruvan.
Jāmadagny'|âbhyanujñātam astre dur|vāra|pauruṣam
agaman no manaḥ Karṇaṃ bandhum ātyayikeṣv iva.
sa hi śakto raṇe rājaṃs trātum asmān mahā|bhayāt
tri|daśān iva Govindaḥ satataṃ su|mahā|bhayāt.

VAIŚAMPĀYANA uvāca.

1.45 tathā Karṇaṃ yudhi varaṃ kīrtayantaṃ punaḥ punaḥ
āśī|viṣavad ucchvasya Dhṛtarāṣṭro 'bravīd idam.
«yat tad Vaikartanaṃ Karṇam agamad vo manas tadā
apy apaśyata Rādheyaṃ sūta|putraṃ tanu|tyajam?
api tan na mṛṣ" âkārṣīd yudhi satya|parākramaḥ
sambhrāntānāṃ tad|ārtānāṃ trastānāṃ trāṇam icchatām?
api tat pūrayāṃ cakre dhanur|dhara|varo yudhi
yat tad vinihate Bhīṣme Kauravāṇām apāvṛtam
tat khaṇḍaṃ pūrayām āsa pareṣām ādadhad bhayam
kṛtavān mama putrāṇāṃ jay'|āśāṃ sa|phalām api?»

My king. Bhishma's mastery of the art of war had been matched by a courage beyond reckoning. He had killed many of the men who fought for Pandu's son. But now this mighty pillar of truth had been toppled, and as marooned sailors hope for a raft your sons hoped for Karna. Karna, they cried, and the cry was echoed by their fellow kings. The time has come, they said. As lost men seek a friend, all our hearts went out to Párashu·rama's favorite, to the one whose skill with the bow no man can compass: to Karna. My king we felt that he alone could save us from our terror, as Go·vinda ever saves the thirty gods from the yet greater terrors that afflict them. 1.40

VAISHAMPÁYANA spoke.

As he listened to Sánjaya's talk of Karna and of his greatness in war, the old snake Dhrita·rashtra let out a sigh like a hiss and spoke. 1.45

"And then? Was the hope in your heart fulfilled? Did you see him come forth, the child of Radha and the horseman, the warrior to whom life is nothing, Karna born of the sun? As you fought on ruined and wild and afraid and desperate for help surely brave and valiant Karna did not come to your aid in vain? Did this greatest of all bearers of the bow close the wound that opened in the Káuravas when Bhishma was brought down? And what of the fear he cast into the enemy's hearts as he did? And of the fruit of my children's victory that through him began to ripen?"

SAMJAYA uvāca.

2.1 ITAM BHĪSMAM ath' Ādhirathir viditvā
bhinnāṃ nāvam iv' âty|a|gādhe Kurūṇām
sodaryavad vyasanāt sūta|putraḥ
saṃtārayiṣyaṃs tava putrasya senām
śrutvā tu Karṇaḥ puruṣ'|êndram a|cyutaṃ
nipātitaṃ Śāṃtanavaṃ mahā|ratham,
ath' ôpayāyāt sahas" âri|karṣaṇo
dhanur|dharāṇāṃ pravaras tadā, nṛ|pa.
hate tu Bhīṣme ratha|sattame parair
nimajjatīṃ nāvam iv' ârṇave Kurūn
pit" êva putrāṃs tvarito 'bhyayāt tataḥ
saṃtārayiṣyaṃs tava putrasya senām.

KARNA uvāca.

yasmin dhṛtir buddhi|parākram'|âujaḥ
satyaṃ smṛti|vīra|guṇāś ca sarve
astrāṇi divyāny atha saṃnatir hrīḥ
priyā ca vāg an|asūyā ca Bhīṣme
2.5 sadā|kṛta|jñe dvi|ja|śatru|ghātake
sanātanaṃ candramas' îva lakṣma.
sa cet praśāntaḥ para|vīra|hantā,
manye hatān eva ca sarva|vīrān.

SÁNJAYA spoke.

NEWS REACHED Ádhirathi that Bhishma had sunk like a broken boat into the churning deep of the Kurus. Out of brotherhood the horseman's son resolved to rescue Duryódhana's army from its plight. O majesty, when he heard that the godlike and invincible warrior the son of Shántanu had been hewn down, Karna best of bowmen and crusher of foes made straight for his side. Duryódhana's supreme protector had been beaten and as a father to his sons Karna hastened to yours to rescue the breeched vessel of the Kurus before the sea swallowed it whole. 2.1

KARNA spoke.

This is a man of his word. A man of blazing and courageous soul. A man of truth. Every quality of a hero of legend is found within him. He wields weapons from heaven, yet he is blessed with humility, perfect modesty, gentle grace and kindness. Bhishma always knew what had to be done. 2.5
Scourge of those who would raise arms against the priests, he was as constant as the mark in the moon. If it is so that this great avenger has been tamed, then I can only think that every warrior on earth lies dead.

n' êha dhruvam kiṃ cana jātu vidyate
loke hy asmin karmaṇo '|nitya|yogāt.
sūry'|ôdaye ko hi vimukta|saṃśayo
bhāvaṃ kurvīt' âdya mahā|vrate hate?
vasu|prabhāge vasu|vīrya|sambhave
gate vasūn eva vasuṃ|dhar'|âdhipe
vasūni putrāṃś ca vasuṃ|dharāṃ tathā
Kurūṃś ca śocadhvam imāṃ ca vāhinīm.

SAṂJAYA uvāca.

mahā|prabhāve varade nipātite
lok'|ēśvare śāstari c' â|mit'|âujasi
parājiteṣu Bharateṣu dur|manāḥ
Karṇo bhṛśaṃ nyaśvasad aśru vartayan.
idaṃ ca Rādheya|vaco niśamya
sutāś ca, rājaṃs, tava sainikāś ca ha
paras|paraṃ cukruśur ārti|jaṃ muhus
tad" âśru netrair mumucuś ca śabdavat.
2.10 pravartamāne tu punar mah"|āhave
vigāhyamānāsu camūṣu pārthivaiḥ
ath" âbravīd dharṣa|karaṃ tadā vaco
ratha'|ṛṣabhān sarva|mahā|ratha'|ṛṣabhaḥ.
«jagaty a|nitye satataṃ pradhāvati
pracintayann a|sthiram adya lakṣaye.
bhavatsu tiṣṭhatsv iha pātito mṛdhe
giri|prakāśaḥ Kuru|puṃ|gavaḥ katham?
nipātite Śāṃtanave mahā|rathe
divā|kare bhū|talam āsthite yathā
na pārthivāḥ soḍhum alaṃ Dhanaṃjayaṃ
giri|pravoḍhāram iv' ânilaṃ drumāḥ.
hata|pradhānaṃ tv idam ārta|rūpaṃ

O but there is nothing that man does in this world that lasts for everything fades. A grand ascetic is no more: who then can be sure that the sun will rise again? A soul of power and luster has departed for the bright lands, a regent of the earth now rests with the gods of heaven. Mourn then your children and mourn your wealth in this world, mourn the rich earth, mourn the Kurus. Mourn these multitudes that stand before you.

SÁNJAYA spoke.

Karna gazed at the broken form of our great savior, our matchless master and teacher, whose splendor had known no end in life. Stricken for a moment at the sufferings of the Bharatas he let out a sharp gasp and tears welled up in his eyes. O lord, both riders and soldiers had listened quietly to his words and now they cried out at one another and wept
for a time as the pain wrung tears from their eyes. But war 2.10
was still upon them and the kings stirred their ranks once again. Then the great warrior Karna addressed his peers. These were the bitter words he spoke.

"I look upon the whirling blur of this passing world and I see nothing in it that remains. How can the bull of the Kurus be torn from his mountainous height down into this cluttered and changing world? The mighty son of Shántanu lies like a sun fallen to earth. You kings who remain can no more survive the blast of Dhanan·jaya than trees can survive a hurricane. This army has had its core plucked out, its frame buckled, its might broken by its enemy. The orphan Kurus have lost their father and now it falls to me to protect them as the great Bhishma once did. It is upon my shoulders that this burden has been placed.

parair hat'|ôtsāham a|nātham adya vai
maya Kurūṇāṃ paripālyam āhave
balaṃ yathā tena mah"|ātmanā tathā.
samāhitaṃ c' ātmani bhāram īdṛśaṃ.
jagat tath" â|nityam idaṃ ca lakṣaye
nipātitaṃ c' āhava|śauṇḍam āhave.
kathaṃ nu kuryām aham īdṛśaṃ bhayam?
2.15 ahaṃ tu tān Kuru|vṛṣabhān a|jihma|gaiḥ
praveśayan Yama|sadanaṃ cayan raṇe
yaśaḥ paraṃ jagati vibhāvya vartitā
parair hato bhuvi śayit" âtha vā punaḥ.
Yudhiṣṭhiro jagati ca satya|saṃdhavān
Vṛkodaro gaja|śata|tulya|vikramaḥ
tath" Ârjunas tri|daśa|var'|ātma|jo yuvā
na tad balaṃ su|jayam ath" âmarair api.
yamau raṇe yatra Yam'|ôpamau bale
sa|Sātyakir yatra ca Devakī|sutaḥ
na tad balaṃ kāpuruṣo 'bhyupeyivān
nivartate mṛtyu|sukhān na c' âsu|bhṛt.
tapo 'bhyudīrṇaṃ tapas" âiva bādhyate
balaṃ balen' âiva tathā manasvibhiḥ,
manaś ca me śatru|nivāraṇe dhruvaṃ
sva|rakṣaṇe v" âcalavad vyavasthitam.
evaṃ c' âiṣāṃ bādhamānaḥ prabhāvaṃ
gatv" âiv' âhaṃ tāñ jayāmy adya, sūta.
mitra|droho marṣaṇīyo na me 'yam
agro sainye yaḥ sameyāt sa mitram.
2.20 kart" âsmy etat sat|puruṣ'|ārya|karma
tyaktvā prāṇān anuyāsyāmi Bhīṣmam.
sarvān saṃkhye śatru|saṃghān haniṣye

I see it now: this world is swiftly passing. Drunk on destruction, it meets its end in the flames. But what is there to fear in that? Driving with arrows the bulls of our kin 2.15
down to Death's kingdom I will fight for revenge and I will either shine on earth bathed in glory or be slain by my adversaries and find my final peace upon the ground.

Yudhi·shthira is the world's pillar to truth, Vrikódara has the strength of a hundred elephants, and young Árjuna is the heir of the thirty gods. Even for the deathless ones victory over our enemy would be hard won. With them fight the twins, mighty as Death, and Sátyaki son of Dévaki. Against them the weak of heart stand no chance. But nothing that draws breath has ever escaped eternity's repose. The wise say that a fire when kindled can be met only with fire, might only with might. My will is firm as a mountain peak. I will fight off my enemies and protect my own. Driver hear me. I go to meet the Pándavas and repel their onslaught and overcome them. He who fights by your side in the heat of battle is your friend, and I will not forget the violence that has been done to mine. I will do what a good man must. I 2.20
turn my back on life and walk in Bhishma's footsteps. Every wave of my enemies I will slay, or if they are to slay me I will fly up to the place where dead heroes dwell. Lest Duryódhana is scorned and must watch his wife and children weep while another man is astride all he holds dear I know what I must do. I will destroy the enemies of my king. O Driver. To bloody war I surrender myself, and guarding the Kurus I will cut to pieces the sons of Pandu and wave by wave my adversaries will fall as I return the kingdom to Dhrita·rashtra's son.

hatas tair vā vīra|lokaṃ prapatsye.
samprākruṣṭe rudita|strī|kumāre
para|bhūte pauruṣe Dhārtarāṣṭre
mayā kṛtyam iti jānāmi, sūta,
tasmād rājñas tv adya śatrūn vijeṣye.
Kurūn rakṣan Pāṇḍu|putrāñ jighāṃsaṃs
tyaktvā prāṇān ghora|rūpe raṇe 'smin
sarvān saṃkhye śatru|saṃghān nihatya
dāsyāmy ahaṃ Dhārtarāṣṭrāya rājyam.
nibadhyatāṃ me kavacaṃ vicitraṃ
haimaṃ śubhraṃ maṇi|ratn'|âvabhāsam
śiras|trāṇaṃ c' ârka|samāna|bhāsaṃ
dhanuḥ śarāṃś c' âgni|viṣ'|âhi|kalpān.
upāsaṅgān ṣoḍaśa yojayantu
dhanūṃṣi divyāni tath" āharantu
asīś ca śaktīś ca gadāś ca gurvīḥ
śaṃkhaṃ ca jāmbūnada|citra|bhāsam.
2.25 imāṃ raukmīṃ nāga|kakṣāṃ vicitrāṃ
dhvajaṃ citraṃ divyam indīvar'|ābham
ślakṣṇair vastrair vipramṛjy' ānayantu
citrāṃ mālāṃ cāru|baddhāṃ sa|lājām.
aśvān agryān pāṇḍur'|âbhra|prakāśān
puṣṭān snātān mantra|pūtābhir adbhiḥ
taptair bhāṇḍaiḥ kāñcanair abhyupetāñ
śīghrāñ śīghraṃ, sūta|putr', ānayasva.
rathaṃ c' âgryaṃ hema|māl"|âvanaddham
ratnaiś citraṃ sūrya|candra|prakāśaiḥ
dravyair yuktaṃ samprahār'|ôpapannair
vāhair yuktaṃ tūrṇam āvartayasva.
citrāṇi cāpāni ca vegavanti

So let me buckle on my spangled armor, shining with
gold and lustered in crystals and gems, my helmet, brilliant as the sun, and my bow and my arrows, deadly as
fiery-venomed cobras. Muster sixteen quivers, and bring
forth my heavenly bows, my swords and spears and stout
maces, my conch that glitters patterned in rivergold and my 2.25
belt like a goldspangled serpent, and bring forth my bright
and heavenly standard, the blossom of the blue lotus. Polish
them all with fine cloth and bring them to me, with wreaths
of many shades delicately woven with sweetsmelling grass.
Bring out my fine horses, strong and swift and glimmering
like pale thunderclouds, groomed and washed in water pu-
rified by mantras and decked in forged harnesses of gold.
Be quick, my son: roll out my great chariot draped with
golden garlands, bright with jewels like pieces of the sun
and moon and hung with the trappings of war and yoke it
at once to its steeds. The bows are bright and strong, the
finest bowstrings ready to be strung. Strap on plate armor
and the great arrowfilled quivers. Go, get all the provisions
we need, bring gourds of gold and copper full to the neck
with milk. Waste no time but raise up garlands and festoon
yourselves, beat the drums of victory. Let us ride out to the 2.30
Diademed Warrior, to Dogbelly,* to Yudhi·shthira and the
twins. We will meet them and fight, and either I will kill
them or be killed myself and go forth from their hands to
where Bhishma is bound.

jyāś c' ôttamāḥ sannahan'|ôpapannāḥ
tūṇāṃś ca pūrṇān mahataḥ śarāṇām
āsādya gātr'|āvaraṇāni c' âiva
prāyātrikaṃ c' ānayat' āśu sarvaṃ
dadhnā pūrṇaṃ vīra|kāṃsyaṃ ca haimam,
ānīya mālām avabadhya c' âṅge
pravādayantv āśu jayāya bherīm.
2.30 prayāhi sūt' āśu yataḥ Kirīṭī
Vṛkodaro Dharma|suto yamau ca
tān vā haniṣyāmi sametya saṃkhye
Bhīṣmāya v" âiṣyāmi hato dviṣadbhiḥ.
yasmin rājā satya|dhṛtir Yudhiṣṭhiraḥ
samāsthito Bhīmasen'|Ârjunau ca
Vāsudevaḥ Sātyakiḥ Sṛñjayāś ca
manye balaṃ tad a|jayyaṃ mahī|paiḥ.
taṃ cen mṛtyuḥ sarva|haro 'bhirakṣate
sad" â|pramattaḥ samare Kirīṭinam
tath" âpi hant" âsmi sametya saṃkhye
yāsyāmi vā Bhīṣma|pathā Yamāya.
na tv ev' âhaṃ na gamiṣyāmi teṣāṃ
madhye śūrāṇāṃ tatra c' âhaṃ bravīmi
mitra|druho dur|bala|śaktayo ye
pāp'|ātmāno na mam' âite sahāyāḥ.»

SAṂJAYA uvāca.

samṛddhimantaṃ ratham uttamaṃ dṛḍhaṃ
sa|kūbaraṃ hema|pariṣkṛtaṃ śubham
patākinaṃ vāta|javair hay'|ôttamair
yuktaṃ samāsthāya yayau jayāya.
2.35 sampūjyamānaḥ Kurubhir mah"|âtmā
ratha'|rṣabho deva|gaṇair yath" Êndraḥ

Mere earthly kings cannot beat an army for whom fight King Yudhi·shthira the bastion of all that is, Bhima·sena and Árjuna, Vasudéva, Sátyaki and Srínjaya. This I know well. But even if Death himself in his eternal vigilance and with his all-reaching arms protects the Diademed Warrior from harm, I will slay him all the same in the midst of battle or else walk the path to Yama that Bhishma now treads.* Make no mistake. I say to all you champions gathered here: I go with no man who cannot muster his loyalty to a friend. The wretched in spirit are no companions of mine."

SÁNJAYA spoke.

The finest horses fleet as the wind were yoked to that great and lustrous and wellwrought chariot with its axle banded in gold and its flags raised high. Karna climbed aboard to
set forth and claim his triumph. Brandishing his fearsome 2.35
bow, the great and taurine Bharata chieftain venerated as if he were Indra by Kurus and by heaven's hosts alike headed for the battlefield. Death awaited him there. As his pennant

yayau tad" āyodhanam ugra|dhanvā
yatr' âvasānaṃ Bharata'|rṣabhasya.
varūthinā mahatā sa|dhvajena
suvarṇa|muktā|maṇi|ratna|mālinā
sad|aśva|yuktena rathena Karṇo
megha|svanen' ârka iv' â|mit'|âujāḥ.
hut'|âśan'|ābhaḥ sa hut'|āśana|prabhe
śubhaḥ śubhe vai su|rathe dhanur|dharaḥ
sthito rarāj' Ādhirathir mahā|rathaḥ
svayaṃ vimāne sura|rāḍ iva sthitaḥ.

SAMJAYA uvāca.

3.1 ŚARA|TALPE mah"|ātmānaṃ śayānam a|mit'|âujasam
mahā|vāta|samūhena samudram iva śoṣitam
dṛṣṭvā pitā|mahaṃ Bhīṣmaṃ sarva|kṣatr'|ântakaṃ gurum
divyair astrair mah"|êṣv|āsaṃ pātitaṃ Savyasācinā
jay'|āśā tava putrāṇāṃ sambhagnā śarma varma ca.
a|pārāṇām iva dvīpam a|gādhe gādham icchatām
srotasā Yāmunen' êva śar'|âugheṇa pariplutam
mahāntam iva Mainākam a|sahyaṃ bhuvi pātitam
nabhaś|cyutam iv' Ādityaṃ patitaṃ dharaṇī|tale
3.5 Śata|kratum iv' â|cintyaṃ purā Vṛtreṇa nirjitam
mohanaṃ sarva|sainyasya yudhi Bhīṣmasya pātanam.
kakudaṃ sarva|sainyānāṃ lakṣma sarva|dhanuṣ|matām
Dhanaṃjaya|śarair vyāptaṃ pitaraṃ te mahā|vratam
taṃ vīra|śayane vīraṃ śayānaṃ puruṣa'|rṣabham
Bhīṣmam Ādhirathir dṛṣṭvā Bharatānāṃ mahā|dyutiḥ
avatīrya rathād ārto bāṣpa|vyākulit'|âkṣaram
abhivādy' âñjaliṃ baddhvā vandamāno 'bhyabhāṣata.

flew above him Karna stood ringed in the wooden ribs of his mighty car encrusted with gold pearls gems and crystals and harnessed to steeds of the noblest breed, and in his measureless splendor he was like a sun bound in lightning. Blazing like fire, he was surrounded by fire; in his gleaming chariot he gleamed, wielding his bow. Warrior of warriors, the son of Ádhiratha stood there and blazed, a king of heaven in a car of the sky.

SÁNJAYA spoke.

ON HIS BED OF arrows Bhishma lay still. He had been 3.1
a man of fathomless soul and power. It was as if a hurricane had emptied the ocean. He had been our refuge and bulwark, and the sight of their patriarch and teacher, nemesis of kings and great archer of heaven's arrows laid out by Árjuna to die, shattered your children's hopes. The island to which sailors far out to sea yearning for a glimpse of land had once looked now lay drowned in a cataract of arrows that had poured down upon him like the waters of the Yámuna. For the troops Bhishma's fall in battle was inconceivable. It was easier to believe that the insuperable peak of Mainàka had collapsed or that the sun loosened from the
sky had plummeted to earth, or that Vritra had overthrown 3.5
Indra whose myriad powers surpass thought itself. There he was, the guiding star to all who had studied the bow, the pinnacle above every soldier, your devout uncle stuck full of the arrows of Dhanan·jaya. Karna son of Ádhiratha and glory of the Bharata race looked once more upon the taurine hero prone on a hero's bed and stricken by the sight stepped down from his chariot as tears welled in his eyes. He

«Karṇo 'ham asmi bhadraṃ te vada mām abhi, Bhārata,
puṇyayā kṣemayā vācā cakṣuṣā c' âvalokaya.
3.10 na nūnaṃ su|kṛtasy' êha phalaṃ kaś cit samaśnute
yatra dharma|paro vṛddhaḥ śete bhuvi bhavān iha.
kośa|saṃcayane mantre vyūhe praharaṇeṣu ca
n' âham anyaṃ prapaśyāmi Kurūṇāṃ, Kuru|sattama.
buddhyā viśuddhayā yukto yaḥ Kurūṃs tārayed bhayāt
yodhāṃs tvam a|plave hitvā pitṛ|lokaṃ gamiṣyasi.

adya prabhṛti saṃkruddhā vyāghrā iva mṛga|kṣayam
Pāṇḍavā, Bharata|śreṣṭha, kariṣyanti Kuru|kṣayam.
adya Gāṇḍīva|ghoṣasya vīrya|jñāḥ Savyasācinaḥ
Kuravaḥ saṃtrasiṣyanti vajra|pāṇer iv' âsurāḥ.
3.15 adya Gāṇḍīva|muktānām aśanīnām iva svanaḥ
trāsayiṣyati bāṇānāṃ Kurūn anyāṃś ca pārthivān.
samiddho 'gnir yathā vīra mahā|jvālo drumān dahet
Dhārtarāṣṭrān pradhakṣyanti tathā bāṇāḥ Kirīṭinaḥ.
yena yena prasarato vāyv|agnī sahitau vane
tena tena pradahato bhūri|gulma|tṛṇa|drumān.
yādṛśo 'gniḥ samudbhūtas tādṛk Pārtho na saṃśayaḥ
yathā vāyur, nara|vyāghra, tathā Kṛṣṇo na saṃśayaḥ.
nadataḥ Pāñcajanyasya rasato Gāṇḍivasya ca
śrutvā sarvāṇi sainyāni trāsaṃ yāsyanti Bhārata.

cupped his hands before Bhishma in salute, and addressed him with reverence.

"O Bhárata. It is I, Karna. I beg that you speak to me
gentle words and look upon me with kind eyes. You are 3.10
the proof that in this world no man reaps the reward his deeds deserve. Despite your age and devotion to what is right you lie here on the ground before me. How will we be able to organize ourselves, form mantras, plan our arrays and our attacks? I see no other Kuru to whom we can turn, for you were the best of them. You go now to the land of the forefathers. Your crew is lost to the swells for you alone had the insight and purity to deliver the Kurus from their terrors.

O best of the Bharatas. Throw deer to tigers and see what will befall the Kurus now. Now they will be given a lesson in power. Now they will shudder at the whisper of Gandíva* in the Left Handed Archer's hands as demons quail
before him who wields the thunderbolt. Now the sound of 3.15
arrows released like forks of lightning from its bowstring will send fear among them and their vassals. My lord as a kindled fire consumes trees in its bright flame the arrows of the Diademed Warrior will tear through the army of Dhrita·rashtra. When wind drives a fire through a forest, it burns up palms and thickets for league upon league upon league. Mark it well, o tiger: Partha is this fire, and Krishna this wind. Every soldier who hears Panchajánya's blare or
Gandíva's hum, every soldier, o Bhárata, will feel the touch
of fear. Without their champion no chieftain will be able to 3.20
bear the tremor as the car flying the banner of the monkey and holding the crusher of foes rides closer. Who of these

3.20 kapi|dhvajasya c' ôtpāte rathasy' â|mitra|karśinaḥ
śabdaṃ soḍhuṃ na śakṣyanti tvām ṛte, vīra, pārthivāḥ.
ko hy Arjunaṃ yoddhayituṃ tvad|anyaḥ pārthivo 'rhati
yasya divyāni karmāṇi pravadanti manīṣiṇaḥ.
a|mānuṣaś ca saṃgrāmas Try|ambakena mah"|ātmanā
tasmāc c' âiva varaṃ prāpto duṣ|prāpam a|kṛt'|ātmabhiḥ.
ko 'nyaḥ śakto raṇe jetuṃ pūrvaṃ yo na jitas tvayā
jito yena raṇe Rāmo bhavatā vīrya|śālinā
kṣatriy'|ânta|karo ghoro deva|dānava|darpa|hā.
tam ady' âhaṃ Pāṇḍavaṃ yuddha|śauṇḍam
    a|mṛṣyamāṇo bhavat" ânuśiṣṭaḥ
āśī|viṣaṃ dṛṣṭi|haraṃ su|ghoram
    śūraṃ śakṣyāmy astra|balān nihantum.»

SAṂJAYA uvāca.

4.1 TASYA LĀLAPYATAḤ śrutvā vṛddhaḥ Kuru|pitā|mahaḥ
deśa|kāl'|ôcitaṃ vākyam abravīt prīta|mānasaḥ.
«samudra iva sindhūnāṃ jyotiṣām iva bhās|karaḥ
satyasya ca yathā santo bījānām iva c' ôrvarā
parjanya iva bhūtānāṃ pratiṣṭhā su|hṛdāṃ tava.
bāndhavās tv" ânujīvantu sahasr'|âkṣam iv' âmarāḥ.
māna|hā bhava śatrūṇāṃ mitrāṇāṃ nandi|vardhanaḥ,
Kauravāṇāṃ bhava gatir yathā Viṣṇur div'|âukasām.
4.5 sva|bāhu|bala|vīryeṇa Dhārtarāṣṭra|jay'|âiṣiṇā
Karṇa Rājapuraṃ gatvā Kāmbojā nirjitās tvayā.
Girivraja|gatāś c' âpi Nagnajit|pramukhā nṛ|pāḥ
Ambaṣṭhāś ca Videhāś ca Gāndhārāś ca jitās tvayā.
himavad|durga|nilayāḥ Kirātā raṇa|karkaśāḥ
Duryodhanasya vaśa|gās tvayā, Karṇa, purā kṛtāḥ.

kings other than you can fight Árjuna? His divine acts are already parables told by seers. The immortal host turned to him and the great Three Eyed God to realize their purpose. How could his soul be less than perfect? Who could defeat someone whom you o master could not? You, who in your might defeated Rama, the bloody annihilator of the warrior caste and tamer of the arrogance of gods and demons both? Yet if o sire you give the command, then I will not hesitate but somehow find the strength in my bow to cut apart this dreadful apparition, this cobra drunk on the venom of war. I will slay the great son of Pandu."

SÁNJAYA spoke.

THE VENERABLE grandfather of the Kurus was touched 4.1
by Karna's lament. He began to speak, choosing his words with care.

"Like the ocean to the river, like the sun to all lights, like good men to the truth, the soil to seeds and the rain-clouds to living things is your constancy to your friends. May those close to you live by you as the deathless gods live by thousandeyed Indra. Humble your enemies and bring joy to those close to your heart: lead the way for the Kurus as Vishnu leads the denizens of heaven. Karna, it was 4.5
for Duryódhana's cause that you traveled to Raja·pura and struck down the Kambójas with just your valor and the might of your own two arms. Then there were the kings of Giri·vraja and their overlord Nágnajit, the Ambáshthas, the Vidéhas and the Gandháras: you overcame them all. It was you, Karna, who long ago brought the hardy Kirátas out of their snowclad lair and under Duryódhana's sway. The

Utkalā Mekalāḥ Pauṇḍrāḥ Kaliṅg'|Ândhrāś ca saṃyuge
Niṣādāś ca Trigartāś ca Bāhlīkāś ca jitās tvayā.
tatra tatra ca saṃgrāme Duryodhana|hit'|āiṣiṇā
bahavaś ca jitā Karṇa tvayā vīrā mah"|âujasā.

4.10 yathā Duryodhanas, tāta, sa|jñāti|kula|bāndhavaḥ.
tathā tvam api sarveṣāṃ Kauravāṇāṃ gatir bhava.
śiven' âbhivadāmi tvāṃ gaccha yudhyasva śatrubhiḥ.
anuśādhi Kurūn saṃkhye, dhatsva Duryodhane jayam.
bhavān pautra|samo 'smākaṃ yathā Duryodhanas tathā
tav' âpi dharmataḥ sarve yathā tasya vayaṃ tathā.
yaunāt sambandhakāl loke viśiṣṭaṃ saṃgataṃ satām
sadbhiḥ saha nara|śreṣṭha pravadanti manīṣiṇaḥ.
sa satya|saṃgato bhūtvā mam' êdam iti niścitam
Kurūṇāṃ pālaya balaṃ yathā Duryodhanas tathā.»

4.15 niśamya vacanaṃ tasya caraṇāv abhivādya ca
yayau Vaikartanaḥ Karṇaḥ samīpaṃ sarva|dhanvinām.
so 'bhivīkṣya nar'|âughāṇāṃ sthānam a|pratimaṃ mahat
vyūḍha|praharaṇ'|ôraskaṃ sainyaṃ tat samabṛṃhayat.
hṛṣitāḥ Kuravaḥ sarve Duryodhana|puro|gamāḥ
upāgataṃ mahā|bāhuṃ sarv'|ânīka|puraḥ|saram
Karṇaṃ dṛṣṭvā mah"|ātmānaṃ yuddhāya samupasthitam
kṣveḍit'|āsphoṭita|ravaiḥ siṃha|nāda|ravair api
dhanuḥ|śabdaiś ca vividhaiḥ Kuravaḥ samapūjayan.

Útkalas, Mékalas, Paundras, Kalíngas and Andhras, the Nishádas, the Tri·gartas and the Bahlíkas: all fell to your sword. Splendored Karna wherever you fought you defeated heroes beyond number and it was all in the service of Duryódhana's cause.

My son. Duryódhana has been a friend to your family 4.10
and your kin. In return you must lead the way for all of the Káuravas.* I implore you, go and fight against your enemies. Guide the Kurus in battle and bring victory to Duryódhana. I look upon you as I look upon Duryódhana—as a grandson. I have taken care to treat you in everything as I treat him. O best of men the wise and the good teach that we prove our worth in this world through our ties of blood and friendship. So be resolute in truth and know to whom you belong. Protect the Káurava army as Duryódhana protects it."

Listening closely to his words, Karna born of the sun 4.15
bent down to touch Bhishma's feet, then went towards the assembled archers. Looking upon the vast array gathered about him, still standing proud with their weapons in their hands, Karna stepped in among their number. As the great warrior of might and majesty took his position alongside them ready for war, Duryódhana and all the Kurus were thrilled at his return and like lions they all roared out their praise, applauding and whooping to the thronging chords plucked on the strings of their bows.

SAMJAYA uvāca.

5.1 RATHA|STHAM puruṣa|vyāghraṃ
dṛṣṭvā Karṇam avasthitam
hṛṣṭo Duryodhano, rājann,
idaṃ vacanam abravīt.
«sa|nātham iva manye 'haṃ bhavatā pālitaṃ balam.
atra kiṃ nu samarthaṃ yadd hitaṃ tat sampradhāryatām.»

KARṆA uvāca.

brūhi naḥ puruṣa|vyāghra tvaṃ hi prājñatamo nṛ|pa
yathā c' ârtha|patiḥ kṛtyaṃ paśyate na tath" êtaraḥ.
te sma sarve tava vacaḥ śrotu|kāmā, nar'|êśvara,
n' â|nyāyyaṃ hi bhavān vākyaṃ brūyād iti matir mama.

DURYODHANA uvāca.

5.5 Bhīṣmaḥ senā|praṇet" āsīd vayasā vikrameṇa ca
śrutena c' ôpasampannaḥ sarvair yodha|guṇais tathā.
ten' ātivayasā Karṇa ghnatā śatru|gaṇān mama
su|yuddhena daś'|âhāni pālitāḥ smo mah"|ātmanā.
tasminn a|sukaraṃ karma kṛtavaty āsthite divam
kaṃ nu senā|praṇetāraṃ manyase tad|anantaram?
na vinā nāyakaṃ senā muhūrtam api tiṣṭhati
āhaveṣv āhava|śreṣṭha karṇa|hīn" êva naur jale.
yathā hy a|karṇa|dhārā nau rathaś c' â|sārathir yathā
draved yath"|êṣṭaṃ tadvat syād ṛte senā|patiṃ balam.
5.10 a|deśiko yathā s'|ârthaḥ sarvaṃ kṛcchraṃ samarcchati
a|nāyakā tathā senā sarvān doṣān samarcchati.
sa bhavān vīkṣya sarveṣu māmakeṣu mah"|ātmasu

SÁNJAYA spoke.

MAJESTY, WHEN Duryódhana saw the tiger Karna standing in his chariot ready to attack, he was delighted and he spoke to him. 5.1

"My lord, with you as its guardian it seems that our army has found its savior. What, then, do you propose we do? We shall take whatever course you advise."

KARNA spoke.

O wisest of kings and tiger in the forest of men, it is you who must now speak. Only a man of worldly power can see what must be done. My king, all who stand before you are eager to hear your command. So come, my liege. Speak to the purpose.

DURYÓDHANA spoke.

Bhishma was our leader, a man equally rich in might, 5.5
courage, holy lore and every virtue that a warrior could have. Over these ten days he has cut with wild force through the ranks of my enemies and we have been safe beneath his aegis. Great warrior though he was it was an arduous task and now he is bound for heaven. Tell me, Karna. Who do you think should be commander in his stead? An army is like a ship on the ocean. Lacking a leader it cannot survive the bloody fighting in which you o Karna so excel, just as a ship cannot sail without a man at its helm. An army without a commander careers out of control like a rudderless ship,*
like a chariot without a driver. Like a caravan lost to fate in 5.10
a foreign land, a leaderless army is lost to calamity. My lord cast your eyes across my brave soldiers. Choose one fit to follow in the wake of Shántanu's son and take us into battle.

paśya senā|patiṃ yuktam anu Śāṃtanavād iha.
yaṃ hi senā|praṇetāraṃ bhavān vakṣyati saṃyuge
taṃ vayaṃ sahitāḥ sarve kariṣyāmo na saṃśayaḥ.

KARṆA uvāca.

sarva eva mah"|ātmāna ime puruṣa|sattamāḥ
senā|patitvam arhanti, n' âtra kāryā vicāraṇā.
kula|saṃhanana|jñānair bala|vikrama|buddhibhiḥ
yuktāḥ kṛta|jñā hrīmanta āhaveṣv a|nivartinaḥ.
5.15 yugapan na tu te śakyāḥ kartuṃ sarve puraḥ|sarāḥ
eka ev' âtra kartavyo yasmin vaiśeṣikā guṇāḥ.
anyonya|spardhināṃ hy eṣāṃ yady ekaṃ yaṃ kariṣyasi
śeṣā vimanaso vyaktaṃ na yotsyante hi Bhārata.
ayaṃ ca sarva|yodhānām ācāryaḥ sthaviro guruḥ
yuktaḥ senā|patiṃ kartuṃ: Droṇaḥ śastra|bhṛtāṃ varaḥ.
ko hi tiṣṭhati dur|dharṣe Droṇe brahma|vid|uttame
senā|patiḥ syād anyo 'smāc Chukr'|Āṅgirasa|darśanāt.
na ca so 'py asti te yodhaḥ sarva|rājasu Bhārata
Droṇaṃ yaḥ samare yāntaṃ n' ânuyāsyati saṃyuge.
5.20 eṣa senā|praṇetṝṇām eṣa śastra|bhṛtām api
eṣa buddhi|matāṃ c' âiva śreṣṭho, rājan, gurus tava.
evaṃ Duryodhan'|ācāryam āśu senā|patiṃ kuru
jigīṣanto 'surān saṃkhye Kārttikeyam iv' âmarāḥ.

SAṂJAYA uvāca.

6.1 KARṆASYA VACANAṂ śrutvā rājā Duryodhanas tadā
senā|madhya|gataṃ Droṇam idaṃ vacanam abravīt.

Be assured that the man you name for this supreme office we will all join to anoint leader.

KARNA spoke.

There can be no doubt that every one of these brave men is worthy of the post. All of them match warcraft, cunning, bravery and strength with humility and loyalty. None would flee the fray. Of course not all of them can 5.15
be elevated to this highest of honors. Yet there is one alone whom you should choose, for his virtues are unique. These men are rivals, o son of Bhárata. If you were to favor one then those you slight in doing so would never agree to fight. The man I suggest is none other than their wise and steadfast teacher: Drona, the master swordsman. He should be appointed commander. What candidate is there besides the unbreakable and peerless seer, in aspect brilliant as one of 5.20
the ancient priests? Who would make a better leader than he? O Bhárata there is no warrior among all your vassals who would not follow Drona into battle. Come now. Make Duryódhana's own instructor commander of this army as when the gods wanted to defeat the demons it was Skanda to whom they turned.

SÁNJAYA spoke.

KING DURYÓDHANA heard Karna's advice. These were the 6.1
words he said to Drona while the whole of the army looked on.

DURYODHANA uvaca.

varṇa|śraiṣṭhyāt kul'|ôtpattyā śrutena vayasā dhiyā
vīryād dākṣyād a|dhṛṣyatvād artha|jñānān nayāj jayāt
tapasā ca kṛta|jñatvād vṛddhaḥ sarva|guṇair api
yukto bhavat|samo goptā rājñām anyo na vidyate.
sa bhavān pātu naḥ sarvān devān iva Śata|kratuḥ,
bhavan|netrāḥ parāñ jetum icchāmo dvi|ja|sattama.
6.5 Rudrāṇām iva Kāpālī Vasūnām iva Pāvakaḥ
Kubera iva yakṣāṇāṃ Marutām iva Vāsavaḥ
Vasiṣṭha iva viprāṇāṃ tejasām iva bhās|karaḥ
pitṝṇām iva Dharmo 'tha, Ādityānām iv' Âmbu|rāṭ
nakṣatrāṇām iva śaśī Diti|jānām iv' Ôśanāḥ
śreṣṭhaḥ senā|praṇetṝṇāṃ sa naḥ senā|patir bhava.
akṣauhiṇyo daś' âikā ca vaśa|gāḥ santu te, 'n|agha,
tābhiḥ śatrūn prativyūhya jah' Îndro dānavān iva.
prayātu no bhavān agre devānām iva Pāvakiḥ
anuyāsyāmahe tv ājau saurabheyā iva' ṛṣabham.
6.10 ugra|dhanvā mah''|êṣv|āso divyaṃ visphārayan dhanuḥ
agre|bhavaṃ tvāṃ tu dṛṣṭvā n' Ârjunaḥ prahariṣyati.
dhruvaṃ Yudhiṣṭhiraṃ saṃkhye
s'|ânubandhaṃ sa|bāndhavam
jeṣyāmi, puruṣa|vyāghra,
bhavān senā|patir yadi.

DURYÓDHANA spoke.

You were born into the highest caste and to a family of noble stock. Your wisdom and power and brilliance of mind are matched in your courage, ingenuity, persistence and prudence. You are a leader and you have known success. You are one of our elders who through discipline has learned the nature of what happens in this world. In you is present all that is good and no man is more fit for the role of guardian of kings than yourself. O protect us now as Indra does the gods. With our eyes on the highest of the twiceborn we will
rise to destroy our opponents. As the skullbearer leads the 6.5
Rudras* and Agni leads the Vasus, as Kubéra leads the *yakshas* and Indra the Maruts, as Vasíshtha leads the brahmins and the sun leads all that is bright, as Dharma* leads our forefathers, as the Lord of Waters leads the children of Áditi, the moon the stars and Úshanas the sons of Diti o leader without equal be our commander now.

O sinless Drona. The eleven battalions all await your command. Draw them up and massacre our enemies as Indra massacred the demons. Lead the charge like Skanda before the gods and let us follow you into battle like a herd
behind its bull. Great archer. When in the heart of the fray 6.10
you loose the enchanted string of your mighty bow, Árjuna will see you and his courage will drain away. With you as my general o tiger in the forest of men I will throw down in battle the steadfast Yudhi·shthira, and all of his brothers and friends.

SAMJAYA uvāca.

evam ukte tato Droṇaṃ jay' êty ūcur nar'|âdhipāḥ
siṃha|nādena mahatā harṣayantas tav' ātma|jam.
sainikāś ca mudā yuktā vardhayanti dvi|j'|ôttamam
Duryodhanaṃ puras|kṛtya prārthayanto mahad yaśaḥ.
Duryodhanaṃ tato, rājan, Droṇo vacanam abravīt.

DROṆA uvāca.

7.1 VEDAṂ ṢAḌ|AṄGAṂ ved' âham artha|vidyāṃ ca mānavīm
Traiyambakam ath' êṣv|astraṃ śastrāṇi vividhāni ca.
ye c' âpy uktā mayi guṇā bhavadbhir jaya|kāṅkṣibhiḥ
cikīrṣus tān ahaṃ sarvān yodhayiṣyāmi Pāṇḍavān.
Pārṣataṃ tu raṇe rājan na haniṣye kathaṃ cana
sa hi sṛṣṭo vadh'|ârthāya mam' âiva puruṣa'|rṣabhaḥ.
yodhayiṣyāmi sainyāni nāśayan sarva|Somakān
na ca māṃ Pāṇḍavā yuddhe yodhayiṣyanti harṣitāḥ.

SAMJAYA uvāca.

7.5 sa evam abhyanujñātaś cakre senā|patiṃ tataḥ
Droṇaṃ tava suto rājan vidhi|dṛṣṭena karmaṇā.
ath' âbhiṣiṣicur Droṇaṃ Duryodhana|mukhā nṛ|pāḥ
senāpatye yathā Skandaṃ purā Śakra|mukhāḥ surāḥ.
tato vāditra|ghoṣeṇa saha puṃsāṃ mahā|svanaiḥ
prādur āsīt kṛte Droṇe harṣaḥ senā|patau tadā.
tataḥ puṇy'|âha|ghoṣeṇa svasti|vāda|svanena ca
saṃstavair gīta|śabdaiś ca sūta|Māgadha|bandinām.

SÁNJAYA spoke.

When Duryódhana finished his address, the chieftains sent up a roar. Your son swelled in his breast at their cries. Their hearts set now on a glorious triumph, the troops cheered on the great twiceborn in excited voices and sang out their praises to the king. Then, o majesty, it was the turn of Drona to speak.

DRONA spoke.

TRUE, DURYÓDHANA: I am well versed in the sixlimbed 7.1
Veda, I understand the laws of the human world and the lore of Rudra. I know well the bow, and every kind of blade.* All that your majesty ascribes to me in his enthusiasm for winning this struggle I would hope to prove I possess in battle with the Pándavas. My king there is one bull in their army that I will never be able to kill, for the grandson of Príshata has been born to end my life. But I will fight their teeming horde and wipe out all the rest of Drúpada's clan.* As for the Pándavas, their courage will fail them when they cross my path.

SÁNJAYA spoke.

Your son had made his decision o majesty and with due 7.5
ceremony he appointed Drona commander. With his brothers the king anointed Drona just as Indra and the gods of old had once anointed Skanda. Elation welled up around their new general to a chorus of drums and flutes and the bellows of men. To the strains of the songs and hymns of the panegyrists and bards and the incantations of the high priests the crowd rippled with expectation. Murmuring benedictions

jaya|śabdair dvi|j'|âgryāṇāṃ su|bhag"|ānartitais tathā
sat|kṛtya vidhinā Droṇaṃ menire Pāṇḍavāñ jitān.

SAMJAYA uvāca.

7.10 senāpatyaṃ tu samprāpya Bhāradvājo mahā|rathaḥ
yuyutsur vyūhya sainyāni prāyāt tava sutaiḥ saha.
Saindhavaś ca Kaliṅgaś* ca Vikarṇaś ca tav' ātma|jaḥ
dakṣiṇaṃ pārśvam āsthāya samatiṣṭhanta daṃśitāḥ.
prapakṣaḥ Śakunis teṣāṃ pravarair haya|sādibhiḥ
yayau Gāndhārakaiḥ sārdhaṃ vimala|prāsa|yodhibhiḥ.
Kṛpaś ca Kṛtavarmā ca Citraseno Viviṃśatiḥ
Duḥśāsana|mukhā yattāḥ savyaṃ pakṣam apālayan.
teṣāṃ prapakṣāḥ Kāmbojāḥ Sudakṣiṇa|puraḥ|sarāḥ
yayur aśvair mahā|vegaiḥ Śakāś ca Yavanaiḥ saha.
7.15 Madrās Trigartāḥ s'|Âmbaṣṭhāḥ pratīcy'|ôdīcya|Mālavāḥ
Śibayaḥ Śūrasenāś ca Śūdrāś ca Maladaiḥ saha.
Sauvīrāḥ Kitavāḥ prācyā dākṣiṇātyāś ca sarvaśaḥ
tav' ātma|jaṃ puras|kṛtya Sūta|putrasya pṛṣṭhataḥ.
harṣayantaḥ sva|sainyāni prāyāt tava sutaiḥ saha
pravaraḥ sarva|yodhānāṃ baleṣu balam ādadhāt.
yayau Vaikartanaḥ Karṇaḥ pramukhe sarva|dhanvinām
tasya dīpto mahā|kāyaḥ svāny anīkāni harṣayan.
hasti|kakṣyo mahā|ketur babhau sūrya|sama|dyutiḥ
na Bhīṣma|vyasanaṃ kaś cid dṛṣṭvā Karṇam amanyata.
7.20 viśokāś c' âbhavan sarve rājānaḥ Kurubhiḥ saha
hṛṣṭāś ca bahavo yodhās tatr' âjalpanta vegataḥ.
«na hi Karṇaṃ raṇe dṛṣṭvā yudhi sthāsyanti Pāṇḍavāḥ.
Karṇo hi samare śakto jetuṃ devān sa|Vāsavān,

and celebrating the luck of the day his soldiers bowed low to Drona. They thought the Pándavas beaten already.

SÁNJAYA spoke.

Keen to start the attack now that he was commander the 7.10
mighty descendant of Bharad·vaja arrayed his troops and prepared to set out with your children. Sáindhava, Kalínga and your son Vikárna formed at the right flank a wall of chainmail. At the tip of their wing and with a group of elite horsemen, Shákuni advanced before the Gandháras, warriors of the sacred arrows. Cautiously guarding the left flank were Kripa, Krita·varman, Chitra·sena and Vivínshati, all led by Duhshásana, and at their edge King Sudákshina led the Kambójas, mounted on swift steeds alongside the
Shakas and the Yávanas. The Madras, the Tri·gartas, the 7.15
Ambáshthas, the Málavas and the peoples of the North and the West, the Shibis, the Shura·senas, Shudras and Máladas, the Sauvíras and Kítavas and the peoples of the East and the South all took up position behind your son and Suta·putra. Compounding force with force their greatest warrior and inspiration stood with Duryódhana at the front of the archers: sunborn Karna, a blaze before their wide eyes tipped with the great flag of the tiger flashing like the sky's orb.

All who saw Karna then forgot about the defeat of Bhishma. Kings and Kurus cast aside their despair. Anxious with 7.20
excitement the soldiers began to whisper to one another. "The Pándavas will turn and run when they see who has returned to the battlefield. Karna could defeat the gods and the Vasus themselves. How much more easily the sons of Pandu will fail when their courage and strength have deserted

kim u Pāṇḍu|sutān yuddhe hīna|vīrya|parākramān.
Bhīṣmeṇa tu raṇe Pārthāḥ pālitā bāhu|śālinā
tāṃs tu Karṇaḥ śarais tīkṣṇair nāśayiṣyati saṃyuge.»

evaṃ bruvantas te 'nyonyaṃ hṛṣṭa|rūpā viśāṃ pate
Rādheyaṃ pūjayantaś ca praśaṃsantaś ca niryayuḥ.
asmākaṃ śakaṭa|vyūho Droṇena vihito 'bhavat.
7.25 pareṣāṃ krauñca ev' āsīd vyūho, rājan, mah"|ātmanām.
prīyamāṇena vihito Dharmarājena, Bhārata.
vyūha|pramukhatas teṣāṃ tasthatuḥ puruṣa'|rṣabhau
vānara|dhvajam ucchritya Viṣvaksena|Dhanaṃjayau.
kakudaṃ sarva|sainyānāṃ lakṣma sarva|dhanuṣmatām
Āditya|patha|gaḥ ketuḥ Pārthasy' â|mita|tejasaḥ
dīpayām āsa tat sainyaṃ Pāṇḍavasya mah"|ātmanaḥ
yathā prajvalitaḥ sūryo yug'|ânte vai vasuṃ|dharām.
yodhānām Arjunaḥ śreṣṭho Gāṇḍīvaṃ dhanuṣāṃ varam
Vāsudevaś ca bhūtānāṃ cakrāṇāṃ ca Sudarśanam
7.30 catvāry etāni tejāṃsi vahañ śveta|hayo rathaḥ
pareṣām agratas tasthau kāla|cakram iv' ôdyatam.

them! Bhishma had kept the Parthas from harm with his mighty reach,* but now the biting arrows of Karna will cut them down."

O king and lord of the Bháratas, these were the things they said as they went forth, thrilled to the marrow. All the while they praised Radha's son and urged him on. Drona set us out in the array of the spearhead while the mildtem-
pered and righteous king drew up our great enemy in the 7.25
formation of the curlew. Leading their force were the twin bulls Vishvak·sena and Dhanan·jaya. Above them flew the army's pinnacle and the star over every bowman: the banner of the monkey. In the path of the sun the standard of vastsplendored Partha mighty son of Pandu lit up his followers as that same sun had once set alight the earth at the end of the last age. A chariot drawn by white horses bore in dazzling quartet Árjuna the master archer, with Gandíva greatest of bows in his grip and Vasudéva lord of all creatures at his side, the discus Sudárshana* a perfect circle in
the god's hands. It hung between us and our enemies like 7.30
the turning wheel of time.

evaṃ tau su|mah"|ātmānau bala|sen"|âgra|gāv ubhau
tāvakānāṃ mukhe Karṇaḥ pareṣāṃ ca Dhanaṃjayaḥ.
tato jay'|âbhisaṃrabdhau paras|para|vadh'|âiṣiṇau
avekṣetāṃ tad" ânyonyaṃ samare Karṇa|Pāṇḍavau.
tataḥ prayāte sahasā Bhāradvāje mahārathe
ārta|nādena ghoreṇa vasudhā samakampata.
tatas tumulam ākāśam āvṛṇot sa|divā|karam
vāt'|ôddhūtaṃ rajas tīvraṃ kauśeya|nikar'|ôpamam.
7.35 vavarṣa dyaur an|abhr" âpi māṃs'|âsthi|rudhirāṇy uta
gṛdhrāḥ śyenā bakāḥ kaṅkā vāyasāś ca sahasraśaḥ.
upary upari senāṃ te tadā paryapatan, nṛ|pa,
go|māyavaś ca prākrośan bhaya|dān dāruṇān ravān.
akārṣur apasavyaṃ ca bahuśaḥ pṛtanāṃ tava
cikhādiṣanto māṃsāni pipāsantaś ca śoṇitam.
apatad dīpyamānā ca sa|nirghātā sa|kampanā
ulkā jvalantī saṃgrāme pucchen' āvṛtya sarvaśaḥ.
pariveṣo mahāṃś c' âpi sa|vidyut|stanayitnumān
bhās|karasy' âbhavad, rājan, prayāte vāhinī|patau.
7.40 ete c' ânye ca bahavaḥ prādur āsan su|dāruṇāḥ
utpātā yudhi vīrāṇāṃ jīvita|kṣaya|kāriṇaḥ.

tataḥ pravavṛte yuddhaṃ paras|para|vadh'|âiṣiṇām
Kuru|Pāṇḍava|sainyānāṃ śabden' âpūrayaj jagat.
te tv anyonyaṃ su|saṃrabdhāḥ Pāṇḍavāḥ Kauravaiḥ saha
abhyaghnan niśitair bāṇair jaya|gṛddhāḥ prahāriṇaḥ.
sa Pāṇḍavānāṃ mahatāṃ mah"|êṣv|āso mahā|dyutiḥ
vegen' âbhyadravat senāṃ kirañ śara|śataiḥ śitaiḥ.
Droṇam abhyudyataṃ dṛṣṭvā Pāṇḍavāḥ saha Sṛñjayaiḥ

Face to face in the van were the two greatest warriors: Karna at the head of your troops, Dhanan·jaya at the head of theirs. For a moment Karna and Pandu's son regarded one another across the battlefield. Each was fired for victory, each bore the other's doom in his eyes. Then all of a sudden as the mighty Drona gave the command the earth lurched with a terrifying and tortured groan and the tumultuous sky and the sun within it were obscured as a hot storm of dust blew upward like a great curtain of silk, and from the cloudless heavens there poured a rain of gore, bones
and blood, and flocks of vultures, hawks, cranes, herons 7.35
and crows wheeled dizzily above the heads of your soldiers, my king, and with eerie, pitiless howls jackals drew deadly circles around us, hungry and thirsty for flesh and blood. Tearing open the air a meteor streaked across the sky and hurtled all the way towards the rearguard before it slammed into the shuddering earth. O majesty, when Drona gave the command the great corona of the sun itself crackled
darkly with lightning. Many and dire were the portents we 7.40
witnessed. All heralded the massacre of heroes in the battle to come.

And so the welter of violence began again. The whole world filled with the sounds of the armies of the Pándavas and the Káuravas. They crashed together in fury beneath arrows loosed to satisfy the hunger of each to destroy the other. The great brightshining archer of the brave Pándavas plunged towards his foes, cascading a hundred shard-like shafts across them as he went. Then, my king, Drona reared up for the attack and seeing him the Pándavas and
the Srínjayas together sent out a tempest of arrows. But 7.45

pratyagṛhṇaṃs tadā, rājañ, śara|varṣaiḥ pṛthak pṛthak.
7.45 vikṣobhyamāṇā Droṇena bhidyamānā mahā|camūḥ
vyaśīryata sa|Pāñcālā vāten' êva balāhakāḥ.
bahūn' îha vikurvāṇo divyāny astrāṇi saṃyuge
apīḍayat kṣaṇen' âiva Droṇaḥ Pāṇḍava|Sṛñjayān.
te vadhyamānā Droṇena Vāsaven' êva dānavāḥ
Pāñcālāḥ samakampanta Dhṛṣṭadyumna|puro|gamāḥ.
tato divy'|âstra|vic chūro Yājñasenir mahā|rathaḥ
abhinac chara|varṣeṇa Droṇ'|ânīkam an|ekadhā.
Droṇasya śara|varṣāṇi śara|varṣeṇa Pārṣataḥ
saṃnivārya tataḥ sarvān Kurūn apy avadhīd balī.
7.50 saṃyamya tu tato Droṇaḥ samavasthāpya c' āhave
svam anīkaṃ mah"|êṣv|āsaḥ Pārṣataṃ samupādravat.
sa bāṇa|varṣaṃ su|mahad asṛjat Pārṣataṃ prati
Maghavān samabhikruddhaḥ sahasā dānaveṣv iva.

te kampyamānā Droṇena bāṇaiḥ Pāṇḍava|Sṛñjayāḥ
punaḥ punar abhajyanta siṃhen' êv' êtare mṛgāḥ.
tathā paryacarad Droṇaḥ Pāṇḍavānāṃ bale balī
alāta|cakravad, rājaṃs, tad adbhutam iv' âbhavat.
kha|cara|nagara|kalpaṃ kalpitaṃ śāstra|dṛṣṭyā
calad|anila|patākaṃ hlāditaṃ valgit'|âśvam
sphaṭika|vimala|ketuṃ trāsanaṃ śātravāṇāṃ
ratha|varam adhirūḍhaḥ saṃjahār' âri|senām.

on Drona came, harrowing and cleaving and scattering like thunderclouds before the wind a great division of the Pándavas and the Panchálas. Now Drona unleashed his divine arsenal and the Pándavas and the Srínjayas were eclipsed beneath his attacks as he went reaving through them like Indra among the demons. While the Panchálas were quaking behind their leader Dhrishta·dyumna, the brave warrior Shikhándin who also knew the heavenly weapons burst showers of arrows from every quarter down onto Drona's battalion. Mighty Dhrishta·dyumna also countered Drona's storms with storms of his own, pouring down ruin upon
the heads of the Kurus. Pausing in the thick of combat to 7.50
gather his wits, the great archer Drona ferocious as Maghavan before the *dánava*s drove his legion on towards Dhrishta·dyumna's, took aim, and sent forth a dense torrent of shafts.

The Pándavas and the Srínjayas were shaken by Drona's attack, shredded again and again in his grip like deer in the jaws of a lion. My king as the mighty Drona sent his great chariot in circles through the Pándavas it became a kind of wonder to behold, a firebrand, decked according to scripture like a dwelling of the spirits of the air, its horses rearing, exultant, its banner dancing like the wind itself and its crest flawless as crystal striking fear into all who beheld it. Standing tall upon his car he closed his enemies in a ring of death.

SAMJAYA uvāca.

8.1 TATHĀ DROṆAM abhighnantaṃ s'|âśva|sūta|ratha|dvi|pān
vyathitāḥ Pāṇḍavā dṛṣṭvā na c' âinaṃ paryavārayan.
tato Yudhiṣṭhiro rājā Dhṛṣṭadyumna|Dhanaṃjayau
abravīt sarvato yattaiḥ kumbha|yonir nivāryatām.
tatr' âinam Arjunaś c' âiva Pārṣataś ca sah'|ânugaḥ
paryagṛhṇaṃs tataḥ sarve samāpetur mahā|rathāḥ:
Kaikeyā Bhīmasenaś ca Saubhadro 'tha Ghaṭotkacaḥ
Yudhiṣṭhiro yamau Matsyā Drupadasy' ātma|jas tathā
8.5 Draupadeyāś ca saṃhṛṣṭā Dhṛṣṭaketuḥ sa|Sātyakiḥ
Cekitānaś ca saṃkruddho Yuyutsuś ca mahā|rathaḥ
ye c' ânye pārthivā, rājan, Pāṇḍavasy' ânuyāyinaḥ
kula|vīry'|ânurūpāṇi cakruḥ karmāṇy an|ekaśaḥ.

saṃgṛhyamāṇāṃ tāṃ dṛṣṭvā Pāṇḍavair vāhinīṃ raṇe
vyāvṛtya cakṣuṣī kopād Bhāradvājo 'nvavaikṣata.
sa tīvraṃ kopam āsthāya rathe samara|dur|madaḥ
vyadhamat Pāṇḍav'|ânīkam abhrāṇ' îva sadā|gatiḥ.
rathān aśvān narān nāgān abhidhāvann itas tataḥ
cacār' ônmattavad Droṇo vṛddho 'pi taruṇo yathā.
8.10 tasya śoṇita|digdh'|âṅgāḥ śoṇās te vāta|raṃhasaḥ
ājāneyā hayā rājann a|viśrāntā dhruvaṃ yayuḥ.
tam antakam iva kruddham āpatantaṃ yata|vratam
dṛṣṭvā samprādravan yodhāḥ Pāṇḍavasya tatas tataḥ.
teṣāṃ prādravatāṃ bhīmaḥ punar āvartatām api
paśyatāṃ tiṣṭhatāṃ c' āsīc chabdaḥ parama|dāruṇaḥ.
śūrāṇāṃ harṣa|janano bhīrūṇāṃ bhaya|vardhanaḥ
dyāvā|pṛthivyor vivaraṃ pūrayām āsa sarvataḥ.

SÁNJAYA spoke.

DRONA TORE ON through elephants, horses, chariots and 8.1
their drivers and the Pándavas reeled at the spectacle, unable to check his advance. King Yudhi·shthira turned to Dhrishta·dyumna and Dhanan·jaya and ordered that the brahmin born of clay* be stopped. They were to engage him on every front. Árjuna, Dhrishta·dyumna and their companions all nodded their assent and the great warriors rushed out towards Drona as one: the Kaikéyas, Bhima·sena, Saubhádra and Ghatótkacha, Yudhi·shthira and the twins, the Matsyas,
Drúpada's eldest and the five ferocious sons of Dráupadi, 8.5
Dhrishta·ketu, Sátyaki and wild Chekitána, mighty Yuyútsu and the numberless other kings o majesty who allied to Pandu had proven their heroism and station with their deeds.

Drona watched from his chariot as the Pándavas bore down upon his army and his eyes misted with anger. Berserk with battle frenzy he drove the Pándavas back before him as if they were clouds upon an everblowing wind. O king their cars horses men and elephants flew from him in all directions. Old Drona quick as a man a fraction his age moved
now as if possessed. His crimson bloodspattered thorough- 8.10
breds swift as the wind charged on and did not seem to tire. The iron holy man fell upon them like merciless Death himself, and when they saw him Yudhi·shthira's warriors ran for their lives. As they fled or turned on their heels or gawped or froze where they stood, an appalling and deafening clamor to thrill the bold and terrify the weak rose up and filled the vast space between heaven and earth.

tataḥ punar api Droṇo nāma viśrāvayan yudhi
akarod raudram ātmānaṃ kirac chara|śataiḥ parān.
8.15 sa tathā teṣv anīkeṣu Pāṇḍu|putreṣu, māriṣa,
kālavad vyacarad Droṇo yuv" êva sthaviro balī
utkṛtya ca śirāṃsy ugro bāhūn api su|bhūṣaṇān
kṛtvā śūnyān rath'|ôpasthān udakrośan mahā|rathaḥ.
tasya harṣa|praṇādena bāṇa|vegena vā vibho
prākampanta raṇe yodhā gāvaḥ śīt"|ârditā iva.
Droṇasya ratha|ghoṣeṇa maurvī|niṣpeṣaṇena ca
dhanuḥ|śabdena c' ākāśe śabdaḥ samabhavan mahān.
ath' âsya dhanuśo bāṇā niścarantaḥ sahasraśaḥ
vyāpya sarvā diśaḥ petur nāg'|âśva|ratha|pattiṣu.
8.20 taṃ kārmuka|mahā|vegam astra|jvalita|pāvakam
Droṇam āsādayāṃ cakruḥ Pāñcālāḥ Pāṇḍavaiḥ saha.
tān sa|kuñjara|patty|aśvān prāhiṇod Yama|sādanam
cakre '|cireṇa ca Droṇo mahīṃ śoṇita|kardamām.
tanvatā param'|âstrāṇi śarān satatam asyatā
Droṇena vihitaṃ dikṣu śara|jālam adṛśyata.
padātiṣu rath'|âśveṣu vāraṇeṣu ca sarvaśaḥ
tasya vidyud iv' âbhreṣu caran ketur adṛśyata.

Become something monstrous, Drona spread a thick rain of arrows upon his foes and spread his renown abroad once
again. My lord, with the vigor of a youth the venerable and 8.15
mighty Drona wheeled like Time among the reams of Pandu's sons and roaring in wrath plucked off heads and tore away arms still banded in gold and left the chariots in his wake mere empty shells. O highness, cowering before his delighted howls and the volleys from his bow his adversaries in that battle were little more than cattle crushed in the track of a plow. The churning of Drona's chariot, the clash of iron and the thrum of his bowstring built to a crescendo that rang through the air as a thousand arrows flitted in a blur from his bow up to clog the sky and tumbled down upon the throng of infantry, chariots, horses and elephants below.

The Pándavas and the Panchálas all streamed towards the 8.20
great wave of his bow and the bright fire of his arrows and Drona dispatched them and their elephants, soldiers and steeds down to Death's kingdom. Soon he had steeped the earth in gore. As he sent arrows soaring endlessly overhead, a lattice of shafts that he had woven appeared across the sky and his banner flashed among soldiers, horses, chariots and elephants like lightning flashing through clouds.

sa Kaikayānāṃ pravarāṃś ca pañca
Pāñcāla|rājaṃ ca śaraiḥ pramathya
Yudhiṣṭhir'|ânīkam a|dīna|sattvo
Droṇo 'bhyayāt kārmuka|bāṇa|pāṇiḥ.
8.25 taṃ Bhīmasenaś ca Dhanaṃjayaś ca
Śineś ca naptā Drupad'|ātma|jaś ca
Śaiby'|ātma|jaḥ Kāśi|patiḥ Śibiś ca
dṛṣṭvā nadanto vyakirac char'|âughaiḥ.
teṣām atho Droṇa|dhanur|vimuktāḥ
patatriṇaḥ kāñcana|citra|puṅkhāḥ
bhittvā śarīrāṇi gaj'|âśva|yūnāṃ
jagmur mahīṃ śoṇita|digdha|vājāḥ.
sā yodha|saṃghaiś ca rathaiś ca bhūmiḥ
śarair vibhinnair gaja|vājibhiś ca
pracchādyamānā patitair babhūva
samāvṛtā dyaur iva kāla|meghaiḥ.
Śaineya|Bhīm'|Ârjuna|vāhinīśaṃ
Saubhadra|Pāñcāla|sa|Kāśi|rājam
anyāṃś ca vīrān samare mamarda
Droṇaḥ sutānāṃ tava bhūti|kāmaḥ.
etāni c' ânyāni ca, Kaurav'|êndra,
karmāṇi kṛtvā samare mah"|ātmā
pratāpya lokān iva kāla|sūryo
Droṇo gataḥ svargam ito hi rājan.
8.30 evaṃ Rukmarathaḥ śūro hatvā śata|sahasraśaḥ
Pāṇḍavānāṃ raṇe yodhān Pārṣatena nipātitaḥ.
akṣauhiṇīm abhyadhikāṃ śūrāṇām a|nivartinām
nihatya paścād dhṛtimān agacchat paramāṃ gatim.
Pāṇḍavaiḥ saha Pāñcālair a|śivaiḥ krūra|karmabhiḥ
hato Rukmaratho, rājan, kṛtvā karma su|duṣ|karam.

Five paladins of the Kékayas and the Panchála king fell under the hail of shafts, and still Drona came on towards Yudhi·shthira's army unchecked. They saw him coming, bow and arrow in hand. Bhima·sena and Dhanan·jaya, the 8.25
scion of Shini and son of Drúpada, King Shibi of Kashi and his prince together sent up a storm of arrows to a chorus of battle cries, but back on fletchings speckled with gold came the winged shafts from Drona's bow to lodge fast in the bodies of elephantriders and horsemen, sending their bloodweltered steeds crashing to the ground beneath them. There were piles of corpses and cars, horses and elephants riddled in arrows. The dead hid the earth as dark skies engloom the day.

Shainéya, Bhima, Árjuna and Dhrishta·dyumna, Abhimányu, the Panchála princes, the king of Kashi and others of their allies all suffered in that battle as Drona defended your sons' cause. O high king of the Káuravas, in his acts that day great Drona was like the sun setting the lands alight when the world is at an end. Now, he is in heaven.

His victims on the Pándava side were legion but the 8.30
heroic Rukma·ratha finally fell, and at Dhrishta·dyumna's hand. He brought devastation almost without end to that mighty army of valiant warriors but o my king at long last he set foot on the final road. O majesty, after all of Rukma·ratha's impossible deeds the Pándavas and Panchálas could slay him only through vicious deceit. And when the preceptor did fall dead upon the plain, a mournful cry rose up into

tato ninādo bhūtānām ākāśe samajāyata
sainyānāṃ ca tato rājann ācārye nihate yudhi.
dyāṃ dharāṃ khaṃ diśo v" âpi pradiśaś c' ânunādayan
aho dhig iti bhūtānāṃ śabdaḥ samabhavan mahān.
8.35 devatāḥ pitaraś c' âiva pūrve ye c' âsya bāndhavāḥ
dadṛśur nihataṃ tatra Bhāradvājaṃ mahā|ratham.
Pāṇḍavās tu jayaṃ labdhvā siṃha|nādān pracakrire
siṃha|nādena mahatā samakampata medinī.

DHṚTARĀṢṬRA uvāca.

9.1 KIṂ KURVĀṆAṂ raṇe Droṇaṃ jaghnuḥ Pāṇḍava|Sṛñjayāḥ
tathā nipuṇam astreṣu sarva|śastra|bhṛtām api?
ratha|bhaṅgo babhūv' âsya dhanur v" âśīryat' âsyataḥ
pramatto v" âbhavad Droṇas tato mṛtyum upeyivān.
kathaṃ nu Pārṣatas, tāta, śatrubhir duṣ|pradharṣaṇam
kirantam iṣu|saṃghātān rukma|puṅkhān an|ekaśaḥ
kṣipra|hastaṃ dvi|ja|śreṣṭhaṃ kṛtinaṃ citra|yodhinam
dūr'|êṣu|pātinaṃ dāntam astra|yuddheṣu pāra|gam
9.5 Pāñcāla|putro nyavadhīd divy'|âstra|dharam a|cyutam
kurvāṇaṃ dāruṇaṃ karma raṇe yattaṃ mahā|ratham?
vyaktaṃ hi daivaṃ balavat pauruṣād iti me matiḥ
yad Droṇo nihataḥ śūraḥ Pārṣatena mah"|ātmanā.
astraṃ catur|vidhaṃ vīre yasminn āsīt pratiṣṭhitam
tam iṣv|astra|dhar'|ācāryaṃ Droṇaṃ śaṃsasi me hatam.
śrutvā hataṃ Rukmarathaṃ vaiyāghra|parivāritam
jātarūpa|pariṣkāraṃ n' âdya śokam upādade.
na nūnaṃ para|duḥkhena mriyate ko 'pi Saṃjaya

the air. And o king it did not come from the armies alone. Echoing in unison through the sky, the earth, the stratosphere, through every quarter of space, was the immense threnody of all living things. Even the gods and the an- 8.35
cestors and the forebears of Bharad·vaja's son looked down upon the great warrior where he lay. Only the Pándavas roared with glee. And the earth shook once again at this mighty sound.

DHRITA·RASHTRA spoke.

IT CANNOT BE. The Pándavas and the Srínjayas slew Dro- 9.1
na? The greatest warrior to have lived? And in the thick of battle? His chariot must have failed, or his bow split as he drew it. Or did mere carelessness offer him Death's hand? O my son. How did Dhrishta·dyumna strike him down? His enemies could barely touch him. There was no weapon he had not mastered. He was a twiceborn without peer who without effort cast from his dancing hands glinting clouds of farflying arrows, a vengeful fighter who wielded the weapons of heaven, whose composure even at the heart of the fray was unshakable. And yet a son of the Panchálas 9.5
slew him.

The power of fate* in the affairs of men is now clear to my eyes. The hero Drona's death at the hand of Príshata's mighty grandson attests to it. You tell me that Rukma·ratha, a man deeply versed in the fourfold art of combat, teacher to all bearers of arrows and swords, clad as much in the finery of perfection as in the tigerskin wrapped about his shoulders—that this man is dead? No. My grief is too great. O Sánjaya it is true that no one dies from feeling pain for

yat tad Droṇaṃ hataṃ śrutvā hato jīvāmi manda|bhāk.
daivam eva paraṃ manye nanv an|arthaṃ hi pauruṣam
9.10 aśma|sāra|mayaṃ nūnaṃ hṛdayaṃ su|dṛḍhaṃ mama
yac chrutvā nihataṃ Droṇaṃ śatadhā na vidīryate.
brāhme daive tath" êṣv|astre yam upāsan guṇ'|ârthinaḥ
brāhmaṇā rāja|putrāś ca sa kathaṃ mṛtyunā hṛtaḥ?
śoṣaṇaṃ sāgarasy' êva Meror iva visarpaṇam
patanaṃ bhās|karasy' êva na mṛṣye Droṇa|pātanam.
dṛptānāṃ pratiṣeddh" āsīd dhārmikānāṃ ca rakṣitā
yo 'hāsīt kṛpaṇasy' ârthe prāṇān api paraṃ|tapaḥ.
mandānāṃ mama putrāṇāṃ jay'|āśā yasya vikrame
Bṛhaspaty|Uśanas|tulyo buddhyā sa nihataḥ katham?
9.15 te ca śoṇā bṛhanto 'śvāś channā jālair hiraṅ|mayaiḥ
rathe vāta|javā yuktāḥ sarva|śastr'|âtigā raṇe
balino hreṣiṇo dāntāḥ Saindhavāḥ sādhu|vāhinaḥ
dṛḍhāḥ saṃgrāma|madhyeṣu kac cid āsan na vihvalāḥ.
kariṇāṃ bṛṃhatāṃ yuddhe śaṅkha|dundubhi|niḥsvanaiḥ
jyā|kṣepa|śara|varṣāṇāṃ śastrāṇāṃ ca sahiṣṇavaḥ
āśaṃsantaḥ parāñ jetuṃ jita|śvāsā jita|vyathāḥ
hayāḥ prajavitāḥ śīghrā Bhāradvāja|rath'|ôdvahāḥ
te sma Rukmarathe yuktā nara|vīra|samāhatāḥ
kathaṃ n' âbhyataraṃs tāta Pāṇḍavānām anīkinīm?

another. But now that I know Drona is no more I feel the pulse of life die in me. One thing is certain. It is that fate alone is supreme, human effort fruitless.

O the man's death blights my own. It is as if I too am no 9.10
more. My heart must be made of solid stone that it does not shatter into a hundred pieces at such tidings. They all went to him: brahmins and princes, all who wanted to learn the art of war or the nature of the gods. How can death have snatched him from us? Has the ocean dried up? Has Meru slid away? The sun fallen from the sky? I cannot accept that he is dead. He brought the proud low and raised up the just. Though the scourge of his foes, he bore the cruelties of life lightly. In his courage lived my own wretched children's dreams of victory. He was brilliant as Brihas·pati or Úshanas. How can he be dead? The tall bays yoked to his char- 9.15
iot and mantled in golden mail galloped swift as the wind past every blade. They were stallions from Sindhu, powerful, whinnying, quickdrawing steeds, indomitable but ever gentle for their master, and stoic even when the fighting was fiercest. The heralds' sounds of conch and drum could not disturb them, they were untroubled before swords and before the arrows flowing from the strings of bows, They were horses fleet and nimble, and breathing mild and easy in limb they stopped the breath of any that rode against them. How can it be, my son, that yoked to Drona's golden car and surrounded by the mightiest of men they did not cross through to the far side of the Pándavas?

9.20 jātarūpa|pariṣkāram āsthāya ratham uttamam
Bhāradvājaḥ kim akarod yudhi satya|parākramaḥ?
vidyāṃ yasy' ôpajīvanti sarva|loka|dhanur|dharāḥ
sa satya|saṃdho balavān Droṇaḥ kim akarod yudhi?
divi Śakram iva śreṣṭhaṃ mahā|mātraṃ dhanur|bhṛtām
ke nu taṃ raudra|karmāṇaṃ yuddhe pratyudyayū rathāḥ?
nanu Rukmarathaṃ dṛṣṭvā prādravanti sma Pāṇḍavāḥ
divyam astraṃ vikurvāṇaṃ raṇe tasmin mahā|balam?
ut' âho sarva|sainyena Dharmarājaḥ sah'|ânujaḥ
Pāñcālya|pragraho Droṇaṃ sarvataḥ samavārayat?
9.25 nūnam āvārayat Pārtho rathino 'nyān a|jihma|gaiḥ
tato Droṇaṃ samārohat Pārṣataḥ pāpa|karma|kṛt.
na hy ahaṃ paripaśyāmi vadhe kaṃ cana śuṣmiṇaḥ
Dhṛṣṭadyumnād ṛte raudrāt pālyamānāt Kirīṭinā.
tair vṛtaḥ sarvataḥ śūraiḥ Pāñcāly'|âpasadas tataḥ
Kekayaiś Cedi|Kārūṣair Matsyair anyaiś ca bhūmi|paiḥ
vyākulī|kṛtam ācāryaṃ pipīlair uragaṃ yathā
karmaṇy a|su|kare saktaṃ jaghān' êti matir mama.
yo 'dhītya caturo vedān s'|âṅgān ākhyāna|pañcamān
brāhmaṇānāṃ pratiṣṭh" āsīt srotasām iva sāgaraḥ.
9.30 kṣatraṃ ca brahma c' âiv' êha yo 'bhyatiṣṭhat paraṃ|tapaḥ
sa kathaṃ brāhmaṇo vṛddhaḥ śastreṇa gatim āptavān?

O tell me my son. With truth as his weapon how fared 9.20
mighty Drona before his death, mounted in his supernal
chariot girt in gold? Tell me of his acts in battle. All in
this world who bear the bow live by their knowledge of the
truth that dwelled within him. What warrior would dare
to go into battle to meet this greatest of archers, this man
terrifying and supreme as the heavenly Indra? Did the Pándavas see the great Rukma·ratha ranging his divine arsenal
before them and ride out against him all the same? Did the
righteous king enclose him within a circle of his brothers
and Panchála friends?

Was it Partha who with his darts hemmed in the other 9.25
warriors while the cruel grandson of Príshata advanced towards Drona? I can think of none with the mettle for this
murderous act except cruel Dhrishta·dyumna, the ward of
the Diademed Warrior. None but the Panchála bastard. I
see him flanked on every side by fighters, by Kékayas and
Chedis, Karúshas, Matsyas and the other chieftains, all over-
whelming Drona like ants crawling on a great snake, trap-
ping him beneath a remorseless onslaught such that Dhri-
shta·dyumna could move in to slay his teacher. Drona was
revered among brahmins as a master of every limb of the five
Vedas,* and they came to study with him as the rivers flow
to the sea. He would not suffer any to cross him, warrior 9.30
or priest. How can a learned man of the book have met his
fate at the tip of the sword?

a|marṣinā marṣitavān kliśyamānān sadā mayā
an|arhamāṇaḥ Kaunteyān karmaṇas tasya tat phalam.
yasya karm' ânujīvanti loke sarva|dhanur|bhṛtaḥ
sa satya|saṃdhaḥ su|kṛtī śrī|kāmair nihataḥ katham?
divi Śakra iva śreṣṭho mahā|sattvo mahā|balaḥ
sa kathaṃ nihataḥ Pārthaiḥ kṣudra|matsyair yathā timiḥ?
kṣipra|hastaś ca balavān dṛḍha|dhanv" âri|mardanaḥ
na yasya jīvit'|ākāṅkṣī viṣayaṃ prāpya jīvati.
9.35 yaṃ dvau na jahataḥ śabdau jīvamānaṃ kadā cana
brāhmaś ca veda|kāmānāṃ jyā|ghoṣaś ca dhanuṣmatām.
a|dīṇaṃ puruṣa|vyāghraṃ hrīmantam a|parājitam
n' âhaṃ mṛṣye hataṃ Droṇaṃ siṃha|dvi|rada|vikramam.

kathaṃ Saṃjaya durdharṣam an|ādhṛṣya|yaśo|balam
paśyatāṃ puruṣ'|êndrāṇāṃ samare Pārṣato 'vadhīt?
ke purastād ayudhyanta rakṣanto Droṇam antikāt
ke nu paścād avartanta gacchato durgamāṃ gatim?
ke 'rakṣan dakṣiṇaṃ cakraṃ savyaṃ ke ca mah"|âtmanaḥ
purastāt ke ca vīrasya yudhyamānasya saṃyuge?
9.40 ke ca tasmiṃs tanūs tyaktvā pratīpaṃ mṛtyum āvrajan
Droṇasya samare vīrāḥ ke 'kurvanta parāṃ dhṛtim?

It was my rash purpose that led to the sufferings of Kunti's children. Drona had sympathy for them throughout—the fate he suffered was undeserved. His wise and truthful example was followed by every man who called himself a warrior. How can men who value majesty have slain him? How can one mighty in soul and arm and great as Indra in heaven be slain by the sons of Pandu, a leviathan devoured by minnows? Perhaps it was because he had a quick hand and strong arms and because before his unbreakable bow his foes knew no quarter. None who came to take Drona's
life survived. There are two sounds which a man never lives 9.35
to forget: the voice of one who knows the Veda and the sigh of a bow in a master's hands. Drona had the bravery of a wild beast, he was a tiger in the forest of men. His force and glory were untrammeled. Dead? It is unthinkable, Sánjaya.

So it was Dhrishta·dyumna who killed Drona while all the other kings watched. But how did he get close enough when no other could approach Drona's splendor and might? Which of Drona's friends at that moment failed to protect him? And after he set foot on that hardest of journeys who took his place? Tell me, who was guarding the right flank of the great man's chariot, who the left? Who was near to
him as he fought? And who threw off his own life and met 9.40
Death early? Which of the heroes around Drona showed the greatest resolve?

kac cin n' âinaṃ bhagān mandāḥ kṣatriyā vyajahan raṇe
rakṣitāras tataḥ śūnye kac cit tair na hataḥ parair?
na sa pṛṣṭham ares trāsād raṇe śauryāt pradarśayet
parām apy āpadaṃ prāpya sa kathaṃ nihataḥ paraiḥ?
etad āryeṇa kartavyaṃ kṛcchrāsv āpatsu, Saṃjaya,
parākramed yathā|śaktyā tac ca tasmin pratiṣṭhitam.
muhyate me manas, tāta, kathā tāvan nivartyatām
bhūyas tu labdha|saṃjñas tvā paripraksyāmi Saṃjaya.

VAIŚAMPĀYANA uvāca.

10.1 EVAṂ PṚṢṬVĀ sūta|putraṃ hṛc|choken' ârdito bhṛśam
jaye nir|āśaḥ putrāṇāṃ Dhṛtarāṣṭro 'patat kṣitau.
taṃ visaṃjñaṃ nipatitaṃ siṣicuḥ paricārakāḥ
jalen' âtyartha|śītena vījantaḥ puṇya|gandhinā.
patitaṃ c' âinam ājñāya samantād Bharata|striyaḥ
parivavrur mahā|rājam aspṛśaṃś c' âiva pāṇibhiḥ.
utthāpya c' âinaṃ śanakai rājānaṃ pṛthivī|talāt
āsanaṃ prāpayām āsur bāṣpa|kaṇṭhyo var'|âṅganāḥ.
10.5 āsanaṃ prāpya rājā tu mūrchay" âbhipariplutaḥ
niś|ceṣṭo 'tiṣṭhata tadā vījyamānaḥ samantataḥ.
sa labdhvā śanakaiḥ saṃjñāṃ vepamāno mahī|patiḥ
punar Gāvalgaṇiṃ sūtaṃ paryapṛcchad yathā|tatham.

How did the measly swordsmen who were his enemies sever him from the bosom of his army? How, indeed, could they fail to finish him when he had none to protect him? His courage was such that whatever disasters befell him or fears beset him he would never have turned his back on his foes. How then did they strike him down? Drona knew well that even in darkest calamity the noble fight on as they can. O my mind is in a whirl. My son, let us cease for a time your tale. I must gather my senses Sánjaya. Then we will talk again.

VAISHAMPÁYANA spoke.

DHRITA·RASHTRA finished speaking and suddenly heart- 10.1
stricken at the hopelessness of his sons' cause he collapsed in a faint to the floor. His attendants sprinkled cold droplets of perfumed water on his face to revive him. The ladies with him were shocked at the sight and rushed to him and laid their hands upon the great king. Necklaced in tears, they gently lifted his body in their beautiful arms and placed
him upon the throne. As they fanned him on all sides he sat 10.5
there unmoving, still deep in his swoon. At last, the lord of the realm slowly opened his eyes. But when he spoke again to his driver Gaválgani his questions were little changed.

DHRITA·RASHTRA uvāca.

yat tad udyann iv' Ādityo jyotiṣā praṇudaṃs tamaḥ
āyād Ajātaśatrur vai kas taṃ Droṇād avārayat?
prabhinnam iva mātaṅgaṃ tathā kruddhaṃ tarasvinam
āsakta|manasaṃ dīptaṃ prati|dvirada|ghātinam
vāśitā|saṃgame yadvad a|jayyaṃ prati|yūthapaiḥ
ati c' ânyān raṇe yodhān vīraḥ puruṣa|sattamaḥ
yo hy eko hi mahā|bāhur nirdahed ghora|cakṣuṣā
kṛtsnaṃ Duryodhana|balaṃ dhṛtimān satya|saṃgaraḥ
10.10 cakṣur|haṇaṃ jaye saktam iṣv|āsa|vara|rakṣitam
dāntaṃ bahu|mataṃ loke ke śūrāḥ paryavārayan?
ke duṣ|pradharṣaṃ rājānam iṣv|āsa|varam a|cyutam
samāsedur nara|vyāghraṃ Kaunteyaṃ tatra māmakāḥ?
taras" âiv' âbhipaty' âtha yo vai Droṇam upādravat
taṃ Bhīmasenam āyāntaṃ ke śūrāḥ paryavārayan?
yad āyāj jala|da|prakhyo rathaḥ parama|vīryavān
parjanya iva Bībhatsus tumulām aśaniṃ sṛjan
vavarṣa śara|varṣāṇi varṣāṇi Maghavān iva
iṣu|sambādham ākāśaṃ kurvan kapi|vara|dhvajaḥ
avasphūrjan diśaḥ sarvās tala|nemi|svanena ca
10.15 cāpa|vidyut|prabho ghoro ratha|gulma|balāhakaḥ
ratha|nemi|ghoṣa|stanitaḥ śara|śabd'|âtibandhuraḥ
roṣa|nirjita|jīmūto mano|'bhiprāya|śīghra|gaḥ
marm'|âti|go bāṇa|dhāras tumulaḥ śoṇit'|ôdakaḥ
samplāvayan mahīṃ sarvāṃ mānavair āstaraṃs tadā

DHRITA·RASHTRA spoke.

The matchless king at his zenith is like the rising sun that drives away darkness with its light. Who kept him from Drona? He has the fury, the potency, the fire of an elephant in must that with singular intent would kill any rival that came near the females of the herd. None of the other bulls could beat him. He is a man bound to truth, strong in arm and steadfast in will. His power so much exceeds any of the warriors he might face that with just a terrible glance from his murderous eyes he could reduce
the whole of Duryódhana's army to cinders. And somehow 10.10
he keeps his humility despite the world's veneration. Who looked into his deadly gaze? Who stood in his path as he came cleaving to victory, ringed in the finest archers? And what of Bhima·sena? He must have been one of the first to rush upon Drona. Who were the warriors who stood in his path? And what happened as that most awesome chariot of them all came into view like a thunderhead or baleful stormcloud forking and crackling with lightningand pouring down wood as Indra pours down hail? How was it for those who watched as Partha approached beneath the banner of the monkey, the air about him thick with arrows?
As the wheels of his chariot squealed across the sky, his 10.15
bow a flashing arc and grim omen above the dense thickets of cars below, his car a tempest driven by wrath and faster than thought or wish and heavy with needles biting to men's marrow? As it came churning with a blood rain and strewing the earth with the dead that now fill it while the wrenching and ghastly noise ever grew and brilliant and victorious and screwed to the purpose Árjuna scattered from the string of

gadā|niṣṭanito raudro Duryodhana|kṛt'|ôdyamaḥ
yuddhe 'bhyaṣiñcad Vijayo gārdhra|patraiḥ śil"|āśitaiḥ
Gāṇḍīvaṃ dhārayan dhīmān kīdṛśaṃ vo manas tadā?
kac cid Gāṇḍīva|śabdena na praṇaśyati vai balam
yad vaḥ sa bhairavaṃ kurvann Arjuno bhṛśam abhyagāt?
10.20 kac cin n' âpānudad Droṇād iṣubhir vo Dhanaṃjayaḥ
vāto meghān iv' āvidhyan pravāñ śara|van'|ânilaḥ
ko hi Gāṇḍīva|dhanvānaṃ naraḥ soḍhuṃ raṇe 'rhati?
yat senāḥ samakampanta yad vīrān aspṛśad bhayam
ke tatra n' ājahur Droṇaṃ ke kṣudrāḥ prādravan bhayāt?
ke vā tatra tanūs tyaktvā pratīpaṃ mṛtyum āvrajan
a|mānuṣāṇāṃ jetāraṃ yuddheṣv api Dhanaṃjayam?
na ca vegaṃ sit'|âśvasya viśakṣyant' îha māmakāḥ
Gāṇḍīvasya ca nirghoṣaṃ prāvṛḍ|jala|da|nisvanam.
viṣvak|seno yasya yantā yoddhā c' âiva Dhanaṃjayaḥ
a|śakyaḥ sa ratho jetuṃ manye dev'|âsurair api.
10.25 su|kumāro yuvā śūro darśanīyaś ca Pāṇḍavaḥ
medhāvī nipuṇo dhīmān yudhi satya|parākramaḥ
ārāvaṃ vipulaṃ kurvan vyathayan sarva|Kauravān
yad" āyān Nakulo dhīmān ke śūrāḥ paryavārayan?
āśī|viṣa iva kruddhaḥ Sahadevo yad" âbhyayāt
śatrūṇāṃ kadanaṃ kurvañ jet" âsau dur|jayo yudhi
ārya|vratam a|mogh'|êṣuṃ hrīmantam a|parājitam
Droṇāy' âbhimukhaṃ yāntaṃ ke śūrāḥ paryavārayan?
yaḥ sa Sauvīra|rājasya pramathya mahatīṃ camūm
ādatta mahiṣīṃ bhojyāṃ kāmyāṃ sarv'|âṅga|śobhanām.

Gandíva stonewhetted shafts tied with vulture feathers all across the plain: o how was your heart then?

Who did not flee when the mere sound of Gandíva's string brought terror among you? And who were they whom Dha- 10.20
nan·jaya's arrows severed from Drona's company as Árjuna rolled like a gust through trembling cloud, a wind through a brake of reeds? What man could stand his ground before the carrier of Gandíva? Whole armies tremble and heroes are filled with dread at his coming. Who stood firm beside Drona? And who were the cowards who fled? Who cast aside his body and went out to meet Death in the shape of Dhanan·jaya, conqueror of warriors not of this earth? Before the charge of his pale horse and the monsoon thunder of Gandíva my mortal soldiers are finished. A chariot holding Dhanan·jaya and manned by Krishna is, I fear, a chariot that neither god nor demon could stop.

Then there is Pandu's youthful fourth son, the handsome 10.25
Nákula. He is a man in his prime, a man brilliant, wise and brave whose war cry fills the Káuravas with fear. Who fought him back when he rode at Drona? Or when fierce Saha·deva came angry as a cobra to take his prey? He is a conquerer that few could overcome, a man of grace and noble covenants, unerring and unstoppable. Who parried Saha·deva's attack? It was Saha·deva who broke King Sauvíra's royal guard and carried off his voluptuous and lovelylimbed queen.

10.30 satyaṃ dhṛtiś ca śauryaṃ ca brahma|caryaṃ ca kevalam
sarvāṇi Yuyudhāne 'smin nityāni puruṣa'|ṛṣabhe.
balinaṃ satya|karmāṇam a|dīnam a|parājitam
Vāsudeva|samaṃ yuddhe Vāsudevād an|antaram
yuktaṃ Dhanaṃjaya|preṣye śūram ācārya|karmaṇi
Pārthena samam astreṣu kas taṃ Droṇād avārayat?
Vṛṣṇīnāṃ pravaraṃ vīraṃ śūraṃ sarva|dhanuṣmatām
Rāmeṇa samam astreṣu yaśasā vikrameṇa ca
satyaṃ dhṛtir damaḥ śauryaṃ brahma|caryam an|uttamam
Sātvate tāni sarvāṇi trailokyam iva Keśave
10.35 tam evaṃ guṇa|sampannaṃ dur|vāram api daivataiḥ
samāsādya mah"|êṣv|āsaṃ ke vīrāḥ paryavārayan?
Pāñcāleṣ' ûttamaṃ śūram uttam'|âbhijana|priyam
nityam uttama|karmāṇam Uttamaujasam āhave
yuktaṃ Dhanaṃjaya|hite mam' ân|arthāya c' ôttamam
Yama|Vaiśravaṇ'|Āditya|Mahendra|Varuṇ'|ôpamam
mahā|ratha|samākhyātaṃ Droṇāy' ôdyantam āhave
tyajantaṃ tumule prāṇān ke śūrāḥ paryavārayan?
eko 'pasṛtya Cedibhyaḥ Pāṇḍavān yaḥ samāśritaḥ
Dhṛṣṭaketuṃ tam āyāntaṃ Droṇāt kaḥ samavārayat?
10.40 yo 'vadhīt Ketumāñ śūro rāja|putraṃ su|darśanam
apar'|ânta|giri|dvāre kas taṃ Droṇād avārayat?
strī|pūrvo yo nara|vyāghro yaḥ sa veda guṇ'|â|guṇān
Śikhaṇḍinaṃ Yājñasenim a|mlāna|manasaṃ yudhi
Devavratasya samare hetuṃ mṛtyor mah"|ātmanaḥ
Droṇāy' âbhimukhaṃ yāntaṃ ke vīrāḥ paryavārayan?
yasminn abhyadhikā vīre guṇāḥ sarve Dhanaṃjayāt
yasminn astrāṇi satyaṃ ca brahma|caryaṃ ca nitya|dā

And the taurine Yuyudhána? All that is eternal rests in him: purity and piety, courage and constancy, harmony itself. He is strong in arm and hale in spirit. None have penetrated his armor of truth. He is Vasudéva's comrade and equal and a devoted peer of Dhanan·jaya, a true master of the art of sword and bow. Who drove him from Drona's midst? 10.30

Who fought back the great Vrishni Sátvata? A hero and paladin, as a warrior he is Rama's equal in valor and fame. In him as the triple world is in Késhava are truth and steadfastness, wisdom, heroism and holiness and a deep knowledge
of the sword and the book. His mettle would be too stern 10.35
even for the gods. Who faced him down? And the baleful Panchála hero Uttamáujas? He is a man beloved of the highborn, whose preternatural might has never failed in war or deed.As loyal and firm in Dhanan·jaya's cause as he is in my downfall, he strives in his whole being against Drona. Reckoned a mere champion, I know him as the equal of the gods of war and death, a warrior who has surrendered his life to the chaos of battle. And the prodigy Dhrishta·ketu, the hero who deserted the Chedis and sought refuge with
the Pándavas after killing the prince of the western reaches 10.40
in a mountain pass? Who drove off his attack?

What of the cause of the great fall of the Paragon, tigerlike Shikhándin? His mind even in the heat of combat is clear as crystal. Born a woman yet become a man, Yajnya·sena's child knows the troubled nature of both. And great Abhimányu? Subhádra's son has inherited all his father's high virtues of war and truth and shining purity. Who drove him from
Drona's reach? In courage he is like Vasudéva, in might 10.45

Vāsudeva|samaṃ vīrye Dhanaṃjaya|samaṃ bale
tejas" Āditya|sa|dṛśaṃ Bṛhaspati|samaṃ matau
10.45 Abhimanyuṃ mah"|ātmānaṃ vyātt'|ānanam iv' ântakam
Droṇāy' âbhimukhaṃ yāntaṃ ke vīrāḥ paryavārayan?
taruṇas tv aruṇa|prakhyaḥ Saubhadraḥ para|vīra|hā
yad" âbhyādravata Droṇaṃ tad" āsīd vo manaḥ katham?
Draupadeyā nara|vyāghrāḥ samudram iva sindhavaḥ
yad Droṇam ādravan saṃkhye ke vīrās tān avārayan?
ye te dvā|daśa varṣāṇi krīḍām utsṛjya bālakāḥ
astr'|ârtham avasan Bhīṣme bibhrato vratam uttamam
Kṣatraṃjayaḥ Kṣatradevaḥ Kṣatradharmā ca māninaḥ
Dhṛṣṭadyumn'|ātma|jā vīrāḥ ke tān Droṇād avārayan?
10.50 śatād viśiṣṭaṃ yaṃ yuddhe samapaśyanta Vṛṣṇayaḥ
Cekitānaṃ mah"|êṣv|āsaṃ kas taṃ Droṇād avārayat?
Vārddhakṣemiḥ Kaliṅgānāṃ yaḥ kanyām āharad yudhi
Anādhṛṣṭir a|dīn'|ātmā kas taṃ Droṇād avārayat?
bhrātaraḥ pañca Kaikeyā dhārmikāḥ satya|vikramāḥ
Indra|gopaka|varṇāś ca rakta|varm'|āyudha|dhvajāḥ
mātṛ|ṣvasuḥ sutā vīrāḥ Pāṇḍavānāṃ jay'|ârthinaḥ
tān Droṇaṃ hantum āyātān ke vīrāḥ paryavārayan?
yaṃ yodhayanto rājāno n' ājayan Vāraṇāvate
ṣaṇ māsān abhisaṃrabdhā jighāṃsanto yudhāṃ patim
10.55 dhanuṣmatāṃ varaṃ śūraṃ satya|saṃdhaṃ mahā|balam
Droṇāt kas taṃ nara|vyāghraṃ Yuyutsuṃ pratyavārayat?
yaḥ putraṃ Kāśi|rājasya Vārāṇasyāṃ mahā|ratham
samare strīṣu gṛdhyantaṃ bhallen' âpaharad rathāt
Dhṛṣṭadyumnaṃ mah"|êṣv|āsaṃ
Pārthānāṃ mantra|dhāriṇam
yuktaṃ Duryodhan'|ân|arthe
sṛṣṭaṃ Droṇa|vadhāya ca

like Dhanan·jaya, like Brihas·pati in intellect, in splendor like the sun, wide-mawed as the Destroyer himself. How did you bear his attack? And Dráupadi's tigers? Who could fight them back when they rushed across the battlefield at Drona like rivers to the ocean? Laying aside the toys of childhood they dwelt for twelve years with Bhishma to study the art of combat and follow the strictest vows. And what about the sons of Dhrishta·dyumna— Kshatran·jaya, Kshatra·deva and noble Kshatra·dharman? Who kept them at bay?
Or the great bowman Chekitána, whom the other Vrishnis 10.50
decree to be a hundred times greater than themselves? Who stopped him?

Who protected Drona from the jubilant Kalínga Ana·dhríshti heir of Vriddha·kshema? I hear he has claimed a wife from the war. And the five righteous brothers born of Kékaya and the sons of their mother's sister? They are bold and heroic and fervent for a Pándava victory. When they came in cloaks the hue of fireflies and beneath the standard of the redarmored warrior, who stood in their path? And what of the warrior lord and strongarmed hero whom the kings of Varanávata desperate for blood fought for six fruitless
months: the best of bowmen and pillar of truth and tiger 10.55
in the forest of men Yuyútsu? Who forced his mighty arms from Drona? And the great archer charged with the Parthas' mantras who in Vαránasi toppled with a barbed arrow the lustful prince of Kashi? As he drove on, scattering soldiers in all directions and fixed on Drona's slaughter and Duryódhana's downfall, who forced Dhrishta·dyumna back? And the stripling grandson of Drúpada? Who fought off the adept in the art of the bow Kshatra·deva son of Shikhándin?

nirdahantaṃ raṇe yodhān dārayantaṃ ca sarvaśaḥ
Droṇāy' âbhimukhaṃ yāntaṃ ke vīrāḥ paryavārayan?
utsaṅga iva saṃvṛddhaṃ Drupadasy' âstra|vittamam
Śaikhaṇḍinaṃ Kṣatradevaṃ ke taṃ Droṇād avārayan?
10.60 ya imāṃ pṛthivīṃ kṛtsnāṃ carmavat samaveṣṭayat
mahatā ratha|vaṃśena mukhy'|âri|ghno mahā|rathaḥ
daś' âśva|medhān ājahre sv|anna|pān'|āpta|dakṣiṇān
nir|argalān sarva|medhān putravat pālayan prajāḥ.
Gaṅgā|srotasi yāvatyaḥ sikatā apy a|śeṣataḥ
tāvatīr gā dadau vīra Uśīnara|suto 'dhvare.
«na pūrve n' âpare cakrur idaṃ ke cana mānavāḥ»
iti saṃcukruśur devāḥ kṛte karmaṇi duṣ|kare.
«paśyāmas triṣu lokeṣu na taṃ saṃsthāsnu|cāriṣu
jātaṃ v" âpi janiṣyaṃ vā dvitīyaṃ v" âpi samprati
10.65 anyam Auśīnarāc Chaibyād dhuro voḍhāram ity» uta.
gatiṃ yasya na yāsyanti mānuṣā loka|vāsinaḥ
tasya naptāram āyāntaṃ Śaibyaṃ kaḥ samavārayat
Droṇāy' âbhimukhaṃ yāntaṃ vyātt'|ānanam iv' ântakam?
Virāṭasya rath'|ânīkaṃ Matsyasy' â|mitra|ghātinaḥ
prepsantaṃ samare Droṇaṃ ke vīrāḥ paryavārayan?
sadyo Vṛkodarāj jāto mahā|bala|parākramaḥ
māyāvī rākṣaso ghoro yasmān mama mahad bhayam
Pārthānāṃ jaya|kāmaṃ taṃ putrāṇāṃ mama kaṇṭakam
Ghaṭotkacaṃ mahā|bāhuṃ kas taṃ Droṇād avārayat?
10.70 ete c' ânye ca bahavo yeṣām arthāya Saṃjaya
tyaktāraḥ saṃyuge prāṇān kiṃ teṣām a|jitaṃ yudhi?
yeṣāṃ ca puruṣa|vyāghraḥ śārṅga|dhanvā vyapāśrayaḥ
hit'|ârthī c' âpi Pārthānāṃ kathaṃ teṣāṃ parājayaḥ?
lokānāṃ gurur atyantaṃ loka|nāthaḥ sanātanaḥ
Nārāyaṇo raṇe nātho divyo divy'|ātmavān prabhuḥ.

There was once a great warrior, and the roar of his chariot 10.60
wheels gathered like a cloak about the earth as he went abroad to destroy his legendary foes. I speak of the bold son of Ushi·nara, who cared for his subjects as if they were his children. Ten horse sacrifices he offered the gods, and he rewarded his priests with generous gifts of food and drink. He spared nothing. He immolated as many cows as there are grains of sand in the Ganges in a rite so awesome that the gods themselves found it hard to believe. "This is an act beyond any man who has come before, and any yet to be," they said. "We look upon the three worlds, on all that is and all that fades: there is none born nor to be born
nor reborn who wields powers such as Shaibya son of Ushi· 10.65
nara." None who live on this earth tread his path. Who then could keep his son, the last in Shibi's line, as he rode at Drona, wide-mawed as Death himself? And when Matsya's protector Viráta brought his troops to spill Drona's blood who drove them back? And I shudder at the thought of Vri·kódara's lastborn and his enormous strength and sorcerous powers. He yearns for the Parthas' triumph. The fiend Gha·tótkacha is the wound in my son's side. But someone kept him at bay. Who was it?

What brief triumph was there for those for whose sake 10.70
so many others abandoned their lives in battle? How was it that the sons of Pritha suffered any kind of defeat when the tiger that bears the horn bow fights to protect them? And what of the divine lord of battle and the highest teacher and eternal master of all worlds and beings, Naráyana? Wise men recount things that he has done that are not of this world.

yasya divyāni karmāṇi pravadanti manīṣiṇaḥ
tāny ahaṃ kīrtayiṣyāmi bhaktyā sthairy'|ârtham ātmanaḥ.

DHṚTARĀṢṬRA uvāca.

11.1 ŚṚṆU DIVYĀNI karmāṇi Vāsudevasya Saṃjaya
kṛtavān yāni Govindo yathā n' ânyaḥ pumān kva cit.
saṃvardhatā go|pa|kule bālen' âiva mah"|ātmanā
vikhyāpitaṃ balaṃ bāhvos triṣu lokeṣu Saṃjaya.
Uccaiḥśravas tulya|balaṃ vāyu|vega|samaṃ jave
jaghāna haya|rājaṃ yo Yamunā|vana|vāsinam.
dānavaṃ ghora|karmāṇaṃ gavāṃ mṛtyum iv' ôtthitam
vṛṣa|rūpa|dharaṃ bālye bhujābhyāṃ nijaghāna ha.
11.5 Pralambaṃ Narakaṃ Jambhaṃ
Pīṭhaṃ v" âpi mah"|âsuram
Muruṃ c' âmara|saṃkāśam
avadhīt puṣkar'|ēkṣaṇaḥ.
tathā Kaṃso mahā|tejā Jarāsaṃdhena pālitaḥ
vikrameṇ' âiva Kṛṣṇena sa|gaṇaḥ pātito raṇe.
Sunāmā raṇa|vikrāntaḥ samagr'|âkṣauhiṇī|patiḥ
Bhoja|rājasya madhya|stho bhrātā Kaṃsasya vīryavān
Baladeva|dvitīyena Kṛṣṇen' â|mitra|ghātinā
tarasvī samare dagdhaḥ sa|sainyaḥ śūra|sena|rāṭ.
Durvāsā nāma vipra'|rṣis tathā parama|kopanaḥ
ārādhitaḥ sa|dāreṇa sa c' âsmai pradadau varān.
11.10 tathā Gāndhāra|rājasya sutāṃ vīraḥ svayaṃ|vare
nirjitya pṛthivī|pālān āvahat puṣkar'|ēkṣaṇaḥ.
a|mṛṣyamāṇā rājāno yasya jātyā hayā iva
rathe vaivāhike yuktāḥ pratodena kṛta|vraṇāḥ.

I will tell you of his deeds now, and of the steadfastness of his heart.*

DHRITA·RASHTRA spoke.

HEAR ME NOW Sánjaya. I will tell you of Vasudéva's wondrous acts. Go·vinda has done thing which no normal man could dream of doing. 11.1

He was born with a lofty soul into a family of herdsmen. While still only a child the strength of his two arms brought him fame across the three worlds. On the wooded banks of the Yámuna he killed the horse king, who had been mighty as Ucchaih·shravas and swift as the racing wind, and though matched in might he slew the beast. Another time the cruel son of Danu came in the form of a bull and brought death among the cattle, and though a mere child the Lotus Eyed God killed him too, with his bare hands.

His next victims were Pralámba, Náraka, Jambha, the great demon Pitha and Muru, more god than devil. Then it was powerful Kansa who despite Jara·sandha's protection fell with his entire army before Krishna's onslaught. The Bhoja chieftain's brother was the legendary Sunáman, a stern and fiery taxiarch and bold king of serried heroes who met his nemesis when the younger brother of Bala·deva cut him down. Krishna bowed with his first wife before the ferocious seer Durvásas and was rewarded for his humility with gifts. 11.5

With many of the earth's regents bent to his will, the hero with lotus eyes took the hand of the Gandhára princess, and yoking to the bridal car the kings he had beaten cracked his whip across their backs as if they were so many steeds. With fiendish trickery mighty Krishna brought down the 11.10

Jarāsaṃdhaṃ mahā|bāhum upāyena Jan'|ârdanaḥ
pareṇa ghātayām āsa samagr'|âkṣauhiṇī|patim.
Cedi|rājaṃ ca vikrāntaṃ rāja|senā|patiṃ balī
arghe vivadamānaṃ ca jaghāna paśuvat tadā.
Saubhaṃ Daitya|puraṃ svasthaṃ Śālva|guptaṃ dur|āsadam
samudra|kukṣau vikramya pātayām āsa Mādhavaḥ.

11.15 Aṅgān Vaṅgān Kaliṅgāṃś ca Māgadhān Kāśi|kauśalān
Vātsya|Gārgya|Karūṣāṃś ca Pauṇḍrāṃś c' âpy ajayad raṇe
Āvantyān Dākṣiṇātyāṃś ca pārvatīyān Daśerakān
Kāśmīrakān Aurasakān Piśācāṃś ca sa|Mandarān
Kāmbojān Vāṭadhānāṃś ca Colān Pāṇḍyāṃś ca, Saṃjaya,
Trigartān Mālavāṃś c' âiva Daradāṃś ca su|dur|jayān
nānā|digbhyaś ca samprāptān Khaśāṃś c' âiva Śakāṃs tathā
jitavān puṇḍarīk'|âkṣo Yavanaṃ ca sah'|ânugaṃ.

pravíśya makar'|āvāsaṃ yādobhir abhisaṃvṛtam
jigāya Varuṇaṃ yuddhe salil'|ântar|gataṃ purā.
11.20 yudhi Pañcajanaṃ hatvā pātāla|tala|vāsinam
Pāñcajanyaṃ Hṛṣī|keśo divyaṃ śaṅkham avāptavān.
Khāṇḍave Pārtha|sahitas toṣayitvā hut'|âśanam
āgneyam astraṃ dur|dharṣaṃ cakraṃ lebhe mahā|balaḥ.
Vainateyaṃ samāruhya trāsayitv" Âmarāvatīm
Mahendra|bhavanād vīraḥ pārijātam upānayat.
tac ca marṣitavāñ Śakro jānaṃs tasya parākramam
rājñāṃ c' âpy a|jitaṃ kaṃ cit Kṛṣṇen' êha na śuśruma.
yac ca tan mahad āścaryaṃ sabhāyāṃ mama Saṃjaya
kṛtavān puṇḍarīk'|âkṣaḥ kas tad|anya ih' ârhati?

great general Jara·sandha and in return for a slight against his hospitality slaughtered like a goat the fierce king of the Chedis, who had been lord of a legion of chieftains. When the sheerwalled city of the demons named Saubha was prospering under Shalva's dominion, Mádhava attacked it and sent it crashing down into the depths of the ocean.

Sánjaya I speak of the conquerer of the Angas, the Va- 11.15
ngas, the Kalíngas and the Mágadhas famed for the city of lights, the Karúshas, Gargyas and Vatsyas, the Paundras, the Avántyas, the people of the South and the people of the mountains, the Dashérakas, Kashmírakas and Áurasakas, the Pisháchas and the peak of Mándara, the Kambójas, Vata·dhanas, the Cholas and Pandyas, the Tri·gartas and Málavas, the hardy Dáradas, the Khashas and the Shakas and Yávana and all her allies.

Long ago Hrishi·kesha entered the sea that teems with
monsters and in its surging depths beat down Váruna. He 11.20
killed Pancha·jana who dwelt in the plains of hell and took from him the sacred conch that bears the demon's name. With Árjuna the mighty Krishna calmed the great Eater of Cerements* in the forest of Khándava, and in return received his murderous disk, weapon of the fire. Mounted on Gáruda the great god terrorized Amarávati, the house of Indra, and tore up from its roots the coral tree that stood in its garden. Shakra knew of his attack and chose not to fight back. How could any king on this earth withstand him? And who could have caused the great miracle* in my throne room? None, o Sánjaya, but the Lotus Eyed God.

11.25 yac ca bhaktyā prapanno 'ham adrākṣaṃ Kṛṣṇam īśvaram
tan me su|viditaṃ sarvaṃ pratyakṣam iva c' āgamat.
n' ânto vikrama|yuktasya buddhyā yuktasya vā punaḥ
karmaṇaḥ śakyate gantuṃ Hṛṣīkeśasya Saṃjaya.
tathā Gadaś ca Sāmbaś ca Pradyumno 'tha Vidūrathaḥ
Āgāvaho 'niruddhaś ca Cārudeṣṇaś ca Sāraṇaḥ
Ulmuko Niśaṭhaś c' âiva Jhallī Babhruś ca vīryavān
Pṛthuś ca Vipṛthuś c' âiva samīko 'th' Ârimejayaḥ
ete vai balavantaś ca Vṛṣṇi|vīrāḥ prahāriṇaḥ
kathaṃ cit Pāṇḍav'|ânīkaṃ śrayeyuḥ samare sthitāḥ
11.30 āhūtā vṛṣṇi|vīreṇa Keśavena mah"|ātmanā.
tataḥ saṃśayitaṃ sarvaṃ bhaved iti matir mama.
nāg'|âyuta|balo vīraḥ Kailāsa|śikhar'|ôpamaḥ
vana|mālī halī rāmas tatra yatra Jan'|ârdanaḥ
yam āhuḥ sarva|pitaraṃ Vāsudevaṃ dvi|jātayaḥ
api vā hy eṣa Pāṇḍūnāṃ yotsyate 'rthāya Saṃjaya.
sa yadā tāta saṃnahyet Pāṇḍav'|ârthāya Keśavaḥ
na tadā pratyanīkeṣu bhavitā tasya kaś cana.
yadi sma Kuravaḥ sarve jayeyuḥ sarva|Pāṇḍavān
Vārṣṇeyo 'rthāya teṣāṃ vai gṛhṇīyāc chastram uttamam.
11.35 tataḥ sarvān nara|vyāghro hatvā nara|patīn raṇe
Kauravāṃś ca mahā|bāhuḥ Kuntyai dadyāt sa medinīm.
yasya yantā Hṛṣīkeśo yoddhā yasya Dhanaṃjayaḥ
rathasya tasya kaḥ saṃkhye pratyanīko bhaved rathaḥ?
na kena cid upāyena Kurūṇāṃ dṛśyate jayaḥ
tasmān me sarvam ācakṣva yathā yuddham avartata.

When I went before him and humbled myself and showed 11.25
him due devotion, the whole universe seemed to hang before my eyes in perfect clarity. Nothing that Hrishi·kesha
does has an end for his every act is born of certainty, of ab-
solute resolve. Gada, Samba, Pradyúmna and Vidu·ratha,
Agávaha, Anirúddha, Charu·deshna and Sárana, Úlmuka,
Níshatha, Jhallin, Babhru, Prithu and Víprithu, Samíka and
Arim·éjaya and all of the other Vrishni fighters have fallen
in among the Pándava legions. They are there because they 11.30
have been summoned to battle by their ram: the great Késhava himself.*

Everything else seems thrown into doubt. The mighty
hero strong as a hundred elephants and tall as Kailása's
peak, Rama the dark harvester necklaced in wildflowers,
goes where his brother goes. And o Sánjaya it is his brother
Janárdana the son of Vasu·deva who fights for the Pándava cause. He is known to the twiceborn as the father of
all things. When Késhava girds himself for their victory
no champion will rise against him. Even if the Kurus could
somehow overcome the Pándavas the tiger Varshnéya would
wield in their name the ultimate weapon and destroying all 11.35
the Káurava regents seize with his might the whole of the
world for Kunti's son. Who or what could ride against the
chariot driven by Hrishi·kesha and defended by Dhanan·
jaya? By no means will the Kurus see their day of triumph.
I ask only that you tell me all that happened during their
struggle.

Arjunaḥ Keśavasy' ātmā Kṛṣṇo 'py ātmā Kirīṭinaḥ
Arjune vijayo nityaṃ Kṛṣṇe kīrtiś ca śāśvatī.
prādhānyena hi bhūyiṣṭham a|meyāḥ Keśave guṇāḥ,
mohād Duryodhanaḥ Kṛṣṇaṃ yan na vett' îha Mādhavam.
11.40 mohito daiva|yogena mṛtyu|pāśa|puras|kṛtaḥ
na veda Kṛṣṇaṃ Dāśārham Arjunaṃ c' âiva Pāṇḍavam.
pūrva|devau mah"|ātmānau Nara|Nārāyaṇāv ubhau
ek'|ātmānau dvidhā|bhūtau dṛśyete mānavair bhuvi.
manas" âpi hi dur|dharṣau senām etāṃ yaśasvinau
nāśayetām ih' êcchantau mānuṣatvāt tu n' êcchataḥ.

yugasy' êva viparyāso lokānām iva mohanam
Bhīṣmasya ca vadhas, tāta, Droṇasya ca mah"|ātmanaḥ.
na hy eva brahma|caryeṇa na ved'|âdhyayanena ca
na kriyābhir na śastreṇa mṛtyoḥ kaś cid vimucyate.
11.45 loka|sambhāvitau vīrau kṛt'|âstrau yuddha|dur|madau
Bhīṣma|Droṇau hatau śrutvā kiṃ nu jīvāmi Saṃjaya?
yāṃ tāṃ śriyam asūyāma purā yātāṃ Yudhiṣṭhire
adya tām anujānīmo Bhīṣma|Droṇa|vadhena ca.
tathā ca mat|kṛte prāptaḥ Kurūṇām eṣa saṃkṣayaḥ
pakvānāṃ hi vadhe sūta vajrāyante tṛṇāny api.
an|anyam idam aiśvaryaṃ loke prāpto Yudhiṣṭhiraḥ
yasya kopān mah"|êṣv|āsau Bhīṣma|Droṇau nipātitau.
prāptaḥ prakṛtito dharmo na dharmo māmakān prati,
krūraḥ sarva|vināśāya kālaḥ samativartate.
11.50 anyathā cintitā hy arthā narais, tāta, manasvibhiḥ

Árjuna is Késhava's very soul, Krishna the Diademed Warrior's heart. Infinite glory rests in Krishna, and Árjuna carries with him triumph and eternity. It is simple: Késhava's virtues are transcendent, measureless, his majesty without equal. But delusion stops Duryódhana from knowing that
Krishna is Mádhava incarnate. Dazed by the power of fate 11.40
and recognizing neither Krishna of Dashárha nor Árjuna of Pandu he puts his neck in Death's noose. Though before their glory minds fail, men know them as the mighty gods of old, Nara and Naráyana. They are one soul split between two bodies. On a whim they could obliterate our troops and it is only their humanity that restrains them.

O my son. Bhishma's murder, and great Drona's. It seems the age is turning and the worlds are soon to be upended. No one can cheat death: not by a pious life nor by studying the
Veda, neither by hand nor by sword. O Sánjaya you tell me 11.45
that Bhishma and Drona, two master swordsmen hallowed across the earth and full of the frenzy of war, are dead. My days then are numbered. With the deaths of Bhishma and Drona all the wealth I have created will now pass to Yudhi·shthira and you and I will have to bring him our begging bowls. Disaster overtakes the Kurus because of what I did long ago. O horseman. For dry twigs and old men, a blade of grass can be as deadly as a lightning bolt.* Yudhi·shthira has attained a magnificence on earth beyond compare and those great archers Bhishma and Drona were victims of his wrath. The world is shaped through its own ordinance and cares not for the efforts of men. Cruel Time destroys
everything and then slips away, and it seems that even the 11.50
wise cannot grasp its secret purpose, that its assignments

anyath" âiva hi gacchanti daivād iti matir mama.
tasmād a|parihārye 'rthe samprāpte kṛcchra uttame
a|pāraṇīye duś|cintye yathā|bhūtaṃ pracakṣva me.

SAṂJAYA uvāca.

12.1 HANTA TE kathayiṣyāmi sarvaṃ pratyakṣa|darśivān
yathā saṃnyapatad Droṇaḥ sāditaḥ Pāṇḍu|Sṛñjayaiḥ.
senā|patitvaṃ samprāpya Bhāradvājo mahā|rathaḥ
madhye sarvasya sainyasya putraṃ te vākyam abravīt.
«yat Kauravāṇām ṛṣabhād Āpageyād an|antaram
senāpatyena māṃ, rājann, adya sat|kṛtavān asi,
sadṛśaṃ karmaṇas tasya phalaṃ āpnuhi, pārthiva.
karomi kāmaṃ kaṃ te 'dya? pravṛṇīṣva yam icchasi.»
12.5 tato Duryodhano rājā Karṇa|Duḥśāsan'|ādibhiḥ
tam ath' ôvāca dur|dharṣam ācāryaṃ jayatāṃ varam.
«dadāsi ced varaṃ mahyaṃ jīva|grāhaṃ Yudhiṣṭhiram
gṛhītvā rathināṃ śreṣṭhaṃ mat|samīpam ih' ānaya.»
tataḥ Kurūṇām ācāryaḥ śrutvā putrasya te vacaḥ
senāṃ praharṣayan sarvām idaṃ vacanam abravīt.
«dhanyaḥ Kuntī|suto rājā yasya grahaṇam icchasi
na vadh'|ârthaṃ su|dur|dharṣa varam anyaṃ prayācase.
kim|arthaṃ ca, nara|vyāghra, na vadhaṃ tasya kāṅkṣasi
n' āśaṃsasi kriyām etāṃ matto Duryodhana dhruvam.
12.10 āho svid Dharmarājasya dveṣṭā tasya na vidyate
yad' îcchasi tvaṃ jīvantaṃ kulaṃ rakṣasi c' ātmanaḥ.

violate even the will of the gods. Yet if these late days are wretched and remorseless and difficult to comprehend, tell me at least what it was that you saw.

SÁNJAYA spoke.

THEN AS I SAW it with my own eyes I will tell you the 12.1
whole story of how Drona was broken by the Pandus and the Srínjayas, and fell. When the mighty son of Bharad·vaja had been appointed commander, he turned to address Duryódhana. The whole army stood and listened.

"My king and lord of the earth. You have today done me a great honor in offering me the leadership of your army and making me the successor to the bull of the Káuravas born to Ápaga. May you reap a fitting reward for your choice. Say now what it is you would have me do, and I will do it."

Before Karna, Duhshásana and the other heroes, King 12.5
Duryódhana then told the hardy teacher of conquerors his wish.

"Grant me this supreme gift: capture alive their titan Yudhi·shthira and so prove yourself the rightful leader of my legions."

The teacher of the Kurus heard your son. His reply sent a ripple through the ranks.

"The king born of Kunti is a lucky man. You want him captured, you say, but not put to death. My intractable sire, tiger in this forest of men, why do you not want him dead? If you do not then Duryódhana you have taken leave of your
senses. The righteous king must have no enemies on earth 12.10
if even you want him alive, want to harbor his dynasty at your bosom. O best of the Bharatas, perhaps once you have

atha vā, Bharata|śreṣṭha, nirjitya yudhi Pāṇḍavān
rājyaṃ samprati dattvā ca saubhrātraṃ kartum icchasi?
dhanyaḥ Kuntī|suto rājā su|jātaṃ c' âsya dhīmataḥ
a|jāta|śatrutā tasya satyaṃ yat snihyate bhavān.»

Droṇena tv evam uktasya tava putrasya, Bhārata,
sahasā niḥsṛto bhāvo yo 'sya nityaṃ hṛdi sthitaḥ.
n' ākāro gūhituṃ śakyo Bṛhaspati|samair api
tasmāt tava suto rājan prahṛṣṭo vākyam abravīt.
12.15 «vadhe Kuntī|sutasy' ājau n', ācārya, vijayo mama.
hate Yudhiṣṭhire Pārtho hanyāt sarvān hi no dhruvam.
na ca śakyo raṇe sarvair nihantum amarair api
ya eva teṣāṃ śeṣaḥ syāt sa ev' âsmān na śeṣayet.
satya|pratijñe tv ānīte punar dyūtena nirjite
punar yāsyanty araṇyāya Pāṇḍavās tam anuvratāḥ.
so 'yaṃ mama jayo vyaktaṃ dīrgha|kālaṃ bhaviṣyati,
ato na vadham icchāmi Dharmarājasya karhi cit.»

tasya jihmam abhiprāyaṃ jñātvā Droṇo 'rtha|tattva|vit
taṃ varaṃ s'|ântaraṃ tasmai dadau saṃcintya buddhimān.

DROṆA uvāca.

12.20 na ced Yudhiṣṭhiraṃ, vīra, pālayaty Arjuno yudhi
manyasva Pāṇḍavaṃ jyeṣṭham ānītaṃ vaśam ātmanaḥ.
na hi śakyo raṇe Pārthaḥ s'|Êndrair dev'|âsurair api
pratyudyātum atas, tāta, n' âitad āmarṣayāmy aham.

defeated the Pándavas you intend to do your brotherly duty and offer them the realm that is rightly theirs? The wise son of Kunti is a fortunate soul. Truly no one wishes him ill.* Even your highness feels such warmth for him."

O Bhárata, at Drona's words the hope that Duryódhana had long kept hidden in his heart suddenly rushed to his lips. My king, even a great sage could not have hidden the excitement that your son felt then. These were the hot words he spoke.

"If Kuntí's son were to fall to the sword, master, then 12.15
victory would never be mine. With Yudhi·shthira gone Árjuna would stop at nothing until every one of us were dead. Even the deathless gods are powerless before him. Even if he were the Pándavas' lone survivor he would spare no man among us. But Yudhi·shthira is true to his word. If we can bring him here and play dice with him again, his luck will desert him, and he and his brothers will return once more to the forest. Then I will surely have my victory, and it will last long. So no. I do not want the good king to die."

In his wisdom Drona could penetrate to the heart of things, and he understood the depths of Duryódhana's trickery. He thought for a moment and then offered the king what he wanted. But there was one condition.

DRONA spoke.

Hero. Consider the eldest of the Pándavas your subject, 12.20
but only if Árjuna does not fight to protect him. As you say, even the gods and demons with Indra at their head could not rise against him and, my son, I for one will not deign to try. He was my student but without question my

a|saṃśayaṃ sa śiṣyo me mat|pūrvaś c' âstra|karmaṇi
taruṇaḥ kīrti|yuktaś ca ek'|âyana|gataś ca ha.
astrāṇ' Îndrāc ca Rudrāc ca bhūyaḥ sa samavāptavān
a|marṣitaś ca te, rājaṃs, tato n' āmarṣayāmy aham.
sa c' âpakramyatāṃ yuddhād yen' ôpāyena śakyate
apanīte tataḥ Pārthe Dharma|rājo jitas tvayā.
12.25 grahaṇaṃ cej jayaṃ tasya manyase puruṣa'|rṣabha
etena c' âbhyupāyena dhruvaṃ grahaṇam eṣyati.
ahaṃ gṛhītvā rājānaṃ satya|dharma|parāyaṇam
ānayiṣyāmi te rājan vaśam adya na saṃśayaḥ.
yadi sthāsyati saṃgrāme muhūrtam api me 'grataḥ
apanīte nara|vyāghre Kuntī|putre Dhanaṃjaye.
Phalgunasya samakṣaṃ tu na hi Pārtho Yudhiṣṭhiraḥ
grahītuṃ samare śakyaḥ s'|Êndrair api sur'|âsuraiḥ.

SAṂJAYA uvāca.

s'|ântaraṃ tu pratijñāte rājño Droṇena nigrahe
gṛhītaṃ tam amanyanta tava putrāḥ su|bāliśāḥ.
12.30 Pāṇḍaveṣu ca s'|âpekṣaṃ Droṇaṃ jānāti te sutaḥ
tataḥ pratijñā|sthairy'|ârthaṃ sa mantro bahulī|kṛtaḥ.
tato Duryodhanen' âpi grahaṇaṃ Pāṇḍavasya tat
sainya|sthāneṣu sarveṣu su|ghoṣitam, ariṃ|dama.

SAṂJAYA uvāca.

13.1 S'|ÂNTARE TU pratijñāte rājño Droṇena nigrahe
tatas te sainikāḥ śrutvā taṃ Yudhiṣṭhira|nigraham
siṃha|nāda|ravāṃś cakrur bāṇa|śaṅkha|ravaiḥ saha.

superior in the discipline of combat. Though but a young man he is renowned because he walks a path that none of us can tread and carries an arsenal the like of which neither Indra nor Rudra has known. My king, his wrath for you is such that I will not be able to stop him. But if Partha can somehow be driven off from the battle or subdued then
you will overwhelm the righteous king. O bull in the field 12.25
of men if you think that victory depends on his capture then this is how to ensure that he is caught. Have no doubt my king: if he comes within my reach for just a moment without the tiger Dhanan·jaya son of Kuntí to protect him, I will capture the king who lives for truth and the law, and he will be yours to command. But with the Fighter of the Red Stars* by his side, Yudhi·shthira the son of Partha would be beyond the reach even of a legion of gods and demons under Indra's command.

SÁNJAYA spoke.

When they heard Drona's promise to the king, your foolish sons ignored its provision and thought Yudhi·shthira
already their prisoner. Of course Duryódhana knew that 12.30
Drona's loyalties were conflicted, and to shore up the brahmin's promise he made much of what Drona had said. O tamer of foes, Duryódhana proclaimed the plan to capture the Pándava to all the troops that stood about them.

SÁNJAYA spoke.

So DRONA's barbed promise to capture the king was 13.1
made. And when the soldiers heard of his intention to trap Yudhi·shthira, horns sounded and arrowshafts clacked and men roared. Before long, spies told the righteous king of the

tat tu sarvaṃ yathā|nyāyaṃ Dharma|rājena, Bhārata,
āptair āśu parijñātaṃ Bhāradvāja|cikīrṣitam.
tataḥ sarvān samānāyya bhrātṝn anyāṃś ca sarvaśaḥ
abravīd Dharma|rājas tu Dhanaṃjayam idaṃ vacaḥ.
«śrutaṃ te, puruṣa|vyāghra, Droṇasy' âdya cikīrṣitam
yathā tan na bhavet satyaṃ tathā nītir vidhīyatām.
13.5 s'|ântaraṃ hi pratijñātaṃ Droṇen' â|mitra|karśiṇā
tac c' ântaram a|mogh'|êṣau tvayi tena samāhitam.
sa tvam adya mahā|bāho yudhyasva mad|an|antaram
yathā Duryodhanaḥ kāmaṃ n' êmaṃ Droṇād avāpnuyāt.»

ARJUNA uvāca.

yathā me na vadhaḥ kārya ācāryasya kadā cana
tathā tava parityāge na me, rājaṃś, cikīrṣitam.
apy evaṃ, Pāṇḍava, prāṇān utsṛjeyam ahaṃ yudhi
pratīyāṃ n' âham ācāryaṃ tvāṃ na jahyāṃ kathaṃ cana.
tvāṃ nigṛhy' āhave, rājan, Dhārtarāṣṭro yam icchati
na sa taṃ jīva|loke 'smin kāmaṃ prāpyet kathaṃ cana.
13.10 prapated dyauḥ sa|nakṣatrā pṛthivī śakalī|bhavet
na tvāṃ Droṇo nigṛhṇīyāj jīvamāne mayi dhruvam.
yadi tasya raṇe sāhyaṃ kurute vajra|bhṛt svayam
Viṣṇur vā sahito devair na tvāṃ prāpsyaty asau mṛdhe.
mayi jīvati, rāj'|êndra, na bhayaṃ kartum arhasi
Droṇād astra|bhṛtāṃ śreṣṭhāt sarva|śastra|bhṛtām api.
anyac ca brūyāṃ, rāj'|êndra, pratijñāṃ mama niś|calām.
na smarāmy an|ṛtāṃ vācaṃ na smarāmi parājayam
na smarāmi pratiśrutya kiṃ cid apy an|ṛtaṃ kṛtam.

exchange, and soon he learned all about Drona's design. He summoned his other brothers and turned to Dhanan·jaya to speak. "Tiger in the forest of men. You have now heard what Drona intends. We must decide what to do to ensure that his plan does not bear fruit. For Drona's boast has a 13.5
flaw, and that flaw, o great archer and burner of foes, is you. With your strong arms fight this day close at my side and we can deny Duryódhana the prize Drona has promised him."

ÁRJUNA spoke.

My king. It is true. Our old teacher cannot defeat me and for that reason I will never desert you. O son of Pandu, I would lay aside my life first. I will neither oblige our sometime mentor nor leave your side, not for anything. Be assured, my king, that however much he might wish it Duryódhana will never on this living earth achieve his desire of capturing you in battle. As long as I breathe, the 13.10
heavens and their stars would fall and the ground would break asunder before Drona takes you as his prisoner. Be sure of it. Even if Vishnu flanked by the gods or the wielder of the thunderbolt himself lent a hand Duryódhana would not have you in his grasp. Though he is a great warrior, perhaps the greatest fighter of them all, while I live you need fear nothing from Drona. And o king of kings I tell you this: I always keep a promise. I do not remember a time that I lied. I do not remember a time I have failed. I do not remember making a promise that I did not keep to the letter.

SAMJAYA uvāca.

tataḥ śaṅkhāś ca bheryaś ca mṛdaṅgāś c' ānakaiḥ saha
prāvādyanta, mahā|rāja, Pāṇḍavānāṃ niveśane.
13.15 siṃha|nādaś ca saṃjajñe Pāṇḍavānāṃ mah"|ātmanām
dhanur|jyā|tala|śabdaś ca gagana|spṛk su|bhairavaḥ.
taṃ śrutvā śaṅkha|nirghoṣaṃ Pāṇḍavasya mah"|âujasaḥ
tvadīyeṣv apy anīkeṣu vāditrāṇy abhijaghnire.
tato vyūḍhāny anīkāni tava teṣāṃ ca Bhārata
śanair upeyur anyonyaṃ yotsyamānāni saṃyuge.
tataḥ pravavṛte yuddhaṃ tumulaṃ loma|harṣaṇam
Pāṇḍavānāṃ Kurūṇāṃ ca Droṇa|Pāñcālyayor api.

yatamānāḥ prayatnena Droṇ'|ânīka|viśātane
na śekuḥ Sṛñjayā yuddhe tadd hi Droṇena pālitam.
13.20 tath" âiva tava putrasya rath'|ôdārāḥ prahāriṇaḥ
na śekuḥ Pāṇḍavīṃ senāṃ pālyamānāṃ Kirīṭinā.
āstāṃ te stimite sene rakṣyamāṇe paras|param
samprasupte yathā naktaṃ vana|rājyau su|puṣpite.
tato Rukmaratho, rājann, arkeṇ' êva virājatā
varūthinīṃ viniṣpiṣya vyacarat pṛtan'|ântare.
tam udyata|rathen' âikam āśu|kāriṇam āhave
an|ekam iva saṃtrāsān menire Pāṇḍu|Sṛñjayāḥ.
tena muktāḥ śarā ghorā viceruḥ sarvato diśam
āsayanto, mahā|rāja, Pāṇḍaveyasya vāhinīḥ.
13.25 madhyaṃ|dinam anuprāpto gabhasti|śata|saṃvṛtaḥ
yathā dṛśyeta gharm'|âṃśus tathā Droṇo vyadṛśyata.
na c' âinaṃ Pāṇḍaveyānāṃ kaś cic chaknoti Bhārata
vīkṣituṃ samare kruddhaṃ Mahendram iva dānavāḥ.
mohayitvā tataḥ sainyaṃ Bhāradvājaḥ pratāpavān

SÁNJAYA spoke.

O great king. Now it was the Pándavas who sounded their horns. The throb of wardrums began. Wild roars from the 13.15
men mingled with the spinechilling thrum of bowstrings cutting the air. The echo of trumpets rolled from the mighty Pándava's host and your own forces o Bhárata struck up in response a battle dirge. The two armies wheeled heavily towards one another, and so began once more the mad and bloody struggle between the Pándavas and the Kurus, between Drona and the Panchálas.

At first the Srínjayas struggled in vain to find a way to approach Drona's defenses and your son's champions could 13.20
not drive their lofty chariots at the soldiers shielded by the Diademed Warrior. Each swayed back from the other and the two armies settled gently into themselves like two tracts of forest blanketed in flowers whose petals had closed for the night. Then o king like a rising sun the Warrior of the Golden Chariot suddenly went forth and collided with the enemy's defenses and hurtled into their midst. Though but a lone man flying in his tall chariot through the fray, he seemed to the Pándavas and the Srínjayas a manyheaded beast. His fearsome arrows flew in every direction from his bow, my king, forcing the Pándava warriors back. Drona 13.25
blazed then like the sun at the meridian circled in a hundred rays, and o Bhárata like demons before the wrath of mighty Indra all the Pándavas had to avert their gaze. Blinding the troops with his brilliance Bharad·vaja's son blasted Dhrishta·dyumna's force with his whetted shafts. He filled the air with trueflying arrows and obscured the whole horizon and

Dhṛṣṭadyumna|balaṃ tūrṇaṃ vyadhaman niśitaiḥ śaraiḥ.
sa diśaḥ sarvato ruddhvā saṃvṛtya kham a|jihma|gaiḥ
Pārṣato yatra tatr' âiva mamṛde Pāṇḍu|vāhinīm.

SAMJAYA uvāca.

14.1 TATAḤ SA Pāṇḍav'|ânīke janayaṃs tumulaṃ mahat
vyacarat pṛtanāṃ Droṇo dahan kakṣam iv' ânalaḥ.
nirdahantam anīkāni sākṣād agnim iv' ôtthitam
dṛṣṭvā Rukmarathaṃ kruddhaṃ samakampanta Sṛñjayāḥ.
pratataṃ kṛṣyataḥ saṃkhye dhanuṣo 'sy' āśu|kāriṇaḥ
jyā|ghoṣaḥ śuśruve 'tyarthaṃ visphūrjitam iv' âśaneḥ.
rathinaḥ sādinaś c' âiva nāgān aśvān padātinaḥ
raudrā hastavatā muktāḥ saṃmṛdnanti sma sāyakāḥ.
14.5 nānadyamānaḥ parjanyaḥ s'|ânilaḥ śuci|saṃkṣaye
aśma|varṣam iv' āvarṣat pareṣām āvahad bhayam.

vyacaran sa tadā, rājan, senāḥ saṃkṣobhayan prabhuḥ
vardhayām āsa saṃtrāsaṃ śātravāṇām a|mānuṣam.
tasya vidyud iv' âbhreṣu cāpaṃ hema|pariṣkṛtam
bhramad|rath'|âmbu|de tasmin dṛśyate sma punaḥ punaḥ.
sa vīraḥ satyavān prājño dharma|nityaḥ su|dāruṇaḥ
yug'|ânta|kāle saṃkruddho raudrāṃ prāvartayan nadīm
amarṣa|vega|prabhavāṃ kravy'|âda|gaṇa|saṃkulām
bal'|âughaiḥ sarvataḥ pūrṇāṃ vīra|vṛkṣ'|âpahāriṇīm
14.10 śoṇit'|ôdāṃ rath'|āvartāṃ hasty|aśva|kṛta|rodhasam
kavac'|ôtpala|saṃyuktāṃ māṃsa|paṅka|samākulām
medo|majj'|âsthi|sikatām uṣṇīṣa|vara|phenilām
saṃgrāma|jala|d'|āpūrṇāṃ prāsa|matsya|samākulām
nara|nāg'|âśva|sambhūtāṃ śara|veg'|âugha|vāhinīm

flattened the Pándava line where the grandson of Príshata rode.

SÁNJAYA spoke.

PANIC SPREAD through the Pándava ranks as Drona tore 14.1
in among them like brushfire through a forest of dry trees. When they saw Rukma·ratha scorching a path of rage towards them like a kindled blaze, and heard everywhere like a peal of thunder before lightning the endless whisper against his hand of the string of his quick bow, the Srínjayas began to tremble with fear. Biting arrows flew from his dexterous fingers and ripped into charioteers, riders, elephants,
horses, soldiers. He brought terror down upon his enemies 14.5
like hail pouring from a black cloud churned by howling wind as the hot season turns to rain.

Majesty, as he traversed your troops mighty Drona spread chaos in his wake. He instilled within us a kind of inhuman dread. Like lightning in the heavens again and again his gilded bow appeared among the swirling banks of chariots on the plain. Wise and truthful and formidable as he was, that unfailing servant of justice now maddened by the closing of the age poured forth an evil river sprung from the aquifers of wrath and thronged with flesheating
ghouls and flowing with blood, deep and teeming with men 14.10
and swirling with chariots, its banks made of elephants and horses, breastplates bobbing upon its surface like lotuses. It was thick with mud and gore and broken bones, it had lymph and marrow for sand, its waters foamed with ribbons of fine cloth, its course swollen by a deluge of warriors, javelin shoals and the bodies of elephants and horses,

śarīra|dāru|saṃghaṭṭāṃ ratha|kacchapa|saṃkulām
uttam'|âṅg'|ôpala|taṭāṃ nistriṃśa|jhaṣa|saṃkulām
ratha|nāga|hrad'|ôpetāṃ nān"|ābharaṇa|nīra|jām
mahā|ratha|śat'|āvartāṃ bhūmi|reṇ'|ūrmi|mālinīm
mahā|vīryavatāṃ saṃkhye su|tarāṃ bhīru|dus|tarām
14.15 śarīra|śata|sambādhāṃ kaṅka|gṛdhra|niṣevitāṃ
mahā|ratha|sahasrāṇi nayantīṃ Yama|sādanam
śūla|vyāla|samākīrṇāṃ prāṇi|vāji|niṣevitām
chinna|cchatra|mahā|haṃsāṃ mukuṭ'|āṇḍa|ja|sevitām
cakra|kūrmāṃ gadā|nakrāṃ śara|kṣudra|jhaṣ'|ākulām
baka|gṛdhra|sṛgālānāṃ ghora|saṃghair niṣevitām
nihatān prāṇinaḥ saṃkhye Droṇena balinā raṇe
vahantīṃ pitṛ|lokāya śataśo rāja|sattama
śarīra|śata|sambādhāṃ keśa|śaivāla|śādvalām
nadīṃ prāvartayad rājan bhīrūṇāṃ bhaya|vardhinīm.
14.20 tarjayantam anīkāni tāni tāni mahā|ratham
sarvato 'bhyadravan Droṇaṃ Yudhiṣṭhira|puro|gamāḥ.
tān abhidravataḥ śūrās tāvakā dṛḍha|kārmukāḥ
sarvataḥ pratyagṛhṇanta tad abhūl loma|harṣaṇam.
śata|māyas tu Śakuniḥ Sahadevaṃ samādravat
sa|niyantṛ|dhvaja|rathaṃ vivyādha niśitaiḥ śaraiḥ.
tasya Mādrī|sutaḥ ketuṃ dhanuḥ sūtaṃ hayān api
n' âtikruddhaḥ śaraiś chittvā ṣaṣṭyā vivyādha mātulam.
Saubalas tu gadāṃ gṛhya pracaskanda rath'|ôttamāt

clusters of arrows in its currents and trunks of dead soldiers, cars floating like turtles, human heads washed up like rocks along its shore, its depths fathomed with chariots and elephants and knives like fish, its waves encrusted with detritus of every kind, swordsmen in their hundreds sucked into its whirlpools, its whole length wreathed in earth and dust, its waters fordless to the faint of heart and risked only by the very brave. It flowed with countless corpses, herons and 14.15
vultures swooping above its lost cargo of warriors in their thousands rolling down to Yama's abode, draw to beasts of prey of feather and fur, lost spears like its predators, broken parasols like swans and crowns like floating birds, wheels for tortoise shells, maces for pearls, flurries of arrowheads for minnows, its banks host to ferocious packs of jackals and flocks of vultures and cranes. Off it bore the legion dead away to their ancestors' shores once Drona had snatched in that bloody reckoning the breath from their throats.

How the weak in spirit trembled before that river, my 14.20
king, its verdant banks of hair and the cadavers that crammed its course. But even as he rose above them those same battalions led by Yudhi·shthira fought back against Drona's might on every front. And in a burst of excitement your stoutbowed archers rushed from all around forward towards their enemies.

Shákuni of a hundred illusions bore down upon Saha·deva and fired sharp arrows into his car, banner and driver. Calm in the fray the son of Madri studded with sixty arrows Shákuni's pennant bow charioteer and team and then finally found behind them the body of his uncle. Then Sáubala grabbed his mace o king and leapt down from his high car

sa tasya gadayā rājan rathāt sūtam apātayat.
14.25 tatas tau virathau, rājan, gadā|hastau mahā|balau
cikrīḍatū raṇe śūrau sa|śṛṅgāv iva parvatau.

Droṇaḥ Pāñcāla|rājānaṃ viddhvā daśabhir āśu|gaiḥ
bahubhis tena c' âbhyastas taṃ vivyādha ṣaṭ'|âdhikaiḥ.
Viviṃśatiṃ Bhīmaseno viṃśatyā niśitaiḥ śaraiḥ
viddhvā n' âkampayad vīras tad adbhutam iv' âbhavat.
Viviṃśatis tu sahasā vy|aśva|ketu|śar'|āsanam
Bhīmaṃ cakre, mahā|rāja, tataḥ sainyāny apūjayan.
sa tan na mamṛṣe vīraḥ śatror vikramam āhave
tato 'sya gadayā dāntān hayān sarvān apātayat.
14.30 hat'|âśvāt sa rathād rājan gṛhya carma mahā|balaḥ
abhyayād Bhīmasenaṃ tu matto mattam iva dvipam.

Śalyas tu Nakulaṃ vīraḥ svasrīyaṃ priyam ātmanaḥ
vivyādha prahasan bāṇair lālayan kopayann iva.
tasy' âśvān ātapa|traṃ ca dhvajaṃ sūtam atho dhanuḥ
nipātya Nakulaḥ saṃkhye śaṅkhaṃ dadhmau pratāpavān.
Dhṛṣṭaketuḥ Kṛpen' âstāñ chittvā bahu|vidhāñ śarān
Kṛpaṃ vivyādha saptatyā lakṣma c' âpy aharat tribhiḥ.
taṃ Kṛpaḥ śara|varṣeṇa mahatā samavārayat
nivārya ca raṇe vipro Dhṛṣṭaketum ayodhayat.
14.35 Sātyakiḥ Kṛtavarmāṇaṃ nārācena stan'|ântare
viddhvā vivyādha saptatyā punar anyaiḥ smayann iva.
taṃ Bhojaḥ sapta|saptatyā viddhvā su|niśitaiḥ śaraiḥ
n' âkampayata Śaineyaṃ śīghro vāyur iv' âcalam.

and with it knocked Shákuni's driver from his post. Bereft of 14.25
their vehicles those strongarmed heroes raised their cudgels and began to sport like horned fish in the game we call battle.

Meanwhile with ten swift shafts Drona pierced the king of the Panchálas and under a hail of reeds the king fired back a hundred and one more. Vivínshati was struck by Bhima·sena's whetted arrows, and Bhima struck back with his own as miraculously he somehow stood his ground. With awesome speed, o king, Vivínshati felled Bhima's foals and knocked away his standard and bow as he did. But in this contest of wills the great Bhima did not submit and crushed
with his mace all of Vivínshati's faithful steeds. His horses 14.30
dead, the great warrior grabbed a shield and leapt down from his car in a frenzy, and onto mad animal Bhima·sena standing before him.

Elsewhere bold Shalya hit with his arrows his own nephew Nákula. He grinned as he did so as if in jest. Nákula blazed up in fury and sounded a note from his conch and brought Shalya's parasol oriflamme driver and bow down into the dirt. And o lord deflecting the volley of arrows from Kripa's bow Dhrishta·ketu pinned him with seventy of his own and then another three, but enveloping Dhrishta·ketu in a great
storm of arrows the brahmin at once fought back. Sátya- 14.35
ki pierced Krita·varman in the center of his chest with an iron arrow then struck him with seventy more, and all the while wore a mocking smile. When Bhoja struck Shainéya with seventy-seven wellwhetted arrows his target remained calm as a mountain in a swift wind. The commander struck Sushárman a savage blow between the joints of his armor,

senā|patiḥ Suśarmāṇaṃ śīghraṃ marmasv atāḍayat
sa c' âpi taṃ tomareṇa jatru|deśe 'bhyatāḍayat.
Vaikartanaṃ tu samare Virāṭaḥ pratyavārayat
saha Matsyair mahā|vīryais tad adbhutam iv' âbhavat.
tat pauruṣam abhūt tatra sūta|putrasya dāruṇam
yat sainyaṃ vārayām āsa śaraiḥ saṃnata|parvabhiḥ.
14.40 Drupadas tu svayaṃ rājā Bhagadattena saṃgataḥ
tayor yuddhaṃ mahā|rāja citra|rūpam iv' âbhavat.
Bhagadattas tu rājānaṃ Drupadaṃ nata|parvabhiḥ
sa|niyantṛ|dhvaja|rathaṃ vivyādha puruṣa'|rṣabhaḥ.
Drupadas tu tataḥ kruddho Bhagadattaṃ mahā|ratham
ājaghān' ôrasi kṣipraṃ śareṇ' ānata|parvaṇā.
yuddhaṃ yodha|varau loke Saumadatti|Śikhaṇḍinau
bhūtānāṃ trāsa|jananaṃ cakrāte 'stra|viśāradau.
Bhūriśravā raṇe rājan Yājñaseniṃ mahā|ratham
mahatā sāyak'|âughena cchādayām āsa vīryavān.
14.45 Śikhaṇḍī tu tataḥ kruddhaḥ Saumadattiṃ viśāṃ pate
navatyā sāyakānāṃ tu kampayām āsa Bhārata.
rākṣasau raudra|karmāṇau Haiḍimb'|Âlambusāv ubhau
cakrāte 'tyadbhutaṃ yuddhaṃ paras|para|jay'|âiṣiṇau.
māyā|śata|sṛjau dṛptau māyābhir itar'|êtarau
antar|hitau ceratus tau bhṛśaṃ vismaya|kāriṇau.
Cekitāno 'nuvindena yuyudhe c' âti|bhairavaḥ
yathā dev'|âsure yuddhe Bala|Śakrau mahā|balau
Lakṣmaṇaḥ Kṣatradevena vimardam akarod bhṛśam
yathā Viṣṇuḥ purā, rājan, Hiraṇyākṣeṇa saṃyuge.

hitting him with a javelin in the collarbone. Viráta and his Matsyas crashed against the child of the cloudsplitting sun and at first somehow drove him back, but with awesome might Karna soon hid them all beneath the mass of his wellwrought shafts.

On another part of the plain King Drúpada met Bhaga· 14.40
datta and majesty their struggle was a dazzling show. Knotless arrows flew from taurine Bhaga·datta's bow towards the chariot bannered in the horsetamer and found Drúpada where they stopped. Fired with anger the king struck the great Bhaga·datta a glancing blow in the chest with a single wellfashioned shaft. The confrontation between the two masters of the bow and best of warriors Soma·datta's son and Shikhándin set fear in the hearts of any who watched. O royal heir of Bhárata and leader of men, heroic Bhuri·shravas hid the great warrior and son of Yajnya·sena behind a
bulky cloud of missiles, and then with ninety shafts wrath- 14.45
ful Shikhándin shook Saumadátti back. Then I saw the two dreadful rakshasas Haidímba and Alámbusa fight a battle beyond belief. Each intent on the other's defeat these wild creatures hurled illusion upon illusion and moved about invisible. O king, like mighty Bala and Shakra Chekitána and Anuvínda fought ferocious as god and demon while Lákshmana crashed against Kshatra·deva like Vishnu grappling with Hiranyáksha.

14.50 tataḥ prajavit'|âśvena vidhivat kalpitena ca
rathen' âbhyapatad rājan Saubhadraṃ Pauravo 'nadat.
tato 'bhyayāt sa tvarito yuddh'|ākāṅkṣī mahā|balaḥ
tena cakre mahad yuddham Abhimanyur ariṃ|damaḥ.
Pauravas tv atha Saubhadraṃ śara|vrātair avākirat
tasy' Ārjunir dhvajaṃ chatraṃ hayāṃś c' ôrvyām apātayat.
Saubhadraḥ Pauravaṃ tv anyair viddhvā saptabhir āśu|gaiḥ
pañcabhis tasya vivyādha hayān sūtaṃ ca sāyakaiḥ.
tataḥ praharṣayan senāṃ siṃhavad vyanadan muhuḥ
samādatt' Ārjunis tūrṇaṃ Paurav'|ânta|karaṃ śaram.
14.55 taṃ tu saṃdhitam ājñāya sāyakaṃ ghora|darśanam
dvābhyāṃ śarābhyāṃ Hārdikyaś ciccheda sa|śaraṃ dhanuḥ.
tad utsṛjya dhanuś chinnaṃ Saubhadraḥ para|vīra|hā
udbabarha sitaṃ khaḍgam ādadānaḥ śar'|âvaram.
sa ten' ân|eka|tāreṇa carmaṇā kṛta|hastavat
bhrānt'|âsir acaran mārgaṃ darśayan vīryam ātmanaḥ.
bhrāmitaṃ punar udbhrāntam ādhūtaṃ punar utthitam
carma|nistriṃśayo, rājan, nir|viśeṣam adṛśyata.
sa Paurava|rathasy' ēṣām āplutya sahasā nadan
Pauravaṃ ratham āsthāya keśa|pakṣe parāmṛśan
14.60 jaghān' âsya padā sūtam asin" âpātayad dhvajam
vikṣobhy' âmbho|nidhiṃ Tārkṣyas taṃ Nāgam iva c' âkṣipat.
tam āgalita|keś'|ântaṃ dadṛśuḥ sarva|pārthivāḥ
ukṣāṇam iva siṃhena pātyamānam a|cetasam.
tam Ārjuni|vaśaṃ prāptaṃ kṛṣyamāṇam a|nāthavat
Pauravaṃ pātitaṃ dṛṣṭvā n' āmṛṣyata Jayadrathaḥ.
sa barhiṇa|mahā|vājaṃ kiṅkiṇī|śata|jālavat

Páurava snarled and spurred on his horses and drove 14.50
his ritually adorned chariot straight at Saubhádra. Mighty
Abhimányu the tamer of foes was eager to fight and he
rode to meet him and another great battle began. Flocked
in arrows from Páurava's bow Árjuna's son sent his foe's
banner pole parasol and some of steeds all tumbling down to
earth. Then Saubhádra loosed seven more arrows at Páurava and five of the shafts pierced his other horses and driver.
Roaring like a lion Abhimányu notched an arrow that would
kill Páurava and strike a great blow for his army's morale.
But Hrídika's son saw the fatal dart terrible to behold and 14.55
with two of his own splintered from Abhimányu's hands
the bow and the arrow too. Throwing aside his shattered
weapon Saubhádra the slayer of foes drew his pale sword and
snatched up his shield and nimble with that starsprent disk
and with his blade whirling he cut out his path so all could
see how fine a warrior he was. His shield and blade were
lost in a blur o king as they rose and flashed and trembled
and rose again, and leaping onto the axle of Páurava's car
he bellowed and grabbed a fistful of his foe's hair at the side
of his head and kicking away his charioteer with his foot 14.60
he hewed down Páurava's standard with his sword. He had
snatched his quarry like Gáruda plucking a snake from the
churning waves of the sea.

All the chieftains watched as Páurava stood with his hair hanging down, like a cowed child. He was crushed in Abhimányu's grip like an ox pinned and insensible in the jaws of a lion. Jayad·ratha could not bear the sight. Taking a shield decorated in peacocks' plumes and strung with a circlet of a hundred small bells he grabbed his sword and

carma c' ādāya khaḍgaṃ ca nadan paryapatad rathāt.
tataḥ Saindhavam ālokya Kārṣṇir utsṛjya Pauravam
utpapāta rathāt tūrṇaṃ śyenavan nipapāta ca.
14.65 prāsa|paṭṭiśa|nistriṃśāc chatrubhiḥ sampracoditān
cicched' âth' âsinā Kārṣṇiś carmaṇā saṃrurodha ca.
saṃdarśayitvā sainyānāṃ sva|bāhu|balam ātmanaḥ
tam udyamya mahā|khaḍgaṃ carma c' âtha punar balī.
Vṛddha|kṣatrasya dāyādaṃ pitur atyanta|vairiṇam
sasār' âbhimukhaḥ śūraḥ śārdūla iva kuñjaram.
tau paras|param āsādya khaḍga|danta|nakh'|āyudhau
hṛṣṭavat samprajahrāte vyāghra|kesariṇāv iva.
sampāteṣv abhighāteṣu nipāteṣv asi|carmaṇoḥ
na tayor antaraṃ kaś cid dadarśa nara|siṃhayoḥ.
14.70 avakṣepo 'si|nirhrādaḥ śastr'|ântara|nidarśanam
bāhy'|ântara|nipātaś ca nir|viśeṣam adṛśyata.
bāhyam ābhyantaraṃ c' âiva carantau mārgam uttamam
dadṛśāte mah"|ātmānau sa|pakṣāv iva parvatau.
tato vikṣipataḥ khaḍgaṃ Saubhadrasya yaśasvinaḥ
śar'|āvaraṇa|pakṣ'|ânte prajahāra Jayadrathaḥ.
rukma|pakṣ'|ântare saktas tasmiṃś carmaṇi bhāsvare
Sindhu|rāja|bal'|ôddhūtaḥ so 'bhajyata mahān asiḥ.
bhagnam ājñāya nistriṃśam avaplutya padāni ṣaṭ
so 'dṛśyata nimeṣeṇa sva|rathaṃ punar āsthitaḥ.
14.75 taṃ Kārṣṇiṃ samarān muktam
āsthitaṃ ratham uttamam
sahitāḥ sarva|rājānaḥ
parivavruḥ samantataḥ.
tataś carma ca khaḍgaṃ ca samutkṣipya mahā|balaḥ
nanād' Ârjuna|dāyādaḥ prekṣamāṇo Jayadratham.

with a cry leapt down from his car. The Dark One 's son* spied the king of Sindhu and let go of Páurava then stepped lightly from the chariot he stood upon and flew at him
like a hawk. Sweeping his sword and blocking with his 14.65
shield every knife, spear and javelin swung by his foes, his brilliance clear to all who beheld him, the mighty child of Árjuna and hero of heroes raised up his heavy blade and his shield and descended upon the son of Vriddha·kshatra and sworn enemy of his father like a panther upon an elephant.

With blade, tooth and nail they came together and each fiercely struck the other like tiger and lion, and as sword and shield collided and swung and fell those feral creatures seemed to blur into one. Their curses, the sough of their
blades and the spaces between their swords with their swings 14.70
and their feints all became indistinguishable. Back and forth they went as they soared, like mountains borne on wings. Then Jayad·ratha brought down his sword upon the very edge of the shield of glorious Saubhádra as he whipped it high, and as it caught its golden rim glinting like the sun's with all the force of the Sindhu king behind it the great blade shattered. He barely glanced at the broken weapon and tossed it six paces distant and then in the blink of an eye was back in his car.

Safe now after his tussle with Abhimányu, all his fellow 14.75
kings pressed in about his chariot to protect him. Raising his sword and shield above his head Árjuna's heir glared at Jayad·ratha and roared with anger. Then the son of Subhádra and killer of heroes abandoned the Sindhu king to rise hot and scorching above other soldiers like the sun above the earth. Shalya flung at him a wroughtiron spear

Sindhu|rājaṃ parityajya Saubhadraḥ para|vīra|hā
tāpayām āsa tat sainyaṃ bhuvanaṃ bhās|karo yathā.
tasya sarv'|āyasīṃ śaktiṃ Śalyaḥ kanaka|bhūṣaṇām
cikṣepa samare ghorāṃ dīptām agni|śikhām iva.
tām avaplutya jagrāha sa|kośaṃ c' âkarod asim
Vainateyo yathā Kārṣṇiḥ patantam ura|g'|ôttamam.
14.80 tasya lāghavam ājñāya sattvaṃ c' â|mita|tejasaḥ
sahitāḥ sarva|rājānaḥ siṃha|nādam ath' ānadan.
tatas tām eva Śalyasya Saubhadraḥ para|vīra|hā
mumoca bhuja|vīryeṇa vaidūrya|vikṛt'|âjirām.
sā tasya ratham āsādya nirmukta|bhuja|g'|ôpamā
jaghāna sūtaṃ Śalyasya rathāc c' âinam apātayat.
tato Virāṭa|Drupadau Dhṛṣṭaketur Yudhiṣṭhiraḥ
Sātyakiḥ Kaikayā Bhīmo Dhṛṣṭadyumna|Śikhaṇḍinau
Yamau ca Draupadeyāś ca sādhu sādhv iti cukruśuḥ.
bāṇa|śabdāś ca vividhāḥ siṃha|nādāś ca puṣkalāḥ
prādur āsan harṣayantaḥ Saubhadram a|palāyinam.
14.85 tan n' âmṛṣyanta putrās te śatror vijaya|lakṣaṇam
ath' âinaṃ sahasā sarve samantān niśitaiḥ śaraiḥ
abhyākiran mahā|rāja jala|dā iva parvatam.
teṣāṃ ca priyam anvicchan sūtasya ca parābhavāt
Ārtāyanir a|mitra|ghnaḥ kruddhaḥ Saubhadram abhyayāt.

DHṚTARĀṢṬRA uvāca.

15.1 BAHŪNI SU|VICITRĀṆI dvandva|yuddhāni Saṃjaya
tvay" ôktāni niśamy' âhaṃ spṛhayāmi sa|cakṣuṣām.
āścarya|bhūtaṃ lokeṣu kathayiṣyanti mānavāḥ
Kurūṇāṃ Pāṇḍavānāṃ ca yuddhaṃ dev'|âsur'|ôpamam.
na hi me tṛptir ast' îha śṛṇvato yuddham uttamam
tasmād Ārtāyaner yuddhaṃ Saubhadrasya ca śaṃsa me.

inlaid with bdellium that flew balefully over the battlefield like a flaring plume of fire. Like Gáruda catching a falling snake Abhimányu jumped down and caught it and slid his own sword back into its scabbard as he did. The feat was 14.80
so wondrous and quick that all the chieftains who saw it yelled their delight. Then with a powerful swing Saubhádra the smasher of foes hurled Shalya's spear, and its shaft set with cat's eyes* flew back towards its owner's chariot like a brightskinned serpent, thudding into Shalya's driver and bringing him slumping down to the base of his car. Viráta and Drúpada, Dhrishta·ketu and Yudhi·shthira, Sátyaki, the Kaikéyas, Bhima, Dhrishta·dyumna and Shikhándin, the twins and the Draupadéyas all hollered with excitement at the scene. As the sound of arrows multiplied and the lions' roars surged about him Saubhádra stood tall and drank in their applause. O majesty your children could not bear their 14.85
enemy's pride and all of them sent their sharp arrows at him like rain bursting on a mountain. Artáyani still clove to our cause. Smarting from the death of his horseman he made once more for Abhimányu to seal the death of his foe. Rage drove him on.

DHRITA·RASHTRA spoke.

LISTENING TO YOU describe these myriad duels, I envy 15.1
those who can see, Sánjaya. One day men will traverse the world telling the wondrous story of the war between the Kurus and the Pándavas as if it were a battle in heaven. But I have yet to hear the end of this great tale. So continue. Tell me of the fight between the sons of Subhádra and Artáyani.

SAMJAYA uvāca.

sāditaṃ prekṣya yantāraṃ Śalyaḥ sarv'|āyasīṃ gadām
samutkṣipya nadan kruddhaḥ pracaskanda rath'|ôttamāt.
15.5 taṃ dīptam iva kāl'|âgniṃ daṇḍa|hastam iv' ântakam
javen' âbhyapatad Bhīmaḥ pragṛhya mahatīṃ gadām.
Saubhadro 'py aśani|prakhyāṃ pragṛhya mahatīṃ gadām
ehy eh' îty abravīc Chalyaṃ yatnād Bhīmena vāritaḥ.
vārayitvā tu Saubhadraṃ Bhīmasenaḥ pratāpavān
Śalyam āsādya samare tasthau girir iv' âcalaḥ.
tath" âiva Madra|rājo 'pi Bhīmaṃ dṛṣṭvā mahā|balam
sasār' âbhimukhas tūrṇaṃ śārdūla iva kuñjaram.
tatas tūrya|ninādāś ca śaṅkhānāṃ ca sahasraśaḥ
siṃha|nādāś ca saṃjajñur bherīṇāṃ ca mahā|svanāḥ.
15.10 paśyatāṃ śataśo hy āsīd anyonya|sama|cetasām
Pāṇḍavānāṃ Kurūṇāṃ ca sādhu sādhv iti nisvanaḥ.
na hi Madr'|âdhipād anyaḥ sarva|rājasu Bhārata
soḍhum utsahate vegaṃ Bhīmasenasya saṃyuge.
tathā Madr'|âdhipasy' âpi gadā|vegaṃ mah"|ātmanaḥ
soḍhum utsahate loke ko 'nyo yudhi Vṛkodarāt.

paṭṭair Jāmbūnadair baddhā babhūva jana|harṣiṇī
prajajvāla tath" āviddhā Bhīmena mahatī gadā.
tath" âiva carato mārgān maṇḍalāni ca bhāgaśaḥ
mahā|vidyut|pratīkāśā Śalyasya śuśubhe gadā.
15.15 tau vṛṣāv iva nardantau maṇḍalāni viceratuḥ
āvarjita|gadā|śṛṅgāv ubhau Śalya|Vṛkodarau.
maṇḍal'|āvarta|mārgeṣu gadā|viharaṇeṣu ca

SÁNJAYA spoke.

His driver laid out on the ground, Shalya yelled in anger,
raised up his mace of solid iron and leapt down from his
high chariot. Bhima saw him flaring up like the fire at the 15.5
end of time, the weapon in his hand like Death's scepter,
and picking up his own heavy mace he was upon him in
a moment. Saubhádra too swept up his mace. It was like
a lightning bolt in his hand. He taunted Shalya to come
to meet him. Bhima struggled to restrain Abhimányu but
when at last he had him under control he turned to do battle
with Shalya himself. Bhima towered above his adversary's
head majestic as a mountain peak but as soon as he saw
him the king of the Madras darted forth as a panther darts
at an elephant. Then the blaring trumpets and conches in
their hundreds and the lionlike roars and deep throb of
drums gathered from the clashing hordes of Kurus and Pá- 15.10
ndavas into a single sound that seemed to rise in praise as
everyone looked on. O Bhárata, the lord of the Madras was
alone among kings the man who might survive Bhima·se-
na's ferocious attack. And who in the world but Dogbelly
could withstand a blow from the great Madra king?

Bhima's huge and beauteous mace was bound with fil-
lets embroidered with Jambu rivergold and it glinted as it
swung. Shalya's mace flashed like lightning as he stepped and
circled. Bristling with clubs for horns Shalya and Vrikódara 15.15
bellowed like bulls and traced arcs each around the other. As
they paced turned and circled and brandished their weapons
there was little to choose between the two lions from the race
of men. Then Bhima landed a blow that smashed fragments
of iron from the fiery and fearsome orb in Shalya's hands.

nir|viśeṣam abhūd yuddhaṃ tayoḥ puruṣa|siṃhayoḥ.
tāḍitā Bhīmasenena Śalyasya mahatī gadā
s'|âgni|jvālā mahā|raudrā gadā|cūrṇam aśīryata.
tath" âiva Bhīmasenasya dviṣat" âbhihatā gadā
varṣā|pradoṣe khadyotair vṛto vṛkṣa iv' ābabhau.
gadā kṣiptā tu samare Madra|rājena Bhārata
vyoma saṃdīpayānā sā sasṛje pāvakaṃ bahu.
15.20 tath" âiva Bhīmasenena dviṣate preṣitā gadā
tāpayām āsa tat sainyaṃ mah"|ôlkā patatī yathā.
te c' âiv' ôbhe gade śreṣṭhe samāsādya paras|param
śvasantyau nāga|kany" êva sasṛjāte vibhā|vasum.
nakhair iva mahā|vyāghrau dantair iva mahā|gajau
tau viceratur āsādya gadābhyāṃ ca paras|param.
tato gad"|âgr'|âbhihatau kṣaṇena rudhir'|ôkṣitau
dadṛśāte mah"|ātmānau puṣpitāv iva kiṃśukau.
śuśruve dikṣu sarvāsu tayoḥ puruṣa|siṃhayoḥ
gad"|âbhighāta|saṃhrādaḥ Śakr'|âśani|rav'|ôpamaḥ.
15.25 gadayā Madra|rājena savya|dakṣiṇam āhataḥ
n' âkampata tadā Bhīmo bhidyamāna iv' âcalaḥ.
tathā Bhīma|gadā|vegais tāḍyamāno mahā|balaḥ
dhairyān Madr'|âdhipas tasthau vajrair girir iv' āhataḥ.
āpetatur mahā|vegau samucchrita|mahā|gadau
punar antara|mārga|sthau maṇḍalāni viceratuḥ.
ath' āplutya padāny aṣṭau saṃnipatya gajāv iva
sahasā loha|daṇḍābhyām anyonyam abhijaghnatuḥ.
tau paras|para|vegāc ca gadābhyāṃ ca bhṛś'|āhatau
yugapat petatur vīrau kṣitāv Indra|dhvajāv iva.
15.30 tato vihvalamānaṃ taṃ niḥśvasantaṃ punaḥ punaḥ
Śalyam abhyapatat tūrṇaṃ Kṛtavarmā mahā|rathaḥ.

Repelled by the shock of his enemy's parry, Bhima·sena's own weapon glowed like a tree hidden by fireflies in a monsoon dusk. Sparks struck from it spewed forth and scorched
the surrounding air. O Bhárata as Bhima brought that blow 15.20
down his mace flashed across the plain like a falling meteor. Their fine weapons found one another and sighed like serpent nymphs and light glanced from them as they locked together. As their clubs crossed the two warriors clawed with their nails like tigers and snapped like elephants with their teeth. With their maces intertwined the bloodflecked shape they made looked for a moment like a flame-of-the-forest in flower, and the crack of their weapons in the hands of those beasts echoed across the whole of the sky as if Indra were knocking together his thunderbolts.

Left and right swung Shalya's mace and beneath its blows 15.25
Bhima was unshaken as stone. The strong Madra king too stood firm as a mountain in a storm. They raised their weapons high and fell upon one another and stood hand to hand, then went in circles, then leapt into the air and came down again. Brutal as elephants they bloodied their clubs on one another until at last, exhausted and crushed beneath each other's pounding blows, they both fell to their knees
and hung like flags of Indra. Shalya staggered and slipped 15.30
and tried to catch his breath, his mace dangling in his hand.

dṛṣṭvā c' âinaṃ mahā|rāja, gaday" âbhinipīḍitam
viceṣṭantaṃ yathā nāgaṃ mūrchay" âbhipariplutam
tataḥ sa|gadam āropya Madrāṇām adhipaṃ ratham
apovāha raṇāt tūrṇaṃ Kṛtavarmā mahā|rathaḥ.
kṣībavad vihvalo vīro nimeṣāt punar utthitaḥ
Bhīmo 'pi su|mahā|bāhur gadā|pāṇir adṛśyata.
tato Madr'|âdhipaṃ dṛṣṭvā tava putrāḥ parāṅ|mukham
sa|nāga|ratha|patty|aśvāḥ samakampanta, māriṣa.
15.35 te Pāṇḍavair ardyamānās tāvakā jita|kāśibhiḥ
bhītā diśo 'nvapadyanta vāta|nunnā ghanā iva.
nirjitya Dhārtarāṣṭrāṃs tu Pāṇḍaveyā mahā|rathāḥ
vyarocanta raṇe rājan dīpyamānā yaśasvinaḥ.
siṃha|nādān bhṛśaṃ cakruḥ śaṅkhān dadhmuś ca harṣitāḥ
bherīś ca vādayām āsur mṛdaṅgāṃś c' ānakaiḥ saha.

O majesty, mighty Krita·varman saw the Madra king beaten down and dizzy with weariness and writhing like a snake, and he made quickly for him and pulled him aboard his chariot and accelerated away from the mess of battle. In the winking of an eye Bhima was up again and hefted his weapon in his mighty grip. His eyes rolled as if he were drunk. O father your children all stood among elephants and infantry and horses and cars and watched in fear as Shalya was carried from the fray. Then they too broke up and 15.35
gave way, driven like shreds of cloud by the rising Pándava wind.

The great Pándava warriors had bettered the sons of Dhrita·rashtra and o king they shone bright in their blazing splendor. Roars and blaring trumpets were the sound of their celebration, and the rumble of countless drums.

16–32
THE DEATH OF THE BEHOLDEN

SAMJAYA uvāca.

16.1 TAD BALAM su|mahad dīrṇam
tvadīyam prekṣya vīryavān
dadhār' âiko raṇe Pāṇḍūn
Vṛṣaseno 'stra|māyayā.
śarā daśa diśo muktā Vṛṣasenena māriṣa
vicerus te vinirbhidya nara|vāji|ratha|dvipān.
tasya dīptā mahā|bāṇā viniśceruḥ sahasraśaḥ
bhānor iva mahā|bāho grīṣma|kāle marīcayaḥ.
ten' ârditā mahā|rāja rathinaḥ sādinas tathā
nipetur urvyāṃ sahasā vāta|nunnā iva drumāḥ.
16.5 hay'|âughāṃś ca rath'|âughāṃś ca
gaj'|âughāṃś ca samantataḥ
apātayad raṇe, rājañ,
śataśo 'tha sahasraśaḥ.

dṛṣṭvā tam evaṃ samare vicarantam a|bhītavat
sahitāḥ sarva|rājānaḥ parivavruḥ samantataḥ.
Nākulis tu Śatânīko Vṛṣasenaṃ samabhyayāt
vivyādha c' âinaṃ daśabhir nārācair marma|bhedibhiḥ.
tasya Karṇ'|ātma|jaś cāpaṃ chittvā ketum apātayat
taṃ bhrātaraṃ parīpsanto Draupadeyāḥ samabhyayuḥ.
Karṇ'|ātma|jaṃ śara|vrātaiś cakruś c' â|dṛśyam añjasā
tān nadanto 'bhyadhāvanta Droṇa|putra|mukhā rathāḥ
16.10 chādayanto mahā|rāja Draupadeyān mahā|rathān
śarair nānā|vidhais tūrṇaṃ parvatāñ jala|dā iva.
tān Pāṇḍavāḥ pratyagṛhṇaṃs tvaritāḥ putra|gṛddhinaḥ
Pāñcālāḥ Kekayā Matsyāḥ Sṛñjayāś c' ôdyat'|āyudhāḥ.
tad yuddham abhavad ghoraṃ tumulaṃ loma|harṣaṇam
tvadīyaiḥ Pāṇḍu|putrāṇāṃ devānām iva dānavaiḥ.
evam uttama|saṃrambhā yuyudhuḥ Kuru|Pāṇḍavāḥ

SÁNJAYA spoke.

GREAT VRISHA·SENA watched the broad army of your sons rent open and began all alone to check the Pándavas with his enchanted bow. Arrows flew over the Pándava horde in ten directions and tore through men, chariots, horses and elephants. Like the sun's rays in the hot season thousands of those burning and heavy shafts from the great man's hand cut through riders and drivers. And pierced through o great king they fell to their knees, trees buckled in the wind. O majesty there were throngs of chariots and horses and elephants in numbers too large to count which he crushed beneath his might. 16.1 16.5

When the other kings saw Vrisha·sena careering fearlessly through the fray they came in around him in a circle. Nákula's boy Shatáníka moved in first and struck him with ten razorsharp wroughtiron shafts. But Karna's son splintered his bow and severed the pole of his standard as the children of Dráupadi closed keenly in around their brother. Soon Vrisha·sena disappeared beneath a thick screen of arrows but then came the warriors under Ashvatthámans command roaring and wheeling and darkening the skies above the mighty Draupadéyas with darts beyond number. They engulfed them as clouds engulf a mountain ridge. Thirsty for Ashvatthámans blood the Pándavas were upon him in a moment and behind them with weapons held high rode Panchálas, Kékayas, Matsyas, Srínjayas. Loud and bloody and full of horror was the fighting that came next as Pandu's sons met your own like gods meeting demons. Their wrath was now at its height. Eye to eye the Kurus and Pándavas stood, and sin for sin they fought. Such was their passion 16.10

paras|param udīkṣantaḥ paras|para|kṛt'|āgasaḥ.
teṣāṃ dadṛśire kopād vapūṃṣy a|mita|tejasām
yuyutsūnām iv' ākāśe patatri|vara|bhoginām.
16.15 Bhīma|Karṇa|Kṛpa|Droṇa|Drauṇi|Pārṣata|Sātyakaiḥ
babhāse sa raṇ'|ôddeśaḥ kāla|sūryair iv' ôditaiḥ.
tad" āsīt tumulaṃ yuddhaṃ nighnatām itar'|êtaram
mahā|balānāṃ balibhir dānavānāṃ yathā suraiḥ.
tato Yudhiṣṭhir'|ânīkam uddhūt'|ârṇava|nisvanam
tvadīyam avadhīt sainyaṃ sampradruta|mahā|ratham.
tat prabhagnaṃ balaṃ dṛṣṭvā śatrubhir bhṛśam arditam,
«alaṃ drutena vaḥ śūrā» iti Droṇo 'bhyabhāṣata.
tataḥ śoṇa|hayaḥ kruddhaś catur|danta iva dvi|paḥ
praviśya Pāṇḍav'|ânīkaṃ Yudhiṣṭhiram upādravat.
16.20 tam avidhyac chitair bāṇaiḥ kaṅka|patrair Yudhiṣṭhiraḥ
tasya Droṇo dhanuś chittvā taṃ drutaṃ samupādravat.
cakra|rakṣaḥ Kumāras tu Pāñcālānāṃ yaśas|karaḥ
dadhāra Droṇam āyāntaṃ vel" êva saritāṃ patim.
Droṇaṃ nivāritaṃ dṛṣṭvā Kumāreṇa dvi|ja'|ṛṣabham
siṃha|nāda|ravo hy āsīt sādhu sādhv iti bhāṣatām.
Kumāras tu tato Droṇaṃ sāyakena mah"|āhave
vivyādh' ôrasi saṃkruddhaḥ siṃhavac c' ānadan muhuḥ.
saṃvārya tu raṇe Droṇaḥ Kumāraṃ vai mahā|balaḥ
śarair an|eka|sāhasraiḥ kṛta|hasto jita|klamaḥ
16.25 taṃ śūram ārya|vratinam astr'|ârtha|kṛta|niśramam
cakra|rakṣam apāmṛdnāt Kumāraṃ dvi|ja|sattamaḥ.

and so unbound their splendor that it seemed like the warriors' wounded bodies were themselves hungrily plucking the feathered arrows from the sky. Bhima, Karna, Kripa, 16.15
Drona, Drauni, Dhrishta·dyumna and Sátyaki: the battlefield shone with them as with suns risen at the end of time. In the crash of battle the killing went on between the great demonic legions and a host divine, before roaring like a stormy sea Yudhi·shthira's army battered the front line of Duryódhana's force. Its champions turned to run.

Drona saw his army gashed by its foe and breaking apart and he called out to his soldiers.

"Heroes! Halt your flight!"

On a horse drenched in blood Drona rode like the four-tusked Airávata into the army of the Pándavas until he reached Yudhi·shthira. As the king's sharp arrows fletched 16.20
in vulture feathers slammed into him Drona drove on, then broke Yudhi·shthira's bow in two and put him to flight. And then as the coast holds back the tide it was Yudhi·shthira's wheelguard* Kumára who to the glory of the Panchálas managed briefly to block Drona's progress. A great roar of excitement swelled around him as Kumára braved the brahmin bull and crying out like an enraged beast sent an arrow across the fray and into Drona's chest. But mighty Drona breathed deep, and with a dense flurry of arrows from his dextrous hand the great twiceborn forced Kumára back. Then despite the wheelguard's heroism and high vows 16.25
and brilliance with the bow, the mighty priest crushed him beneath his attack.

sa madhyaṃ prāpya senāyāḥ sarvāḥ paricaran diśaḥ
tava sainyasya gopt" āsīd Bhāradvājo ratha'|rṣabhaḥ.
Śikhaṇḍinaṃ dvā|daśabhir viṃśatyā c' Ôttamaujasam
Nakulaṃ pañcabhir viddhvā Sahadevaṃ ca saptabhiḥ
Yudhiṣṭhiraṃ dvā|daśabhir Draupadeyāṃs tribhis tribhiḥ
Sātyakiṃ pañcabhir viddhvā Matsyaṃ ca daśabhiḥ śaraiḥ
vyakṣobhayad raṇe yodhān yathā|mukhyān abhidravan
abhyavartata samprepsuḥ Kuntī|putraṃ Yudhiṣṭhiram.
16.30 Yugaṃdharas tato, rājan, Bhāradvājaṃ mahā|ratham
vārayām āsa saṃkruddhaṃ vāt'|ôddhūtam iv' ârṇavam.
Yudhiṣṭhiraṃ sa viddhvā tu śaraiḥ saṃnata|parvabhiḥ
Yugaṃdharaṃ ca bhallena ratha|nīḍād apāharat.
tato Virāṭa|Drupadau Kaikeyāḥ Sātyakiḥ Śibiḥ
Vyāghradattaś ca Pāñcālyaḥ Siṃhasenaś ca vīryavān
ete c' ânye ca bahavaḥ parīpsanto Yudhiṣṭhiram
āvavrus tasya panthānaṃ kirantaḥ sāyakān bahūn.
Vyāghradattaś ca Pāñcālyo Droṇaṃ vivyādha mārgaṇaiḥ
pañcāśadbhiḥ śitai, rājaṃs, tata uccukruśur janāḥ.
16.35 tvaritaṃ Siṃhasenas tu Droṇaṃ viddhvā mahā|ratham
prāhasat sahasā hṛṣṭas trāsayan vai yata|vratam.
tato visphārya nayane dhanur|jyām avamṛjya ca
tala|śabdaṃ mahat kṛtvā Droṇas taṃ samupādravat.
tatas tu Siṃhasenasya śiraḥ kāyāt sa|kuṇḍalam
Vyāghradattasya c' ākramya bhallābhyām aharad balī.
tān pramṛdya śara|vrātaiḥ Pāṇḍavānāṃ mahā|rathān
Yudhiṣṭhira|samabhyāśe tasthau mṛtyur iv' ântakaḥ.

Bharad·vaja's taurine son was proving your army's savior.
Reaching the center of foe's troops, he aimed by turns in every direction. Shikhándin he struck with twelve of his arrows
then Uttamáujas with twenty then Nákula with five and Sa-
ha·deva with seven. Twelve more pierced Yudhi·shthira as
three hit each of the Draupadéyas and five reached Sátyaki
and he struck Matsya with ten. He threw the warriors about
him into turmoil, all the while making urgently for their
leader the son of Kuntí. Great Drona was like a tempest- 16.30
driven sea, and next it was Yugan·dhara who stepped into
his furious path. Sending his trueworked arrows straight at
Yudhi·shthira, Drona knocked Yugan·dhara from the seat
of his car with a single spearheaded shaft.

Yudhi·shthira was in danger. Together with their comrades Viráta, Drúpada and the Kaikéyas, Sátyaki, Shibi,
the Panchála Vyaghra·datta and hero Sinha·sena scattered
Drona's course with their many missiles and arrows to protect their king from harm. O majesty the Panchála went at
Drona with fifty of his biting shafts while his friends spir-
ited Yudhi·shthira away. Sinha·sena found his mark with a 16.35
speedy shot and burst into excited laughter to have grazed
the great ascetic. But mighty Drona plucked the string of his
own bow and as it sang in the air his spearlike shafts sheared
the bejewelled heads of Vyaghra·datta and Sinha·sena away
from their necks. Unceasing he ravaged the paladins of the
Pándavas with his volleys and now he stood near Yudhi·sh-
thira's chariot like Death come to bear him off. O majesty,
cries of alarm went up from Yudhi·shthira's troops. With
sternvowed Drona so close to him the warriors all thought
their king dead. As he reared up to Yudhi·shthira they said 16.40

tato 'bhavan mahā|śabdo rājan Yaudhiṣṭhire bale
hṛto rāj" êti yodhānāṃ samīpa|sthe yata|vrate.
16.40 abruvan sainikās tatra dṛṣṭvā Droṇasya vikramam,
adya rājā Dhārtarāṣṭraḥ kṛt'|ârtho vai bhaviṣyati
āgamiṣyati no nūnaṃ Dhārtarāṣṭrasya saṃyuge.
evaṃ saṃjalpatāṃ teṣāṃ tāvakānāṃ mahā|rathaḥ
āyāj javena Kaunteyo ratha|ghoṣeṇa nādayan
śoṇit'|ôdāṃ rath"|āvartāṃ kṛtvā viśasane nadīm
śūr'|âsthi|caya|saṃkīrṇāṃ preta|kūl'|âpahāriṇīm
tāṃ śar'|âugha|mahā|phenāṃ prāsa|matsya|samākulām
nadīm uttīrya vegena Kurūn vidrāvya Pāṇḍavaḥ
tataḥ Kirīṭī sahasā Droṇ'|ânīkam upādravat
chādayann iṣu|jālena mahatā mohayann iva.
16.45 śīghram abhyasyato bāṇān saṃdadhānasya c' âniśam
n' ântaraṃ dadṛśe kaś cit Kaunteyasya yaśasvinaḥ.
na diśo n' ântar|ikṣaṃ ca na dyaur n' âiva ca medinī
adṛśyata, mahā|rāja, bāṇa|bhūtam iv' âbhavat.
n' âdṛśyata tadā rājaṃs tatra kiṃ cana saṃyuge
bāṇ'|ândha|kāre mahati kṛte Gāṇḍīva|dhanvanā.
sūrye c' âstam anuprāpte rajasā c' âbhisaṃvṛte
n' âjñāyata tadā śatrur na su|hṛn na ca kiṃ cana.
tato 'vahāraṃ cakrus te Droṇa|Duryodhan'|ādayaḥ.
16.50 tān viditvā bhṛśaṃ trastān a|yuddha|manasaḥ parān
svāny anīkāni Bībhatsuḥ śanakair avahārayat.
tato 'bhituṣṭuvuḥ Pārthaṃ prahṛṣṭāḥ Pāṇḍu|Sṛñjayāḥ
Pāñcālāś ca mano|jñābhir vāgbhiḥ sūryam iva' ṛṣayaḥ
evaṃ sva|śibiraṃ prāyāj jitvā śatrūn Dhanaṃjayaḥ
pṛṣṭhataḥ sarva|sainyānāṃ mudito vai sa|Keśavaḥ.

to themselves, Now Duryódhana's wish will come to pass and then, as Drona promised Dhrita·rashtra's son, he will come for us.

But even as such words were on their lips, with the wheels of his chariot grinding, the mighty warrior and son of Kunti was quickly among your own, rising suddenly out of the river rife with shoals of arrows foaming to its surface and all crowded with ghosts and thick with the trunks and bones of dead heroes, the river that fountained from the havoc Drona had brought. The Diademed Warrior scattered Kurus before him and made straight for Drona's guard and cast across them a wide and bewildering net of arrows as he
went. Quick and unrelenting flew his missiles as over and 16.45
over he notched another onto his string. Soon the very shape of the fabled son of Kunti vanished before our eyes. O king the horizon itself could no more been seen, nor could the space near or far above our heads, nor the earth beneath our feet. The last moments of sunset were invisible through the dust and under that wooden darkness spread upon us by the bow Gandíva the battlefield too had disappeared. There were only arrows.

We could make out neither friend nor enemy. Drona, Duryódhana and the other Kuru generals signaled the retreat. When he realized that the terror he had whipped up 16.50
among them had forced them to cease battle, slowly and contemptuously Árjuna drew back his own men. The Pandus, the Srínjayas and the Panchálas were overjoyed. They poured their praise on Partha in beautiful words like sages in thrall to the sun. With his foes defeated and Késhava at his side, Dhanan·jaya son of Pandu made his way back in high

masāra|galv|arka|suvarṇa|rūpyair
vajra|pravāla|sphaṭikaiś ca mukhyaiḥ
citre rathe Pāṇḍu|suto babhāse
nakṣatra|citre viyat' îva candraḥ.

SAMJAYA uvāca.

17.1 TE SENE ŚIBIRAM gatvā nyaviśetāṃ, viśāṃ pate,
yathā|bhāgaṃ yathā|nyāyaṃ yathā|gulmaṃ ca sarvaśaḥ.
kṛtv" âvahāraṃ sainyānāṃ Droṇaḥ parama|durmanāḥ
Duryodhanam abhiprekṣya sa|vrīḍam idam abravīt.
«uktam etan mayā pūrvaṃ: na tiṣṭhati Dhanaṃjaye
śakyo grahītuṃ saṃgrāme devair api Yudhiṣṭhiraḥ.
iti tad vaḥ prayatatāṃ kṛtaṃ Pārthena saṃyuge.
mā viśaṅkīr vaco mahyam a|jeyau Kṛṣṇa|Pāṇḍavau.
17.5 apanīte tu yogena kena cic chveta|vāhane
tata eṣyati te, rājan, vaśam adya Yudhiṣṭhiraḥ.
kaś cid āhvayatāṃ saṃkhye deśam anyaṃ prakarṣatu
tam a|jitvā na Kaunteyo nivarteta kathaṃ cana.
etasminn antare śūnye Dharma|rājam ahaṃ nṛ|pa
grahīṣyāmi camūṃ bhittvā Dhṛṣṭadyumnasya paśyataḥ.
Arjunena vihīnas tu yadi n' ôtsṛjate raṇam
mām upāyāntam ālokya gṛhītaṃ viddhi Pāṇḍavaṃ.
evaṃ te 'haṃ, mahā|rāja, dharma|putraṃ Yudhiṣṭhiram
samāneṣyāmi sa|gaṇaṃ vaśam adya na saṃśayaḥ.
17.10 yadi tiṣṭhati saṃgrāme muhūrtam api Pāṇḍavaḥ
ath' âpayāti saṃgrāmād vijayāt tad viśiṣyate.»

spirits to his tent at the rear of the camp. Atop his chariot spangled in the finest quartz and coral and diamonds interwrought with gold, crystals and sapphires, he shone like the moon among a million stars.

SÁNJAYA spoke.

THE TWO ARMIES went back to their tents and everyone 17.1
retired to the different quarters of the camp. But having forced this stalemate with the enemy Drona was plunged into deep despair. He raised his eyes to Duryódhana and his words were tinged with shame.

"What I said before has been proven true. As long as Dhanan·jaya is by his side Yudhi·shthira can be taken only by the gods. And so all your struggles Partha rendered in vain. Be sure of what I say: Krishna and Árjuna are invincible.
But if their white horses can be drawn off somehow, then in 17.5
a moment, my king, Yudhi·shthira will be yours. Someone must challenge Árjuna and lure him to somewhere far from the midst of the fray, since the heir born to Kunti will not weaken as long as Árjuna remains unbowed. If the good king were alone for just a brief time then my lord I could break his line and snatch him from Dhrishta·dyumna's vigilant gaze. As long as he keeps to the field even when bereft of Árjuna, you can be assured that when you see me next I will have Yudhi·shthira in chains. Believe me great king. I will bring the child of righteousness and all his cohorts under
your command, and I will do so soon. If the son of Pandu 17.10
stays on the plain for just a passing moment then he will leave the war and any hope of victory behind him."

SAMJAYA uvāca.

Droṇasya tad vacaḥ śrutvā Trigart'|âdhipatis tataḥ
bhrātṛbhiḥ sahito, rājann, idaṃ vacanam abravīt.
«vayaṃ vinikṛtā rājan sadā Gāṇḍīva|dhanvanā
an|āgaḥsv api c' āgas|kṛd asmāsu Bharata'|rṣabha.
te vayaṃ smaramāṇās tān vinikārān pṛthag|vidhān
krodh'|âgninā dahyamānā na śemahi sadā niśi.
sa no diṣṭy" âstra|sampannaś cakṣur|viṣayam āgataḥ
kartāraḥ sma vayaṃ karma yac cikīrṣāma hṛd|gatam.
17.15 bhavataś ca priyaṃ yat syād asmākaṃ ca yaśas|karam
vayam enaṃ haniṣyāmo nikṛṣy' āyodhanād bahiḥ.
ady' âstv an|Arjunā bhūmir a|Trigart" âtha vā punaḥ
satyaṃ te pratijānīmo n' âitan mithyā bhaviṣyati.»
evaṃ Satyarathaś c' ôktvā Satyadharmā ca Bhārata
Satyavrataś ca Satyeṣuḥ Satyakarmā tath" âiva ca
sahitā bhrātaraḥ pañca rathānām ayutena ca
nyavartanta mahā|rāja kṛtvā śapatham āhave.
Mālavās Tuṇḍikerāś ca rathānām ayutais tribhiḥ
Suśarmā ca nara|vyāghras Traigartaḥ Prasthal'|âdhipaḥ
17.20 Māvellakair Lalitthaiś ca sahito Madrakair api
rathānām ayuten' âiva so 'gamad bhrātṛbhiḥ saha
nānā|jana|padebhyaś ca rathānām ayutaṃ punaḥ
samutthitaṃ viśiṣṭānāṃ śapath'|ârtham upāgamat.
tato jvalanam ānāyya kṛtvā sarve pṛthak pṛthak
jagṛhuḥ kuśa|cīrāṇi citrāṇi kavacāni ca.

SÁNJAYA spoke.

O king, the lord of the Tri·gartas and his brothers heard what Drona said. Suśarman turned to address Duryódhana.*

"O king and bull of the Bharatas. Although we commit no sin, every day we suffer the abuse of that evildoer who bears the bow Gandíva. When we meditate on his many insults in the dead of night we burn in flames of anger that consume our hours of rest. If he raises his bow once more at us then we will surely be the authors of that deed for which we have hoped in the innermost chambers of our hearts.
May our promise please you and may it bring us fame. We 17.15
will kill him and drag his corpse off the plain. This will not be undone: the world will no longer hold both Árjuna and the brothers Tri·garta."

And so it was o Bhárata that with these words a sacred vow was sworn between his five brothers Satya·ratha, Satya·dharman, Satya·vrata, Satyéshu and Satya·karman. They came forth with their thousand chariots. At the head of the Málavas and Tundikéras and his own massive armies the Tri·garta tiger Sushárman lord of Prasthala went in step
with brothers. Then came the panoplies of the Mavéllakas, 17.20
the Lalítthas and the Mádrakas, and a final great legion made up of folk tatterdemalion. The sealing of the vow in that mighty assembly began. A pyre was built high, and with bunches of sacred grass and bright chips of bark each performed his rite. Their armor was bound with ribbons and anointed with oil. They took bunches of grass in their hands and tied girdles of hemp around their waists. Those heroes of unreckonable gifts were sacrificers with heirs and

te ca baddha|tanu|trāṇā ghṛt'|âktāḥ kuśa|cīriṇaḥ
maurvī|mekhalino vīrāḥ sahasra|śata|dakṣiṇāḥ
yajvānaḥ putriṇo lokyāḥ kṛta|kṛtyās tanu|tyajaḥ
yokṣyamāṇās tad" ātmānam yaśasā vijayena ca
17.25 brahma|carya|śruti|mukhaiḥ kratubhiś c' āpta|dakṣiṇaiḥ
prāpya lokān su|yuddhena kṣipram eva yiyāsavaḥ
brāhmaṇāṃs tarpayitvā ca niṣkān dattvā pṛthak pṛthak
gāś ca vāsāṃsi ca punaḥ samābhāṣya paras|param
prajvālya kṛṣṇa|vartmānam upāgamya raṇe vratam
tasminn agnau tadā cakruḥ pratijñāṃ dṛḍha|niścayāḥ.
śṛṇvatāṃ sarva|bhūtānām uccair vāco babhāṣire
dhṛtāṃ Dhanaṃjaya|vadhe pratijñāṃ c' âpi cakrire.
«ye vai lokāś c' ân|ṛtināṃ ye ca vai brahma|ghātināṃ
madya|pasya ca ye lokā guru|dāra|ratasya ca
17.30 brahma|sva|hāriṇaś c' âiva rāja|piṇḍ'|âpahāriṇaḥ
śaraṇ'|āgataṃ ca tyajato yācamānaṃ tathā ghnataḥ
agāra|dāhināṃ c' âiva ye ca gāṃ nighnatām api
apakāriṇāṃ ca ye lokā ye ca brahma|dviṣām api
sva|bhāryām ṛtu|kāleṣu mohād vai n' âbhigacchatām
śrāddha|maithunikānāṃ ca ye c' âpy ātm'|âpahāriṇām
nyās'|âpahāriṇāṃ ye ca śrutaṃ nāśayatāṃ ca ye
klībena yudhyamānānāṃ ye ca nīc'|ânusāriṇām
nāstikānāṃ ca ye lokā ye 'gni|mātṛ|pitṛ|tyajāṃ
tān āpnuyāmahe lokān ye ca pāpa|kṛtām api
17.35 yady a|hatvā vayaṃ sarve nivartema Dhanaṃjayam
tena c' âbhyarditās trāsād bhavema hi parāṅ|mukhāḥ.
yadi tv a|su|karaṃ loke karma kuryāma saṃyuge
iṣṭāl lokān prāpnuyāmo vayam adya na saṃśayaḥ.»

domains, men of duty, warriors who had abandoned life and turned their hearts to glory and triumph. Through pious 17.25
and solemn rites rich with largesse they prepared for the realms where battle would bring them, and now were eager to fight on. They rewarded their priests with gifts of coins, cows and cloth, and speaking once more among themselves agreed on their oath and set alight the fire that brings all to black.

With iron wills they forged their promise in those flames. To make even firmer their resolve to kill Dhanan·jaya they declaimed these words to all who could hear them.

"There are men who break the law. Who kill and cast 17.30
out priests and plunder kings. Drunks who toy with their teachers' wives. Men who turn away the needy, who kill beggars, who slaughter cows and burn down homes, who scorn the gods or lie with their wives when it is forbidden or fornicate at the funerals of their fathers. Men who skirmish with the weak, who hang on the words of idiots, infidels who walk away from their hearths and their elders. There are men who destroy themselves and the rules by which we live. May we share their fate if in fear we turn our backs to 17.35
our task. But we say this: if in battle we achieve our arduous goal then we will ascend to the places where the blessed dwell."

evam uktvā tato, rājaṃs, te 'bhyavartanta saṃyuge
āhvayanto 'rjunaṃ vīrāḥ pitṛ|juṣṭāṃ diśaṃ prati
āhūtas tair nara|vyāghraiḥ Pārthaḥ para|puraṃ|jayaḥ
Dharma|rājam idaṃ vākyam a|pad'|ântaram abravīt.
«āhūto na nivarteyam iti me vratam āhitam
Saṃśaptakāś ca māṃ rājann āhvayanti mahā|mṛdhe.
17.40 eṣa ca bhrātṛbhiḥ sārdhaṃ Suśarm" āhvayate raṇe,
vadhāya sa|gaṇasy' âsya mām anujñātum arhasi.
n' âitac chaknomi saṃsoḍhum āhvānaṃ, puruṣa'|rṣabha,
satyaṃ te pratijānāmi hatān viddhi parān yudhi.»

YUDHIṢṬHIRA uvāca.

śrutaṃ te tattvatas, tāta, yad Droṇena cikīrṣitaṃ
yathā tad an|ṛtaṃ tasya bhavet tat tvaṃ samācara.
Droṇo hi balavāñ śūraḥ kṛt'|âstraś ca jita|śramaḥ
pratijñātaṃ ca ten' âitad grahaṇaṃ me, mahā|ratha.

ARJUNA uvāca.

ayaṃ vai Satyajid, rājann, adya tvā rakṣitā yudhi
dhriyamāṇe tu Pāñcālye n' ācāryaḥ kāmam āpsyati.
17.45 hate tu puruṣa|vyāghre raṇe Satyajiti, prabho,
sarvair api sametair vā na sthātavyaṃ kathaṃ cana.

SAMJAYA uvāca.

anujñātas tato rājñā pariṣvaktaś ca Phalgunaḥ
premṇā dṛṣṭaś ca bahudhā hy āśiṣaś c' âsya yojitaḥ
vihāy' âinaṃ tataḥ Pārthas Trigartān pratyayād balī
kṣudhitaḥ kṣud|vighāt'|ârthaṃ siṃho mṛga|gaṇān iva.
tato Dauryodhanaṃ sainyaṃ mudā paramayā yutam
ṛte 'rjunaṃ bhṛśaṃ kruddhaṃ Dharmarājasya nigrahe.

O majesty, with these words the mighty brothers went forth and called out Árjuna's name south across the land. When he heard their tiger's roars Partha the conqueror of cities spoke to the good king these urgent words.

"My king I have vowed never to refuse a challenge. Beholden* are summoning me. Sushárman and his brothers 17.40
are calling me out to fight. You must grant me leave to crush them and their troops. Bull in the herd of men I cannot resist this challenge, but I can promise that a handful of your foes are as good as dead."

YUDHI·SHTHIRA spoke.

Brother. You have heard exactly what it is that Drona intends: make sure that his aim remains a hollow one. You are a great warrior, but Drona is a mighty hero too, a master of the bow who suffers hardship unbending, and he it is who has vowed to capture me.

ÁRJUNA spoke.

You have a protector here before you, majesty, in Sátyajit. While this son of Pancháli lives our teacher's desire will
remain unfulfilled. O king, the tiger Sátyajit will fall only 17.45
when no warrior on earth still stands.

SÁNJAYA spoke.

The king granted the Red Star Fighter his leave and then embraced him with deep affection. Equipped with his blessing alone, brave Partha left the king and rode out for the Tri·gartas like a lion at a herd of deer ravening to quell its hunger. And Duryódhana's army swelled in frenzy, inflamed with the prospect of capturing the good king once Árjuna had been dispatched. The two armies crashed together like

tato 'nyonyena te sene samājagmatur ojasā
Gaṅgā|Sarayvau vegena prāvṛṣ' îv' ôlbaṇ'|ôdake.

SAṂJAYA uvāca.

18.1 TATAḤ SAṂŚAPTAKĀ, rājan, same deśe vyavasthitāḥ
vyūhy' ânīkaṃ rathair eva candr'|ākāraṃ mudā yutāḥ.
te Kirīṭinam āyāntaṃ dṛṣṭvā harṣeṇa māriṣa
udakrośan nara|vyāghrāḥ śabdena mahatā tadā.
sa śabdaḥ pradiśaḥ sarvā diśaḥ khaṃ ca samāvṛṇot
āvṛtatvāc ca lokasya n' āsīt tatra pratisvanaḥ.
atīva samprahṛṣṭāṃs tān upalabhya Dhanaṃjayaḥ
kiṃ cid abhyutsmayan Kṛṣṇam idaṃ vacanam abravīt.
18.5 «paśy' âitān Devakī|mātar mumūrṣūn adya saṃyuge
bhrātṝṃs Traigartakān eva roditavye praharṣitān.
atha vā harṣa|kālo 'yaṃ Traigartānām a|saṃśayaṃ
ku|narair dur|avāpān hi lokān prāpsyanty an|uttamān.»
evam uktvā mahā|bāhur Hṛṣīkeśaṃ tato 'rjunaḥ
āsasāda raṇe vyūḍhāṃ Trigartānām anīkinīṃ.
sa Devadattam ādāya śaṅkhaṃ hema|pariṣkṛtaṃ
dadhmau vegena mahatā ghoṣeṇ' āpūrayan diśaḥ.
tena śabdena vitrastā Saṃśaptaka|varūthinī
niś|ceṣṭ" âvasthitā saṃkhye hy aśma|sāra|mayī yathā.
18.10 vāhās teṣāṃ vivṛtt'|âkṣāḥ stabdha|karṇa|śiro|dharāḥ
viṣṭabdha|caraṇā mūtraṃ rudhiraṃ ca prasusruvuḥ.
upalabhya tataḥ saṃjñām avasthāpya ca vāhinīm
yugapat Pāṇḍu|putrāya cikṣipuḥ kaṅka|patriṇaḥ.
tāny Arjunaḥ sahasrāṇi daśa pañcabhir āśu|gaiḥ
an|āgatāny eva śaraiś cicched' āśu|parākramaḥ.
tato 'rjunaṃ śitair bāṇair daśabhir daśabhiḥ punaḥ

the Ganges and Sárayu plunging their rainswollen waters into the immensity of the ocean.

SÁNJAYA spoke.

O MAJESTY. The Beholden were drawn up together, their 18.1
chariots arranged in the figure of the moon. They bristled with anticipation. When those tigers laid their eyes on the Diademed Warrior as he rode near they let out a delirious cry so loud that it filled every quarter of the sky and smothered its own echo. Dhanan·jaya observed their excitement. He smiled slightly, turned to Krishna and spoke.

"Look at them o son of Dévaki: the brothers Tri·garta, so 18.5
soon to meet their end. Giddy with joy when they should be weeping. Or perhaps it is time for the Tri·gartas to rejoice, since they are bound for realms beyond the reach of fools."

With these words to Hrishi·kesha, strongarmed Árjuna rode into battle against the serried ranks of the Tri·gartas. Raising the conch Deva·datta to his lips he blew deep and filled the air with its sound. Its note blared out above the army of the Beholden and fear stole across every one of them. For a moment they froze still on the battlefield as if
cast in iron. Their horses rolled their eyes, necks and ears 18.10
stiffening, motionless but for the bloodcolored piss running down their shanks.

Then the brothers Tri·garta gathered their wits. They rallied their troops and as one loosed their heronfeathered arrows at Pandu's son. But before they even reached him Árjuna nimbly split the hundredfold volley with swift shafts of his own. Ten whetted darts then ten again they let fly at Árjuna, and Partha knocked them all away. Back he shot

pratyavidhyaṃs tataḥ Pārthas tān avidhyat tribhis tribhiḥ.
ek'|âikas tu tataḥ Pārthaṃ rājan vivyādha pañcabhiḥ
sa ca tān prativivyādha dvābhyāṃ dvābhyāṃ parākramī.
18.15 bhūya eva tu saṃkruddhās te 'rjunaṃ saha|Keśavaṃ
āpūrayan śarais tūrṇaṃ taṭākam iva vṛṣṭibhiḥ.
tataḥ śara|sahasrāṇi prāpatann Arjunaṃ prati
bhramarāṇām iva vrātāḥ phullaṃ druma|gaṇaṃ vane.
tataḥ Subāhus triṃśadbhir adri|sāra|mayair dṛḍhaiḥ
avidhyad iṣubhir gāḍhaṃ Kirīṭe Savyasācinam.
taiḥ Kirīṭī kirīṭa|sthair hema|puṅkhair a|jihma|gaiḥ
śāta|kumbha|may'|āpīḍo babhau yūpa iv' ûcchritaḥ.
hast'|āvāpaṃ Subāhos tu bhallena yudhi Pāṇḍavaḥ
ciccheda taṃ c' âiva punaḥ śara|varṣair avākirat.
18.20 tataḥ Suśarmā daśabhiḥ Surathaś ca Kirīṭinam
Sudharmā Sudhanuś c' âiva Subāhuś ca samārpayan.
tāṃs tu sarvān pṛthag bāṇair
vānara|pravara|dhvajaḥ
pratyavidhyad dhvajāṃś c' âiṣāṃ
bhallaiś ciccheda kāñcanān.
Sudhanvano dhanuś chittvā hayāṃś c' âsy' âvadhīc charaiḥ
ath' âsya sa|śiras|trāṇaṃ śiraḥ kāyād apāharat.

three and three again. O majesty, each Tri·garta struck Partha with five of his arrows but with twin shafts he struck back at each. In a tumult of anger they poured their missiles 18.15
unrelentingly on Árjuna and on Késhava, rain upon a pool, and hundreds of them plummeted down as when swarms of bees in a forest descend on swaths of openpetalled flowers. Subáhu sent thirty arrows of solid iron into the crown Árjuna wore, and with his head studded in those goldfeathered and trueflying shafts Kirítin stood tall like a sacrificial stake capped in ingots of river gold.

The son of Pandu fought back. With a barbed missile he cracked apart the very guard protecting Subáhu's hand and then let fly a downpour of darts upon his head. Ten arrows 18.20
flew back at the Diademed Warrior from the five bows of Sushárman, Súratha, Sudhárman, Subáhu and Súdhanus. Yet while the flag of the monkey fluttered over his head one by one with his barbed arrows Árjuna pierced and tattered each of their golden oriflammes, and then he split Súdhanus' bow in two, transfixed his horse and at last tore the warrior's still-helmeted head from his neck.

tasmiṃs tu patite vīre trastās tasya pad'|ânugāḥ
vyadravanta bhayād bhītā yena Dauryodhanaṃ balam.
tato jaghāna saṃkruddho Vāsavis tāṃ mahā|camūṃ
śara|jālair a|vicchinnais tamaḥ sūrya iv' âṃśubhiḥ.
18.25 tato bhagne bale tasmin vipralīne samantataḥ
Savyasācini saṃkruddhe Traigartān bhayam āviśat.
te vadhyamānāḥ Pārthena śaraiḥ saṃnata|parvabhiḥ
amuhyaṃs tatra tatr' âiva trastā mṛga|gaṇā iva.
tatas Trigarta|rāṭ kruddhas tān uvāca mahā|rathān.
«alaṃ drutena vaḥ, śūrā, na bhayaṃ kartum arhatha.
śaptv" âtha śapathān ghorān
sarva|sainyasya paśyataḥ
gatvā Dauryodhanaṃ sainyaṃ
kiṃ vai vakṣyatha mukhyaśaḥ.
n' âvahāsyāḥ kathaṃ loke karmaṇā tena saṃyuge
bhavema sahitāḥ sarve nivartadhvaṃ yathā|balam.»
18.30 evam uktās tu te, rājann, udakrośan muhur muhuḥ
śaṅkhāṃś ca dadhmire vīrā harṣayantaḥ paras|param.
tatas te saṃnyavartanta Saṃśaptaka|gaṇāḥ punaḥ
Nārāyaṇāś ca Gopālā mṛtyuṃ kṛtvā nivartanaṃ.

SAMJAYA uvāca.

19.1 DṚṢṬVĀ TU SAṂNIVṚTTĀṂS tān Saṃśaptaka|gaṇān punaḥ
Vāsudevaṃ mah"|ātmānam Arjunaḥ samabhāṣata.
«coday' âśvān, Hṛṣīkeśa, Saṃśaptaka|gaṇān prati
n' âite hāsyanti saṃgrāmaṃ jīvanta iti me matiḥ.
paśya me 'dya balaṃ ghoraṃ bāhvor iṣv|asanasya ca
ady' âitān pātayiṣyāmi Rudraḥ paśu|gaṇān iva.»

Terror struck his companions as Súdhanus' trunk fell to earth. They turned to fly back beneath Duryódhana's wing. But with his blood aflame the son of Indra sent arrows in unbroken lines through those mighty battalions like rays of
the sun cutting through darkness. With their force scattered 18.25
and broken, horror at the Left Handed Archer's wrath possessed the Tri·gartas. Harrowed by the wellwhittled arrows from Partha's bow they stumbled about in confusion like a herd of frightened deer. But Satya·ratha was furious and he called out to his warriors.

"Stand your ground! You are heroes. Fear does not become you. We have taken solemn oaths and every member of this army bore witness to them. What words will you find when you face Duryódhana's men? When report of our deeds in this war travels abroad, what will we become but a laughing stock? We must be strong together. We must fight as one."

At their king's words a cry went up, then another. They 18.30
blew into their shells and rallied a second time. Once more the Beholden attacked. Once more the Naráyanas and the Go·palas chose to make death their final retreat.

SÁNJAYA spoke.

SEEING THE MASS of the Beholden wheeling to face him 19.1
Árjuna addressed great Vasudéva.

"Spur on the horses, Hrishi·kesha. It seems the Beholden will not cease from this battle alive. See now the fearsome might of my arm and my bow. It is time that I immolate them as Rudra immolates his flock."

tataḥ Kṛṣṇaḥ smitaṃ kṛtvā pratinandya śivena tam
prāveśayata dur|dharṣo yatra yatr' āicchad Arjunaḥ.
19.5 babhrāje sa ratho 'tyartham uhyamāno raṇe tadā
uhyamānam iv' ākāśe vimānaṃ pāṇḍurair hayaiḥ.
maṇḍalāni tataś cakre gata|pratyāgatāni ca
yathā Śakra|ratho rājan yuddhe dev'|âsure purā.
atha Nārāyaṇāḥ kruddhā vividh'|āyudha|pāṇayaḥ
chādayantaḥ śara|vrātaiḥ parivavrur Dhanaṃjayam.
a|dṛśyaṃ ca muhūrtena cakrus te, Bharata'|rṣabha,
Kṛṣṇena sahitaṃ yuddhe Kuntī|putraṃ Dhanaṃjayam.
kruddhas tu Phalgunaḥ saṃkhye dvi|guṇī|kṛta|vikramaḥ
Gāṇḍīvaṃ dhanur ākṛṣya tūrṇaṃ jagrāha saṃkule.
19.10 baddhvā ca bhru|kuṭīṃ vaktre krodhasya pratilakṣaṇaṃ
Devadattaṃ mahā|śaṅkhaṃ pūrayām āsa Pāṇḍavaḥ.
ath' âstram ari|saṃgha|ghnaṃ Tvāṣṭram abhyasyad Arjunaḥ.
tato rūpa|sahasrāṇi prādur āsan pṛthak pṛthak.
ātmanaḥ pratirūpais tair nānā|rūpair vimohitāḥ
anyonyam Arjunaṃ matvā svam ātmānaṃ ca jaghnire.
ayam Arjuno 'yaṃ Govinda imau Yādava|Pāṇḍavau,
iti bruvāṇāḥ saṃmūḍhā jaghnur anyonyam āhave.
mohitāḥ param'|âstreṇa kṣayaṃ jagmuḥ paras|param
aśobhanta raṇe yodhāḥ puṣpitā iva kiṃśukāḥ.
19.15 tataḥ śara|sahasrāṇi tair vimuktāni bhasmasāt
kṛtvā tad astraṃ tān vīrān anayad Yama|sādanam.
atha prahasya Bībhatsur Lalitthān Mālavān api
Māvellakāṃs Trigartāṃś ca Yaudheyāṃś c' ārdayac charaiḥ.

At this, proud Krishna smiled and assented, loyal as ever to Árjuna. Borne through the fray by its white steeds their 19.5
chariot glittered like a vessel of the skies and it traced circles that vanished and reappeared, and o majesty it was like the chariot Indra rode in the celestial battle of old. With weapons bristling in their hands the cruel Naráyanas pressed in around Dhanan·jaya, covering him with a canopy of arrows, and for a moment o bull of the Bharatas the fierce son of Kuntí and Warrior of the Red Stars Dhanan·jaya disappeared beneath their attack. In the chaos Pandu's son brandished Gandíva. His brow darkened as a cloud of anger 19.10
passed across his face. He blew hard into the great conch Deva·datta, and then he unleashed the smasher of the enemy horde that is men know as the Tvashtri weapon.

Out of nowhere stepped a thousand figures, one by one, each a double of Árjuna. Bewildered by these apparations the Naráyanas mistook one another for their foe and set upon their own kind, crying out in confusion, It is Árjuna! And there is Go·vinda! Over there—Pándava and Yádava! With each cry another was slaughtered. Deranged by his spectacular attack warriors perished together in the dance of war, and as they fell they were as beautiful as lilies in flower. The Tvashtri weapon reduced to ash thousands of 19.15
arrows and sent the archers who fired them away to Yama's abode. Árjuna laughed in disgust as his shafts scattered the Lalítthas and Málavas, the Mavéllakas and the Tri·gartas and the Yaudhéyas.

te hanyamānā vīreṇa kṣatriyāḥ kāla|coditāḥ
vyasṛjañ śara|varṣāṇi Pārthe nānā|vidhāni ca.
tato n' âiv' Ârjunas tatra na ratho na ca Keśavaḥ
pratyadṛśyanta ghoreṇa śara|varṣeṇa saṃvṛtāḥ.
tatas te labdha|lakṣyatvād anyonyam abhicukruśuḥ
hatau Kṛṣṇāv iti prītā vāsāṃsy ādudhuvus tadā.
19.20 bherī|mṛdaṅga|śaṅkhāṃś ca dadhmur vīrāḥ sahasraśaḥ
siṃha|nāda|ravāṃś c' ôgrāṃś cakrire tatra, māriṣa.
tataḥ prasiṣvide Kṛṣṇaḥ khinnaś c' Ârjunam abravīt.
«kv' âsi Pārtha? na paśye tvāṃ. kaś cij jīvasi śatru|han?»
tasya tad bhāṣitaṃ śrutvā tvaramāṇo Dhanaṃjayaḥ
Vāyavy'|âstreṇa tair astāṃ śara|vṛṣṭim apāharat.
tataḥ Saṃśaptaka|vrātān s'|âśva|dvipa|rath'|āyudhān
uvāha bhagavān vāyuḥ śuṣka|parṇa|cayān iva.
uhyamānās tu te rājan bahv aśobhanta vāyunā
uḍḍīnāḥ pakṣiṇaḥ kāle vṛkṣebhya iva, māriṣa.
19.25 tāṃs tathā vyākulī|kṛtya tvaramāṇo Dhanaṃjayaḥ.
śirāṃsi bhallair aharad bāhūn api ca s'|āyudhān
hasti|hast'|ôpamāṃś c' ôrūñ śarair urvyām apātayat.
pṛṣṭha|cchinnān vicaraṇān bāhu|pṛṣṭh'|ēkṣaṇ'|ākulān
nān"|âṅg'|âvayavair hīnāṃś cakār' ârīn Dhanañjayaḥ.
gandharva|nagar'|ākārān vidhivat kalpitān rathān
śarair viśakalī|kurvaṃś cakre vy|aśva|ratha|dvipān.
muṇḍa|tāla|vanān' îva tatra tatra cakāśire
chinna|dhvaja|ratha|vrātāḥ ke cit ke cit kva cit kva cit.
s'|ôttarīyavato nāgāḥ sa|patāk'|âṅkuś'|āyudhāḥ
petuḥ Śakr'|âśani|hatā drumavanta iv' âcalāḥ.

But time drove them on. Despite his crushing blows they
brewed another rising storm of arrows and once more Árjuna, Késhava and their chariot disappeared into its squalls.
Their enemies felt the thrill of victory within reach, some
throwing off their cloaks and crying out to one another
that the Krishnas were dead,* others sounding and pound- 19.20
ing and hammering a hundred trumpets and drums. They
bellowed in triumph, my king. Krishna labored on wearily,
sweat pouring from his brow, and called out to his friend.

"O son of Pandu where are you? I cannot see you. O deathbringer are you still among the living?"

Árjuna was quickened by his cry, and invoking now the
Vayávya weapon he began to blow back the arrow rain that
was falling. The holy wind picked up swords, cars, horses,
elephants and piles of the Beholden and carried them away
like dry leaves. They glittered in the air, my king, like flights
of birds leaving the trees when the season has turned. As he 19.25
gathered speed Árjuna brought disaster down upon them.
His iron barbs took off heads and hands still clenching
swords and brought the long trunks of the tallest elephants
tumbling upon the broad earth. Mashing brokenbacked or
legless figures into arms, thighs and eyes he tore his enemies
limb from limb. He broke with his arrows each chariot
decked to look like a city of spirits and sundered man from
elephant and from steed and from car.

It was like looking upon a vast forest of palms with their
fronds cut away. Everywhere were piles of shattered chariots and ruined standards. Among flags hooks and spears 19.30
elephants lay resplendent in their armor like wooded mountains blasted by Indra's thunderbolt. Horses lay with their

19.30 cāmar'|āpīḍa|kavacāḥ srast'|ântra|nayan'|âsavaḥ
s'|ārohās tura|gāḥ petuḥ Pārtha|bāṇa|hatāḥ kṣitau.
vipraviddh'|âsi|nakharāś chinna|varma'|rṣṭi|śaktayaḥ
pattayaś chinna|varmāṇaḥ kṛpaṇāḥ śerate hatāḥ.
tair hatair hanyamānaiś ca patadbhiḥ patitair api
bhramadbhir niṣṭanadbhiś ca krūram āyodhanaṃ babhau.
rajaś ca mahad udbhūtaṃ śāntaṃ rudhira|vṛṣṭibhiḥ
mahī c' âpy abhavad durgā kabandha|śata|saṃkulā.
tad babhau raudra|bībhatsaṃ Bībhatsor yānam āhave
ākrīḍa iva Rudrasya ghnataḥ kāl'|âtyaye paśūn.
19.35 te vadhyamānāḥ Pārthena vyākul'|âśva|ratha|dvipāḥ
tam ev' âbhimukhāḥ kṣīṇāḥ Śakrasy' âtithitāṃ gatāḥ.
sā bhūmir, Bharata|śreṣṭha, nihatais tair mahā|rathaiḥ
āstīrṇā sambabhau sarvā pretī|bhūtaiḥ samantataḥ.
etasminn antare c' âiva pramatte Savyasācini
vyūḍh'|ânīkas tato Droṇo Yudhiṣṭhiram upādravat.
taṃ pratyagṛhṇaṃs tvaritā vyūḍh'|ânīkāḥ prahāriṇaḥ
Yudhiṣṭhiraṃ parīpsantas tad" āsīt tumulaṃ mahat.

SAMJAYA uvāca.

20.1 PARIṆĀMYA NIŚĀṂ tāṃ tu Bhāradvājo mahā|rathaḥ
uktvā su|bahu, rāj'|êndra, vacanāṃ vai Suyodhanaṃ
vidhāya yogaṃ Pārthena Saṃśaptaka|gaṇaiḥ saha
niṣkrānte ca tadā Pārthe Saṃśaptaka|vadhaṃ prati
vyūḍh'|ânīkas tato Droṇaḥ Pāṇḍavānāṃ mahā|camūm
abhyayād Bharata|śreṣṭha Dharma|rāja|jighṛkṣayā.

riders still clad in breastplates, chaplets and chowries, dashed to earth under Partha's shafts, their entrails unwound, their eyes out, their breath departed. Men's daggers were bent, their swords, lances and mail all snapped and crushed. Foot-soldiers lay dead in broken armor. A pitiful sight. Dead and dying and falling and fallen they stumbled and moaned. How dark a place that plain was. Clouds of dust rose and fell with the bloody rain and the earth was so thick with the trunks of men that there was nowhere left to stand. Picking one's way across that horror was a feat too gruesome even for men who dwelt in gore. It was like the pleasure grove of
Rudra, killer of the flock at the hour of time's passing. Any 19.35
whom Partha reached were no more. Their chariots, horses and elephants were lost, and they themselves waned away, bound for Indra's halls. All across that land, o best of the Bharatas, across every foot of it, were strewn dead heroes emptied of their souls. But even as the Left Handed Archer's madness was at its height, Drona drove his legions at Yu-dhi·shthira, and gathered as one their attack was swift, for they were desperate to have the king in their grasp. Another great battle began.

SÁNJAYA spoke.

O KING OF KINGS. Now that Árjuna had set forth to 20.1
destroy the Beholden, the strategy that Drona had hatched with them and Suyódhana during their long discussion the previous night was underway. At the head of his array the son of Bharad·vaja rode for the great Pándava host. His aim o best of the Bharatas was the capture of the righteous king.

vyūhaṃ dṛṣṭvā Suparṇaṃ tu Bhāradvāja|kṛtaṃ tadā
vyūhena maṇḍal'|ârdhena pratyavyūhad Yudhiṣṭhiraḥ.
20.5 mukham tv āsīt su|parṇasya Bhāradvājo mahā|rathaḥ
śiro Duryodhano rājā sodaryaiḥ s'|ânugair vṛtaḥ
cakṣuṣī Kṛtavarmā ca Gautamaś c' âsya bhās|karaḥ
Bhūtaśarmā Kṣemaśarmā Karakarṣaś ca vīryavān
Kaliṅgāḥ Siṃhalāḥ prācyāḥ śūr'|Ābhīrā Daśerakāḥ
Śakā Yavana|Kāmbojās tathā haṃsa|pathāś ca ye
grīvāyāṃ Śūrasenāś ca Daradā Madra|Kekayāḥ
gaj'|âśva|ratha|patty|oghās tasthuḥ parama|daṃśitāḥ.
Bhūriśravās tathā Śalyaḥ Somadattaś ca Bāhlikaḥ
akṣauhiṇyā vṛtā vīrā dakṣiṇaṃ pakṣam āsthitāḥ.
20.10 Vind'|Ânuvindāv Āvantyau Kāmbojaś ca Sudakṣiṇaḥ
vāmaṃ pārśvaṃ samāśritya Droṇa|putr'|âgratāḥ sthitāḥ.
pṛṣṭhe Kaliṅgāḥ s'|Âmbaṣṭhā Māgadhāḥ Pauṇḍra|Madrakāḥ
Gāndhārāḥ Śakunāḥ prācyāḥ pārvatīyā Vasātayaḥ.
pucche Vaikartanaḥ Karṇaḥ sa|putra|jñāti|bāndhavaḥ
mahatyā senayā tasthau nānā|jana|pad'|ôtthayā.
Jayadratho Bhīmarathaḥ sāṃyātrika|sabho jayaḥ
Bhūmiṃjayo Vṛṣaḥ Krātho Naiṣadhaś ca mahā|balaḥ

Yudhi·shthira had drawn his own troops up in a halfcircle
when he had seen Drona's choice of the Gáruda configura-
tion. Bharad·vaja's mighty son formed the bird's beak and 20.5
in its head rode King Duryódhana with his kith and kin.
Krita·varman and Gáutama the sun were its eyes and along
its neck marched row upon row of soldiers, cars, horses and
elephants, all clad in the finest mail, from Bhuta·sharman
and Kshema·sharman and valiant Kara·karsha through the
Kalíngas and Sínhalas and the people of the East, the brave
Abhíras, the Dashérakas and Shakas, the Yávanas and Kambójas and the people from the lands of the swan, and
then the Shura·senas, Dáradas, Madras and the Kékayas.
Spanning the one wing with their legions were the heroes
Bhuri·shravas, Shalya, Soma·datta and Báhlika, and span- 20.10
ning the other with Drona's son at their head were Vinda
and Anuvínda of Avánti and the Kambója king Sudákshina. The bird's back was made of the Kalíngas and the Ambáshthas, the Mágadhas and Paundras and Mádrakas, the
Gandháras and Shákunas and the peoples of the mountains
in the East and those who dwell beyond them. In its tail
were Karna born of the sun with his folk and friends, all
men of grand and venerable stock from many and distant
lands. And in the bird's belly my king stood lords of war
clad for paradise and ringed in mighty troops. They were
Jayad·ratha and Bhima·ratha whose halls rise towards the
dawn, and Bhumin·jaya and Vrisha and Kratha the great
Níshadha chieftain.

vṛtā balena mahatā brahma|loka|pariṣkṛtāḥ
vyūhasy' ôrasi te rājan sthitā yuddha|viśāradāḥ.
20.15 Droṇena vihito vyūhaḥ padāty|aśva|ratha|dvipaiḥ
vāt'|ôddhūt'|ârṇav'|ākāraḥ pravṛtta iva lakṣyate.
tasya pakṣa|prapakṣebhyo niṣpatanti yuyutsavaḥ
sa|vidyut|stanitā meghāḥ sarva|digbhya iv' ôṣṇa|ge.
tasya Prāgjyotiṣo madhye vidhivat kalpitaṃ gajam
āsthitaḥ śuśubhe rājann aṃśumān udaye yathā.
mālya|dāmavatā rājan śveta|cchatreṇa dhāryatā
Kṛttikā|yoga|yuktena paurṇamāsyām iv' êndunā
nīl'|âñjana|caya|prakhyo mad'|ândho dvi|rado babhau
ativṛṣṭo mahā|meghair yathā syāt parvato mahān.
20.20 nānā|nṛ|patibhir vīrair vividh'|āyudha|bhūṣaṇaiḥ
samanvitaḥ pārvatīyaiḥ Śakro deva|gaṇair iva
tato Yudhiṣṭhiraḥ prekṣya vyūhaṃ tam atimānuṣam
a|jayyam aribhiḥ saṃkhye Pārṣataṃ vākyam abravīt.
«brāhmaṇasya vaśaṃ n' âham iyām adya yathā prabho
pārāvata|sa|varṇ'|âśva tathā nītir vidhīyatām.»

DHṚṢṬADYUMNA uvāca.

Droṇasya yatamānasya vaśaṃ n' âiṣyasi, su|vrata,
aham āvārayiṣyāmi Droṇam adya sah'|ânugam.
mayi jīvati Kauravya n' ôdvegaṃ kartum arhasi
na hi śakto raṇe Droṇo vijetuṃ māṃ kathaṃ cana.

SAṂJAYA uvāca.

20.25 evam uktvā kiran bāṇān Drupadasya suto balī
pārāvata|sa|varṇ'|âśvaḥ svayaṃ Droṇam upādravat.
an|iṣṭa|darśanaṃ dṛṣṭvā Dhṛṣṭadyumnam avasthitam

Drona's rows of men and horses and cars and beasts unfurled like the face of the ocean ruffled by the wind. From shoulder to tip the array of eager warriors rolled on like clouds in hot weather gathering with lightning and thunder across the sky. And o king as if touched by the dawn of a rising sun Prag·jyótisha sat resplendent at their very center atop his perfectly laden steed. The vast elephant was the color of black antimony and it streamed from its temples like a mountain drenched by a great rain.* It was lit up by its rider, who with his garlands and snowy parasol hung above the creature like the moon cradled in the Pleiades. 20.15

Meanwhile like Shakra before the Himalayan gods Yudhi· 20.20
shthira stood before the great flashing swords and jewels that picked out his own broad army of mighty kings. He gazed upon the unearthly and invincible horde that approached him, and then he turned to Príshata's grandson and spoke.

"O rider of the turtledovecolored horses. Whatever course you choose my liege make sure that the priest does not have me in chains by the day's end."

DHRISHTA·DYUMNA spoke.

Drona may try but he will not have his way, good king. I will drive Drona back and all his kind with him. As long as I live, o son of Kuru, you have nothing to fear. Drona cannot better me in battle.

SÁNJAYA spoke.

At this promise Drúpada's mighty son drove his turtle- 20.25
dovecolored steeds at Drona, scattering arrows as he went. The unwelcome sight of Dhrishta·dyumna swam before the priest's eyes and for just a moment a flicker of dismay fell

kṣaṇen' âiv' âbhavad Droṇo n' âti|hṛṣṭamanā iva.
taṃ tu samprekṣya putras te Durmukhaḥ śatru|karśanaḥ
priyaṃ cikīrṣur Droṇasya Dhṛṣṭadyumnam avārayat.
sa samprahāras tumulaḥ su|ghoraḥ samapadyata
Pārṣatasya ca śūrasya Durmukhasya ca Bhārata.
Pārṣataḥ śara|jālena kṣipraṃ pracchādya Durmukham
Bhāradvājaṃ śar'|âugheṇa mahatā samavārayat.
20.30 Droṇam āvāritaṃ dṛṣṭvā bhṛś'|āyastas tav' ātma|jaḥ
nānā|liṅgaiḥ śara|vrātaiḥ Pārṣataṃ samamohayat.
tayor viṣaktayoḥ saṃkhye
Pāñcālya|Kuru|mukhyayoḥ
Droṇo Yaudhiṣṭhiraṃ sainyaṃ
bahudhā vyadhamac charaiḥ
anilena yath" âbhrāṇi vicchinnāni samantataḥ
tathā Pārthasya sainyāni vicchinnāni kva cit kva cit.
muhūrtam iva tad yuddham āsīn madhura|darśanam
tata unmattavad rājan nir|maryādam avartata.
n' âiva sve na pare rājann ajñāyanta paras|paraṃ
anumānena saṃjñābhir yuddhaṃ tat samavartata.
20.35 cūḍāmaṇiṣu niṣkeṣu bhūṣaṇeṣv api varmasu
teṣām āditya|varṇ'|ābhā raśmayaḥ pracakāśire.
tat prakīrṇa|patākānāṃ ratha|vāraṇa|vājinām
balākā|śabal'|âbhr'|ābhaṃ dadṛśe rūpam āhave.
narān eva narā jaghnur udagrāś ca hayā hayān
rathāṃś ca rathino jaghnur vāraṇā vara|vāraṇān.
samucchrita|patākānāṃ gajānāṃ parama|dvipaiḥ
kṣaṇena tumulo ghoraḥ saṃgrāmaḥ samapadyata.
teṣāṃ saṃsakta|gātrāṇāṃ karṣatām itar'|êtaram
danta|saṃghāta|saṃgharṣāt sa|dhūmo 'gnir ajāyata.
20.40 viprakīrṇa|patākās te viṣāṇa|janit'|âgnayaḥ

across them. Your son Dúrmukha bane of foes also saw Dhrishta·dyumna's sally and he rode out to meet him in defense of his commander. O Bhárata a loud and bloody struggle began between Dúrmukha and the grandson of
Príshata. In moments Dhrishta·dyumna had cast a net of 20.30
arrows across him and a great mass of shafts upon Bharad·vaja's son. Laboring beneath his attack your Dúrmukha looked across at Drona and saw him vanishing in arrows and sent at Dhrishta·dyumna a dizzying volley of his own myriad darts. The Kuru and Panchála warriors fought close while Drona pulled away and reaved Yudhi·shthira's host, and as he opened fissures everywhere in Partha's ranks like banks of cloud split by a gale for a moment my king the battle took on a wild beauty of its own, before madness and chaos engulfed it once again.

Neither friend nor foe could be told apart o majesty and 20.35
we could but cry out and guess at who stood before us. Light brighter than rays of the sun flashed from head jewels and medallions and armor and chains. Pennants fluttered among beasts and cars and horses like cranes scattered across a dark sky. Men slew men and horses kicked high and killed horses and cars crushed cars and elephants slew elephants. Bearing their tattered flags the huge beasts filled the fray
with blood and noise as they tangled legs and dragged one 20.40
another behind them and struck tusks that sparked with fire and smoke. Between torn banners and the sparks thrown from their jaws they loomed like crackling thunderheads, and like a dark autumn sky the earth was thick with them roaring and rolling and streaming in musth.

babhūvuḥ khaṃ samāsādya sa|vidyuta iv' âmbu|dāḥ.
vikṣaradbhir nadadbhiś ca nipatadbhiś ca vāraṇaiḥ
sambabhūva mahī kīrṇā meghair dyaur iva śāradī.
teṣām āhanyamānānāṃ bāṇa|tomara|vṛṣṭibhiḥ
vāraṇānāṃ ravo jajñe meghānām iva samplave.
tomar'|âbhihatāḥ ke cid bāṇaiś ca parama|dvipāḥ
vitresuḥ sarva|nāgānāṃ śabdam ev' âpare 'vrajan.
viṣāṇ'|âbhihatāś c' âpi ke cit tatra gajā gajaiḥ
cakrur ārta|svaraṃ ghoram utpāta|jala|dā iva.
20.45 pratīpāḥ kriyamāṇāś ca vāraṇā vara|vāraṇaiḥ
unmathya punar ājagmuḥ preritāḥ param'|âṅkuśaiḥ.
mahā|mātrair mahā|mātrās tāḍitāḥ śara|tomaraiḥ
gajebhyaḥ pṛthivīṃ jagmur mukta|praharaṇ'|âṅkuśāḥ.
nir|manuṣyāś ca mātaṅgā vinadantas tatas tataḥ
chinn'|âbhrāṇ' îva sampetuḥ sampraviśya paras|param.
hatān parivahantaś ca patitān patit'|āyudhān
diśo jagmur mahā|nāgāḥ ke cid eka|carā iva.
tāḍitās tāḍyamānāś ca tomara'|ṛṣṭi|paraśvadhaiḥ
petur ārta|svaraṃ kṛtvā tadā viśasane gajāḥ.
20.50 teṣāṃ śail'|ôpamaiḥ kāyair nipatadbhiḥ samantataḥ
āhatā sahasā bhūmiś cakampe ca nanāda ca.
sāditaiḥ sa|gaj'|ārohaiḥ sa|patākaiḥ samantataḥ
mātaṅgaiḥ śuśubhe bhūmir vikīrṇair iva parvataiḥ.
gaja|sthāś ca mahā|mātrā nirbhinna|hṛdayā raṇe
rathibhiḥ pātitā bhallair vikīrṇ'|âṅkuśa|tomarāḥ.
krauñcavad vinadanto 'nye nārāc'|âbhihatā gajāḥ
parān svāṃś c' âpi mṛdnantaḥ paripetur diśo daśa.
gaj'|âśva|ratha|yodhānāṃ śarīr'|âugha|samāvṛtā
babhūva pṛthivī, rājan, māṃsa|śoṇita|kardamā.
20.55 pramathya ca viṣāṇ'|âgraiḥ samutkṣiptāś ca vāraṇaiḥ

The cries of those magnificent beasts as spear and javelin
and shaft went into them were like the roars of clouds in a
storm. I saw elephants tremble as they were pierced through
by lances and arrows, others running in pursuit of the death
wails of their kind. I saw hides torn open by tusks. The 20.45
sounds of pain were as chilling as omens in the heavens.
Galloping together they crashed against one another and
then carried on beneath the sharp bite of the goad as riders
struck riders with spear and arrow and toppled to earth with
their steeds, weapons and hooks flying from their lifeless
hands. Riderless elephants blared and galloped among one
another like shredded clouds and the great things dragged
the dead and fallen and fallen swords with them as they
coursed together across the plain and fell in howls of pain
from wounds old or fresh from clubs and spears and lances.

The slaughter was immense. The earth shook and re- 20.50
sounded beneath an endless avalanche of bodies, and like a
jagged mountain range elephants and riders and flags were
heaped up upon it. Elephantriders were struck in the heart
by archers' arrows and dropping their hooks or pikes fell
from their seats, the elephants beneath them transfixed by
irons and screeching like birds and trampling their own
and their foes as they galloped away any way they could. O 20.55
majesty. The earth was a mire of blood and gore full of the
corpses of soldiers and bowmen and elephants and horses
mangled by foot or tusk, a mire across which the survivors
ground their wheels or if their wheels were gone merely
dragged the shells of their cars. Everywhere there were chariots without drivers, horses without horsemen, panicked

sa|cakrāś ca vi|cakrāś ca rathair eva mahā|rathāḥ.
rathāś ca rathibhir hīnā nir|manuṣyāś ca vājinaḥ
hat'|ārohāś ca mātaṅgā diśo jagmur bhay'|āturāḥ.
jaghān' âtra pitā putraṃ putraś ca pitaraṃ tathā
ity āsīt tumulaṃ yuddhaṃ na prajñāyata kiṃ cana.
ā gulphebhyo 'vasīdante narā lohita|kardamaiḥ
dīpyamānaiḥ parikṣiptā dāvair iva mahā|drumāḥ.
śoṇitaiḥ sicyamānāni vastrāṇi kavacāni ca
chatrāṇi ca patākāś ca sarvaṃ raktam adṛśyata.
20.60 hay'|âughāś ca rath'|âughāś ca nar'|âughāś ca nipātitāḥ
saṃkṣuṇṇāḥ punar āvṛtya bahudhā ratha|nemibhiḥ.
sa gaj'|âugha|mahā|vegaḥ par'|âsu|nara|śaivalaḥ
rath'|âugha|tumul'|āvartaḥ prababhau sainya|sāgaraḥ.
taṃ vāhana|mahā|naubhir yodhā jaya|dhan'|âiṣiṇaḥ
avagāhy' âpy a|majjanto vaira|mohaṃ pracakrire.
śara|varṣ'|âbhivṛṣṭeṣu yodheṣv añcita|lakṣmasu
na hi sva|cittatāṃ lebhe kaś cid āhata|lakṣaṇaḥ.
vartamāne tathā yuddhe ghora|rūpe bhayaṃ|kare
mohayitvā parān Droṇo Yudhiṣṭhiram upādravat.

SAMJAYA uvāca.

21.1 TATO YUDHIṢṬHIRO Droṇaṃ dṛṣṭv" ântikam upāgatam
mahatā śara|varṣeṇa pratyagṛhṇād a|bhītavat.
tato halahalā|śabda āsīd Yaudhiṣṭhire bale
jighṛkṣati mahā|siṃhe gajānām iva yūtha|pam.
dṛṣṭvā Droṇaṃ tataḥ śūraḥ Satyajit satya|vikramaḥ
Yudhiṣṭhiraṃ pariprepsur ācāryaṃ samupādravat.
tata ācārya|Pāñcālyau yuyudhāte mahā|balau
vikṣobhayantau tat sainyam Indra|Vairocanāv iva.

elephants with their riders hanging dead in their stirrups. Son felled father and father felled son as the roar of battle drowned out all else. Men black as burnt trees with mud and gore sank ankledeep in the swamp, their armor and silk 20.60
beblooded and their parasols and flags all the same scarlet. Piles of horses and piles of chariots and the fallen dead were turned over and torn again by the endless rolling of wheels. The battlefield became an ocean that bore in its great tides clumps of beasts and unbreathing men like weeds. Knots of chariots swirled in its currents. Warriors took to its waters in vessels that drew deep and somehow stayed afloat, but instead of the wealth and fame they had sought they found only the madness of war. Noble faces were no more, cut to pieces under the hail of arrows. No one could even recognise himself any more.

It was Drona who had caused this pandemonium among his foes. And as the appalling welter of violence went on, he made his way towards Yudhi·shthira.

SÁNJAYA spoke.

YUDHI·SHTHIRA SAW Drona approach. He was not afraid 21.1
and sent at him a torrent of arrows, but a ululation rose above his army like the sound made by an elephant herd when a lion eyes its bull.* Mighty Sátyajit set his eyes upon Drona and keen to save his king rode out bravely for his teacher. Two warriors great as Indra and Viróchana's son, the Panchála met his master in a contest that we watched with awe.

21.5 tato Droṇaṃ mah"|êṣv|āsaḥ Satyajit satya|vikramaḥ
avidhyan niśit'|âgreṇa param'|âstraṃ vidarśayan.
tath" âsya sāratheḥ pañca śarān sarpa|viṣ'|ôpamān
amucyad antaka|prakhyān sammumoh' âsya sārathiḥ.
ath' âsya sahas" âvidhyadd hayān daśabhir āśu|gaiḥ
daśabhir daśabhiḥ kruddha ubhau ca pārṣṇi|sārathī.
maṇdalaṃ tu samāvṛtya vicaran pṛtanā|mukhe
dhvajaṃ ciccheda ca kruddho Droṇasy' â|mitra|karṣaṇaḥ.
Droṇas tu tat samālokya caritaṃ tasya saṃyuge
manasā cintayām āsa prāpta|kālam ariṃ|damaḥ.
21.10 tataḥ Satyajitaṃ tīkṣṇair daśabhir marma|bhedibhiḥ
avidhyac chīghram ācāryaś chittv" âsya sa|śaraṃ dhanuḥ.
sa śīghrataram ādāya dhanur anyat pratāpavān
Droṇam abhyahanad, rājaṃs, triṃśadbhiḥ kaṅka|patribhiḥ.
jñātvā Satyajitā Droṇaṃ grasyamānam iv' āhave
Vṛkaḥ śara|śatais tīkṣṇaiḥ Pāñcālyo Droṇam ardayat.
saṃchādyamānaṃ samare Droṇaṃ dṛṣṭvā mahā|ratham
cukruśuḥ Pāṇḍavā rājan vastrāṇi dudhuvuś ca ha.
Vṛkas tu parama|kruddho Droṇaṃ ṣaṣṭyā stan'|ântare
vivyādha balavān rājaṃs tad adbhutam iv' âbhavat.
21.15 Droṇas tu śara|varṣeṇa chādyamāno mahā|rathaḥ
vegaṃ cakre mahā|vegaḥ krodhād udvṛtya cakṣuṣī.
tataḥ Satyajitaś cāpaṃ chittvā Droṇo Vṛkasya ca
ṣaḍbhiḥ sa|sūtaṃ sa|hayaṃ śarair Droṇo 'vadhīd Vṛkam.
ath' ânyad dhanur ādāya Satyajid vegavattaram
s'|âśvaṃ sa|sūtaṃ viśikhair Droṇaṃ vivyādha sa|dhvajam
sa tan na mamṛṣe Droṇaḥ Pāñcālyen' ârdito mṛdhe

Bold beyond bounds the great bowman Sátyajit found his 21.5
target first, with an arrow whetted to a point and loosed with
wondrous skill. He followed it with five deadly shafts like
snakes' tongues and they found Drona's driver and knocked
his senses from him. Without pause with ten swift shafts he
pierced Drona's horses and with ten and ten again he vented
his fury on Drona's flankriders,* before wheeling furiously
in a broad arc through the fray Sátyajit punisher of foes cut
straight through the pole upon which Drona's oriflamme
flew. Drona watched his handiwork and deciding that the
moment had come to tame his adversary the Teacher split 21.10
the bow and arrows he held in his hands and with ten
sharp shafts biting to the marrow pierced Sátyajit himself.
But fiery Sátyajit lightly raised another bow my king and
sent at Drona thirty vulturefeathered shafts. And Vrika saw
Drona in Sátyajit's jaws and with his own sharp arrows in
myriad the Panchála added to Drona's pain. As the priest
disappeared beneath their joint attack the Pándavas watched
and whooped and pulled off their armor. Majesty it was
difficult to believe one's eyes as Vrika now in an ecstasy of
violent rage sent sixty arrows thudding into Drona's chest.

Shadowed beneath an arrow storm Drona rolled his eyes 21.15
in fury and with all his power unleashed his attack. He
broke Sátyajit's bow in two and then did the same to Vrika's
and then sent six shafts straight at him and his driver and
his horses. With a wild gesture Sátyajit swept up another
bow and struck back at Drona and his arrows found the
brahmin's horses and horseman and the pole of his flag. As
Drona felt the force of the Panchála prince, his patience with
the battle was gone and he loosed a great volley to finish off

tatas tasya vināśāya sa|tvaraṃ vyasṛjac charān.
hayān dhvajaṃ dhanur muṣṭim ubhau ca pārṣṇi|sārathī
avākirat tato Droṇaḥ śara|varṣaiḥ sahasraśaḥ.
21.20 tathā saṃchidyamāneṣu kārmukeṣu punaḥ punaḥ
Pāñcālyaḥ param'|âstra|jñaḥ śoṇ'|âśvaṃ samayodhayat.
sa Satyajitam ālokya tath" ôdīrṇaṃ mah"|āhave
ardha|candreṇa ciccheda śiras tasya mah"|ātmanaḥ.

tasmin hate mahā|mātre Pāñcālānāṃ mahā|rathe
apāyāj javanair aśvair Droṇāt trasto Yudhiṣṭhiraḥ.
Pāñcālāḥ Kekayā Matsyāś Cedi|Kārūṣa|Kosalāḥ
Yudhiṣṭhiram abhīpsanto dṛṣṭvā Droṇam upādravan.
tato Yudhiṣṭhiraṃ prepsur ācāryaḥ śatru|pūga|hā
vyadhamat tāny anīkāni tūla|rāśim iv' ânilaḥ.
21.25 nirdahantam anīkāni tāni tāni punaḥ punaḥ
Droṇaṃ Matsyād avara|jaḥ Śatānīko 'bhyavartata.
sūrya|raśmi|pratīkāśaiḥ
karmāra|parimārjitaiḥ
ṣaḍbhiḥ sa|sūtaṃ sa|hayaṃ
Droṇaṃ viddhv" ânadad bhṛśam.
krūrāya karmaṇe yuktaś cikīrśuḥ karma duṣ|karam
avākirac chara|vrātair Bhāradvājaṃ mahā|rathaṃ.
tasya nānadato Droṇaḥ śiraḥ kāyāt sa|kuṇḍalam
kṣureṇ' âpāharat tūrṇaṃ tato Matsyāḥ pradudruvuḥ.
Matsyāñ jitv" âjayac Cedīn Kārūṣān Kekayān api
Pāñcālān Sṛñjayān Pāṇḍūn Bhāradvājaḥ punaḥ punaḥ.

his foe. A huge shower of arrows fell onto Sátyajit's steeds and standard, bow, quiver and both his flankriders but as 21.20
bow upon bow broke in his grasp such was the Panchála's skill that again and again he fought back at the red horses of Drona. Yet at last his hubris did prove his undoing. With an arrowtip curved like a halfmoon Drona finally severed the great man's head.

Terror took Yudhi·shthira when he saw Drona slay one of the best warriors and greatest leaders that the Panchálas could boast, and he drove his swift steeds into retreat as the Panchálas and Kékayas and Matsyas, the Chedis, Karúshas and Kósalas all saw what was happening and rode in to protect him. Making for Yudhi·shthira the Teacher rode on through his foes and flattened the lines arrayed before him like wind through a meadow's grass. As he plowed through 21.25
line upon line it was Shataníka, the younger brother of Matsya, who set out to stop him. With six arrows still warm from the blacksmith's forge and bright as rays of the sun he found Drona and his horses and his driver. Eager to try his hand at the highest prize he clove to the deed and seeking Drona's blood sent a shower of arrows down upon the head of Bharad·vaja's son. But with a single sharp and deadly blow Drona struck from his body the man's head still framed by rings and still roaring. Next came the Matsyas and the Matsyas fell and then came the Chedis and the Chedis fell and the Karúshas and the Kékayas, the Panchálas, Srínjayas and the Pandus. On Drona went, burning through the thickets of men like a fire raging through a forest.

21.30 tam̩ dahantam anīkāni kruddham agnim̩ yathā vanam
dr̥ṣṭvā Rukmaratham̩ vīram̩ samakampanta Sr̥ñjayāḥ.
uttamam̩ hy ādadānasya dhanur asy' āśu|kāriṇaḥ
jyā|ghoṣo nighnato '|mitrān dikṣu sarvāsu śuśruve.
nāgān aśvān padātīm̩ś ca rathino gaja|sādinaḥ
raudrā hastavatā muktāḥ pramathnanti sma sāyakāḥ.
nānadyamānaḥ parjanyo miśra|vāto him'|âtyaye
aśma|varṣam iv' āvarṣat pareṣām̩ bhayam ādadhat.
sarvā diśaḥ samacalat sainyam̩ vikṣobhayann iva
balī śūro mah"|êṣv|āso mitrāṇām a|bhayam̩|karaḥ.
21.35 tasya vidyud iv' âbhreṣu cāpam̩ hema|pariṣkr̥tam
dikṣu sarvāsu paśyāmo Droṇasy' â|mita|tejasaḥ.
śobhamānām̩ dhvaje c' âsya vedīm adrākṣma Bhārata
himavac|chikhar'|ākārām̩ carataḥ sam̩yuge bhr̥śam.
Droṇas tu Pāṇḍav'|ânīke cakāra kadanam̩ mahat
yathā Daitya|gaṇe Viṣṇuḥ sur'|âsura|namas|kr̥taḥ.
sa śūraḥ satya|vāk prājño balavān satya|vikramaḥ
mah'|ânubhāvaḥ kalp'|ânte raudrām̩ bhīru|vibhīṣaṇām
kavac'|ōrmi|dhvaj'|āvartām̩ martya|kūl'|âpahāriṇīm
gaja|vāji|mahā|grāhām asi|mīnām̩ dur|āsadām
21.40 vīr'|âsthi|śarkarām̩ raudrām̩ bherī|muraja|kacchapām
carma|varma|plavām̩ ghorām̩ keśa|śaivala|śāḍvalām
śar'|âughiṇīm̩ dhanuḥ|srotām̩ bāhu|pallava|sam̩kulām
raṇa|bhūmi|vahām̩ tīvrām̩ Kuru|Sr̥ñjaya|vāhinīm
manuṣya|śīrṣa|pāṣāṇām̩ śakti|mīnām̩ gad"|ôḍupām
uṣṇīṣa|phena|vasanām̩ vikīrṇ'|ântra|sarīsr̥pām̩

The surviving Sríñjayas saw what the mighty Warrior 21.30
of the Golden Chariot was doing, and they were afraid. All about us was the sigh of the string of the fine bow he brandished as his light fingers sent death among his foes. His hands worked quickly and out flew his cruel arrows through elephants and their riders, through horses, horsemen, men. Drona rushed on like a cloud wrapped in wind and roaring at the cold season's end, and fear fell upon us like hailstones. Churning through the men before him the great and merciful and mighty bowman wheeled across the
plain. We looked to the horizon and there we saw Drona's 21.35
goldfiligreed bow like lightning between clouds, and as he flew enveloped in splendor on through the fray we saw the fire altar blazing atop his standard, like snow gleaming on a mountain peak.

The destruction Drona wrought upon the Pándavas was like the ruin that Vishnu reverend to god and demon once brought upon the children of Diti. True in courage and true in word and mighty in his wisdom, he was a warrior of the highest eminence and now as the end of things approached Drona poured forth a river of death. Only the brave could look upon it. In its waves were pieces of armor and in its currents flagpoles bumped against the bodies of men. Not fish but swords swam in its fordless waters, and elephants
and horses were where sharks might have been. In its ghastly 21.40
flow were pebbles of human bone, drums and tambourines like tortoises, and breastplates and greaves were its boats and its evil verdure skeins of hair like weeds. Thick with arrows, sluggish with bows and budding limbs, its hot waves bore Kurus and Sríñjayas across the bed of the battlefield

vīr'|âpahāriṇīm ugrāṃ māṃsa|śoṇita|kardamām
hasti|grāhāṃ ketu|vṛkṣāṃ kṣatriyāṇāṃ nimajjanīm
krūrāṃ śarīra|saṃghaṭṭāṃ sādi|nakrāṃ dur|atyayāṃ
Droṇaḥ prāvartayat tatra nadīm antaka|gāminīm
21.45 kravy'|âda|gaṇa|saṃjuṣṭāṃ śva|śṛgāla|gaṇ'|âyutām
niṣevitāṃ mahā|raudraiḥ piśit'|âśaiḥ samantataḥ.

tam dahantam anīkāni rath'|ôdāraṃ kṛt'|ântavat
sarvato 'bhyadravan Droṇaṃ Kuntī|putra|puro|gamāḥ.
te Droṇaṃ sahitāḥ śūrāḥ sarvataḥ pratyavārayan
gabhastibhir iv' ādityaṃ tapantaṃ bhuvanaṃ yathā.
taṃ tu śūraṃ mah"|êṣv|āsaṃ tāvak" âbhyudyat'|āyudhāḥ
rājāno rāja|putrāś ca samantāt paryavārayan.

Śikhaṇḍī tu tato Droṇaṃ pañcabhir nata|parvabhiḥ
Kṣatradharmā ca viṃśatyā Vasudānaś ca pañcabhiḥ
21.50 Uttamaujās tribhir bāṇaiḥ Kṣatradevaś ca saptabhiḥ
Sātyakiś ca śaten' ājau Yudhāmanyus tath" âṣṭabhiḥ
Yudhiṣṭhiro dvā|daśabhir Droṇaṃ vivyādha sāyakaiḥ
Dhṛṣṭadyumnaś ca daśabhiś Cekitānas tribiḥ śaraiḥ.
tato Droṇaḥ satya|saṃdhaḥ prabhinna iva kuñjaraḥ
abhyatītya rath'|ânīkaṃ dṛḍha|senam apātayat.
tato rājānam āsādya praharantam a|bhītavat
avidhyan navabhiḥ Kṣemaṃ sa hataḥ prāpatad rathāt.
sa madhyaṃ prāpya sainyānāṃ sarvāḥ pravicaran diśaḥ

between banks lined with human skulls, while on its surface clubs bobbed like rafts and in its depths spears were its fish. It foamed with the ribbons of turbans and unraveled entrails were its watersnakes and blood and gore formed its gruesome clay. Away went the bodies of dead heroes and beneath the floating staves like felled trees went elephants like gharials and other warriors and riders whose corpses the river's bloody waters had swallowed like so many creepers
and crocodiles, while along its distant shores loped eaters of 21.45
carrion and packs of dogs and jackals and throngs of things awful and strange that hungered for human meat.

Drona tore his deadly course through their army as the great sons of Kuntí tried to stop him. Your own kings and princes all raised their bows and kept close to our valiant and mighty champion as the Pándavas pressed together to meet him. It was like trying to compass the sun that scorches the earth beneath its rays.

They struck Drona in turn, Shikhándin with five true-worked arrows and Kshatra·dharman with twenty and Va-
su·dana with five, then Uttamáujas with three of his own 21.50
and Kshatra·deva with seven. Sátyaki sent a whole volley down upon him and Yudha·manyu found Drona with seven arrows, while twelve missiles from Yudhi·shthira's bow struck home, and Dhrishta·dyumna loosed ten and Chekitána three. But Drona rode on and broke through and fell wild as an elephant upon the densely packed chariot line before him. King Kshema rode forth but Drona pinned him with nine of his arrows and he collapsed dead from his car. Wheeling across the plain Drona was now right at the enemy's center, riding through them as our savior, and he

trātā hy abhavad anyeṣāṃ na trātavyaḥ kathaṃ cana.
21.55 Śikhaṇḍinaṃ dvā|daśabhir viṃśatyā c' Ôttamaujasam
Vasudānaṃ ca bhallena praiṣayad Yama|sādanam.
aśītyā Kṣatradharmāṇaṃ ṣaḍ|viṃśatyā Sudakṣiṇam
Kṣatradevaṃ tu bhallena ratha|nīḍād apātayat.
Yudhāmanyuṃ catuḥ|ṣaṣṭyā triṃśatā c' âiva Sātyakim
viddhvā Rukmarathas tūrṇaṃ Yudhiṣṭhiram upādravat.
tato Yudhiṣṭhiraḥ kṣipraṃ Kitavo rāja|sattamaḥ
apāyāj javanair aśvaiḥ Pāñcālyo Droṇam abhyayāt
taṃ Droṇaḥ sa|dhanuṣkaṃ tu s'|âśva|yantāram akṣiṇot
sa hataḥ prāpatad bhūmau rathāj jyotir iv' âmbarāt.
21.60 tasmin hate rāja|putre Pāñcālānāṃ yaśas|kare
hata Droṇaṃ hata Droṇam ity āsīn niḥsvano mahān.
tāṃs tathā bhṛśa|saṃrabdhān Pāñcālān Matsya|Kekayān
Sṛñjayān Pāṇḍavāṃś c' âiva Droṇo vyakṣobhayad balī.
Sātyakiṃ Cekitānaṃ ca Dhṛṣṭadyumna|Śikhaṇḍinau
Vārddhakṣemiṃ Caitraseniṃ Senābinduṃ Suvarcasam
etāṃś c' ânyāṃś ca su|bahūn nānā|jana|pad'|ēśvarān
sarvān Droṇo 'jayad yuddhe Kurubhiḥ parivāritaḥ.
tāvakās ca, mahā|rāja, jayaṃ labdhvā mah"|āhave
Pāṇḍaveyān raṇe jaghnur dravamāṇān samantataḥ.
21.65 te dānavā iv' Êndreṇa vadhyamānā mah"|ātmanā
Pāñcālāḥ Kekayā Matsyāḥ samakampanta, Bhārata.

DHṚTARĀṢṬRA uvāca.

22.1 BHĀRADVĀJENA bhagneṣu Pāṇḍaveṣu mahā|mṛdhe
Pāñcāleṣu ca sarveṣu kaś cid anyo 'bhyavartata.
āryāṃ yuddhe matiṃ kṛtvā kṣatriyāṇāṃ yaśas|karīm
a|sevitāṃ kāpuruṣaiḥ sevitāṃ puruṣa'|rṣabhaiḥ

needed no refuge where he stood. Twelve arrows he sent at 21.55
Shikhándin and twenty at Uttamáujas and with a barbed tip he ushered Vasu·dana into Death's realm. Eighty found Kshatra·dharman and six and twenty Sudákshina and with another hooked shaft he knocked Kshatra·deva from the seat of his car. Four and sixty Rukma·ratha loosed at Yudha·manyu and thirty at Sátyaki and then he charged straight at his quarry. As he did, the great Panchála chieftain Kítava drove his swift steeds at Drona to protect Yudhi·shthira. But his bow and horse and driver all fell before the priest's attack and then Kítava himself fell dead from his car like a star falling from the sky.

The howl for Drona's blood went up as the glorious prince 21.60
of the Panchálas crashed down dead. But despite their rage Drona rippled through them, through Matsya and Kékaya and Srínjaya and Pándava. Sátyaki and Chekitána and Dhrishta·dyumna and Shikhándin, Varddhakshémi and Chaitraséni and Sena·bindu and Suvárchas and all the other countless kings from lands beyond mention all lost to Drona and his Kurus that hour. Grasping at their great triumph your army struck down the stock of Pandu as they ran for
their lives. O majesty and scion of Bhárata. That hour it 21.65
was the Panchálas, the Kékayas and the Matsyas who shook like demons beneath mighty Indra's blows.

DHRITA·RASHTRA spoke.

A GREAT BATTLE. Did any of the Pándavas or Panchálas 22.1
broken beneath Bharad·vaja's attack rise again? The noble glory of war brings warriors their renown. It is hallowed by the mighty and looms above the mean. And great Dro-

aho n' āsīt pumān kaś cid dṛṣṭvā Droṇaṃ vyavasthitam
jṛmbhamāṇam iva vyāghraṃ prabhinnam iva kuñjaram
tyajantam āhave prāṇān saṃnaddhaṃ citra|yodhinam
mah"|êṣv|āsaṃ nara|vyāghraṃ dviṣatām bhaya|vardhanam
22.5 kṛta|jñaṃ satya|nirataṃ Duryodhana|hit'|âiṣiṇam.
Bhāradvājaṃ tath" ânīke dṛṣṭvā śūram avasthitam
ke śūrāḥ saṃnyavartanta? tan mam' ācakṣva Saṃjaya.

SAṂJAYA uvāca.

tān dṛṣṭvā calitān saṃkhye praṇunnān Droṇa|sāyakaiḥ
Pāñcālān Pāṇḍavān Matsyān Sṛñjayāṃś Cedi|Kekayān
Droṇa|cāpa|vimuktena śar'|âugheṇ' âsu|hāriṇā
Sindhor iva mah"|âughena hriyamāṇān yathā plavān
Kauravāḥ siṃha|nādena nānā|vādya|svanena ca
ratha|dvipa|narāṃś c' âiva sarvataḥ samavārayan.
tān paśyan sainya|madhya|stho rājā sva|jana|saṃvṛtaḥ
Duryodhano 'bravīt Karṇaṃ prahṛṣṭaḥ prahasann iva.

DURYODHANA uvāca.

22.10 paśya Rādheya Pāñcālān praṇunnān Droṇa|sāyakaiḥ
siṃhen' êva mṛgān vanyāṃs trāsitān dṛḍha|dhanvanā.
n' âite jātu punar yuddham īheyur iti me matiḥ
yathā tu bhagnā Droṇena vāten' êva mahā|drumāḥ.
ardyamānāḥ śarair ete rukma|puṅkhair mah"|ātmanā
pathā n' âikena gacchanti ghūrṇamānās tatas tataḥ.
saṃniruddhāś ca Kauravyair Droṇena ca mah"|ātmanā

na was a fighter clad in all the finery of battle. He was a supreme archer feared by his enemies. He was a man of action and a lover of truth and his devotion to Duryódhana was complete, for he had delivered up his life to war. There must have been fighters who saw dauntless Drona before them like a yawning tiger or an elephant in musth and yet still contended against him for fame. Tell me, Sánjaya. Tell 22.5
me too of those who when the great son of Bharad·vaja was among them ran for their lives.

SÁNJAYA spoke.

They all quailed and quivered beneath Drona's volleys: the Panchálas and the Pándavas and Matsyas and Srínjayas and the Chedis and Kékayas. On the torrent of lifestealing arrows that poured from Drona's bow they were carried off like driftwood on the high waves of the Sindhu. The Káuravas roared at the sight and with cries and shouts pressed in closer around the Pándava chariots, beasts and men. Surrounded by his guard at the very heart of his host, King Duryódhana looked on and called across to Karna, excitement and delight in his eyes.

DURYÓDHANA spoke.

Look at them o son of Radha. The Panchálas crouched 22.10
in fear beneath the arrows of Drona's bow like forest deer before a lion. I doubt that they will trouble me again soon. They have been broken by our commander like tall trees broken by the wind. They are being crushed beneath the great archer's golden shafts. Look at them, at their disarray, how they twist and turn. We Káuravas and highsouled Drona have raked them up for burning. Look at how they back

ete 'nye maṇḍalī|bhūtāḥ pāvaken' êva kuñjarāḥ.
bhramarair iva c' āviṣṭā Droṇasya niśitaiḥ śaraiḥ
anyonyaṃ samalīyanta palāyana|parāyaṇāḥ.
22.15 eṣa Bhīmo dṛḍha|krodho hīnaḥ Pāṇḍava|Sṛñjayaiḥ
madīyair āvṛto yodhaiḥ, Karṇa, nandayat' îva mām.
vyaktaṃ Droṇa|mayaṃ lokam adya paśyati dur|matiḥ
nir|āśo jīvitān nūnam adya rājyāc ca Pāṇḍavaḥ.

KARṆA uvāca.

n' âiṣa jātu mahā|bāhur jīvann āhavam utsṛjet
na c' êmān, puruṣa|vyāghra, siṃha|nādān sahiṣyati.
na c' âpi Pāṇḍavā yuddhe majjerann iti me matiḥ
śūrāś ca balavantaś ca kṛt'|âstrā yuddha|dur|madāḥ.
viṣ'|âgni|dyūta|saṃkleśān vana|vāsaṃ ca Pāṇḍavāḥ
smaramāṇā na hāsyanti saṃgrāmam iti me matiḥ.
22.20 nikṛto hi mahā|bāhur a|mit'|âujā Vṛkodaraḥ
varān varān hi Kaunteyo rath'|ôdārān haniṣyati.
asinā dhanuṣā śaktyā hayair nāgair narai rathaiḥ
āyasena ca daṇḍena vrātān vrātān haniṣyati.
tam enam anuvartante Sātyaki|pramukhā rathāḥ
Pāñcālāḥ Kekayā Matsyāḥ Pāṇḍavāś ca viśeṣataḥ.
śūrāś ca balavantaś ca vikrāntāś ca mahā|rathāḥ
vinighnantaś ca Bhīmena saṃrabdhen' âbhicoditāḥ.
te Droṇam abhivartante sarvataḥ Kuru|puṃ|gavāḥ
Vṛkodaraṃ parīpsantaḥ sūryam abhra|gaṇā iva.
22.25 ek'|âyana|gatā hy ete pīḍayeyur yata|vratam

into a circle like elephants ringed in fire. Drona's sharp arrows swarm among them like bees and each man scrabbles about desperate to save his skin. Look at Bhima quaking 22.15
with anger. All alone in the thick of my army, no Pándava or Sríñjaya in sight. How this in particular amuses me, Karna. Today Bhima must look with sad eyes upon a world remade in Drona's image. And he will have to abandon all hope he might have still for dominion, or for his life.

KARNA spoke.

O tiger in the forest of men. As long as he breathes, strongarmed Bhima will not surrender. Nor will he tolerate these roars he hears about him. None of the Pándavas will simply give way in this battle for they are mighty warriors and there is no weapon they cannot wield. Their minds are warped by bloodlust. They fight in the memory both of their time in the wilderness and of their many sufferings from poison and from fire and from the dice. I tell you
this: the Pándavas will never abandon the battlefield. Bhi- 22.20
ma's valor has never been checked. The strongarmed son of Kunti will not lie down until he has slain hero upon hero. The very greatest fighters that now live will fall. By sword by bow and by spear he will crush them, beneath horse and elephant hooves and chariot wheels and the feet of men and beneath arrows and beneath staves horde upon horde will die. Sátyaki's guard is at his side, and so too are the Panchálas, Kékayas and Matsyas. Then there are the other four Pándavas, supreme warriors of bravery and might. They will go forth to kill with Bhima's furious cries in their ears. Vrikódara's will is what they seek to make good and they

a|rakṣyamāṇaṃ śalabhā yathā dīpaṃ mumūrṣavaḥ.
a|saṃśayaṃ kṛt'|âstrāś ca paryāptāś c' âpi vāraṇe
ati|bhāram ahaṃ manye Bhāradvāje samāhitam.
te śīghram anugacchāmo yatra Droṇo vyavasthitaḥ
kokā iva mahā|nāgaṃ mā vai hanyur yata|vrataṃ.

SAÑJAYA uvāca.

Rādheyasya vacaḥ śrutvā rājā Duryodhanas tataḥ
bhrātṛbhiḥ sahito, rājan, prāyād Droṇa|rathaṃ prati.
tatr' ārāvo mahān āsīd ekaṃ Droṇaṃ jighāṃsatām
Pāṇḍavānāṃ nivṛttānāṃ nānā|varṇair hay'|ôttamaiḥ.

DHṚTARĀṢṬRA uvāca.

23.1 SARVEṢĀM EVA ME brūhi ratha|cihnāni, Saṃjaya,
yad Droṇam abhyavartanta kruddhā Bhīma|puro|gamāḥ.

SAṂJAYA uvāca.

ṛśya|varṇair hayair dṛṣṭvā vyāyacchantaṃ Vṛkodaram
rajat'|âśvas tataḥ śūraḥ Śaineyaḥ saṃnyavartata.
sār'|âṅg'|âśvo Yudhāmanyuḥ svayaṃ pratvarayan hayān
paryavartata dur|dharṣaḥ kruddho Droṇa|rathaṃ prati.
pārāvata|sa|varṇais tu hema|bhāṇḍair mahā|javaiḥ
Pāñcāla|rājasya suto Dhṛṣṭadyumno nyavartata.
23.5 pitaraṃ tu pariprepsuḥ Kṣatradharmā yata|vrataḥ

will gather about Drona like banks of cloud about the sun. They are men bound by a single goal. Like moths that live 22.25
but a moment in this world they will descend upon the flame that is our noble commander and he will have no one to protect him. Remember this. Their mastery of the arts of war is matched only by their resilience. Something great and terrible hangs over Bharad·vaja's son. We must stay close to the course that Drona takes, lest like wolves hunting an elephant the Pándavas reach him and tear him apart.

SÁNJAYA spoke.

O majesty, King Duryódhana listened to Radha's son and with his brothers rolled up alongside Drona's chariot. Then a great clamor arose and the Pándavas rode out as one behind fine steeds of many shades. And their hearts burned for the death of Drona.

DHRITA·RASHTRA spoke.

TELL ME, SÁNJAYA, of all the banners and the chariots 23.1
that Bhima's wild host brought at Drona.

SÁNJAYA spoke.

Glimpsing Vrikódara behind his brindled horses, the mighty son of Shini swung about his silver steeds. Hardy Yudha·manyu angrily spurred on his dappled horses and wheeled towards Drona's chariot, while behind dovecolored horses fleet of foot and harnessed in gold there appeared Dhrishta·dyumna, prince of the Panchálas. Kshatra·dhar- 23.5
man turned his bay team and made straight for his old teacher, for he was sworn to the warrior code and clung to his noble calling. On came Shikhándin's son Kshatra·deva,

siddhiṃ c' âsya parāṃ kāṅkṣan śoṇ'|âṣvaḥ saṃnyavartata.
padma|pattra|nibhāṃś c' âśvān mallik'|ākṣān sv|alaṃ|kṛtān
Śaikhaṇḍiḥ Kṣatradevas tu svayaṃ pratvarayan yayau.
darśanīyās tu Kāmbojāḥ śuka|pattra|paricchadāḥ
vahanto Nakulaṃ śīghraṃ tāvakān abhidudruvuḥ.
kṛṣṭās tu megha|saṅkāśā avahann Uttamaujasam
dur|dharṣāy' âbhisaṃdhāya kruddhaṃ yuddhāya Bhārata.
tathā tittira|kalmāṣā hayā vāta|samā jave
avahaṃs tumule yuddhe Sahadevam udāyudham.
23.10 danta|varṇās tu rājānaṃ kāla|vālā Yudhiṣṭhiram
bhīma|vegā nara|vyāghram avahan vāta|raṃhasaḥ.
hem'|ôttama|praticchannair hayair vāta|samair jave
abhyavartanta sainyāni sarvāṇy eva Yudhiṣṭhiram.
rājñas tv an|antaro rājā Pāñcālyo Drupado 'bhavat
jāta|rūpa|paricchannaḥ sarvais tair abhirakṣitaḥ.
lalāmair haribhir yuktaiḥ sarva|śabda|kṣamair yudhi
rājñāṃ madhye mah"|êṣv|āsaḥ śānta|bhīr abhyavartata.
taṃ Virāṭo 'nvayāc chīghraṃ saha sarvair mahā|rathaiḥ.
23.15 Kaikayāś ca Śikhaṇḍī ca Dhṛṣṭaketus tath" âiva ca
svaiḥ svaiḥ sainyaiḥ parivṛtā Matsya|rājānam anvayuḥ.
taṃ tu pāṭala|puṣpāṇāṃ sama|varṇā hay'|ôttamāḥ
vahamānā vyarājanta Matsyasy' â|mitra|ghātinaḥ.
haridra|sama|varṇāś ca javanā hema|mālinaḥ
putraṃ Virāṭa|rājasya sa|tvarāḥ samudāvahan.
Indra|gopaka|varṇaiś ca bhrātaraḥ pañca Kaikayāḥ
jāta|rūpa|sam'|ābhāsaḥ sarve lohitaka|dhvajāḥ.
te hema|mālinaḥ śūrāḥ sarve yuddha|viśāradāḥ
varṣanta iva jīmūtāḥ pratyadṛśyanta daṃśitāḥ.

driving on wellbedecked horses the colour of lotus petals and with spots white as jasmine flowers around their eyes. The quick Kambója breeds that bore Nákula down upon us wore harnesses of parrot feathers beautiful to behold. Wrathful Uttamáujas was carried straight into the dense fray o Bhárata as if on driven clouds, and into the crash of battle with his sword upraised horses speckled like partridges and quick as squalls bore Saha·deva. The steeds of 23.10
the tiger Yudhi·shthira had black tails and coats white as ivory and they raced on swift as the wind, and swift as the wind were the horses draped in the finest gold that carried the troops around him.

Next to the king stood another, the mighty bowman Drúpada, king of the Panchálas, swathed in gold and ringed by his sentinel troop, borne magisterially into that royal array on gentle steeds, starred palominos mild and nimble however loud the din of battle became. Viráta arrived swiftly in their wake, and other champions, the Kaikéyas, Shikhán- 23.15
din, Dhrishta·ketu, each surrounded by his guard and each drawing up alongside the Matsya lord. The fine steeds that drew the vengeful king blazed like the trumpet flower. His son's fleetfooted team were banded in gold, their coats yellow as sandalwood, and under ruby pennants and behind beasts the color of cochineal those valiant masters of war the brothers Kaikéya glinted in their mail, golden chains festooning their necks. They were stormclouds dense with rain.

23.20 āma|pātra|nikāśās tu Pāñcālyam a|mit'|âujasam
dāntās tāmr'|âruṇā yuktāḥ Śikhaṇḍinam udāvahan.
tathā dvā|daśa|sāhasrāḥ Pāñcālānāṃ mahā|rathāḥ
teṣāṃ tu ṣaṭ|sahasrāṇi ye Śikhaṇḍinam anvayuḥ.
putraṃ tu Śiśupālasya nara|siṃhasya, māriṣa,
ākrīḍanto vahanti sma sāraṅga|śabalā hayāḥ.
Dhṛṣṭaketuś ca Cedīnām ṛṣabho 'tibal'|ôditaḥ
Kāmbojaiḥ śabalair aśvair abhyavartata dur|jayaḥ.
Bṛhatkṣatraṃ tu Kaikeyaṃ su|kumāraṃ hay'|ôttamāḥ
palāla|dhūma|saṃkāṣāḥ Saindhavāḥ śīghram āvahan.
23.25 mallik'|âkṣāḥ padma|varṇā Bāhli|jātāḥ sv|alaṃ|kṛtāḥ
śūraṃ Śikhaṇḍinaḥ putram Ṛkṣadevam udāvahan.
rukma|bhāṇḍa|praticchannāḥ Kauśeya|sa|dṛśā hayāḥ
kṣamāvanto 'vahan saṃkhye Senābindum ariṃ|damam.
yuvānam avahan yuddhe krauñca|varṇā hay'|ôttamāḥ
Kāśyasy' âbhimukhaṃ putraṃ su|kumāraṃ mahā|ratham.
śvetās tu Prativindhyaṃ taṃ kṛṣṇa|grīvā mano|javāḥ
yantuḥ prīti|karā rājan rāja|putram udāvahan.
Sutasomaṃ tu yaṃ somāt Pārthaḥ putram ayācata
māṣa|puṣpa|sa|varṇās tam avahan vājino raṇe.
23.30 sahasra|soma|pratimo babhūva
pure Kurūṇām Udayendu|nāmni
tasmiñ jātaḥ soma|saṃkranda|madhye
yasmāt tasmāt Sutasomo 'bhavat saḥ.
Nākuliṃ tu śat'|ânīkaṃ śāla|puṣpa|nibhā hayāḥ

Yoked before his chariot, mild horses coppery red like 23.20
the dawn or unkilned clay drew the Panchála prince Shikhándin, his splendors untrammeled, and behind him came six of the twelve hundred Panchála champions. The horses belonging to the son of the lion Shishu·pala were patterned like antelope and they danced, my lord, as they drew his car.

The bull of the Chedis fabled for his might, invincible Dhrishta·ketu, drove dapples from Kambója, and fine breeds from Sindhu the shade of strawsmoke galloped before Brihat·kshatra, the young Kékaya prince. Shikhándin's 23.25
other son brave Riksha·deva drove roans the color of lotuses born in Balkh with spots of white around their eyes and rich livery about their hides, as brightharnessed gentletempered horses with coats like silk bore through the fray Sena·bindu, burner of foes, and steeds dotted like curlews took the young and tender son of the king of Kashi, a warrior now but barely a man, deep into the field of battle. Prativíndhya's horses were white with black necks, and my king those gorgeous creatures carried their prince along with the swiftness of thought itself.

Stallions white as gram blossom took Suta·soma into war, the son with the light of a thousand moons whom Bhima·sena owed to Soma. The boy was born while the *soma** roared, 23.30
in the city of the Kurus known as Udayéndu, and thus he got his name. Like rosemallow and the flower of calotropis were the horses so beloved to their master Shatáníka son of Nákula. Dráupadi's second son the tiger Shruta·karman answered the call to battle with turquoise roans and charioteers hidden in gold, and her third, Shruta·kirti, a well of wisdom and

Āditya|taruṇa|prakhyāḥ ślāghanīyam udāvahan.
kāñcan'|âpihitair yoktrair mayūra|grīva|saṃnibhāḥ
Draupadeyaṃ nara|vyāghraṃ Śrutakarmāṇam āhave.
Śrutakīrtiṃ śruta|nidhiṃ Draupadeyaṃ hay'|ôttamāḥ
ūhuḥ Pārtha|samaṃ yuddhe cāṣa|pattra|nibhā hayāḥ.
yam āhur adhyardha|guṇaṃ Kṛṣṇāt Pārthāc ca saṃyuge
Abhimanyuṃ piśaṅgās taṃ kumāram avahan raṇe.
23.35 ekas tu Dhārtarāṣṭrebhyaḥ Pāṇḍavān yaḥ samāśritaḥ
taṃ bṛhanto mahā|kāyā Yuyutsum avahan raṇe.
palāla|kāṇḍa|varṇās tu Vārddhakṣemiṃ tarasvinam
ūhuḥ su|tumule yuddhe hayā hṛṣṭāḥ sv|alaṃ|kṛtāḥ.
kumāraṃ śiti|pādās tu rukma|pattrair uraś|chadaiḥ
Saucittim avahan yuddhe yantuḥ preṣya|karā hayāḥ.
rukma|pṛṣṭh'|âvakīrṇās tu kauśeya|sa|dṛśā hayāḥ
suvarṇa|mālinaḥ kṣāntāḥ Śreṇimantam udāvahan.
astrāṇāṃ ca dhanur|vede brāhme vede ca pāra|gam
taṃ Satyadhṛtim āyāntam aruṇāḥ samudāvahan.
23.40 yaḥ sa Pāñcāla|senā|nīr Droṇam aṃśam akalpayat
pārāvata|sa|varṇās taṃ Dhṛṣṭadyumnam udāvahan.
tam anvayāt Satyadhṛtiḥ Saucittir yuddha|dur|madaḥ
Śreṇimān Vasudānaś ca putraḥ Kāśyasya c' Âbhibhūḥ.
yuktaiḥ parama|Kāmbojair javanair hema|mālibhiḥ
bhīṣayanto dviṣat|sainyaṃ Yama|Vaiśravaṇ'|ôpamāḥ
prabhadrakās tu Kāmbojāḥ ṣaṭ|sahasrāṇy udāyudhāḥ
nānā|varṇair hayaiḥ śreṣṭhair hema|varṇa|ratha|dhvajāḥ
śara|vrātair vidhunvantaḥ śatrūn vitata|kārmukāḥ
samāna|mṛtyavo bhūtvā Dhṛṣṭadyumnaṃ samanvayuḥ.

Partha's likeness, was borne by the finest horses touched by
the color of the bluejay's wing. Across the field galloped the
bays of Prince Abhimányu, Krishna and Partha twinned in
one man, and tall and powerful were the stallions that drew 23.35
Yuyútsu, who had left behind his ninety-nine brothers and
chosen fight for the Pándava cause.

Into that welter came brilliant Varddhakshémi, before
whom cantered caparisoned steeds strawstalk pale, and the
whitefooted warmbloods of Prince Sáuchitti went mild into
battle in armor pinioned in gold, gold too the armor that
plated the silken backs of Shrénimat's tranquil chargers,
and gold the chains about their necks. Chestnut horses galloped before Satya·dhriti, maven of heaven bow and spear,
alongside the grays the shade of the turtledove that drew 23.40
Dhrishta·dyumna lord of the Panchála army, who had chosen Drona as his share. He it was whom they followed,
Satya·dhriti and wardrunk Sáuchitti, Shrénimat, Vasu·dana
and Kashi's son Ábhibhu, and with their teams of Kambója
thoroughbreds fleet and ribboned in gold, terrible as the
spirits of death and darkness, six thousand noble Kambójas, with swords upraised and their banners and chariots
glinting in gold. On they drove their fine steeds of many
shades as they rolled behind Dhrishta·dyumna, and bows
bent they were ready to cast arrows upon their foes. They
were men for whom death was but a trifle.

23.45 babhru|kauśeya|varṇās tu suvarṇa|vara|mālinaḥ
ūhur a|glāna|manasaś Cekitānaṃ hay'|ôttamāḥ
Indr'|āyudha|sa|varṇais tu Kuntibhojo hay'|ôttamaiḥ
āyāt su|vaśyaiḥ Purujin mātulaḥ Savyasācinaḥ.
antar|ikṣa|sa|varṇās tu tārakā|citritā iva
rājānaṃ Rocamānaṃ te hayāḥ saṃkhye samāvahan.
ye tu puṣkara|nālasya sama|varṇā hay'|ôttamāḥ
jave śyena|samāś citrāḥ Sudāmānam udāvahan.
śaśa|lohita|varṇās tu pāṇḍur'|ôdgata|rājayaḥ
Pāñcālyaṃ go|pateḥ putraṃ Siṃhasenam udāvahan.
23.50 Pāñcālānāṃ nara|vyāghro yaḥ khyāto Janamejayaḥ
tasya sarṣapa|puṣpāṇāṃ tulya|varṇā hay'|ôttamāḥ.
māṣa|varṇāś ca javanā bṛhanto hema|mālinaḥ
dadhi|pṛṣṭhāś candra|mukhāḥ Pāñcālyam avahan Drutam.
śūrāś ca bhadrakāś c' âiva śara|kāṇḍa|nibhā hayāḥ
padma|kiñjalka|varṇ'|ābhā Daṇḍadhāram udāvahan.
rāsabh'|âruṇa|varṇ'|ābhā pṛṣṭhato mūṣika|prabhāḥ
valganta iva saṃyattā Vyāghradattam udāvahan.
harayaḥ kālakāś citrāś citra|mālya|vibhūṣitāḥ
Sudhanvānaṃ nara|vyāghraṃ Pāñcālyaṃ samudāvahan.
23.55 Indr'|âśani|sama|sparśā Indra|gopaka|saṃnibhāḥ
kāye citr'|ântarāś citrāś Citrāyudham udāvahan.
bibhrato hema|mālās tu cakra|vāk'|ôdarā hayāḥ
Kosal'|âdhipateḥ putraṃ Sukṣatraṃ vājino 'vahan.
śabalās tu bṛhanto 'śvā dāntā jāmbūnada|srajaḥ
yuddhe satya|dhṛtiṃ Kṣemim avahan prāṃśavaḥ śubhāḥ.
eka|varṇena sarveṇa dhvajena kavacena ca
aśvaiś ca dhanuṣā c' âiva śuklaiḥ Śuklo 'bhyavartata.
Samudrasena|putraṃ tu sāmudrā rudra|tejasam
aśvāḥ śaś'|âṅka|sa|dṛśāś Candrasenam udāvahan.

Encircled in pure gold and with coats like liverbrown 23.45
silk the great steeds of Chekitána galloped unwearied, and
Púrujit, chief of the Kuntis and uncle of Árjuna, drove beasts
faithful and fine with striae like rainbows, while horses star-
bright like pieces of the firmament carried King Rochamána
into the fray against us. Roans soaring like eagles and with
the luster of the blue lotus pulled Sudáman, skewbalds red
as hares with streaks white as dhaora blooms bore Sinha·
sena, the son of a Panchála cowherd, and the horses that 23.50
drew glorious Janam·éjaya tiger of the Panchálas were the
color of mustardseed flowers. The bud of the black gram
bloomed in the milkwhite backs and moonpale faces of the
strong and swift steeds garlanded in gold that Druta the
Panchála drove. Handsome and vigorous were the horses
bearing Danda·dhara, their coats the color of reed stalks
touched with the hue of lotus anthers. As if dancing into
war, duns brown as donkeys and striped like the trunks of
raintrees along their backs drew Vyaghra·datta, and speckled bright and black were the bays of Sudhánvan, tiger of
the Panchálas, and bright the wreaths that decorated them.

Aglow as with lightning and sparkling like fireflies, the 23.55
bright shapes of Chitráyudha's steeds dazzled the eye, and
the stallions that bore up Sukshátra son of the Kósala king
wore glittering chains about hides spotted like sheldrakes,
and tall and resplendent beasts, mild dapples with manes
and tails braided in rivergold drew the pious Kshemi. In
one tone, all white were Shukla's mares, banner, breastplate
and bow, white he was as he rode. And horses of the coast
aglow like the moon bore up ferocious Chandra·sena son
of Samúdra·sena.

23.60 nīl'|ôtpala|sa|varṇās tu tapanīya|vibhūṣitāḥ
Śaibyaṃ Citrarathaṃ saṃkhye citra|māly" âvahan hayāḥ.
kalāya|puṣpa|varṇās tu śveta|lohita|rājayaḥ
Rathasenaṃ haya|śreṣṭhāḥ samūhur yuddha|dur|madam.
yaṃ tu sarva|manuṣyebhyaḥ prāhuḥ śūrataraṃ nṛ|pam
taṃ Paṭaccarahantāraṃ śuka|varṇ" âvahan hayāḥ.
citr'|āyudhaṃ Citramālyaṃ citra|varm'|āyudha|dhvajam
ūhuḥ kiṃśuka|puṣpāṇāṃ sama|varṇā hay'|ôttamāḥ.
eka|varṇena sarveṇa dhvajena kavacena ca
dhanuṣā ratha|vāhaiś ca nīlair Nīlo 'bhyavartata.
23.65 nānā|rūpai ratna|cihnair varūtha|dhvaja|kārmukaiḥ
vāji|dhvaja|patākābhiś citraiś Citro 'bhyavartata.
ye tu puṣkara|pattrasya tulya|varṇā hay'|ôttamāḥ
te Rocamānasya sutaṃ Hemavarṇam udāvahan.
yodhāś ca bhadrakārāś ca śara|daṇḍ'|ânudaṇḍyāḥ
śvet'|âṇḍāḥ kukkuṭ'|âṇḍ'|ābhā Daṇḍaketuṃ hay" âvahan.

Keśavena hate saṃkhye pitary athā nar'|âdhipe
bhinne kapāṭe Pāṇḍyāṇāṃ vidruteṣu ca bandhuṣu
Bhīṣmād avāpya c' âstrāṇi Droṇād Rāmāt Kṛpāt tathā
astraiḥ samatvaṃ samprāpya Rukmi|Karṇ'|Ârjun'|Âcyutaiḥ
23.70 iyeṣa Dvārakāṃ hantuṃ kṛtsnāṃ jetuṃ ca medinīm
nivāritas tataḥ prājñaiḥ su|hṛdbhir hita|kamyayā
vair'|ânubandham utsṛjya sva|rājyam anuśāsti yaḥ
sa sāraṅga|dhvajaḥ Pāṇḍyaś candra|raśmi|nibhair hayaiḥ
Vaidūrya|jāla|saṃchannair vīrya|draviṇam āśritaḥ
divyaṃ visphārayaṃś cāpaṃ Droṇam abhyadravad balī.
āṭarūṣaka|varṇ'|ābhā hayāḥ Pāṇḍy'|ânuyāyinām
avahan ratha|mukhyānām ayutāni catur|daśa.

Bright garlands and wellburnished gold bound the roans 23.60
the color of the blue lotus that took Chitra·ratha son of Shibi into the melee, and noble breeds of dark blossom* fretted in white and brown bore battlecrazed Ratha·sena. Patácchara·hantri whom men call hero of heroes rode behind steeds versicolored as birds of paradise, and with armor, sword and standard all rainbowbright as the weapons in his hands Chitra·malya came on behind fine horses vivid as flame-of-the-forest. In one tone, all dark were Nila's team, banner, breastplate and bow, dark he was as he rode. Gemlike burst 23.65
Chitra's bow, banner and mail with scintillae, bright his horse's livery and drapes, bright he was as he rode. Fine steeds blue as waterlily petals drew Hema·varna son of Rochamána and whiteballed purebred warhorses the color of hens' eggs and striped like reed stems along their spines bore Danda·ketu.

When his father and king of his folk was slain by Késhava and his door hung broken and his friends had all fled, Pandya had gone to study the art of combat with Bhishma, Drona, Rama and Kripa. And when his skill matched the skill of Rukmin, Karna, Árjuna and even Krishna, he yearned to 23.70
smash the City of Doors and wage a war across the whole of the broad earth. But his elders discouraged him, and out of compassion for his friends he set aside his old animosity and settled down to rule his kingdom. Wealth and power had come to him. Now, carrying the sign of the antelope, he bore down on Drona with his celestial bow drawn in his hands. Horses clad in mail from Vidúra glowed before his car with the light of moonbeams, and horses the hue of waterwillow drew fourteen legions in his train.

nānā|rūpeṇa varṇena nān"|ākṛti|mukhā hayāḥ
ratha|cakra|dhvajaṃ vīraṃ Ghaṭotkacam udāvahan.
23.75 Bhāratānāṃ sametānām utsṛjy' âiko matāni yaḥ
gato Yudhiṣṭhiraṃ bhaktyā tyaktvā sarvam abhīpsitam
lohit'|âkṣaṃ mahā|bāhuṃ Bṛhantaṃ tam Araṭṭa|jāḥ
sahā|sattvā mahā|kāyāḥ sauvarṇa|syandane sthitaṃ.
suvarṇa|varṇā dharma|jñam anīka|sthaṃ Yudhiṣṭhiram
rāja|śreṣṭhaṃ haya|śreṣṭhāḥ sarvataḥ pṛṣṭhato 'nvayuḥ.
varṇair ucc'|âvacair anyaiḥ sad|aśvānāṃ prabhadrakāḥ
saṃnyavartanta yuddhāya bahavo deva|rūpiṇaḥ.

te yattā Bhīmasenena sahitāḥ kāñcana|dhvajāḥ
pratyadṛśyanta, rāj'|êndra, s'|Êndrā iva div'|âukasaḥ.
23.80 atyarocata tān sarvān Dhṛṣṭadyumnaḥ samāgatān
sarvāṇy ati ca sainyāni Bhāradvājo vyarocata.
atīva śuśubhe tasya dhvajaḥ kṛṣṇ'|âjin'|ôttaraḥ,
kamaṇḍalur, mahā|rāja, jāta|rūpa|mayaḥ śubhaḥ.
dhvajaṃ tu Bhīmasenasya Vaidūrya|maṇi|locanaṃ
bhrājamānaṃ mahā|siṃhaṃ rājataṃ dṛṣṭavān ahaṃ.
dhvajaṃ tu Kuru|rājasya Pāṇḍavasya mah"|âujasaḥ
dṛṣṭavān asmi sauvarṇaṃ somaṃ graha|gaṇ'|ânvitam
mṛdaṅgau c' âtra vipulau divyau Nand'|Ôpanandakau
yantreṇ' āhanyamānau ca su|svanau harṣa|vardhanau.
23.85 śarabhaṃ pṛṣṭha|sauvarṇaṃ Nakulasya mahā|dhvajam
apaśyāma rathe 'ty|ugraṃ bhīṣayāṇam avasthitam.
haṃsas tu rājataḥ śrīmān dhvaje ghaṇṭā|patākavān

Under the banner of the chariot wheel there came the legendary Ghatótkacha behind horses of mysterious aspect, their origin arcane. Then there was the man who alone 23.75
ignored the censure of all the assembled council of Bháratas and who turned his back on his own dreams and came to Yudhi·shthira on bended knee. That man was Brihánta of the bloodred eyes and mighty arms and now he stood on a golden car yoked to powerful muscled breeds from Arátta. Golden horses massed behind wise Yudhi·shthira where he stood at the head of his host, rare king among rare creatures. His men rode out for war together, noble and godlike and rippling with the different colors of their fabulous steeds.

With their glittering banners Bhima·sena with his fierce devotees looked my king like Indra and the denizens of heaven. Dhrishta·dyumna outshone all who rode near him 23.80
but brighter than even he was Bharad·vaja's son. The staff of his standard was all dark luster, majesty, wrapped in the skin of a black antelope, and his ascetic's gourd was inlaid intricately with gold. On Bhima·sena's standard I saw a great lion made of silver* whose eyes were jewels from Vidúra. I saw on the chariot pole of the mighty Pándava and overlord of Kurus a brilliant image of the moon ringed in planets and alongside it I saw the two broad drums called Joy and Rejoicing from whose skins terror beat forth. On Nákula's 23.85
car I saw raised high a great carven goldbacked *shárabha*, fierce and fell to behold. A silver flamingo trailing pennants and bells crowned Saha·deva's stout pole and atop the staves of the sons of Dráupadi were images of Dharma, Vayu, Indra and the Ashvins. A golden hornbill forged in enchanted

Sahadevasya dur|dharṣe dviṣatāṃ śoka|vardhanaḥ.
pañcānāṃ Draupadeyānāṃ pratimā|dhvaja|bhūṣaṇam
Dharma|Māruta|Śakrāṇām Aśvinoś ca mah"|ātmanoḥ.
Abhimanyoḥ kumārasya śārṅga|pakṣī hiraṇ|mayaḥ
rathe dhvaja|varo, rājaṃs, tapta|vāmī|kar'|ôjjvalaḥ.
Ghatotkacasya rāj'|ēndra dhvaje gṛdhro vyarocata
aśvāś ca kāma|gās tasya Rāvaṇasya purā yathā.
23.90 māhendraṃ ca dhanur divyaṃ Dharma|rāje Yudhiṣṭhire
Vāyavyaṃ Bhīmasenasya dhanur divyam abhūn, nṛ|pa.
trailokya|rakṣaṇ'|ârthāya Brahmaṇā sṛṣṭam āyudham
tad divyam Ajaraṃ c' âiva Phālgun'|ârthāya vai dhanuḥ.
Vaiṣṇavaṃ Nakulāy' âtha Sahadevāya c' Âśvinam
Ghatoṭkacāya Paulastyaṃ dhanur divyaṃ bhayānakam
Raudram Āgneya|Kauberaṃ Yāmyaṃ Giriśam eva ca
pañcānāṃ Draupadeyānāṃ dhanū|ratnāni, Bhārata.
Raudraṃ dhanur|varaṃ śreṣṭhaṃ lebhe yad Rohiṇī|sutaḥ
tat tuṣṭaḥ pradadau Rāmaḥ Saubhadrāya mah"|ātmane.
23.95 ete c' ânye ca bahavo dhvajā hema|vibhūṣitāḥ
tatr' âdṛśyanta śūrāṇāṃ dviṣatāṃ śoka|vardhanāḥ.
tad abhūd dhvaja|sambādham a|kāpuruṣa|sevitaṃ
Droṇ'|ânīkaṃ, mahā|rāja, paṭe citram iv' ârpitaṃ.
śuśruvur nāma|gotrāṇi vīrāṇāṃ saṃyuge tadā
Droṇam ādravatāṃ, rājan, svayaṃ|vara iv' āhave.

DHṚTARĀṢṬRA uvāca.

24.1 VYATHAYEYUR IME senāṃ devānām api, Saṃjaya,
āhave ye nyavartanta Vṛkodara|mukhā nṛ|pāḥ.
samprayuktaḥ kil' âiv' âyaṃ diṣṭe bhavati pūruṣaḥ
tasminn eva tu sarv'|ârthāḥ pradṛśyante pṛthag|vidhāḥ.

flame adorned Abhimányu's standerd, and atop Ghatótkacha's there roosted a vulture, sign of the car drawn by horses wild as Rávana's were of old.

Then there were the weapons. The righteous King Yu- 23.90
dhi·shthira held the celestial bow of Indra and the celestial bow in Bhima's hands came from the god of the wind. The bow crafted of heaven's stuff that Phálguna held had been fashioned by Brahma for the protection of the three worlds, while Nákula and Saha·deva received theirs from Vishnu and the Ashvins. The fearsome magic bow that Ghatótkacha held came from Pulástya, and the jewels of archery borne by the Draupadéyas were named Raudra, Agnéya, Kaubéra, Yamya and Giri·sha. Subhádra's son had earned the respect of Rama son of Róhini and o king he had given the boy the fine and fearsome weapon that he now held in his hands.

These and many like them were the standards and statues 23.95
whose patterns were bright above the heads of our foes and signed the coming of our sorrows. We too stood beneath our banners and no coward stood among us. Drona's force was as full of color as painted canvas. You could hear the names of the heroes echoing across the plain as they rode at Drona, and my king to hear them you may have thought you were at a wedding rather than a war.

DHRITA·RASHTRA spoke.

O SÁNJAYA. EVEN the army of heaven would grow weak 24.1
with fear at the sight of Vrikódara and his fellow kings steeled for war. Be certain that this man is well acquainted with destiny. In him are all the myriad enigmas of this life

dīrghaṃ viproṣitaḥ kālam araṇye jaṭilo 'jinī
a|jñātaś c' âiva lokasya vijahāra Yudhiṣṭhiraḥ.
sa eva mahatīṃ senāṃ samāvartayad āhave.
kim anyad daiva|saṃyogān mama putrasya c' âbhavat?
24.5 yukta eva hi bhāgyena dhruvam utpadyate naraḥ,
sa tath" ākṛṣyate tena na yathā svayam icchati.
dyūta|vyasanam āsādya kleśito hi Yudhiṣṭhiraḥ
sa punar bhāga|dheyena sahāyān upalabdhavān.
«ardhaṃ me Kekayā labdhāḥ Kāśikāḥ Kosalāś ca ye
Cedayaś c' âpare Vaṅgā mām eva samupāśritāḥ.
pṛthivī bhūyasī, tāta, mama Pārthasya no tathā»
iti mām abravīt, sūta, mando Duryodhanaḥ purā.
tasya senā|samūhasya madhye Droṇaḥ su|rakṣitaḥ
nihataḥ Pārṣaten' ājau kim anyad bhāga|dheyataḥ.
24.10 madhye rājñāṃ mahā|bāhuṃ sadā yuddh'|âbhinandinam
sarv'|âstra|pāra|gaṃ Droṇaṃ kathaṃ Mṛtyur upeyivān?
samanuprāpta|kṛcchro 'haṃ saṃmohaṃ paramaṃ gataḥ
Bhīṣma|Droṇau hatau śrutvā n' âhaṃ jīvitum utsahe.
yan mā Kṣatt" ābravīt, tāta, prapaśyan putra|gṛddhinam
Duryodhanena tat sarvaṃ prāptaṃ sūta mayā saha.
nṛśaṃsaṃ tu paraṃ tat syāt tyaktvā Duryodhanaṃ yadi
putra|śeṣaṃ cikīrṣeyaṃ kṛcchraṃ na maraṇaṃ bhavet.

foreclosed. His residence in exile was long. His brother Yudhi·shthira wore a beard and animal skin and dwelt in the wilderness, and there he languished, forgotten by all the world. Now he rides at the head of the great army he has summoned to war. What else could be born of my son's encounter with fate?

It is true that a man is formed only after he has come up 24.5
against his destiny. What befalls him is never what he would wish for himself. The dice brought misery and ruin upon Yudhi·shthira but chance gave him friends again. "The Kékayas, the men of Kashi, the Kósalas, the Chedis and the kings of Vanga have all taken up my cause. My allies are countless, father. Partha cannot say the same." This was what my unhappy son once told me, Sánjaya. If Príshata's grandson reached past the strong defenses before him and into the midst of our massive army and struck Drona dead,
then what can we call it but fate? Drona was a great master 24.10
of every weapon in the world who fought exultant beside kings. How could Death even step close to him? O blackest calamity. My head swims. If Bhishma and Drona are dead then I want no more of life. Sánjaya you are my eyes and my hands. I fear for my sons. O Sánjaya. Vídura* warned me about the dreams I had for my sons. His prophecies have all come true for Duryódhana, and for myself. I have lost Duryódhana to the cruelties of his foes. But if I can still have a father's hope then I pray that a wretched death is not the fate that befalls all of my children.

yo hi dharmaṃ parityajya bhavaty artha|paro naraḥ
so 'smāc ca hīyate lokāt kṣudra|bhāvaṃ ca gacchati.
24.15 adya c' âpy asya rāṣṭrasya hat'|ôtsāhasya Saṃjaya
avaśeṣaṃ na paśyāmi kakude mṛdite sati.
kathaṃ syād avaśeṣaṃ hi dhuryayor abhyatītayoḥ
yau nityam upajīvāmaḥ kṣamiṇau puruṣa'|rṣabhau?
vyaktam eva ca me śaṃsa yathā yuddham avartata.
ke 'yudhyan ke vyapākarṣan ke kṣudrāḥ prādravan bhayāt?
Dhanaṃjayaṃ ca me śaṃsa yad yac cakre ratha'|rṣabhaḥ
tasmād bhayaṃ no bhūyiṣṭaṃ bhrātṛvyāc ca Vṛkodarāt.
yath" āsīc ca nivṛtteṣu Pāṇḍaveyeṣu, Saṃjaya,
mama sainy'|âvaśeṣasya saṃnipātaḥ su|dāruṇaḥ.
24.20 kathaṃ ca vo manas tāta nivṛtteṣv abhavat tadā?
māmakānāṃ ca ye śūrāḥ ke kāṃs tatra nyavārayan?

SAṂJAYA uvāca.

25.1 MAHAD BHAIRAVAM āsīn naḥ
saṃnivṛtteṣu Pāṇḍuṣu
dṛṣṭvā Droṇaṃ chādyamānaṃ
tair bhās|karam iv' âmbu|daiḥ.
taiś c' ôddhūtaṃ rajas tīvram avacakre camūṃ tava
tato hatam amaṃsyāma Droṇaṃ dṛṣṭi|pathe hate.
tāṃs tu śūrān mah"|êṣv|āsān krūraṃ karma cikīrṣataḥ
dṛṣṭvā Duryodhanas tūrṇaṃ sva|sainyaṃ samacūcudat.
«yathā|śakti yath"|ôtsāhaṃ yathā|sattvaṃ nar'|âdhipāḥ
vārayadhvaṃ yathā|yogaṃ Pāṇḍavānām anīkinīm.»

A man who turns his back on what is right is but a fool grasping at pennies, lost to the world. He makes his bed among the worms. O Sánjaya. What is left of this wide 24.15
realm now that its lifeblood has been stopped and its great example crushed into the earth? I see nothing. There can be nothing when the two that made it great with their grace and to whose example the rest of us always aspired have departed from it.

Tell me how the battle went. Who fought on? Who was too weak to fight and turned and fled? Tell me how the bull Dhanan·jaya fared in battle and of the terrors that deadly Vrikódara brought against us. Tell me how my men dwindled in their ranks and collapsed dead upon the dead of the Pándavas. What went through your mind when you stood 24.20
among the dead? Who of my warriors felled whom?

SÁNJAYA spoke.

DISASTER LOOMED before us as the Pándavas gathered 25.1
themselves together once again. We watched Drona disappearing behind them as if they were clouds rushing to engulf the sun. A hot wind rose up and filled our eyes with dust. Gone from our gaze for a time we thought Drona gone from the earth as well.

Duryódhana saw the dark intentions of the mighty archers as they rolled towards us and he spoke sharply to his warriors.

"Rulers of men. I call on all your power and all the will that is in you and which gives you life for as has been ordained the Pándavas are now upon us. Stand your ground."

25.5 tato Durmarṣaṇo Bhīmam abhyagacchat sutas tava
ārād dṛṣṭvā kiran bāṇair icchan Droṇasya jīvitam.
bāṇair samācinod Bhīmaṃ kruddho mṛtyur iv' āhave
taṃ ca Bhīmo 'tudad bāṇais tad" āsīt tumulaṃ mahat.

ta īśvara|samādiṣṭāḥ prājñāḥ śūrāḥ prahāriṇaḥ
rājyaṃ mṛtyu|bhayaṃ tyaktvā pratyatiṣṭhan parān yudhi.

Kṛtavarmā Śineḥ pautraṃ Droṇaṃ prepsuṃ, viśāṃ pate,
paryavārayad āyāntaṃ śūraṃ samara|śobhinam.
taṃ Śaineyaḥ śara|vrātaiḥ kruddhaḥ kruddham avārayat
Kṛta|varmā ca Śaineyaṃ matto mattam iva dvipam.
25.10 Saindhavaḥ Kṣatradharmāṇam āyāntaṃ niśitaiḥ śaraiḥ
ugra|dhanvā mah"|êṣv|āsaṃ yatto Droṇād avārayat.
Kṣatra|dharmā Sindhu|pateś chittvā ketana|kārmuke
nārācair daśabhiḥ kruddhaḥ sarva|marmasv atāḍayat.
ath' ânyad dhanur ādāya Saindhavaḥ kṛta|hastavat
vivyādha Kṣatradharmāṇaṃ raṇe sarv'|āyasaiḥ śaraiḥ.
Yuyutsuṃ Pāṇḍav'|ârthāya yatamānaṃ mahā|ratham
Subāhur bhrātaraṃ śūraṃ yatto Droṇād avārayat.
Subāhoḥ su|dhanur bāṇau vyasyataḥ parigh'|ôpamau
Yuyutsuḥ śita|pītābhyāṃ kṣurābhyām acchinad bhujau.
25.15 rājānaṃ Pāṇḍava|śreṣṭhaṃ dharm'|ātmānaṃ Yudhiṣṭhiram
vel" êva sāgaraṃ kṣubdhaṃ Madra|rāṭ samavārayat.
taṃ Dharma|rājo bahubhir marma|bhidbhir avākirat

Spying Bhima in the distance Durmárshana raised his 25.5
bow and fired and rode off to meet him in combat and
thus make safe Drona's life. Mad as Death come to this rite
of blood, he heaped arrows upon Bhima's head, and as he
rushed towards him Bhima stung him back with arrows of
his own. So it was that the pandemonium began once again.

On each side were heroes mighty and wise and loyal to
the wishes of their kings. They stood face to face with their
foes and none of them any longer feared for his own fate or
feared for the fate of the kingdom.

O majesty. First it was Shini's son who rode bold and
ablaze across the plain and while it was Drona whom he
sought none but Krita·varman stood in his path. They met
in fury as volley struck volley and the two of them came
at one another mad as elephants in must. Kshatra·dharman 25.10
bore down upon the prince of Sindhu, but he was ready
for him and he raised his mighty bow and drove his great
foe back and away from Drona beneath a flock of whetted
shafts. Fury blazed up in Kshatra·dharman. He split the bow
held in the prince's hands and tore holes in his banner and
sent ten heavy shafts through all the joints in the crafting
of his armor. But in the dance of battle Sáindhava was still
light on his feet and he swept up another bow and the
arrows cast in iron that he loosed found their target. On
came bold and strong Yuyútsu loyal to the Pándava cause
and brother to the warrior Subáhu, who stood ready to meet
him. Beneath a hail of his kin's shafts Yuyútsu raised high his
own fine bow and struck Subáhu in both of his arms with
twin arrows strong as a gate's bolts and tipped in gleaming
burrs. Elsewhere like a barque weathering the stormy sea 25.15

Madr'|ēśas taṃ catuḥ|ṣaṣṭyā śarair viddhv" ânadad bhṛśam.
tasya nānadataḥ ketum uccakarta ca kārmukam
kṣurābhyāṃ Pāṇḍavo jyeṣṭhas tata uccukruśur janāḥ.

tath" âiva rājā Bāhlīko rājānaṃ Drupadaṃ śaraiḥ
ādravantaṃ sah'|ânīkaḥ sah'|ânīkaṃ nyavārayat.
tad yuddham abhavad ghoraṃ vṛddhayoḥ saha|senayoḥ
yathā mahā|yūtha|payor dvipayoḥ samprabhinnayoḥ.

25.20 Vind'|Ânuvindāv Āvantyau Virāṭaṃ Matsyam ārcchatām
saha|sainyau sah'|ânīkaṃ yath" Êndr|Âgnī purā Balim.
tad utpiñjalakaṃ yuddham āsīd dev'|âsur'|ôpamam
Matsyānāṃ Kekayaiḥ sārdham a|bhīt'|âśva|ratha|dvipam.

Nākuliṃ tu Śatānīkaṃ bhūta|karmā sabhā|patiḥ
asyantam iṣu|jālāni yāntaṃ Droṇād avārayat.
tato Nakula|dāy'|ādas tribhir bhallaiḥ su|saṃśitaiḥ
cakre vi|bāhu|śirasaṃ Bhūtakarmāṇam āhave.
Sutasomaṃ tu vikrāntam āyāntaṃ taṃ śar'|âughiṇaṃ
Droṇāy' âbhimukhaṃ vīraṃ Viviṃśatir avārayat.

25.25 Sutasomas tu saṃkruddhaḥ sva|pitṛvyam a|jihma|gaiḥ
Viviṃśatiṃ śarair viddhvā n' âbhyavartata daṃśitaḥ.

the Madra monarch fought with the best of the Pándavas Yudhi·shthira, whose essence is the order of things. The righteous king buried the lord of the Madras in a flurry of biting shafts, but then with a cry the Madra lord struck him back hard a full four and sixty times. Nonetheless Pandu's will would not be bettered and drawing two barbed darts he let them fly and cut Madra's flag away from its pole and knocked the bow from his hands. His victim's cries redoubled. Those who watched roared their acclaim.

At the head of his troops came King Drúpada and it was Bahlíka and his guard whose hail of arrows held him back. These two great men and their soldiers fought a bloody battle. The two kings were like elephants wild and inflamed as they strove to defend their herds. Vinda and Anuvínda 25.20
born in the land of Avánti brought their legions towards the Matsyas led by King Viráta as Bali once led his army against Agni and Indra. And when Kékaya met Matsya the violence was as great as when god ever met demon, for fear rode in that battle with no one, not in saddle nor palanquin nor car.

Down came Shatáníka son of Nákula, weaving nets of arrows across the sky, and it was Bhuta·karman lord of the halls who stood firm to meet him. But Nákula's heir aimed three of his ironclad arrows with a perfect eye and when he loosed his bowstring they flew and took Bhuta·karman's head and two arms from his body. Suta·soma also fought his way towards Drona, dashing forward in a cloud of his arrows. It was his father's brother Vivínshati this time who slowed his valiant assault. His blood fired by the heat of 25.25
battle, Suta·soma was poised to strike a death blow, yet when

atha Bhīmarathaḥ Śālvam āśu|gair āyasaiḥ śitaiḥ
ṣaḍbhiḥ s'|âśva|niyantāram anayad Yama|sādanam.
Śrutakarmāṇam āyāntaṃ mayūra|sa|dṛśair hayaiḥ
Caitrasenir mahā|rāja tava pautraṃ nyavārayat.
tau pautrau tava dur|dharṣau paras|para|vadh'|âiṣiṇau
pitṝṇām artha|siddhy|arthaṃ cakratur yuddham uttamam.
tiṣṭhantam agre taṃ dṛṣṭvā Prativindhyaṃ mah"|āhave
Drauṇir mānaṃ pituḥ kurvan mārgaṇaiḥ samavārayat.
25.30 taṃ kruddhaḥ prativivyādha Prativindhyaḥ śitaiḥ śaraiḥ
siṃha|lāṅgūla|lakṣmāṇaṃ pitur arthe vyavasthitam.
pravapann iva bījāni bīja|kāle nara'|rṣabha
Drauṇāyaniṃ Draupadeyāḥ śara|varṣair avākiran.
Ārjuniṃ Śrutakīrtiṃ tu Draupadeyaṃ mahā|rathaṃ
Droṇāy' âbhimukhaṃ yāntaṃ Dauḥśāsanir avārayat.
tasya Kṛṣṇa|samaḥ Kārṣṇis tribhir bhallaiḥ su|saṃśitaiḥ
dhanur dhvajaṃ ca sūtaṃ ca chittvā Droṇ'|ântikaṃ yayau.
yas tu śūratamo rājan ubhayoḥ senayor mataḥ
taṃ Paṭaccarahantāraṃ Lakṣmaṇaḥ samavārayat.
25.35 sa Lakṣmaṇasy' êṣv|asanaṃ chittvā lakṣma ca Bhārata
lakṣmaṇe śara|jālāni visṛjan bahv aśobhata.
Vikarṇas tu mahā|prājño Yājñaseniṃ Śikhaṇḍinam
paryavārayad āyāntaṃ yuvānaṃ samare yuvā.
tatas tam iṣu|jālena Yājñaseniḥ samāvṛṇot

he had found his uncle with his trueflying shafts he chose not to ride in and finish him off. Six of Bhima·ratha's swift and iron shafts sent Shalva down to lodge at Yama's abode, and his horse and driver followed close behind. Tending steeds bright as peacocks Shruta·karman rode towards us too and his opponent o my king was none other than your other grandson Chaitraséni. Each of these two of your formidable heirs strove hard, as each sought the other's death and each had the hopes of a father for which to fight.

While the battle raged about him Drona's son saw Prativíndhya standing near and minded of his own father's will he loosed his arrows. Flaring up in anger Prativíndhya sent his 25.30
own sharp darts against Ashvattháman where he stood firm in his father's cause beneath the banner of the lion's tail. At the same time o great lord the Draupadéyas scattered their arrows outpouring from their bows like seeds strewn in the spring. As Shruta·kirti the mighty son of Dráupadi and Árjuna made his way towards Drona it was Duhshásana's son who was there to meet him. The Dark One's equal born of the god's sister sent three wellaimed arrows cleaving through Dauhshásani's bow and standard and then rode on ever closer to where Drona would be found. The hero of heroes Patácchara·hantri whose honor is known by the men of both the armies bore down, o king, upon Lákshmana.

Lákshmana managed to hold him back for a moment. 25.35
But o Bhárata the bow that Lákshmana held was cracked in two as his standard fell and his foe sent a dazzling tide of arrows down upon him. Then youth met youth as Shikhándin son of Yajnya·sena bore down upon quickwitted Vikárna. The priest's son cast a veil of darts upon your own

vidhūya tad|bāṇa|jālaṃ babhau tava suto balī.
Aṅgado 'bhimukhaṃ vīram Uttamaujasam āhave
Droṇāy' âbhimukhaṃ yāntaṃ śar'|âugheṇa nyavārayat.
sa samprahāras tumulas tayoḥ puruṣa|siṃhayoḥ
sainikānāṃ ca sarveṣāṃ tayoś ca prīti|vardhanaḥ.
25.40 Durmukhas tu mah"|êṣv|āso vīraṃ Purujitaṃ balī
Droṇāy' âbhimukhaṃ yāntaṃ vatsa|dantair avārayat.
sa Durmukhaṃ bhruvor madhye nārācen' âbhyatāḍayat
tasya tad vibabhau vaktraṃ sa|nālam iva paṅka|jam.
Karṇas tu Kaikayān bhrātṝn pañca lohitaka|dhvajān
Droṇāy' âbhimukhaṃ yātāñ śara|varṣair avārayat.
te c' âinaṃ bhṛśa|saṃtaptāḥ śara|varṣair avākiran
sa ca tāṃś chādayām āsa śara|jālaiḥ punaḥ punaḥ.
n' âiva Karṇo na te pañca dadṛśur bāṇa|saṃvṛtāḥ
s'|âśva|sūta|dhvaja|rathāḥ paras|para|śar'|ācitāḥ.
25.45 putras te Durjayaś c' âiva Jayaś ca Vijayaś ca ha
Nīla|Kāśya|ja|Yatsenāṃs trayas trīn pratyavārayan.
tad yuddham abhavad ghoram īkṣitṛ|prīti|vardhanam
siṃha|vyāghra|tarakṣūṇāṃ yatha" ṛkṣa|mahiṣa'|ṛṣabhaiḥ.
Kṣemadhūrti|Bṛhantau tau bhrātarau Sātvataṃ yudhi
Droṇāy' âbhimukhaṃ yāntaṃ śarais tīkṣṇais tatakṣatuḥ.
tayos tasya ca tad yuddham
atyl|adbhutam iv' âbhavat
siṃhasya dvipa|mukhyābhyāṃ
prabhinnābhyāṃ yathā vane.

but Vikárna shook it off in a fiery display of might. Ángada too made for Drona and Uttamáujas drove him back with the force of his volleys. Two lions they were and they and all their soldiery fought a harsh struggle that was a sight awesome to behold.

Valiant Púrujit rode at Drona, and it was the might and 25.40
the hooked darts of the great archer Dúrmukha that slowed his attack. Púrujit fired a single arrow and it landed dead between Dúrmukha's brows. There his face hung like a lotus atop its stem. Beneath the red flashes of their pennants the five brothers Kaikéya rode for Drona and it was Karna who sent his showers of wood down upon their heads. Blasted by the force of his attack, they sent back showers of their own before Karna hid them all once again behind the torrents flowing from his bow. Those reeds closed over them all, and soon Karna and the brothers disappeared as their arrows heaped up above drivers, flags and chariots.
Two trios struck one another as your own sons Dúrjaya, 25.45
Jaya and Víjaya came against Nila, the prince of Kashi and Yatséna. Their encounter was a fierce one and we watched in wonder, for it was as if a lion, a tiger and a hyena had met a buffalo, a bull and a bear. Sátvata too made for Drona but the brothers Kshema·dhurti and Brihánta whittled him with their keen darts. It was like two elephants wild with the season finding a lion in the woods and it too was a wondrous sight to see.

rājānaṃ tu tath" Âmbaṣṭham
ekaṃ yuddh'|âbhinandinam
Cedi|rājaḥ śarān asyan
kruddho Droṇād avārayat.

25.50 tam Ambaṣṭho 'sthi|bhedinyā niravidhyac chalākayā
sa tyaktvā sa|śaraṃ cāpaṃ rathād bhūmim upāgamat.
Vārddhakṣemiṃ tu Vārṣṇeyaṃ Kṛpaḥ Śāradvataḥ śaraiḥ
a|kṣudraḥ kṣudrakair Droṇāt kruddha|rūpam avārayat.
yudhyantau Kṛpa|Vārṣṇeyau ye 'paśyaṃś citra|yodhinau
te yuddh'|āsakta|manaso n' ânyāṃ bubudhire kriyām.
Saumadattis tu rājānaṃ Maṇimantam a|tandritam
paryavārayad āyāntaṃ yaśo Droṇasya vardhayan.
sa Saumadattes tvaritaś citr'|êṣv|asana|ketane
punaḥ patākāṃ sūtaṃ ca cchatraṃ c' âpātayad rathāt.

25.55 ath' āplutya rathāt tūrṇaṃ Yūpaketur a|mitra|hā
s'|âśva|sūta|dhvaja|rathaṃ taṃ cakarta var'|âsinā.
rathaṃ ca svaṃ samāsthāya
dhanur ādāya c' âparam
svayaṃ yacchan hayān, rājan,
vyadhamat Pāṇḍavīṃ camūm.
Pāṇḍyam Indram iv' āyāntam asurān prati dur|jayam
samarthaḥ sāyak'|âughena Vṛṣaseno nyavārayat.

The king of the Chedis fought fiercely and fired high to keep back from Drona Ambáshtha, devotee of war. But 25.50
Ambáshtha struck the king with a single marrowpiercing bolt carved from bone and he dropped his bow and quiver and fell from his chariot to the earth. And Kripa of the high stock of Sharádvat firing reeds thin as splinters drove back from Drona's circle the wrathful Vrishni Varddhakshémi. Dazzling fighters both, the sight of them locked in combat was a vision to eclipse all others and any who watched were unable to look away. Glory it was that Bhuri·shravas son of Soma·datta earnt for Drona as he made his stand against the tireless King Mánimat. But Mánimat cracked his whip across the backs of his steeds and knocking away his enemy's flashing bow sent his banner, driver and parasol flying clear
from his car. With a blow from his tempered sword vengeful 25.55
Bhuri·shravas sent Mánimat tumbling from his chariot and then hastily despatched his steed and standard and the very planks on which he had stood. Planting his feet firmly he took up another bow, gathered the reins and drove his horses straight, my king, for the Pándava line. Hardy Pandya flew at Vrisha·sena like Indra flying against the demon horde, but Vrisha·sena stilled his passage with a cluster of his shafts.

gadā|parigha|nistriṃśa|paṭṭiś'|âyo|van'|ôpalaiḥ
kaḍaṅgarair bhuśuṇḍībhiḥ prāsais tomara|sāyakaiḥ
musalair mudgaraiś cakrair bhiṇḍipāla|paraśvadhaiḥ
pāṃsu|vāt'|âgni|salilair bhasma|loṣṭha|tṛṇa|drumaiḥ
25.60 ārujan prarujan bhañjan nighnan vidrāvayan kṣipan
senāṃ vibhīṣayann āyād Droṇa|prepsur Ghaṭotkacaḥ.
tam tu nānā|praharaṇair nānā|yuddha|viśeṣaṇaiḥ
rākṣasaṃ rākṣasaḥ kruddhaḥ samājaghne hy Alambusaḥ.
tayos tad abhavad yuddhaṃ rakṣo|grāmaṇi|mukhyayoḥ
tādṛg yādṛk purā vṛttaṃ Śambar'|âmara|rājayoḥ.

evaṃ dvandva|śatāny āsan ratha|vāraṇa|vājinām
padātīnāṃ ca bhadraṃ te tava teṣāṃ ca saṃkulam.
n' âitādṛśo dṛṣṭa|pūrvaḥ saṃgrāmo n' âiva ca śrutaḥ
Droṇasy' â|bhāva|bhāve tu prasaktānāṃ yath" âbhavat.
25.65 idaṃ ghoram idaṃ citram idaṃ raudram iti prabho
tatra yuddhāny adṛśyanta pratatāni bahūni ca.

DHṚTARĀṢṬRA uvāca.

26.1 TEṢV EVAṂ saṃnivṛtteṣu pratyudyāteṣu bhāgaśaḥ
kathaṃ yuyudhire Pārthā māmakāś ca tarasvinaḥ?
kim Arjunaś c' âpy akarot Saṃśaptaka|balaṃ prati?
Saṃśaptakā vā Pārthasya kim akurvata, Saṃjaya?

With blocks and bars and knives and spears and stones and iron and wood, and with daggers and hammers and wheels and sticks and clubs, with sand and wind, fire, water, with piles of ash and clods of earth and palm trees
pulled from the soil, Ghatótkacha smashed and blasted and 25.60
crushed and scattered the terrified army before him.* On he went in search of Drona. But fiend against fiend Alámbusa came to meet him and as he came he hurled at him his own vast arsenal of weapons and missiles. These two were the greatest of their strange stock and they fought a battle akin to the contest of old between Shámbara and the king of the deathless gods.

In tumult and beauty the war raged between the Pándavas and your own. In their hundreds soldiers and riders and elephants and chariots fought duels in a gathering the like of which had been neither known nor seen before. At stake was the survival or death of Drona and it was on his
fate that we all hung. O great king. Such were the many 25.65
battles spread out across the plain. And they were awful and manycolored and cruel.

DHRITA·RASHTRA spoke.

As DUEL AFTER duel played out that day, how did my 26.1
own bold children fare against the sons of Pritha? O Sánjaya. What befell the Beholden at Árjuna's hands? And him at theirs?

SAMJAYA uvāca.

tathā teṣu nivṛtteṣu pratyudyāteṣu bhāgaśaḥ
svayam abhyadravad Bhīmaṃ nāg'|ânīkena te sutaḥ.
sa nāga iva nāgena go|vṛṣeṇ' êva go|vṛṣaḥ
samāhūtaḥ svayaṃ rājñā nāg'|ânīkam upādravat.
26.5 sa yuddha|kuśalaḥ Pārtho bāhu|vīryeṇa c' ânvitaḥ
abhinnat kuñjar'|ânīkam a|cireṇ' âiva, māriṣa.
te gajā giri|saṃkāśāḥ kṣarantaḥ sarvato madam
Bhīmasenasya nārācair vimukhā vimadī|kṛtāḥ.
vidhamed abhra|jālāni yathā vāyuḥ samuddhataḥ
vyadhamat tāny anīkāni tath" âiva pavan'|ātma|jaḥ.
sa teṣu visṛjan bāṇān Bhīmo nāgeṣv aśobhata
bhuvaneṣv iva sarveṣu gabhastīn udito raviḥ.
te bhīma|bāṇ'|âbhihatāḥ saṃsyūtā vibabhur gajāḥ
gabhastibhir iv' ârkasya vyomni nānā|balāhakāḥ.
26.10 tathā gajānāṃ kadanaṃ
kurvāṇam anil'|ātma|jam
kruddho Duryodhano 'bhyetya
pratyavidhyac chitaiḥ śaraiḥ.
tataḥ kṣaṇena kṣiti|paṃ kṣata|ja|pratim"|ēkṣaṇaḥ
kṣayaṃ ninīṣur niśitair Bhīmo vivyādha patribhiḥ.
sa śar'|ârpita|sarv'|âṅgaḥ kruddho vivyādha Pāṇḍavam
nārācair arka|raśmy|ābhair Bhīmasenaṃ smayann iva.
tasya nāgaṃ maṇi|mayaṃ ratna|citraṃ dhvaje sthitam
bhallābhyāṃ kārmukaṃ c' âiva kṣipraṃ ciccheda Pāṇḍavaḥ.

SÁNJAYA spoke.

So indeed did hero meet hero. For his part your son Duryódhana led the elephants at his command against Bhima. As when wild beasts spar whether elephants or bulls Bhima heard the king's challenge and rode out to meet his force. O father. The might of Bhima's two arms and the 26.5
wisdom of his warcraft were too much for those creatures. Almost no time passed before Pritha's son broke through the wall of elephants. In musth they streamed from their mountainous heights as Bhima's iron arrows brought them low and stilled their frenzy. Like a wind whirling through rainclouds Bhima son of fire and air simply blew their ranks apart. Radiating arrows through those beasts he shone like the risen sun that casts its beams upon the living world, and like so many dark clouds hanging veined in light those gray beasts were picked out by his deadly shafts. As the 26.10
warrior sprung from the wind wrought destruction upon his herd, Duryódhana came in close and fired at him his sharp arrows. But Bhima's eyes twinkled like drops of blood and he barely paused before sending back his own sharpened and feathered darts to drive Duryódhana into Death's arms. Duryódhana was pierced in every limb. But still he burned with anger, and with a grim smile on his face struck Bhima·sena once again with arrows aglow like rays of the sun. With one shaft Pandu's son tore through the jeweled serpent glittering with gems that adorned Duryódhana's flag, and then with another sliced through the curve of his bow.

Duryodhanaṃ pīḍyamānaṃ dṛṣṭvā Bhīmena, māriṣa,
cukṣobhayiṣur abhyāgād Aṅgo mātaṅgam āsthitaḥ.
26.15 tam āpatantaṃ nāg'|êndram ambu|da|pratima|svanam
kumbh'|ântare Bhīmaseno nārācen' ārdayad bhṛśam.
tasya kāyaṃ vinirbhidya nyamajjad dharaṇī|tale
tataḥ papāta dvi|rado vajr'|āhata iv' âcalaḥ.
tasy' āvarjita|nāgasya mlecchasya ca patiṣyataḥ
śiraś ciccheda bhallena kṣipra|kārī Vṛkodaraḥ.
tasmin nipatite vīre samprādravata sā camūḥ
sambhrānt'|âśva|dvipa|rathā padātīn avamṛdnatī.
tеṣv anīkeṣu sarveṣu vidravatsu samantataḥ
Prāgjyotiṣas tato Bhīmaṃ kuñjareṇa samādravat.
26.20 yena nāgena Maghavān ajayad daitya|dānavān
sa nāga|pravaro Bhīmaṃ sahasā samupādravat.
caraṇābhyām atho dvābhyāṃ saṃhatena kareṇa ca
vyāvṛtta|nayanaḥ kruddhaḥ pramathann iva Pāṇḍavam
Vṛkodara|rathaṃ s'|âśvam a|viśeṣam acūrṇayat.
padbhyāṃ Bhīmo 'py atho dhāvaṃs tasya gātreṣv alīyata
jānann añjalik'|āvedhaṃ n' âpākrāmata Pāṇḍavaḥ.
gātr'|âbhyantara|go bhūtvā kareṇa tāḍayan muhuḥ
kālayām āsa taṃ nāgaṃ vadh'|ākāṅkṣiṇam a|vyayaṃ.
26.25 kulāla|cakravan nāgas tadā tūrṇam ath' âbhramat
nāg'|âyuta|balaḥ śrīmān kālayāno Vṛkodaram.

O sire, all this time Anga had been watching Duryódhana's travails against Bhima from his perch atop his steed and
at that moment rode out to attack. Anga's elephant came 26.15
towards Bhima·sena like a thunderous cloud. But as it came the Pándava sank an arrow deep into its skull and on it tore right through its body and sank into the ground behind it. Like a rock knocked from a ridge by a lightning bolt the creature sagged and buckled beneath its rider and before the man's body could strike the earth Dogbelly deftly severed the head of that barbarian king with a single lethal shaft. As soon as the mighty Anga fell, the whole rest of his division of horses and elephants and chariots scattered and fled, and more soldiers lost their lives in the crush of foot wheel and hoof.

While all around him line upon line broke and fell away, one man stood his ground. Prag·jyótisha spurred his bull at
Bhima and it pounded towards him like the creature upon 26.20
whose back Indra had ridden to victory over the spawn of Diti and Danu. Coiling its truck and rolling its eyes the wild beast leapt at the Pándava and brought its two forelegs down hard upon his car, crushing it to splinters and killing all his horses. Bhima was now on foot and he slipped and disappeared beneath the forequarters of the creature. The Pándava knew full well that another's arrow had wounded the beast and he did not run but darted alongside it and struck it sharply with his hand, riling the vast bloodcrazed
beast still further. At his blow the creature suddenly spun 26.25
its huge and mighty bulk about like a potter's wheel and made straight for Vrikódara. Now unsheltered Bhima stood within inches of its great head and it swung its trunk and

Bhīmo 'pi niṣkramya tataḥ su|pratīk'|âgrato 'bhavat
Bhīmaṃ kareṇ' âvanamya jānubhyām abhyatāḍayat.
grīvāyāṃ veṣṭayitv" âinaṃ sa gajo hantum aihata
kara|veṣṭaṃ Bhīmaseno bhramaṃ dattvā vyamocayat.
punar gātrāṇi nāgasya praviveśa Vṛkodaraḥ.
yāvat pratigaj'|āyātaṃ sva|bale pratyavaikṣata
Bhīmo 'pi nāga|gātrebhyo viniḥsṛty' âpayāj javāt.
26.30 tataḥ sarvasya sainyasya nādaḥ samabhavan mahān
aho dhig nihato Bhīmaḥ kuñjareṇ' êti māriṣa.
tena nādena saṃtrastā Pāṇḍavānām anīkinī
sahas" âbhyadravad rājan yatra tasthau Vṛkodaraḥ.
tato Yudhiṣṭhiro rājā hataṃ matvā Vṛkodaram
Bhagadattaṃ sa|Pāñcālaḥ sarvataḥ samavārayat.
taṃ rathaṃ rathināṃ śreṣṭhāḥ parivārya paraṃ|tapāḥ
avākirañ śarais tīkṣṇaiḥ śataśo 'tha sahasraśaḥ.
sa vighātaṃ pṛṣatkānām aṅkuśena samācaran
gajena Pāṇḍu|Pāñcālān vyadhamat parvat'|ēśvaraḥ.
26.35 tad adbhutam apaśyāma Bhagadattasya saṃyuge
tathā vṛddhasya caritaṃ kuñjareṇa, viśāṃ pate.
tato rājā Daśārṇānāṃ Prāgjyotiṣam upādravat
tiryag|yātena nāgena sa|maden' āśu|gāminā.
tayor yuddhaṃ samabhavan nāgayor bhīma|rūpayoḥ
sa|pakṣayoḥ parvatayor yathā sa|drumayoḥ purā.
Prāgjyotiṣa|pater nāgaḥ saṃnivṛty' âpavṛtya ca
pārśve Daśārṇ'|âdhipater bhittvā nāgam aghātayat.
tomaraiḥ sūrya|raśmy|ābhair Bhagadatto 'tha saptabhiḥ
jaghāna dvi|rada|sthaṃ taṃ śatruṃ pracalit'|āsanam.

struck him on his knees then wrapped it around his neck and began to strangle him to death. But Bhima·sena twisted about and slithered from its noose and leapt down once more beneath its body. He waited and watched until his own army's elephant line was near enough, and then he slipped from his hiding place and made quickly for its protection.

It was at that moment my lord that the cry went up for 26.30
all to hear. Bhima had died, they said, beneath the feet of an elephant. Panic at the words flew through the Pándava ranks my king, and they all rushed to the place where Dogbelly had stood. King Yudhi·shthira heard that his brother was dead and brought the Panchálas in a great circle about Bhaga·datta. Around Bhaga·datta's chariot there now stood the deadliest and greatest of his enemy. They sent a hundred then a thousand arrows up into the sky.

Swinging his hooked goad the mountain king gathered up the fleet darts as they fell and then spurred on his bull at
the Pandus and Panchálas who stood before him. O lord of 26.35
these fields, the bravery with which old Bhaga·datta fought from his steed was awesome to watch. First to meet him was the king of the Land of the Ten Lakes, who cut galloping across the plain towards him on the back of his own wild beast. The two monstrous animals clashed like the mountains mantled in trees and borne on wings in battles of old. King Prag·jyótisha turned his creature about and it stepped aside as the other came past and it drove its tusk to make a mortal wound through the flank of Dashárnava's steed. The palanquin slipped from the animal's back, and with seven spears like the rays of the sun Bhaga·datta transfixed the foe that it held.

26.40 vyavacchidya tu rājānaṃ Bhagadattaṃ Yudhiṣṭhiraḥ
rath'|ânīkena mahatā sarvataḥ paryavārayat.
sa kuñjara|stho rathibhiḥ śuśubhe sarvato vṛtaḥ
parvate vana|madhya|stho jvalann iva hut'|âśanaḥ.
maṇḍalaṃ sarvataḥ śliṣṭaṃ rathinām ugra|dhanvinām
kiratāṃ śara|varṣāṇi sa nāgaḥ paryavartata.
tataḥ Prāgjyotiṣo rājā parigṛhya mahā|gajam
preṣayām āsa sahasā Yuyudhāna|rathaṃ prati.
Śineḥ pautrasya tu rathaṃ parigṛhya mahā|dvipaḥ
aticikṣepa vegena Yuyudhānas tv apākramat.
26.45 bṛhataḥ Saindhavān aśvān samutthāpya tu sārathiḥ
tasthau Sātyakim āsādya samplutas taṃ rathaṃ punaḥ.
sa tu labdhv" ântaraṃ nāgas tvarito ratha|maṇḍalāt
niścakrāma tataḥ sarvān paricikṣepa pārthivān.
te tv āśu|gatinā tena trāsyamānā nara'|ṛṣabhāḥ
tam ekaṃ dvi|radaṃ saṃkhye menire śataśo nṛ|pāḥ.
te gaja|sthena kālyante Bhagadattena Pāṇḍavāḥ
Airāvata|sthena yathā deva|rājena dānavāḥ.
teṣāṃ pradravatāṃ bhīmaḥ Pāñcālānām itas tataḥ
gaja|vāji|kṛtaḥ śabdaḥ su|mahān samajāyata.
26.50 Bhagadattena samare kālyamāneṣu Pāṇḍuṣu
Prāgjyotiṣam abhikruddhaḥ punar Bhīmaḥ samabhyayāt.
tasy' âbhidravato vāhān hasta|muktena vāriṇā
siktvā vyatrāsayan nāgas te Pārtham aharaṃs tataḥ.
tatas tam abhyayāt tūrṇaṃ Ruciparvā Kṛtī|sutaḥ
pravarṣan śara|varṣeṇa ratha|stho 'ntaka|saṃnibhaḥ.

But as he did so Yudhi·shthira brought his great division of chariots closer to King Bhaga·datta, cutting him off entirely from the Kurus. Surrounded by warriors in their chariots Bhaga·datta blazed atop his steed like a fire dancing in a mountain wood. The beast prowled at the center of that dense and terrible circle of warriors as they raised their bows and sent up showers of arrows. King Prag·jyótisha gathered in the reins and drove the great elephant straight at the chariot of Yuyudhána. The beast grabbed the car still holding Shini's son and hurled it violently back, sending Yuyudhána spinning into retreat. But his horseman mastered 26.40
the strong Sindhu steeds and made for Sátyaki and there drew to a halt at his side. As he did, Bhaga·datta's elephant found an opening and rushed through and past the ring of chariots and crashed among the soldiers behind. 26.45

They scattered in all directions. Even the mightiest of men felt the pulse of terror and though a single beast thundered at their heels they thought it a hundredhead of soldiers in pursuit. In olden times the king of the gods had mounted his elephant Airávata and beaten back the demons, and now Bhaga·datta beat back the Pándavas from atop his own steed as a vast and horrible noise gathered from the hooves and feet of the Panchálas' horses and elephants fleeing wherever they could. With the Pandus racing past him Bhima commandeered another chariot and charged once more in a mad attack at Prag·jyótisha, but when he was close enough the creature doused his steeds in a trumpet of water from its trunk and they pulled him off course in panic. Then it was Ruchi·parvan son of Kritin who attacked, tall as Death in his car. He let down a shower of arrows. But with a single 26.50

tataḥ sa Ruciparvāṇaṃ śareṇ' ānata|parvaṇā
su|varcāḥ parvata|patir ninye Vaivasvata|kṣayaṃ.
tasmin nipatite vīre Saubhadro Draupadī|sutāḥ
Cekitāno Dhṛṣṭaketur Yuyutsuś c' ārdayan dvipam.
26.55 ta enaṃ śara|dhārābhir dhārābhir iva toya|dāḥ
siṣicur bhairavān nādān vinadanto jighāṃsavaḥ.
tataḥ pārṣṇy|aṅkuś'|âṅguṣṭhaiḥ kṛtinā codito dvipaḥ
prasārita|karaḥ prāyāt stabdha|karṇ'|ēkṣaṇo drutam.
so 'dhiṣṭhāya padā vāhān Yuyutsoḥ sūtam ārujat
Yuyutsus tu rathād rājann apākrāmat tvar'|ânvitaḥ.
tataḥ Pāṇḍava|yodhās te nāga|rājaṃ śarair drutam
siṣicur bhairavān nādān vinadanto jighāṃsavaḥ.

putras tu tava sambhrāntaḥ Saubhadrasy' āpluto ratham
sa kuñjara|stho visṛjann iṣūn ariṣu pārthivaḥ.
26.60 babhau raśmīn iv' Ādityo bhuvaneṣu samutsṛjan.
tam Ārjunir dvā|daśabhir Yuyutsur daśabhiḥ śaraiḥ
tribhis tribhir Draupadeyā Dhṛṣṭaketuś ca vivyadhuḥ.
so 'ri|yatn'|ârpitair bāṇair ācito dvi|rado babhau
saṃsyūta iva sūryasya raśmibhir jala|do mahān.
niyantuḥ śilpa|yatnābhyāṃ prerito 'ri|śar'|ârditaḥ
pariciksepa tān nāgaḥ sa ripūn savya|dakṣiṇam.
go|pāla iva daṇḍena yathā paśu|gaṇān vane
āveṣṭayata tāṃ senāṃ Bhagadattas tathā muhuḥ.
26.65 kṣipraṃ śyen'|âbhipannānāṃ vāyasānām iva svanaḥ
babhūva Pāṇḍaveyānāṃ bhṛśaṃ vidravatāṃ svanaḥ.

wellfashioned shaft the splendored mountain king sent Ruchi·parvan away to the broken harbor of the sun.* Another hero dead, and then it was the turn of Saubhádra to attack. He came against the beast with the other sons of Dráupadi and with Chekitána, Dhrishta·ketu and Yuyútsu. Like 26.55
clouds streaming rain they poured sheets of arrows down upon their quarry and bellowed and bayed for his blood. With his thumbs and his heels and his hook Prag·jyótisha held his steed fast and drove it on and it went quickly with its ears rigid and its eyes fixed and its trunk winding in the air, and then my king it brought down its foot on Yuyútsu's horses and crushed the life from his driver as Yuyútsu leapt in terror from his car, and still my lord came the baying and the bellowing as once more the Pándava warriors poured arrows flowing down upon that king of beasts.

I saw your son fly past Saubhádra's car as from his high
seat King Bhaga·datta cast down arrows upon his foes and 26.60
shone there bright as the sun with its beams fanned through the living world. They struck back at him, Árjuna's son with twelve arrows and Yuyútsu with ten, and with three and three again the Draupadéyas and Dhrishta·ketu found their target. Thick with the spines driven into him by his foes the elephant shone like a great raincloud woven with the rays of the sun. But with mettle and skill Prag·jyótisha drove the creature on, and though suffering from their blows still the beast sent its foes flying left and right as it went. For a time Bhaga·datta drove their army as a cowherd drives with his
staff his animals through the woods, and the noise of the 26.65
progeny of Pandu in desperate flight rang like the cries of a bird snatched in an eagle's talons.

sa nāga|rājaḥ pravar'|âṅkuś'|āhataḥ
    purā sa|pakṣo 'dri|varo yathā, nṛ|pa.
bhayaṃ tadā ripuṣu samādadhad bhṛśaṃ
    vaṇig|janānāṃ kṣubhito yath" ârṇavaḥ.
tato dhvanir dvi|rada|rath'|âśva|pārthivair
    bhayād dravadbhir janito 'ti|bhairavaḥ
kṣitiṃ viyad dyāṃ vidiśo diśas tathā
    samāvṛṇot pārthiva saṃyuge tataḥ.
sa tena nāga|pravareṇa pārthivo
    bhṛśaṃ jagāhe dviṣatām anīkinīm
purā su|guptāṃ vibudhair iv' āhave
    Virocano deva|varūthinīm iva.
bhṛśaṃ vavau jvalana|sakho viyad rajaḥ
    samāvṛṇon muhur api c' âiva sainikān
tam eka|nāgaṃ gaṇaśo yathā gajān
    samantato drutam atha menire janāḥ.

SAMJAYA uvāca.

27.1 YAN MĀṂ PĀRTHASYA saṃgrāme karmāṇi paripṛcchasi
tac chṛṇuṣva mahā|bhāga Pārtho yad akaron mṛdhe.
rajo dṛṣṭvā samudbhūtaṃ śrutvā ca jana|nisvanam
Bhagadatte vikurvāṇe Kaunteyaḥ Kṛṣṇam abravīt.
«yathā Prāgjyotiṣo rājā gajena Madhu|sūdana
tvaramāṇo 'bhiniṣkrānto dhruvaṃ tasy' âiṣa nisvanaḥ.
Indrād an|avaraḥ saṃkhye gaja|yāna|viśāradaḥ
prathamo vā dvitīyo vā pṛthivyām iti me matiḥ.
27.5 sa c' âpi dvi|rada|śreṣṭhaḥ sadā|pratigajo yudhi
sarva|śastr'|âtigaḥ saṃkhye kṛta|karmā jita|klamaḥ.
sahaḥ śastra|nipātānām agni|sparśasya c' ân|agha
sa Pāṇḍava|balaṃ sarvam ady' âiko nāśayiṣyati.
na c' āvābhyām ṛte 'nyo 'sti śaktas taṃ pratibādhitum

O king. Goaded on by that curved hook the lord of the elephant kingdom like a winged mountain of legend sent fear among his foes. They were like seafarers on a wild ocean. O majesty a great thunder born of the terror and the horses and chariots and elephants and kings that churned the plain in flight spread across the earth and filled all the zones of the sky. A mighty beast had carried one king deep into the fold of his despisers as once long ago Viróchana had been enrobed in the protections of his priests and traveled deep in battle into the army of the gods. All across the plain, dust and fire billowed and blew and engulfed the men as they fought, and somewhere among them but a single beast seemed to multiply into a hundred of its kind.

SÁNJAYA spoke.

O ILLUSTRIOUS KING you asked of Partha's acts in the war. 27.1
Listen now and I will tell you what he did that day.

As Bhaga·datta flew through the Pándavas' midst the risen dust filled Árjuna's eyes and the cries of men his ears. He turned and spoke to Krishna.

"O slayer of Madhu. King Bhaga·datta flies abroad on his steed: this sound presages his work. An elephantrider of the caliber of the gods, he has few if any peers on this
earth whom I could name. The tusked beast he rides is one 27.5
of the strongest of its kind, an animal of war unbowed by fatigue and untamed by any blade raised against it. It heeds neither the bite of swords nor the lick of flame for to be sure o Pure One it could destroy by itself this wide army of Pandu's sons. There are only two who can withstand it and they are you and I. So let us make haste for the King of Lights. He is an arrant believer in his strength and his

tvaramāṇas tato yāhi yataḥ Prāgjyotiṣ'|âdhipaḥ.
dṛptaṃ saṃkhye dvipa|balād vayasā c' âpi vismitam
ady' âinaṃ preṣayiṣyāmi Bala|hantuḥ priy'|âtithim.»
vacanād atha Kṛṣṇas tu prayayau Savya|sācinaḥ
dāryate Bhagadattena yatra Pāṇḍava|vāhinī.
27.10 taṃ prayāntaṃ tataḥ paścād āhvayanto mahā|rathāḥ
Saṃśaptakāḥ samārohan sahasrāṇi catur|daśa.
daś' âiva tu sahasrāṇi Trigartānāṃ mahā|rathāḥ
catvāri ca sahasrāṇi Vāsudevasya c' ânugāḥ.
dīryamāṇāṃ camūṃ dṛṣṭvā Bhagadattena, māriṣa,
āhūyamānasya ca tair abhavadd hṛdayaṃ dvidhā
kiṃ nu śreyas|karaṃ karma bhaved ady' êti cintayan
iha vā vinivarteyaṃ, gaccheyaṃ vā Yudhiṣṭhiram?
tasya buddhyā vicāry' âivam Arjunasya Kur'|ûdvaha
abhavad bhūyasī buddhiḥ Saṃśaptaka|vadhe sthirā.
27.15 sa saṃnivṛttaḥ sahasā kapi|pravara|ketanaḥ
eko ratha|sahasrāṇi nihantuṃ Vāsavī raṇe.
sā hi Duryodhanasy' āsīn matiḥ Karṇasya c' ôbhayoḥ
Arjunasya vadh'|ôpāye tena dvaidham akalpayat.
sa tu dolāyamāno 'bhūd dvaidhī|bhāvena Pāṇḍavaḥ
vadhena tu nar'|âgryāṇām akarot tāṃ mṛṣā tadā.
tataḥ śata|sahasrāṇi śarāṇāṃ nata|parvaṇām
vyasṛjann Arjune rājan Saṃśaptaka|mahā|rathāḥ.
n' âiva Kuntī|sutaḥ Pārtho n' âiva Kṛṣṇo Janārdanaḥ
na hayā na ratho rājan dṛśyante sma śaraiś citāḥ.
27.20 yadā moham anuprāptaḥ siṣvide hi Janārdanaḥ
tatas tān prāyaśaḥ Pārtho brahm'|âstreṇa nijaghnivān.
śataśaḥ pāṇayaś chinnāḥ s'|êṣu|jyā|tala|kārmukāḥ

steed. Wild though he is I will send him as a welcome guest to the home of Bala's killer."

Krishna heard the Left Handed Archer and brought the chariot around to where the Pándavas were being forced asunder beneath Bhaga·datta's attack. As he did so, from 27.10
behind they heard the mocking cries of the Beholden riding after in pursuit. Fourteen thousand they were, ten thousand Tri·gartas and four thousand others who had once followed Vasudéva. Watching his army buckling beneath Bhaga·datta's onslaught while his challengers jeered at his back Árjuna's heart was pulled in two, my king. He asked himself whether he ought to go to or from his brother's side and his mind raced between the two courses before him, until o sire of the Kurus it was his will to fight the Beholden that proved the sterner. The banner of the monkey fluttered above his 27.15
head as Indra's son turned briskly about to make for the myriad chariots ranged behind him. This was exactly what Duryódhana had hoped for. Árjuna's confusion had been part of their plan. He had resolved his dilemma and chosen to seek the blood of his great foes, but in doing so he sprung their trap.

The mighty Beholden loosed at Árjuna a seething mass of wellwrought arrows and beneath it the son of Kuntí and Krishna the reaver of men and their horses and their chariot all disappeared from view. Then, as panic gripped Janárdana 27.20
and sweat broke out on his brow, Pritha's son invoked the weapon of Brahma and blasted the sky all but clear. His foes began to fall in their hundreds. Severed hands still holding bows, bowstrings and arrows, and poles and horses and drivers fell to the earth. Elephants collapsed beneath dead

ketavo vājinaḥ sūtā rathinaś c' âpatan kṣitau.
drum'|âcal'|âgr'|âmbu|dharaiḥ sama|kāyāḥ su|kalpitāḥ
hat'|ārohāḥ kṣitau petur dvipāḥ Pārtha|śar'|āhatāḥ.
vipraviddha|kuthā|ballāś chinna|bhāṇḍāḥ par'|âsavaḥ
s'|ārohās tura|gāḥ petur mathitā mārgaṇair bhṛśam.
sa'|rṣṭi|prās'|âsi|nakharāḥ sa|mudgara|paraśvadhāḥ
vicchinnā bāhavaḥ petur nṛṇāṃ bhallaiḥ Kirīṭinā.
27.25 bāl'|Ādity'|âmbu|j'|êndūnāṃ tulya|rūpāṇi māriṣa
saṃchinnāny Arjuna|śaraiḥ śirāṃsy urvyāṃ prapedire.
jajvāl' âlaṃ|kṛtaiḥ senā patribhiḥ prāṇa|bhojanaiḥ
nānā|rūpais tad" â|mitrān kruddhe nighnati Phalgune.
kṣobhayantaṃ tathā senāṃ dvi|radaṃ nalinīm iva
Dhanaṃjayaṃ bhūta|gaṇāḥ sādhu sādhv ity apūjayan.
dṛṣṭvā tat karma Pārthasya Vāsavasy' êva Mādhavaḥ
vismayaṃ paramaṃ gatvā prāñjalis tam uvāca ha.
«karm' âitat Pārtha Śakreṇa Yamena Dhanadena ca
duṣ|karaṃ samare yat te kṛtam ady' êti me matiḥ.
27.30 yugapac c' âiva saṃgrāme śataśo 'tha sahasraśaḥ
patitā eva me dṛṣṭāḥ Saṃśaptaka|mahā|rathāḥ.»
tataḥ Saṃśaptakān hatvā bhūyiṣṭhā ye vyavasthitāḥ
«Bhagadattāya yāh'» îti Kṛṣṇam Pārtho 'bhyacodayat.

riders and lay upon the ground in their finery in piles of tree green and mountain gray and raincloud blue. Out they breathed their lives and out trailed their harnesses flailing and their reins and caparisons all torn to ribbons as the horses and horsemen cut into pieces by those keen arrows fell down dead to the earth. O my king then upon them 27.25
came down the broken bodies of soldiers fallen beneath the iron shafts of the Diademed Warrior, and in their death grips were swords and spears, daggers, hammers and battle-axes. Heads the color of the morning sun and of the water lotus and the watery moon were cut away by Árjuna's arrows and tumbled down to the ground. And those fine arrows flashed across the host in a million hues like flames from his rage as they flew on their feathers to sup the breath of his foes. The whole army of the Beholden shook like a lotus pond turned over beneath the hooves of an elephant.

All the denizens of heaven and earth sang Dhanan·jaya's praises that day. Mádhava watched Partha son of Indra do his work. He raised his hands in reverence and when he spoke his voice was full of wonder.

"These are things that would even test the might of Kubéra or Yama or Indra. In their hundreds and thousands I 27.30
have seen the very best of the Beholden fall as one."

Indeed he had killed more of the Beholden than the number that still stood when Partha spoke to Krishna his next command.

"Make for Bhaga·datta," he said.

SAMJAYA uvāca.

28.1 YIYĀSATAS TATAḤ Kṛṣṇaḥ Pārthasy' âśvān mano|javān
sampraiṣīdd hema|saṃchannān Droṇ'|ânīkāya pāṇḍurān.
taṃ prayāntaṃ Kuru|śreṣṭhaṃ svān bhrātṝn Droṇa|tāpitān
Suśarmā bhrātṛbhiḥ sārdhaṃ yuddh'|ârthī pṛṣṭhato 'nvayāt.
tataḥ śveta|hayaḥ Kṛṣṇam abravīd a|jitaṃ jayaḥ.
«eṣa māṃ bhrātṛbhiḥ sārdhaṃ Suśarm" āhvayate, 'cyuta.
dīryate c' ôttareṇ' âiva tat sainyaṃ Madhu|sūdana,
dvaidhī|bhūtaṃ mano me 'dya kṛtaṃ Saṃśaptakair idam.
28.5 kiṃ nu Saṃśaptakān hanmi svān rakṣāmy a|hit'|ârditān
iti me tvaṃ mataṃ vetsi tatra kiṃ su|kṛtaṃ bhavet?»
evam uktas tu Dāśārhaḥ syandanaṃ pratyavartayat
yena Trigart'|âdhipatiḥ Pāṇḍavaṃ samupāhvayat.
tato 'rjunaḥ Suśarmāṇaṃ viddhvā saptabhir āśu|gaiḥ
dhvajaṃ dhanuś c' âsya raṇe kṣurābhyāṃ samakṛntata.
Trigart'|âdhipateś c' âpi bhrātaraṃ ṣaḍbhir āyasaiḥ
s'|âśvaṃ sa|sūtaṃ tvaritaḥ Pārthaḥ praiṣīd Yama|kṣayam.
tato bhuja|ga|saṃkāśāṃ Suśarmā śaktim āyasīm
cikṣep' Ârjunam ādiśya Vāsudevāya tomaram.
28.10 śaktiṃ tribhiḥ śaraiś chittvā tomaraṃ tribhir Arjunaḥ
Suśarmāṇaṃ śara|vrātair mohayitvā nyavartayat.
taṃ Vāsavam iv' āyāntaṃ bhūri|varṣa|śar'|âughiṇam
rājaṃs tāvaka|sainyānāṃ n' ôgraṃ kaś cid avārayat.
tato Dhanaṃjayo bāṇaiḥ sarvān eva mahā|rathān

SÁNJAYA spoke.

PARTHA WAS KEEN to ride out and Krishna spurred forth 28.1
the pale steeds swift as thought and mantled in gold and
they flew towards Drona's line. As the best of the Kurus
sallied forth to save his brothers from the flames of Drona
so with his own brothers Sushárman followed in his wake.
The paladin of the white horses turned then and spoke to
his indomitable friend.

"Áchyuta. Sushárman and his brothers have challenged
me to fight but our army is crumbling on its northern front.
O slayer of Madhu my resolve is divided for the Beholden
have riven it in two. Should I go to destroy them once 28.5
and for all? Or should I help my suffering kin? Such is my
dilemma. But you know which course we must take."

Without a word the chieftain of the Dashárhas brought
the chariot about to the place to where the Tri·garta lord
called out his challenge to Pandu's son. Seven swift arrows
from Árjuna's hands slammed into Sushárman and then two
barbed shafts rent apart the warrior's standard and bow and
another six tipped in iron hastened the king's brother down
to Death's withered kingdom. But Sushárman took aim and
he flung a spear at Vasudéva and a javelin of iron deadly as
a snake straight at Árjuna. Three arrows from Árjuna's bow 28.10
cut apart the javelin and three more the spear and then he
canopied Sushárman in a dizzying storm of reeds and my
king as he raced on like the Thunderer beneath that gathering roiling mass there were none in your son's ranks who
could halt his terrible advance. Like a fire through brush-
wood Dhanan·jaya rolled back across the plain and any
warrior however great whom his arrows struck fell dead. No

āyād vinighnan Kauravyān dahan kakṣam iv' ânalaḥ.
tasya vegam a|sahyaṃ tu Kuntī|putrasya dhīmataḥ
n' āśaknuvaṃs te saṃsoḍhuṃ sparśam agner iva prajāḥ.
saṃveṣṭayann anīkāni śara|varṣeṇa Pāṇḍavaḥ
Suparṇa|pātavad rājann āyāt Prāgjyotiṣaṃ prati.
28.15 yat tad ānāmayaj Jiṣṇur Bharatānām a|pāpinām
dhanuḥ kṣema|karaṃ saṃkhye dviṣatām aśru|vardhanam,
tad eva tava putrasya rājan dur|dyūta|devinaḥ
kṛte kṣatra|vināśāya dhanur āyacchad Arjunaḥ.
tathā vikṣobhyamāṇā sā Pārthena tava vāhinī
vyaśīryata, mahā|rāja, naur iv' āsādya parvatam.
tato daśa|sahasrāṇi nyavartanta dhanuṣmatām
matiṃ kṛtvā raṇe krūrā vīrā jaya|parājaye.
vyapeta|hṛdaya|trāsa āpad|dharm'|âtigo rathaḥ
ārchat Pārtho guruṃ bhāraṃ sarva|bhāra|saho yudhi.
28.20 yathā nala|vanaṃ kruddhaḥ prabhinnaḥ ṣaṣṭi|hāyanaḥ
mṛdnīyāt tadvad āyastaḥ Pārtho 'mṛdnāc camūṃ tava.
tasmin pramathite sainye Bhagadatto nar'|âdhipaḥ
tena nāgena sahasā Dhanaṃjayam upādravat.
taṃ rathena nara|vyāghraḥ pratyagṛhṇād Dhanaṃjayaḥ
sa saṃnipātas tumulo babhūva ratha|nāgayoḥ.
kalpitābhyāṃ yathā|śāstraṃ rathena ca gajena ca
saṃgrāme ceratur vīrau Bhagadatta|Dhanaṃjayau.
tato jīmūta|saṃkāśān nāgād Indra iv' âbhibhuḥ
abhyavarṣac char'|âugheṇa Bhagadatto Dhanaṃjayam.
28.25 sa c' âpi śara|varṣaṃ tac chara|varṣeṇa Vāsaviḥ
a|prāptam eva ciccheda Bhagadattasya vīryavān.

creature can withstand the touch of fire and so it was that none could survive the high son of Kuntí as he rushed along, and bearing down on Prag·jyótisha o majesty he rained arrows in a deluge upon the throngs that he found, flying through the air like broadwinged Gáruda.

Árjuna rose above them all. His bow was bent in a curve 28.15
that brought sanctuary to those tribes of Bharata still without sin and tears to the eyes of his foes. For its aim in that war my king was the ruin of the house of your crooked son. O majesty, as Partha shook the host before him it shattered like a ship smashed against a rock. Ten thousand archers cruel and brave despaired of victory and defeat alike while opposite them without a trace of fear in his heart and now far beyond the bounds of reason Partha shouldered the great burden that was his as he had shouldered all those which
had come before in that war, and like a young elephant in 28.20
must trampling a brake of reeds into the ground he broke the men in his path like twigs.

Yet from out of that ruined horde King Bhaga·datta came rearing towards Dhanan·jaya atop his great steed. Dhanan·jaya stood his ground and elephantrider crashed against chariotwarrior, each bedecked car and beast as scripture dictates. From high upon his elephant, like the supreme king of the gods atop a cloud, Bhaga·datta poured a sheet
of arrows down onto Dhanan·jaya but arrow for arrow In- 28.25
dra's son matched him and broke up his attack. O Bhárata, Prag·jyótisha blocked Árjuna's wooden rain and struck Partha and Krishna with arrows of his own. He bound them both in a warp of his darts then he drove his heels into the flanks of his steed and rode on to trample them dead.

tataḥ Prāgjyotiṣo rājā śara|varṣaṃ nivārya tat
śarair jaghne mahā|bāhuṃ Pārthaṃ Kṛṣṇaṃ ca, Bhārata.
tataḥ sma śara|jālena mahat" âbhyavakīrya tau
codayām āsa taṃ nāgaṃ vadhāy' Âcyuta|Pārthayoḥ.
tam āpatantaṃ dvi|radaṃ dṛṣṭvā kruddham iv' ântakam
cakre 'pasavyaṃ tvaritaḥ syandanena jan'|ârdanaḥ.
taṃ prāptam api n' êyeṣa
    parāvṛttaṃ mahā|dvipam
s'|ārohaṃ mṛtyusāt kartuṃ
    smaran dharmaṃ Dhanaṃjayaḥ.
28.30 sa tu nāgo dvipa|rathān hayāṃś c' āmṛdya māriṣa
prāhiṇon mṛtyu|lokāya tataḥ kruddho Dhanaṃjayaḥ.

DHṚTARĀṢṬRA uvāca.

29.1 TATHĀ KRUDDHAḤ kim akarod Bhagadattasya Pāṇḍavaḥ
Prāgjyotiṣo vā Pārthasya? tan me śaṃsa yathā|tatham.

SAṂJAYA uvāca.

Prāgjyotiṣena saṃsaktāv ubhau Dāśārha|Pāṇḍavau
mṛtyu|daṃṣṭr'|ântikaṃ prāptau sarva|bhūtāni menire.
tathā sma śara|varṣāṇi pātayaty a|niśaṃ prabho
gaja|skandhān mahā|rāja Kṛṣṇayoḥ syandana|sthayoḥ.
atha kārṣṇāyasair bāṇaiḥ pūrṇa|kārmuka|niḥsṛtaiḥ
avidhyad Devakī|putraṃ hema|puṅkhaiḥ śilā|śitaiḥ.
29.5 agni|sparśa|samās tīkṣṇā Bhagadattena coditāḥ
nirbhidya Devakī|putraṃ kṣitiṃ jagmuḥ su|vāsasaḥ.
tasya Pārtho dhanuś chittvā śar'|âvāpaṃ nihatya ca
lālayann iva rājānaṃ Bhagadattam ayodhayat.
so 'rka|raśmi|nibhāṃs tīkṣṇāṃs tomarān vai catur|daśa
prerayan Savyasācī tu tridh" âik'|âikam ath' âcchinat.
tato nāgasya tad varma vyadhamat Pākaśāsaniḥ

But the reaver of men saw the elephant bearing down upon
them mad as Death and he quickly swung the chariot about
and away to its right. As the elephant flew past them Árjuna had it before him. Yet at the last moment he stayed true
to what was right and chose not to deliver over the beast
and its burden to their end. As it rode on, o father, horses 28.30
and chariots and others of its kind fell one after another
beneath its hooves and down into Death's kingdom. And as
Dhanan·jaya watched, his anger rose.

DHRITA·RASHTRA spoke.

WHAT VIOLENCE DID the wrathful Pándava do next to 29.1
Bhaga·datta? Or Prag·jyótisha to Partha? Tell me all that
happened.

SÁNJAYA spoke.

At that moment both Dashárha and Pandu's son were
in Prag·jyótisha's grasp and they seemed to us held fast in
death's jaws. My lord and king, from his perch between his
steed's shoulders Bhaga·datta rained down arrows onto the
Krishnas' chariot in an endless downpour. He drew back his
bow, and arrows of dark iron fletched in gold flew through
the air and sank their stonewhetted points into Dévaki's
son. So sharp were those arrows which Bhaga·datta loosed 29.5
that they went right through him like flames and then fell
finefeathered to the earth. Then Partha struck back and
began almost to toy with Bhaga·datta as he fought. He
destroyed his bow and the quiver that held his arrows. Now
fourteen spears like the rays of the sun came flying from the
king's hand, but the Left Handed Archer shot back and cut
each of them in three. With a torrent of arrows the son of the

śara|jālena mahatā tad vyaśīryata bhū|tale.
viśīrṇa|varmā sa|gajaḥ śaraiḥ su|bhṛśam arditaḥ
babhau dhārā|nipāt'|âkto vy|abhraḥ parvata|rāḍ iva.
29.10 tataḥ Prāgjyotiṣaḥ śaktiṃ hema|daṇḍām ayas|mayīm
vyasṛjad Vāsudevāya dvidhā tām Arjuno 'cchinat.
tataś chattraṃ dhvajaṃ c' âiva chittvā rājño 'rjunaḥ śaraiḥ
vivyādha daśabhis tūrṇam utsmayan parvat'|êśvaram.
so 'tividdho 'rjuna|śaraiḥ su|puṅkhaiḥ kaṅka|patribhiḥ
Bhagadattas tataḥ kruddhaḥ Pāṇḍavasya jan'|âdhipa.
vyasṛjat tomarān mūrdhni śvet'|âśvasy' ônnanāda ca
tair Arjunasya samare kirīṭaṃ parivartitam.
parivṛttaṃ kirīṭaṃ taṃ yamayann eva Phalgunaḥ,
«su|dṛṣṭaḥ kriyatāṃ loka» iti rājānam abravīt.
29.15 evam uktas tu saṃkruddhaḥ śara|varṣeṇa Pāṇḍavam
abhyavarṣat sa|Govindaṃ dhanur ādāya bhāsvaram.
tasya Pārtho dhanuś chittvā tūṇīrān saṃnikṛtya ca
tvaramāṇo dvi|saptatyā sarva|marmasv atāḍayat.
viddhas tath" âpy a|vyathito Vaiṣṇav|âstram udīrayan
abhimantry' âṅkuśaṃ kruddho vyasṛjat Pāṇḍav'|ôrasi.
visṛṣṭaṃ Bhagadattena tad astraṃ sarva|ghāti vai
urasā pratijagrāha Pārthaṃ saṃchādya Keśavaḥ.
vaijayanty abhavan mālā tad astraṃ Keśav'|ôrasi
padma|koṣa|vicitr'|āḍhyā sarva'|rtu|kusum'|ôtkaṭā
jvalan'|ârk'|êndu|varṇ'|ābhā pāvak'|ôjjvala|pallavā.

Punisher of Fools broke up the armor plating Bhaga·datta's elephant and it clattered down to the ground. Though his own raiment hung tattered and he and his elephant were furrowed deep in wounds Bhaga·datta stayed solid as the stone sovereign Himálaya, cloudless though drenched in rain. Prag·jyótisha hurled at Vasudéva an iron javelin inlaid 29.10
with gold and again Árjuna split it in two. Then as a smile played across his lips Árjuna struck at the mountain king with ten arrows of his own that lodged in his parasol and standard. Bhaga·datta's anger flared my king. Badly injured by Árjuna's arrows finely fletched in vulture feathers he cried out and cast yet more spears at the head of the warrior of the white horses and they struck and skewed the diadem he wore on his head.

The Red Star Fighter steadied his dislodged crown and called across to the king.

"Take a last look at this world."

So high was Bhaga·datta's choler raised at this remark 29.15
that sweeping up a bright bow he poured a deluge of shafts down onto Go·vinda and Pándava. But once more Partha cracked his bow in two and burst apart his quivers and in only a moment with two and seventy darts Árjuna struck every hole in his mail. Then somehow despite his injuries the king raised up an iron hook and whispering the Váishnava enchantment across it launched it straight at Pándava's breast. Nothing can survive the Váishnava's blow. As it made its way through the air Késhava stepped before Partha and took it full in his own chest. And there it bloomed into a garland of triumph. Twined with bright lotus sepals and thick with flowers of every season it glowed like the sun

29.20 tayā padma|palāśinyā vāta|kampita|pattrayā
śuśubhe 'bhyadhikaṃ Śaurir atasī|puṣpa|saṃnibhaḥ.
tato 'rjunaḥ klānta|manāḥ Keśavaṃ pratyabhāṣata.
«a|yudhyamānas tura|gān saṃyant" âsmi tav', ân|agha,
ity uktvā Puṇḍarīkākṣa pratijñāṃ svāṃ na rakṣasi.
yady ahaṃ vyasanī vā syām a|śakto vā nivāraṇe
tatas tvay" âivaṃ kāryaṃ syān na tu kāryaṃ mayi sthite.
sa|bāṇaḥ sa|dhanuś c' âhaṃ sa|sur'|âsura|mānavān
śakto lokān imāñ jetuṃ tac c' âpi viditaṃ tava.»
29.25 tato 'rjunaṃ Vāsudevaḥ pratyuvāc' ârthavad vacaḥ.
«śṛṇu guhyam idaṃ Pārtha purā vṛttaṃ yath" ân|agha
catur|mūrtir ahaṃ śaśval loka|trāṇ'|ârtham udyataḥ
ātmānaṃ paribhajy' êha lokānāṃ hitam ādadhe.
ekā mūrtis tapaś|caryāṃ kurute me bhuvi sthitā
aparā paśyati jagat kurvāṇaṃ sādhv|a|sādhunī.
aparā kurute karma mānuṣaṃ lokam āśritā
śete caturthī tv aparā nidrāṃ varṣa|sahasrikām.
y" âsau varṣa|sahasr'|ânte mūrtir uttiṣṭhate mama
var'|ârhebhyo varāñ śreṣṭhāṃs tasmin kāle dadāti sā.
29.30 taṃ tu kālam anuprāptaṃ viditvā pṛthivī tadā
āyācata varaṃ yaṃ māṃ Narak'|ârthāya taṃ śṛṇu.

moon or fire and blossomed with tongues of flame. Blue 29.20
as flax in the field, Shauri shone wrapped in lotuses, their petals trembling in the wind.

But Árjuna was troubled, and spoke then to Késhava.

"O sinless one. Your promise was to drive the horses and not to fight. But Pundarikáksha you broke that promise. If I fall or if I cannot defend myself then perhaps you could help me. But I still stand. And you know well that with my arrows and my bow there is no god demon or man whom I cannot overcome."

Késhava replied to Árjuna and his words were full of 29.25
meaning.

"Hear me now o blameless son of Pritha, and I will tell you of a mystery that came to pass long ago. My everlasting task is the protection of the world and for this purpose I split my being apart into four figures and bestowed my graces on its different realms. One of my incarnations arose on this earth and lives a life of burning austerity. Another looks upon the good and evil of men. The third performs the work of men and moves among them. The fourth slumbers through a night that lasts a thousand summers. And when the end of those thousand summers comes near, it is this incarnation which grants wondrous things to those of the
time that are worthy of them. Long ago the Earth herself 29.30
knew that one such time was at hand and she asked me to do something for her future child. She was to be mother of Náraka. Hear now what she said.

‹devānām asurāṇāṃ ca hy a|vadhyas tanayo 'stu me
upeto Vaiṣṇav'|âstreṇa tan me tvaṃ dātum arhasi.›
evaṃ varam ahaṃ śrutvā jagatyās tanaye tadā
a|mogham astram prāyacchaṃ Vaiṣṇavaṃ paramaṃ purā.
avocaṃ c' ‹âitad astraṃ vai hy a|moghaṃ bhavatu kṣame
Narakasy' âbhirakṣ"|ârthaṃ. n' âinaṃ kaś cid vadhiṣyati.
anen' âstreṇa te guptaḥ sutaḥ para|bal'|ârdanaḥ
bhaviṣyati dur|ādharṣaḥ sarva|lokeṣu sarvadā.›
29.35 tath" êty uktvā gatā devī kṛta|kāmā manasvinī
sa c' âpy āsīd dur|ādharṣo Narakaḥ śatru|tāpanaḥ.
tasmāt Prāgjyotiṣaṃ prāptaṃ tad astraṃ Pārtha māmakam
n' âsy' â|vadhyo 'sti lokeṣu s'|Êndra|Rudreṣu, māriṣa.
tan mayā tvat|kṛte hy etad anyathā vyapanāyitaṃ
viyuktaṃ param'|âstreṇa jahi Pārtha mah"|âsuraṃ.
vairiṇaṃ yudhi dur|dharṣaṃ Bhagadattaṃ sura|dviṣam
yath" âhaṃ jaghnivān pūrvaṃ hit'|ârthaṃ Narakaṃ tathā.»
evam uktas tataḥ Pārthaḥ Keśavena mah"|ātmanā
Bhagadattaṃ śitair bāṇaiḥ sahasā samavākirat.
29.40 tataḥ Pārtho mahā|bāhur a|sambhrānto mahā|manāḥ
kumbhayor antare nāgaṃ nārācena samārpayat.
sa samāsādya taṃ nāgaṃ bāṇo vajra iv' âcalam
abhyagāt saha puṅkhena valmīkam iva panna|gaḥ.

'May I be given a son whom neither demon nor divinity can slay. The arrow of Vishnu is yours and you are the one who can grant me this wish.'

I heard Earth's request and so it was that all that time ago I laid upon Earth's son the supreme and unerring arrow of Vishnu.

'I place the arrow of Vishnu before Earth for the sake of Náraka's protection. None will be able to defeat him now. With this arrow as his talisman Earth's son will strike down any blow that is raised against him. He will be invincible in all places and among all things.'

After I had spoken wise Earth was pleased and she de- 29.35
parted. Náraka her son was indeed invincible and the scourge of all his foes. O Partha, it was from Náraka that Prag·jyótisha took my weapon. And my son there are none that dwell with Indra or Rudra whom he could not have destroyed with it. It was for you that I broke my promise and drew it from him. The weapon of weapons is no longer his. Strike him dead Partha. He is an archdemon. Enmity is his passion. As I in the end slew Náraka himself for the sake of the good of things so strike dead the cruel warrior and despiser of gods King Bhaga·datta."

Partha listened to what the great Késhava said. Quickly
he began to sow sharp shafts above Bhaga·datta's head. With 29.40
his mighty arms and steady heart and hand, Partha sent an arrow to pierce the forehead of Bhaga·datta's steed and it drove deep as lightning upon a clifftop and disappeared right up to its nock like a serpent into a mound of earth. For a few steps more Bhaga·datta drove the creature on, but like the words of a poor man in his wife's ears, the

sa karī Bhagadattena preryamāṇo muhur muhuḥ
na karoti vacas tasya daridrasy' êva yoṣitā.
sa tu viṣṭabhya gātrāṇi dantābhyām avaniṃ yayau
nadann ārta|svaraṃ prāṇān utsasarja mahā|dvipaḥ.
tato Gāṇḍīva|dhanvānam abhyabhāṣata Keśavaḥ.
«ayaṃ mahattaraḥ, Pārtha, palitena samāvṛtaḥ.
29.45 valī|saṃchanna|nayanaḥ śūraḥ parama|dur|jayaḥ
akṣṇor unmīlan'|ârthāya baddha|paṭṭo hy asau nṛ|paḥ.»
deva|vākyāt praciccheda śareṇa bhṛśam Arjunaḥ
chinna|mātr'|âṃśuke tasmin ruddha|netro babhuva saḥ.
tamo|mayaṃ jagan mene Bhagadattaḥ pratāpavān
tataś candr'|ârdha|bimbena bāṇena nata|parvaṇā
bibheda hṛdayaṃ rājño Bhagadattasya Pāṇḍavaḥ.
sa bhinna|hṛdayo rājā Bhagadattaḥ Kirīṭinā
śar'|âsanaṃ śarāṃś c' âiva gat'|âsuḥ pramumoca ha.
śirasas tasya vibhraṣṭaṃ prapapāta var'|âṃśukaṃ
nāla|tāḍana|vibhraṣṭaṃ palāśaṃ nalinād iva.
29.50 sa hema|mālī tapanīya|bhāṇḍāt
papāta nāgād giri|saṃnikāśāt
su|puṣpito māruta|vega|rugṇo
mahī|dhar'|âgrād iva karṇikāraḥ.
nihatya taṃ nara|patim Indra|vikramaṃ
sakhāyam Indrasya tath" Āindrir āhave
tato 'parāṃs tava jaya|kāṅkṣiṇo narān
babhañja vāyur balavān drumān iva.

king's commands were not heard. The great beast tried for a moment to steady its limbs, then down it came to the ground and it howled as it fell on its tusks and heaved out its final breath.

Késhava spoke to the bearer of Gandíva.

"Look at this one, Partha. Venerable warrior behind long locks of gray. Awesome champion with lines etched about 29.45
his eyes. See how he has bound back his hair beneath his turban to keep his eyes clear."

Árjuna did not hesitate but at the god's word sent forth an arrow that tore through the king's headdress. Bhaga·datta could no longer see, his world woven with darkness.

With a flatjointed shaft shaped like a halfmoon Pándava pierced the king's heart and Bhaga·datta let fall from his hands his bow and his arrow and, from his heart skewered by Kirítin's arrow, his life. Down fluttered the fine scarf as it came away from his neck, like a petal plucked roughly from the stalk of a lotus, and still garlanded in gold he 29.50
tumbled from the great height of his elephant's back and its firebeaten harness like a bayur tree in full bloom plucked from a mountain peak by a gust of wind. And so it was that a son of Indra slew in battle one who had been a friend to the lord of the gods, a king of men brave as Indra. And when he had done so he rose through your zealous son's sorry troop as a strong wind rises through the trees.

SAMJAYA uvāca.

30.1 PRIYAM INDRASYA satataṃ sakhāyam a|mit'|âujasam
hatvā Prāgjyotiṣaṃ Pārthaḥ pradakṣiṇam avartata.
tato Gāndhāra|rājasya sutau para|puraṃ|jayau
ārdetām Arjunaṃ saṃkhye bhrātarau Vṛṣak'|Âcalau.
tau samety' Ârjunaṃ vīrau puraḥ paścāc ca dhanvinau
avidhyetāṃ mahā|vegair niśitair āśu|gair bhṛśam.
Vṛṣakasya hayān sūtaṃ dhanuś chattraṃ rathaṃ dhvajam
tilaśo vyadhamat Pārthaḥ Saubalasya śitaiḥ śaraiḥ.
30.5 tato 'rjunaḥ śara|vrātair nānā|praharaṇair api
Gāndhārān ākulāṃś cakre Saubala|pramukhān punaḥ.
tataḥ pañca|śatān vīrān Gāndhārān udyat'|āyudhān
prāhiṇon mṛtyu|lokāya kruddho bāṇair Dhanaṃjayaḥ.
hat'|âśvāt tu rathāt tūrṇam avatīrya mahā|bhujaḥ
āruroha rathaṃ bhrātur anyac ca dhanur ādade.
tāv ekaṃ ratham ārūḍhau bhrātarau Vṛṣak'|Âcalau
śara|varṣeṇa Bībhatsum avidhyetāṃ muhur muhuḥ.
syālau tava mah"|ātmānau rājānau Vṛṣak'|Âcalau
bhṛśaṃ nijaghnatuḥ Pārtham Indraṃ Vṛtra|balāv iva.
30.10 labdha|lakṣyau tu Gāndhārāv ahatāṃ Pāṇḍavaṃ punaḥ
nidāgha|vārṣikau māsau lokaṃ gharm'|âṃśubhir yathā.
tau ratha|sthau nara|vyāghrau rājānau Vṛṣak'|Âcalau
saṃśliṣṭ'|âṅgau sthitau rājan jaghān' âik'|êṣuṇ" Ârjunaḥ.
tau rathāt siṃha|saṃkāśau lohit'|âkṣau mahā|bhujau
gat'|âsū petatur vīrau sodaryāv eka|lakṣaṇau.

SÁNJAYA spoke.

HIS MIGHT HAD BEEN measureless and he was Indra's longtreasured friend, but Prag·jyótisha had been slain. As Árjuna circled his corpse out of respect, the two sons of the Gandhára king, the sackers of cities named Vríshaka and Áchala, made across the fray toward him. One of those heroes came from the front and one from behind and as they rode on and raised their bows they struck Árjuna with a sudden gust of arrows sharp and swift. But Partha answered Vríshaka son of Súbala with a blast of his own whetted shafts and away went his horses driver bow parasol chariot and banner like seed scattered on the wind. Then with arrows like a thousand hailstones Árjuna rippled the column of Gandháras behind Vríshaka and a full five hundred he hammered into hell, swords still raised high above their heads.
30.1
30.5

Broad Vríshaka leapt quickly from his chariot and its dead steeds and he climbed aboard his brother's and took up another bow. From their single car Vríshaka and Áchala poured down upon their sworn foe a heavy arrow rain. With all their might those great kings and brothers of your wife struck at Partha as Vritra and Bala once struck Indra. The Gandháras pinned the Pándava beneath their deadly aim. He was like the earth needled by sunbeams during the months of heat and rain. Yet even as Vríshaka and Áchala stood there atop their chariot in a cluster of limbs, a single arrow from Árjuna's bow passed clean through the two mighty kings. Redeyed lions who had shared the same hopes as they had shared the same womb, those heroes tumbled down from their chariot to join those who are no
30.10

tayor bhūmiṃ gatau dehau rathād bandhu|jana|priyau
yaśo daśa diśaḥ puṇyaṃ gamayitvā vyavasthitau.
dṛṣṭvā vinihatau saṃkhye mātulāv a|palāyinau
bhṛśaṃ mumucur aśrūṇi putrās tava viśāṃ pate.
30.15 nihatau bhrātarau dṛṣṭvā māyā|śata|viśāradaḥ
Kṛṣṇau sammohayan māyāṃ vidadhe Śakunis tataḥ.
laguḍ'|âyo|guḍ'|âśmānaḥ śataghnyaś ca sa|śaktayaḥ
gadā|parigha|nistriṃśa|śūla|mudgara|paṭṭiśāḥ
sa|kampana'|ṛṣṭi|nakharā musalāni paraśvadhāḥ
kṣurāḥ kṣurapra|nālīkā vatsa|dant'|âsthi|sandhayaḥ
cakrāṇi viśikhāḥ prāsā vividhāny āyudhāni ca
prapetuḥ śataśo digbhyaḥ pradigbhyaś c' Ârjunaṃ prati.
khar'|ôṣṭra|mahiṣāḥ siṃhā vyāghrāḥ sṛmara|cillikāḥ
ṛkṣāḥ sālāvṛkā gṛdhrāḥ kapayaś ca sarīsṛpāḥ
30.20 vividhāni ca rakṣāṃsi kṣudhitāny Arjunaṃ prati
saṃkruddhāny abhyadhāvanta vividhāni vayāṃsi ca.
tato divy'|âstra|vic chūraḥ Kuntī|putro Dhanaṃjayaḥ
visṛjann iṣu|jālāni sahasā tāny atāḍayat.
te hanyamānāḥ śūreṇa pravaraiḥ sāyakair dṛḍhaiḥ
viruvanto mahā|rāvān vineśuḥ sarvato hatāḥ.
tatas tamaḥ prādur abhūd Arjunasya rathaṃ prati
tasmāc ca tamaso vācaḥ krūrāḥ Pārtham abhartsayan.
tat tamo bhairavaṃ ghoraṃ bhayaṃ|kartṛ mah"|āhave
uttam'|âstreṇa mahatā Jyotiṣkeṇ' Ârjuno 'vadhīt.
30.25 hate tasmiñ jal'|âughās tu prādur āsan bhayānakāḥ
ambhasāṃ tu vināś'|ârtham Ādity'|âstram ath' Ârjunaḥ
prāyukt'; âmbhas tatas tena prāyaśo 'streṇa śoṣitam

more. Two bodies so dear to their kin and four strong arms that had hewn glorious fame from the four corners of the earth fell from their car to the soil and rolled and came to rest. Tears flowed from your sons' eyes my lord when they saw their brave uncles struck down thus.

Shákuni also watched as they were felled. From his bounty 30.15
of a hundred tricks he began to bewitch the two Krishnas with his magic. From a hundred directions on Árjuna fell sticks, iron balls, stones and fireballs and spears, clubs, bludgeons, knives, pikes, hammers, tridents, bonebreakers, swords, scimitars, maces and axes, daggers, arrows with barbed heads and jointed in calves' teeth, discuses, javelins and darts and weapons of yet stranger kinds. Camels, donkeys and buffalo, lions, tigers, yaks and insects,
jackals, wolves, vultures, monkeys and serpents, all kinds 30.20
of fiends and flocks of winged things hungry and cruel all rushed upon him then. But Dhanan·jaya son of Kuntí was a hero wise in the weapons of heaven and without waiting he cast his net of arrows and snared them all within it. Pierced by the hero's fine adamantine shafts, everywhere the creatures' screams rose up and they fell down dead.

Darkness came next across Árjuna's chariot and from out of that darkness a deathly susurrus. Grim and terrible that darkness was and it struck fear into us all, but with the vast and brilliant weapon named Jyotíshka* Árjuna drove it
off. Then a terrifying swell of water massed overhead, and 30.25
Árjuna loosed the arrow of the sun to destroy it. As it cut across it the great cloud turned to vapor, and so the myriad sorcery of Súbala's son was dispelled. A smile played across his lips as Árjuna began with the might of his arms to press

evaṃ bahu|vidhā māyāḥ Saubalasya kṛtāḥ kṛtāḥ.
jaghān' âstra|balen' āśu prahasann Arjunas tadā
tathā hatāsu māyāsu trasto 'rjuna|śar'|āhataḥ
apāyāj javanair aśvaiḥ Śakuniḥ prākṛto yathā.
tato 'rjuno 'stra|vic chaighryaṃ darśayann ātmano 'riṣu
abhyavarṣac char'|âugheṇa Kauravāṇām anīkinīm.
sā hanyamānā Pārthena tava putrasya vāhinī
dvaidhī|bhūtā, mahā|rāja, Gaṅg" êv' āsādya parvatam.
30.30 Droṇam ev' ânvapadyanta ke cit tatra nara'|ṛṣabhāḥ
ke cid Duryodhanaṃ rājann ardyamānāḥ Kirīṭinā.
n' âpaśyāma tatas tv enaṃ sainye vai rajas" āvṛte
Gāṇḍīvasya ca nirghoṣaḥ śruto dakṣiṇato mayā.
śaṅkha|dundubhi|nirghoṣaṃ vāditrāṇāṃ ca niḥsvanam
tataḥ punar dakṣiṇataḥ saṃgrāmaś citra|yodhinām.
su|yuddham Arjunasy' āsīd ahaṃ tu Droṇam anviyām,
Yaudhiṣṭhirāṇy anīkāni praharanti tatas tataḥ.
nānā|vidhāny anīkāni putrāṇāṃ tava Bhārata
Arjuno vyadhamat kāle div' îv' âbhrāṇi mārutaḥ.
30.35 taṃ Vāsavam iv' āyāntaṃ bhūri|varṣaṃ śar'|âughiṇaṃ
mah"|êṣv|āsaṃ nara|vyāghraṃ n' ôgraṃ kaś cid avārayat.
te hanyamānāḥ Pārthena tvadīyā vyathitā bhṛśam
svān eva bahavo jaghnur vidravantas tatas tataḥ.
te 'rjunena śarā muktāḥ kaṅka|patrās tanu|cchidaḥ
śalabhā iva sampetuḥ saṃvṛṇvānā diśo daśa.
tura|gaṃ rathinaṃ nāgaṃ padātim api māriṣa
vinirbhidya kṣitiṃ jagmur valmīkam iva panna|gāḥ.
na ca dvitīyaṃ vyasṛjat kuñjar'|âśva|nareṣu saḥ
pṛthag eka|śar'|â|rugṇā nipetus te gat'|âsavaḥ.

swift and hard upon his foe. His enchantments destroyed, Shákuni suffered beneath Árjuna's arrows and wheeled his galloping horses about and fled away in fear like a fool. Árjuna's mastery was dazzling and quick. He tipped a mass of arrows across the Káurava line and o great king like the Ganges forking at the foot of a mountain the torrent of your son's army was split in two by the Diademed Partha's attack,
some heading after Drona and others after Duryódhana as 30.30
his blows rained down upon them. O lord we could not even see him through the battlefield's cloak of dust. But I heard the sigh of Gandíva's string somewhere to my right and I could hear the sound of horns and drums and the blare of trumpets and then again on my right I heard the clatter of arms. Árjuna's onslaught went on as I followed Drona. From all around, Yudhi·shthira's troops pushed towards us while one after another Árjuna cast asunder your son's arrays
as on a dark day the wind parts the clouds. More tiger than 30.35
man the great bowman came like Indra aflight, a vast storm pouring out arrows, and no one was able to make him pause.

Twisting beneath Partha's onslaught many of your men trampled their own as they escaped any way they could. Those razorsharp shafts fletched in vulture feathers flew from Árjuna's fingers and they billowed like locusts through every inch of the sky. Through horse, rider elephant and soldier they went and then plunged into the earth like snakes into a colony of ants. None did he strike twice, whether elephant, horse or man, but each gasped his last breath and fell transfixed by a single shaft.

30.40 hatair manuṣyair dvi|radaiś ca sarvataḥ
śar'|âbhimṛṣṭaiś ca hayair nipātitaiḥ
tadā śva|go|māyu|bal'|âbhināditaṃ
vicitram āyodha|śiro babhūva tat.
pitā sutaṃ tyajati su|hṛd|varaṃ su|hṛt
tath" âiva putraḥ pitaraṃ śar'|āturaḥ
sva|rakṣaṇe kṛta|matayas tadā janās
tyajanti vāhān api Pārtha|pīḍitāḥ.

DHṚTARĀṢṬRA uvāca.

31.1 TEṢV ANĪKEṢU bhagneṣu Pāṇḍu|putreṇa Saṃjaya
calitānāṃ drutānāṃ ca katham āsīn mano hi vaḥ?
anīkānāṃ prabhagnānām avasthānam a|paśyatām
duṣ|karaṃ pratisaṃdhānaṃ tan mam' ācakṣva, Saṃjaya.

SAṂJAYA uvāca.

tath" âpi tava putrasya priya|kāmā, viśāṃ pate,
yaśaḥ|pravīrā lokeṣu rakṣanto Droṇam anvayuḥ.
samudyateṣu śastreṣu samprāpte ca Yudhiṣṭhire
a|kurvann ārya|karmāṇi bhairave saty a|bhītavat.
31.5 antaraṃ Bhīmasenasya prāpatann a|mit'|âujasaḥ
Sātyakeś c' âiva vīrasya Dhṛṣṭadyumnasya vā vibho.
Droṇaṃ Droṇam iti krūrāḥ Pāñcālāḥ samacodayan
mā Droṇam iti putrās te Kurūn sarvān acodayan.
Droṇaṃ Droṇam iti hy eke mā Droṇam iti c' âpare
Kurūṇāṃ Pāṇḍavānāṃ ca Droṇa|dyūtam avartata.
yaṃ yaṃ pramathate Droṇaḥ Pāñcālānāṃ ratha|vrajam
tatra tatra tu Pāñcālyo Dhṛṣṭadyumno 'bhyavartata.
tathā bhāga|viparyāsaiḥ saṃgrāme bhairave sati
vīrāḥ samāsadan vīrān kurvanto bhairavaṃ ravam.

Corpses and dead elephants lay all around and horses 30.40
with broken forms all quilted in arrows. Our heads filled then with the howls of jackals and dogs intermingling with the caws of the crows, as sick with wounds father abandoned son, son abandoned father, friend deserted friend and riders left their horses to die. Each strove to save himself when Partha struck that day.

DHRITA·RASHTRA spoke.

SO THEY FLED IN disarray, lines broken by Pandu's son. 31.1
What went through their minds then? And how did they regroup when all about them were the signs of their shattered former shape? Tell me Sánjaya.

SÁNJAYA spoke.

O lord of men. Despite what had happened the Kuru paladins came back once more at Drona, for they were loyal to your son and more than that it was their fame on earth that was at stake. With their swords raised high overhead they rode at Yudhi·shthira, and despite the horror
around them they remained noble and fearless. Majesty 31.5
they attacked the measureless splendor of Bhima and went against valiant Sátyaki and Dhrishta·dyumna. While the savage Panchálas bayed for Drona's blood your sons cried out at the Kuru soldiers to defend their commander. The Pándavas strove for his end and the Kurus for his protection. And so the contest for Drona went on. Wherever Drona rattled the Panchála ranks their prince Dhrishta·dyumna was there to meet him. Reverse followed reverse as that grim struggle wore on, and grim were the battle cries as
hero clashed with hero. But the Pándavas were unshaken. 31.10

31.10 a|kampanīyāḥ śatrūṇāṃ babhūvus tatra Pāṇḍavāḥ
akampayann anīkāni smarantaḥ kleśam ātmanaḥ.
te '|marṣa|vaśa|samprāptā hrīmantaḥ sattva|coditāḥ
tyaktvā prāṇān nyavartanta ghnanto Droṇaṃ mah"|āhave.

ayasām iva sampātaḥ śilānām iva c' âbhavat
dīvyatāṃ tumule yuddhe prāṇair a|mita|tejasām.
na tu smaranti saṃgrāmam api vṛddhās tathā|vidham
dṛṣṭa|pūrvaṃ, mahā|rāja, śruta|pūrvam ath' âpi vā.
prākampat' êva pṛthivī tasmin vīr'|âvasādane
pravartatā bal'|âughena mahatā bhāra|pīḍitā.
31.15 ghūrṇato 'pi bal'|âughasya divaṃ stabdhv" êva niḥsvanaḥ
Ajātaśatros tat|sainyam āviveśa su|bhairavaḥ.

samāsādya tu Pāṇḍūnām anīkāni sahasraśaḥ
Droṇena caratā saṃkhye prabhagnāni śitaiḥ śaraiḥ.
teṣu pramathyamāneṣu Droṇen' âdbhuta|karmaṇā
paryavārayad āyasto Droṇaṃ senā|patiḥ svayam.
tad adbhutam apaśyāma Droṇa|Pāñcālayos tadā
n' âiva tasy' ôpamā kā cid iti me niścitā matiḥ.

It was their turn to send ripples through the mass of their foe as the memory of what they had suffered rose up anew, and overcome by the force of their own rage and wild with shame at what had befallen them it was the deepest part of their souls that drove them on to greater violence. They cast down their own lives and staked them on Drona's death. They played at survival with a throw of the dice.

O majesty, in the crash of battle warriors whose splendor knew no end fell to the earth like lumps of iron or stone in a struggle the like of which none old or young had known before. Beneath its teeming freight of the dead the earth itself seemed to tremble in sympathy with the hearts of
those heroes. The rumble of the great roiling mass of men 31.15
filled the sky above and then fell to earth and shook through the columns of the matchless king's army.

Drona careered across the plain between the serried lines of Pándavas and broke holes in their thousand links with his whetted shafts. As he wrought another miraculous feat of war and ground his victims beneath him the commander of the Pandus himself labored through the fray to meet him. The struggle that followed between Dhrishta·dyumna and Drona was astonishing and ferocious. Words fail me as I try to tell it.

tato Nīlo 'nala|prakhyo dadāha Kuru|vāhinīm
śara|sphuliṅgaś cāp'|ârcir dahan kakṣam iv' ânalaḥ.
31.20 taṃ dahantam anīkāni Droṇa|putraḥ pratāpavān
pūrv'|âbhibhāṣī su|ślakṣṇaṃ smayamāno 'bhyabhāṣata.
«Nīla, kiṃ bahubhir dagdhais tava yodhaiḥ śar'|ârciṣā.
may" âikena hi yudhyasva, kruddhaḥ prahara c' āśu mām.»
tam padma|nikar'|ākāraṃ padma|pattra|nibh'|ēkṣaṇam
vyākośa|padm'|ābha|mukhaṃ Nīlo vivyādha sāyakaiḥ.
ten' âtividdhaḥ sahasā Drauṇir bhallaiḥ śitais tribhiḥ
dhanur dhvajaṃ ca chattraṃ ca dviṣataḥ sa nyakṛntata.
sa plutaḥ syandanāt tasmān Nīlaś carma|var'|âsi|bhṛt
Droṇāyaneḥ śiraḥ kāyādd hartum aicchat patatrivat.
31.25 tasy' ônnat'|âṃsaṃ su|nasaṃ śiraḥ kāyāt sa|kuṇḍalam
bhallen' âpāharad Drauṇiḥ smayamāna iv' ân|agha.
sampūrṇa|candr'|ābha|mukhaḥ padma|pattra|nibh'|ēkṣaṇaḥ
prāṃśur utpala|garbh'|ābho nihato nyapatat kṣitau.
tataḥ pravivyathe senā Pāṇḍavī bhṛśam ākulā
ācārya|putreṇa hate Nīle jvalita|tejasi.
acintayaṃś ca te sarve Pāṇḍavānāṃ mahā|rathāḥ
kathaṃ no Vāsavis trāyāc chatrubhya iti māriṣa.
dakṣiṇena tu senāyāḥ kurute kadanaṃ balī
Saṃśaptak'|âvaśeṣasya Nārāyaṇa|balasya ca.

Elsewhere Nila tore like a fire through the Kuru horde, his bow the flame and arrows the flying sparks, like a fire tearing through dry wood. And as he rolled through the 31.20
army's avenues Drona's hot son spoke to him with words whose blandishments soon gave way to a crooked smile.

"Nila. Enough with all these tindersticks blackened by your burning reeds. I am he whom you must fight now, alone. Bring down all your speed and fury upon me o little one."

Like a bunch of lotuses was Ashvatthámán's fair form and his eyes were the shape of lotus leaves and his face a lotus in bloom, and Nila pierced him through each with his arrows. Though marred by those shafts Drauni with three sharp and tearing iron darts of his own cut through his foe's bow and his parasol and tore the flag above his head. Then down fluttered Nila like a bird from his car and sword and shield in hand he strove to sever his opponent's head. But o 31.25
sinless one there was then a smile on Drauni's lips, and with a single arrow he parted from the knotted shoulders upon which it rested Nila's beringed and nobly formed head. And fine as a lotus calyx, its eyes the shape of lotus leaves and its face bright as the flushed moon, down it fell to the ground.

Despair rushed through the Pándava army when the dancing flame that was Nila was snuffed out between the fingers of the teacher's son. And there was no Pándava that did not then wonder how even the scion of Indra would protect them from a foe such as this. Indeed Árjuna was not there. He was off to the south, still crushing beneath his main all that was left of the Beholden, and the Naráyana phalanxes at their side.

SAMJAYA uvāca.

32.1 PRATIGHĀTAM TU sainyasya n' āmṛṣyata Vṛkodaraḥ,
so 'bhyāhanad gurum ṣaṣṭyā Karṇam ca daśabhiḥ śaraiḥ.
tasya Droṇaḥ śitair bāṇais tīkṣṇa|dhārair a|jihma|gaiḥ
jīvit'|ântam abhiprepsur marmaṇy āśu jaghāna ha.
Karṇo dvā|daśabhir bāṇair Aśvatthāmā ca saptabhiḥ
ṣaḍbhir Duryodhano rājā tata enam ath' âkirat.
Bhīmaseno 'pi tān sarvān pratyavidhyan mahā|balaḥ
Droṇam pañcāśat" êṣūṇām Karṇam ca daśabhiḥ śaraiḥ
32.5 Duryodhanam dvā|daśabhir Drauṇim c' âṣṭābhir āśu|gaiḥ
ārāvam tumulam kurvann abhyavartata tān raṇe.
tasmin saṃtyajati prāṇān mṛtyu|sādhāraṇī|kṛte
Ajātaśatrus tān yodhān Bhīmam trāt' êty acodayat.
te yayur Bhīmasenasya samīpam a|mit'|âujasaḥ
Yuyudhāna|prabhṛtayo Mādrī|putrau ca Pāṇḍavau.
te sametya su|saṃrabdhāḥ sahitāḥ puruṣa'|rṣabhāḥ
mah"|êṣv|āsa|varair guptam Droṇ'|ânīkam bibhitsavaḥ
samāpetur mahā|vīryā Bhīma|prabhṛtayo rathāḥ.
tān pratyagṛhṇād a|vyagro Droṇo 'pi rathinām varaḥ.
32.10 mahā|rathān atibalān vīrān samara|yodhinaḥ
bāhyam mṛtyu|bhayam kṛtvā tāvakān Pāṇḍavā yayuḥ.
sādinaḥ sādino 'bhyaghnaṃs tath" âiva rathino rathān
āsīc chakty|asi|sampāto yuddham āsīt paraśvadhaiḥ.
prakṛṣṭam asi|yuddham ca babhūva kaṭuk'|ôdayam
kuñjarāṇām ca sampāte yuddham āsīt su|dāruṇam.
apatat kuñjarād anyo hayād anyas tv avāk|śirāḥ
naro bāṇa|vinirbhinno rathād anyaś ca māriṣa.

SÁNJAYA spoke.

OUR BRIEF ASCENDANCE was too much for Bhima to bear. 32.1
With sixty arrows he struck at his teacher and then fired ten more at Karna. But Drona sent arrows swift and sharp dead through the air at the joints in Bhima's armor, striving to put an end to his disciple's life. Their fiery points bit deep. Then a dozen came from Karna and seven from Ashvattháman and six more arced and dropped from King Duryódhana's bow. Yet Bhima·sena struck back at them all. With his cry tearing the air above he loosed a brace of fifty shafts at Drona and ten at Karna, then twelve at Duryódhana and eight 32.5
more at Drona's son. Even so, Bhima bled out his life and stood then at death's edge. The matchless king ordered his fighters to Bhima's side, and with Yuyudhána and the Pándavas born of Madri at the head of their mighty group they made their way towards him. Bulls in the herd of men driven by their hatred for Drona's army and the archers so great and strong who ringed it, those mighty heroes led by Bhima with their blood up bore down upon their quarries. As their warriors fierce and wild came towards us our very best awaited them: Drona. Peace was in his eyes. Yet any fear 32.10
of death they may have harbored themselves the Pándavas had driven from their hearts, and thus they were upon us.

Warrior crashed against warrior and car against car and spear fell upon sword and axe locked with axe. The time of battle stretched as long and cruel as the blades drawn from their scabbards. The clash between the elephants was perhaps the most fierce. I saw one man tumbling from an elephant's back and another from his horse and another I saw torn by arrows as he stood in his car. An elephant

tatr' ânyasya ca sammarde patitasya vivarmaṇaḥ
śiraḥ pradhvaṃsayām āsa vakṣasy ākramya kuñjaraḥ.

32.15 aparāṃś c' âpare 'mṛdnan vāraṇāḥ patitān narān
viṣāṇaiś c' âvaniṃ gatvā vyabhindan rathino bahūn
nar'|ântraiḥ ke cid apare viṣāṇ'|ālagna|saṃsrayaiḥ
babhramuḥ samare nāgā mṛdnantaḥ śataśo narān.
kārṣṇāyasa|tanu|trāṇān nar'|âśva|ratha|kuñjarān
patitān pothayāṃ cakrur dvipāḥ sthūla|nalān iva.

gṛdhra|pattr'|âdhivāsāṃsi śayanāni nar'|âdhipāḥ
hrīmantaḥ kāla|samparkāt su|duḥkhāny anuśerate.
hanti sm' âtra pitā putraṃ rathen' âbhyativartate
putraś ca pitaraṃ mohān nir|maryādam avartata.

32.20 akṣo bhagno dhvajaś chinnaś chattram urvyāṃ nipātitam.
yug'|ârdhaṃ chinnam ādāya pradudrāva tathā hayaḥ.
s'|âsir bāhur nipatitaḥ śiraś chinnaṃ sa|kuṇḍalam
gajen' ākṣipya balinā rathaḥ saṃcūrṇitaḥ kṣitau.
rathinā tāḍito nāgo nārācen' âpatad vy|asuḥ
s'|ârohaś c' âpatad vājī gajen' ātāḍito bhṛśam.

crossing the slaughter trampled the chest of the crumpled
and stripped corpse of a man and then crushed his head
beneath its foot. Others trampled other of the dead, and 32.15
numberless were the fallen that those beasts impaled as they
were dragged low to the ground by the ravened entrails
that snagged their tusks. Yet more of the beasts wandered
aimlessly across the plain toiling among the hundredhigh
heaps of the slaughtered, of men and horses and cars and
other elephants all fallen and plated in dark iron and all
flattened and broken beneath their feet as if nothing more
than a field of snapped reeds.

I saw lords of men humbled by their encounter with
time who had taken their final rest upon sorrowing beds
decked in the feathers of vultures. Father murdered son and
then rode on and son murdered father for in this nightmare
nothing of order remained. There a shattered wheel, here a 32.20
tattered flag or a lone parasol on the broad earth. A horse
runs past dragging a buckled halfwheel behind it. A severed
hand clutching a sword, a head with gold rings still in its
ears, a chariot that had felt the kick of a beast's heavy foot
lying mangled in the mud. An elephant transfixed by an iron
arrow from some archer's bow crumples lifeless to earth, and
another kicks out at a horse and it folds with its rider before
the shock.

nirmaryādaṃ mahad yuddham avartata su|dāruṇam.
hā tāta hā putra sakhe kv' âsi? tiṣṭha! kva dhāvasi?
prahar' āhara! jahy enaṃ! smita|kṣveḍita|garjitaiḥ
ity evam uccaranti sma śrūyante vividhā giraḥ.
32.25 narasy' âśvasya nāgasya samasajjata śoṇitam
upāśāmyad rajo bhaumaṃ bhīrūn kaśmalam āviśat.
cakreṇa cakram āsādya vīro vīrasya saṃyuge
atīteṣu pathe kāle jahāra gadayā śiraḥ.
āsīt keśa|parāmarśo muṣṭi|yuddhaṃ ca dāruṇaṃ
nakhair dantaiś ca śūrāṇām a|dvīpe dvīpam icchatām.
tatr' ācchidyata śūrasya sa|khaḍgo bāhur udyataḥ
sa|dhanuś c' âparasy' âpi sa|śaraḥ s'|âṅkuśas tathā.
ākrośad anyam anyo 'tra tath" ânyo vimukho 'dravat
anyaḥ samasya c' ânyasya śiraḥ kāyād apāharat.
32.30 sa|śabdam adravac c' ânyaḥ śabdād anyo 'trasad bhṛśam
svān anyo 'tha parān anyo jaghāna niśitaiḥ śaraiḥ.
giri|śṛṅg'|ôpamaś c' âtra nārācena nipātitaḥ
mātaṅgo nyapatad bhūmau nadī|rodha iv' ôṣṇage.
tath" âiva rathinaṃ nāgaḥ kṣaran girir iv' ārujan
abhyatiṣṭhat padā bhūmau sah'|âśvaṃ saha|sārathiṃ.
śūrān praharato dṛṣṭvā kṛt'|âstrān rudhir'|ôkṣitān
bahūn apy āviśan moho bhīrūn hṛdaya|dur|balān.
sarvam āvignam abhavan na prājñāyata kiṃ cana
sainye ca rajasā dhvaste nir|maryādam avartata.

That day the war became something vast and awful beyond compass. Garbled cries burst out and resounded.
Screams for a father, a son, a friend: Where are you? Wait!
Where are you going? Stand and fight! Stop! Finish him!
Blood of man and horse and beast flowed together and a 32.25
foul cloud of dust stirred from the earth settled on their
wretched forms. On the black path of the dead a warrior
slammed his chariot into another's and knocked off his head
with a club. They clutched at one another's hair and hammered with fists and used nails and teeth as each sought for
solid ground in the sinking morass. A man's arm that held
a sword high was cut clean away and then one that held a
bow, an arrow, a hook. Someone screamed at someone else
and someone fled in terror and someone found another just
like himself and tore his head from his shoulders. A man 32.30
thundered past and another ran from the awful noise and
beneath a hail of sharp arrows a man killed his own while
another killed his foe. Like a rock in a mountainslide down
came an elephant pierced by an iron arrow, and it settled
to earth as it might at leisure into the cool waters of a river
in the summer heat. Like a falling stone another was pulled
over and its foot came down upon a warrior and his car and
driver. The sight of all these brilliant warriors drenched in
blood with arms flailing filled many who were weak and sick
at heart with utter despair. The whole scene was upended
and it was impossible in the chaos to make anything out
through the dust that rolled before everything.

32.35 tataḥ senā|patiḥ śīghram «ayaṃ kāla» iti bruvan
nity'|âbhitvaritān eva tvarayām āsa Pāṇḍavān.
kurvantaḥ śāsanaṃ tasya Pāṇḍavā bāhu|śālinaḥ
saro haṃsā iv' āpetur ghnanto Droṇa|rathaṃ prati.
gṛhṇīt'! ādravat'! ânyonyaṃ vibhītā! vinikṛntata!
ity āsīt tumulaḥ śabdo dur|dharṣasya rathaṃ prati.
tato Droṇaḥ Kṛpaḥ Karṇo Drauṇī rājā Jayadrathaḥ
Vind'|Ânuvindāv Āvantyau Śalyaś c' âinān avārayan
te tv ārya|dharma|saṃrabdhā dur|nivāryā dur|āsadāḥ
śar'|ārtā na jahur Droṇaṃ Pāñcālāḥ Pāṇḍavaiḥ saha.
32.40 tato Droṇo 'bhisaṃkruddho visṛjañ śataśaḥ śarān
Cedi|Pāñcāla|Pāṇḍūnām akarot kadanaṃ mahat.
tasya jyā|tala|nirghoṣaḥ śuśruve dikṣu māriṣa
vajra|saṃhrāda|saṃkāśas trāsayan mānavān bahūn.
etasminn antare Jiṣṇur jitvā Saṃśaptakān bahūn
abhyayāt tatra yatr' âsau Droṇaḥ Pāṇḍūn pramardati.
tāñ śar'|âugha|mah"|āvartān śoṇit'|ôdān mahā|hradān
tīrṇaḥ Saṃśaptakān hatvā pratyadṛśyata Phalgunaḥ.
tasya kīrtimato lakṣma sūrya|pratima|tejasaḥ
dīpyamānam apaśyāma tejasā vānara|dhvajam.
32.45 Saṃśaptaka|samudraṃ tam ucchoṣy' âstra|gabhastibhiḥ
sa Pāṇḍava|yug'|ânt'|ârkaḥ Kurūn apy abhyatītapat.
pradadāha Kurūn sarvān Arjunaḥ śastra|tejasā,
yug'|ânte sarva|bhūtāni dhūma|ketur iv' ôtthitaḥ.

But somehow from within it all their commander's voice cried out: "Now is the time!" 32.35

And so Dhrishta·dyumna rallied the ever vigorous Pándavas and following his order they raised their mighty arms and like swans on the wind flew without fear upon Drona's chariot to destroy it. The clamor grew about the mighty teacher's car: Grab him! Be quick! Be brave! Cut him to pieces! Drona and Kripa and Karna and Ashvattháman and King Jayad·ratha and the two Avántis Vinda and Anuvínda and Shalya all stood their ground, but unstoppable and unreachable and proud in their noble calling the Pándavas and the Panchálas shrugged off their suffering and kept their eyes on their teacher.

Fury blazed in Drona. And he wrought a terrible violence 32.40
upon the Chedis and the Panchálas and the Pandus as arrows flew from his bow in their hundreds. All across the sky its string crackled like lightning and the sound o father filled frail hearts with fear. Having felled the Beholden in droves high Jishnu made his way to where Drona ravaged the Pandus to stop him. The Warrior of the Red Stars appeared suddenly for he had made his way through the arrowdeep gulfs of bloodred roaring surge that was all that was left of the Beholden and we saw like the searing flame of the sun the glint of his crown and the dazzling colors of the banner
of the monkey. The whole ocean of the Beholden the thirsty 32.45
rays of his arrows had drunk up, and now Árjuna son of Pandu and sun risen at the end of time set the Kurus alight as he sent the flame of his sword's blade blistering through the entire army, and we were like the living world on fire beneath the smokebannered orb when the age turns. Hair wild and

tena bāṇa|sahasr'|âughair gaj'|âśva|ratha|yodhinaḥ
tāḍyamānāḥ kṣitiṃ jagmur mukta|keśāḥ śar'|ārditāḥ.
ke cid ārta|svaraṃ cakrur vineśur apare punaḥ
Pārtha|bāṇa|hatāḥ ke cin nipetur vigat'|âsavaḥ.
teṣām utpatitān kāṃś cit patitāṃś ca parāṅ|mukhān
na jaghān' Ârjuno yodhān yodha|vratam anusmaran.
32.50 te vikīrṇa|rathāś citrāḥ prāyaśaś ca parāṅ|mukhāḥ
Kuravaḥ Karṇa Karṇ' êti hā h" êti ca vicukruśuḥ.
tam Ādhirathir ākrandaṃ vijñāya śaraṇ'|âiṣiṇām
«mā bhaiṣṭ'» êti pratiśrutya yayāv abhimukho 'rjunaṃ.
sa Bhārata|ratha|śreṣṭhaḥ sarva|Bhārata|harṣaṇaḥ
prāduś cakre tad" Āgneyam astram astra|vidāṃ varaḥ.
tasya dīpta|śar'|âughasya dīpta|cāpa|dharasya ca
śar'|âughāñ śara|jālena vidudhāva Dhanaṃjayaḥ.
tath" âiv' Ādhirathis tasya bāṇāñ jvalita|tejasaḥ
astram astreṇa saṃvārya prāṇadad visṛjañ śarān.
32.55 Dhṛṣṭadyumnaś ca Bhīmaś ca Sātyakiś ca mahā|rathaḥ
vivyadhuḥ Karṇam āsādya tribhis tribhir a|jihma|gaiḥ.
Arjun'|âstraṃ tu Rādheyaḥ saṃvārya śara|vṛṣṭibhiḥ
teṣāṃ trayāṇāṃ cāpāni ciccheda vi|śikhais tribhiḥ.
te nikṛtt'|āyudhāḥ śūrā nir|viṣā bhuja|gā iva
rathāt śaktīḥ samutkṣipya bhṛśaṃ siṃhā iv' ânadan.
tā bhuj'|âgrair mahā|vegā visṛṣṭā bhuja|g'|ôpamāḥ
dīpyamānā mahā|śaktyo jagmur Ādhirathiṃ prati.

bodies torn by arrows, soldiers and chariots and horses and elephants crashed beneath the rolling volleys of his arrows and fell down dead to the earth. Some fell cursing and some just vanished and some arrowed in Partha's shafts were dead before they struck the ground. Others staggered upright or stumbled away from him and Árjuna held to his code
and did not strike them down without mercy. Spared for 32.50
now they wandered bereft of their chariots while yet others scattered from his path and called out in moans formless or shaped in Karna's name.

Ádhiratha's son heard the plaintive wails of these desperate souls and we heard him call out to them: "Fear not!" He turned towards Árjuna and rode at him.

All in the land of Bhárata urged on the best warrior the Bharatas had known. Sage of war that he was, he invoked then the Weapon of Fire. But with sorcery of his own Dhanan·jaya cut through the bind of arrows from the brightburning bowman wreathed in bright shafts. Then attack smothered attack as roaring and arrows flying Ádhirathi struck down the shafts that came flamed in splendor from
his foes. Three arrows came from Dhrishta·dyumna and 32.55
three from Bhima and three from the mighty Sátyaki and each of them flew true and found him. He buried Árjuna's arrows in a welter of his own and then with only three slim reeds he split each of the others' three bows in two. Their weapons knocked from their hands for a moment, they were like snakes without tongues, yet in a moment more they raised up spears and as one they rode and roared like animals before sending those great staves long as serpents hurtling through the air with all the power of their arms.

tā nikṛtya śitair bāṇais tribhis tribhir a|jihma|gaiḥ
nanāda balavān Karṇaḥ Pārthāya visṛjañ śarān.
32.60 Arjunaś c' âpi Rādheyaṃ viddhvā saptabhir āśu|gaiḥ
Karṇād avara|jaṃ bāṇair jaghāna niśitais tribhiḥ.
tataḥ Śatruṃjayaṃ hatvā Pārthaḥ ṣaḍbhir a|jihma|gaiḥ
jahāra sadyo bhallena Vipāṭasya śiro rathāt
paśyatāṃ Dhārtarāṣṭrāṇām eken' âiva Kirīṭinā
pramukhe Sūta|putrasya sodaryā nihatās trayaḥ.
tato Bhīmaḥ samutpatya sva|rathād Vainateyavat
var'|âsinā Karṇa|pakṣāñ jaghāna daśa pañca ca.
punas tu ratham āsthāya dhanur ādāya c' âparam
vivyādha daśabhiḥ Karṇaṃ sūtam aśvāṃś ca pañcabhiḥ.
32.65 Dhṛṣṭadyumno 'py asi|varaṃ carma c' ādāya bhāsvaram
jaghāna Candravarmāṇaṃ Bṛhatkṣatraṃ ca Naiṣadhaṃ.
tataḥ sva|ratham āsthāya Pāñcālyo 'nyac ca kārmukam
ādāya Karṇaṃ vivyādha tri|saptatyā nadan raṇe.
Śaineyo 'py anyad ādāya dhanur indu|sama|dyutiḥ
sūta|putraṃ catuḥ|ṣaṣṭyā viddhvā siṃha iv' ānadan
bhallābhyāṃ sādhu|muktābhyāṃ
chittvā Karṇasya kārmukam
punaḥ Karṇaṃ tribhir bāṇair
bāhvor urasi c' ârpayat.

They flashed towards Karna. Three shafts and then three again whittled the wind and cut the spars from the arc of their flight as strong Karna bellowed and from his bow sent another volley at Partha.

But with seven swift shafts Árjuna stuck Radha's son and 32.60
three slammed hard and deadly sharp into one of Karna's brothers. And down fell Shatrun·jaya dead beneath six more arrows flying true. In the same second Partha took the head from Vipáta's shoulders with an ironclad dart and left his body still standing in its car. Three brothers were slain by the lone hand of the Diademed Warrior, and all before the very eyes of the horseman's son, as the sons of Dhrita·rashtra looked dumbly on.

Then Bhima leapt from his chariot up into the air, swept like Gáruda upon Karna and struck down fifteen of his guard with his great sword. He climbed onto another car and sweeping up a new bow sent ten arrows at Karna and with five studded his horseman and steeds. king of the Pan- 32.65
chálas Dhrishta·dyumna took up a fine sword and gleaming shield and rained down blow upon blow on Chandra·varman and Brihat·kshatra the Níshadha, before he too leapt back onto his car and hefting another bow and roaring exultant sent three and seventy shafts at Karna. Lustered Shini's son raised his bow and bellowing like a wild beast struck the son of the horseman with sixty-four of his arrows and with two more heavy shafts deftly loosed split Karna's bow in his hands, then pierced his arms and chest with three more. As Sátyaki's flood threatened to engulf him, Duryódhana and Drona and King Jayad·ratha all rushed to

tato Duryodhano Droṇo rājā c' âiva Jayadrathaḥ
nimajjamānaṃ Rādheyam ujjahruḥ Sātyak'|ârṇavāt.
32.70 pattyaś ca ratha|mātaṅgās tvadīyāḥ śataśo 'pare
Karṇam ev' âbhyadhāvanta trāsayānāḥ prahāriṇaḥ.
Dhṛṣṭadyumnaś ca Bhīmaś ca Saubhadro 'rjuna eva ca
Nakulaḥ Sahadevaś ca Sātyakiṃ jugupū raṇe.

evam eṣa mahā|raudraḥ kṣay'|ârthaṃ sarva|dhanvinām
tāvakānāṃ pareṣāṃ ca tyaktvā prāṇān abhūd raṇaḥ.
padāti|ratha|nāg'|âśvā gajāś ca ratha|pattibhiḥ
rathino nāga|patty|aśvai ratha|pattī ratha|dvi|paiḥ
aśvair aśvā gajair nāgā rathino rathibhiḥ saha
saṃsaktāḥ samadṛśyanta pattayaś c' âpi pattibhiḥ.
32.75 evaṃ su|kalilaṃ yuddham āsīt kravy'|âda|harṣaṇam
mahadbhis tair a|bhītānāṃ Yama|rāṣṭra|vivardhanam.
tato hatā nara|ratha|vāji|kuñjarair
an|ekaśo dvipa|ratha|patti|vājinaḥ
gajair gajā rathibhir udāyudhai rathā
hayair hayāḥ patti|gaṇaiś ca pattayaḥ.
rathair dvipā dvi|rada|varair mahā|hayā
hayair narā vara|rathibhiś ca vājinaḥ
nirasta|jihvā|daśan'|ēkṣaṇāḥ kṣitau
kṣayaṃ gatāḥ pramathita|varma|bhūṣaṇāḥ.
tathā parair bahu|karaṇair var'|āyudhair
hatā gatāḥ pratibhaya|darśanāḥ kṣitim
vipothitā haya|gaja|pāda|tāḍitā
bhṛś'|ākulā ratha|mukha|nemibhiḥ kṣatāḥ.

defend him. A great and fearsome phalanx of your soldiers, 32.70
chariots and elephants heaved towards Karna while piling forward to save Sátyaki came Dhrishta·dyumna and Bhima and Abhimányu, and Árjuna, Nákula and Saha·deva.

How the battle was then. A gruesome contest for the theft of the breath and the being of every warrior on your side and on theirs. What stood revealed upon the plain was a vast interlocking of elephants and horses and soldiers and chariots, with more soldiers and more chariots, and warriors with horses and footmen and elephants and footmen and chariots with elephants and cars, and horses with horses and elephants with elephants and warriors with warriors and
soldiers with soldiers. Crammed with the dead the conflict 32.75
between those bold and mighty men had yielded its bounty to carrioneaters and swelled Death's kingdom. The dead were numberless. Horses and soldiers and cars and elephants tangled with elephants and horses and chariots and men in numbers that defied reckoning. There were elephants fallen on elephants and chariots upon warriors with arms still holding weapons to the sky, and horses on horses and soldiers on mounds of soldiers. Raising your eyes you saw more elephants entwined with the debris of chariots, the huge bodies of horses beneath the massive bulk of yet more, and men beneath those horses and horses embracing heroes with eyes and teeth out and tongues in ribbons on the ground and armor and finery all broken up, then more and more countless weapons and wellmade swords shattered and sad to behold, all lying on the earth crushed and buckled beneath foot and hoof and beast and covered with wheels and the shattered ribs of the cars.

pramodane śvā|pada|pakṣi|rakṣasāṃ
jana|kṣaye vartati tatra dāruṇe
mahā|balās te kupitāḥ paras|paraṃ
niṣūdayantaḥ pravicerur ojasā.
32.80 tato bale bhṛśa|lulite paras|paraṃ
nirīkṣamāṇe rudhir'|âugha|samplute
divā|kare 'staṃ|girim āsthite śanair
ubhe prayāte śibirāya Bhārata.

As this terrible vanishment of men brought joy to fiends, birds and wild beasts, still the great warriors who survived were fighting on in rage and violence and the need to destroy one another. They stood face to face deep in the vaults of 32.80
the surging ocean of blood, until at long last o Bhárata the sun set, and night sent the two armies back to their camps.

33–54
THE DEATH OF ABHIMÁNYU

SAMJAYA uvāca.

33.1 PŪRVAM ASMĀSU bhagneṣu Phalgunen' â|mit'|âujasā
Droṇe ca mogha|saṃkalpe rakṣite ca Yudhiṣṭhire
sarve vidhvasta|kavacās tāvakā yudhi nirjitāḥ
rajasvalā bhṛś'|ôdvignā vīkṣamāṇā diśo daśa.
avahāraṃ tataḥ kṛtvā Bhāradvājasya sammate
labdha|lakṣyaiḥ parair hīnā bhṛś'|âvahasitā raṇe
ślāghamāneṣu bhūteṣu Phalgunasy' â|mitān guṇān
Keśavasya ca sauhārde kīrtyamāne 'rjunaṃ prati
33.5 abhiśastā iv' âbhūvan dhyāna|mūkatvam āsthitāḥ.
tataḥ prabhāta|samaye Droṇaṃ Duryodhano 'bravīt
praṇayād abhimānāc ca dviṣad|vṛddhyā ca dur|manāḥ
śṛṇvatāṃ sarva|bhūtānāṃ saṃrabdho vākya|kovidaḥ.
«nūnaṃ vayaṃ vadhya|pakṣe bhavato brahma|vittama
tathā hi n' âgrahīḥ prāptaṃ samīpe 'dya Yudhiṣṭhiram.
icchatas te na mucyeta cakṣuḥ|prāpto raṇe ripuḥ
jighṛkṣato rakṣyamāṇaḥ s'|âmarair api Pāṇḍavaiḥ.
varaṃ dattvā mama prītaḥ paścād vikṛtavān asi
āśā|bhaṅgaṃ na kurvanti bhaktasy' āryāḥ kathaṃ cana.»
33.10 tato hrītas tath" ôktaḥ sa Bhāradvājo 'bravīn nṛ|pam.

Sánjaya spoke.

WE HAD BEEN crushed beneath the Red Star Fighter's measureless might. Drona's plan had failed and Yu-dhi·shthira was safe. We had been defeated. The men stood in tattered armor, caked in grime, eyes glancing wildly about them. With Drona's leave they laid their weapons upon the ground. We had been terribly humiliated by our adversaries. It had been their day. People described with admiration Ár-juna's infinite gifts and spoke with wonder of the concern that Késhava had shown towards his friend. Then like con- 33.5
demned men everyone fell into the oblivion of sleep.

33.1

At daybreak Duryódhana spoke to Drona. Although almost out of his wits with fury at his enemy's triumphs he spoke with eloquence, tempering his anger with a haughty affection. We listened to what he said.

"It would seem o greatest of seers that our side is fated to lose. You come close enough to touch Yudhi·shthira yet you do not. If any foe of yours made the mistake of showing himself to you then I know that even with the help of the deathless gods the Pándavas would not be able to save him from your grasp. If, that is, you truly wanted to capture him. In the past you have done as I have asked, and you are dear to me for that. But a man of honor takes care not to wreck the hopes of one who has entrusted himself to his charge."

Bharad·vaja's son listened to the king. There was shame 33.10
in his voice when he spoke.

«n' ârhase māṃ tathā jñātuṃ ghaṭamānaṃ tava priye.
sa|sur'|âsura|gandharvāḥ sa|yakṣ'|ôra|ga|rākṣasāḥ
n' âlaṃ lokā raṇe jetuṃ pālyamānaṃ Kirīṭinā.
viśva|sṛg yatra Govindaḥ pṛtanā|nīs tath" Ârjunaḥ,
tatra kasya balaṃ krāmed anyatra Try|ambakāt, prabho?
satyaṃ, tāta, bravīmy adya n' âitaj jātv anyathā bhavet
ath" âiṣāṃ pravaraṃ vīraṃ pātayiṣye mahā|ratham.
taṃ ca vyūhaṃ vidhāsyāmi yo '|bhedyas tri|daśair api
yogena kena cid, rājann, Arjunas tv apanīyatām.
33.15 na hy a|jñātam a|sādhyaṃ vā tasya saṃkhye 'sti kiṃ cana
tena hy upāttaṃ sa|kalaṃ sarva|jñānam itas tataḥ.»

Droṇena vyāhṛte tv evaṃ Saṃśaptaka|gaṇāḥ punaḥ
āhvayann Arjunaṃ saṃkhye dakṣiṇām abhito diśam.
tato 'rjunasy' âtha paraiḥ sārdhaṃ samabhavad raṇaḥ
tādṛśo yādṛśo n' ânyaḥ śruto dṛṣṭo 'pi vā kva cit.
tato Droṇena vihito rājan vyūho vyarocata
caran madhyaṃ|dine sūryaḥ pratapann iva dur|dṛśaḥ.
taṃ c' Âbhimanyur vacanāt pitur jyeṣṭhasya Bhārata
bibheda dur|bhidaṃ saṃkhye cakra|vyūham an|ekadhā
33.20 sa kṛtvā duṣ|karaṃ karma hatvā vīrān sahasraśaḥ
ṣaṭsu vīreṣu saṃsakto Dauḥśāsani|vaśaṃ gataḥ.
Saubhadraḥ, pṛthivī|pāla, jahau prāṇān paraṃ|tapaḥ
vayaṃ parama|saṃhṛṣṭāḥ Pāṇḍavāḥ śoka|karśitāḥ
Saubhadre nihate, rājann, avahāram akurmahi.

"You might hold me in higher regard for I am struggling to bring your wishes to pass. Even with an army of gods and devils flanked by genies, spirits and demons no man could make something his when Kirítin is its guardian. Where Go·vinda the creator goes so too does great Árjuna. Tell me my king: who except the Three Eyed God could defeat their combined might? But my son I say this to you, for it will be so nor be denied. I will today hew their high king from their number. I will draw up the army into an array that even the gods could not breach. All the same, o lord, Árjuna
must somehow be drawn away from the battlefield because 33.15
in the reckoning to come nothing is outside the reach of his heart or arm. Piece by piece he has gathered his wisdom in war and now there is nothing that he cannot do."

When Drona had spoken the Beholden again hurled out their challenge off to the south where Árjuna was to be found. There took place a battle between Árjuna and his foes the like of which had never been seen nor heard of before. Drona's chosen formation shone blinding as the sun burning along its meridian. But that day o Bhárata at his uncle's behest Abhimányu broke apart the unbreakable strength of
the Káurava wheel. Thousands fell before him as he went 33.20
about his impossible task. In the end, six of his adversaries surrounded him and he was brought to his knees before Duhshásana's son. O lord of this earth, the son of Subhádra and firebrand to his foes breathed out his last that day. How grave was the sorrow that fell upon the Pándavas then, and how we rejoiced. Yet we too lay down our swords when Abhimányu died, o king.

DHṚTARĀṢṬRA uvāca.

putraṃ puruṣa|siṃhasya, Saṃjay', â|prāpta|yauvanam
raṇe vinihataṃ śrutvā bhṛśaṃ me dīryate manaḥ.
dāruṇaḥ kṣatra|dharmo 'yaṃ vihito dharma|kartṛbhiḥ
yatra rājy'|ēpsavaḥ śūrā bāle śastram apātayan.
33.25 bālam atyanta|sukhinaṃ vicarantam a|bhītavat
kṛt'|âstrā bahavo jaghnur brūhi Gāvalgaṇe katham?
bibhitsatā rath'|ânīkaṃ Saubhadreṇ' â|mit'|âujasā
vikrīḍitaṃ yathā saṃkhye tan mam' ācakṣva, Saṃjaya.

SAṂJAYA uvāca.

yan māṃ pṛcchasi, rājendra, Saubhadrasya nipātanam
tat te kārtsnyena vakṣyāmi śṛṇu rājan samāhitaḥ.
vikrīḍitaṃ kumāreṇa yath' ânīkaṃ bibhitsatā
ārugṇāś ca yathā vīrā duḥ|sādhyāś c' âpi viplave.
dāv'|âgny|abhiparītānāṃ bhūri|gulma|tṛṇa|drume
van'|âukasām iv' âraṇye tvadīyānām abhūd bhayam.

SAṂJAYA uvāca.

34.1 SAMARE 'TYUGRA|karmāṇaḥ karmabhir vyañjita|śramāḥ
sa|Kṛṣṇāḥ Pāṇḍavāḥ pañca devair api dur|āsadāḥ.
sattva|karm'|ânvayair buddhyā kīrtyā ca yaśasā śriyā
n' âiva bhūto na bhavitā n' âiva tulya|guṇaḥ pumān.
satya|dharma|rato dānto vipra|pūj"|ādibhir guṇaiḥ
sad" âiva tri|divaṃ prāpto rājā kila Yudhiṣṭhiraḥ.

DHRITA·RASHTRA spoke.

Sánjaya. Your words rend my heart. That the son of so great a man could be cut down in the prime of life, in war. The laws of a warrior's life are harsh. And how grotesque it is to any who strive for the good of things that men who lust for power could bring down a sword upon a child's head. A child rambles through a world free from horror 33.25
and full of the purest bliss. How could these six swordsmen kill him? Tell me o son of Gaválgana. And tell me too how the brilliant son of Subhádra played with our chariots as if they were toys when he fought his way through our ranks. Come Sánjaya. Speak.

SÁNJAYA spoke.

Great king, you ask me to describe to you Saubhádra's fall. I will tell you the whole story and o majesty I ask that you hear me. Indeed the youth made playthings with the cars through which he battled and on that black day he crushed the most hale of heroes. That day fear came among your men and it seized them as it might villagers in a forest far from anywhere when a great fire comes tearing through the dense palm thickets about them.

SÁNJAYA spoke.

AS THEY CAME FORTH invincible as gods, the five Pánda- 34.1
vas and Krishna all bore the signs of the violence that they had done and that had been done to them. First among them was he to whom in wondrousness and greatness and splendor and wisdom and all that suffuses the noble in deed no man who has lived or ever will live can be compared. Virtue and truth are his passion, and his humility hides

yug'|ânte c' ântako rājañ Jāmadagnyaś ca vīryavān
ratha|stho Bhīmasenaś ca kathyante sa|dṛśās trayaḥ.
34.5 pratijñā|karma|dakṣasya raṇe Gāṇḍīva|dhanvanaḥ
upamāṃ n' âdhigacchāmi Pārthasya sa|dṛśīṃ kṣitau.
guru|vātsalyam atyantaṃ naibhṛtyaṃ vinayo damaḥ
Nakule '|prātirūpyaṃ ca śauryaṃ ca niyatāni ṣaṭ.
śruta|gāmbhīrya|mādhurya|sattva|vīrya|parākramaiḥ
sa|dṛśo devayor vīraḥ Sahadevaḥ kil' Âśvinoḥ.
ye ca Kṛṣṇe guṇāḥ sphītāḥ Pāṇḍaveṣu ca ye guṇāḥ
Abhimanyau kil' âika|sthā dṛśyante guṇa|saṃcayāḥ.
Yudhiṣṭhirasya dhairyeṇa Kṛṣṇasya caritena ca
karmabhir Bhīmasenasya sa|dṛśo bhīma|karmaṇaḥ
34.10 Dhanaṃjayasya rūpeṇa vikrameṇa śrutena ca
vinayāt Sahadevasya sa|dṛśo Nakulasya ca.

DHṚTARĀṢṬRA uvāca.

Abhimanyum ahaṃ, sūta, Saubhadram a|parājitam
śrotum icchāmi kārtsnyena. katham āyodhane hataḥ?

SAṂJAYA uvāca.

sthiro bhava mahā|rāja śokaṃ dhāraya dur|dharam.
mahāntaṃ bandhu|nāśaṃ te kathayiṣyāmi tac chṛṇu.

the nobility of a man who reveres the twiceborn before all others. I speak of King Yudhi·shthira, who even now has touched the highest realms of heaven. O majesty it is he and the great scion of Jamad·agni who brings death at the age's end and Bhima·sena high in his car whom they call the
Perfect Three. And never will I meet a man on this earth the 34.5
measure of the one who carries Gandíva through the fray: Partha, brilliant in mind and hand. His brother Nákula is beholden only to himself. Mildness and modesty, honesty, peace and power, and a total devotion to his elders make six the strictures that bind him. In courage, might, truth and grace, depth of soul and wisdom, the warrior Saha·deva can stand without shame alongside the twin Horse Gods of heaven. And all the virtues in Krishna and the blessings of the sons of Pandu appear united in the figure of Abhimányu. In steadfastness he is like Yudhi·shthira, in speed
like Krishna, in deed wild as Bhima·sena, his discipline he 34.10
shares with the twins and in form and gait and voice he is the very image of his father.

DHRITA·RASHTRA spoke.

O horseman, it is the tale of Abhimányu the triumphant son of Subhádra that now I wish to hear. How was he slain in battle?

SÁNJAYA spoke.

Steel yourself great king and dam the flood of your grief. Hear me, for I tell of the death of your brother's grandson.

cakra|vyūho, mahā|rāja, hy Ācāryeṇ' âbhikalpitaḥ
tatra Śakr'|ôpamāḥ sarve rājāno viniveśitāḥ.
ār'|āsthāneṣu vinyastāḥ kumārāḥ sūrya|varcasaḥ
saṃghāto rāja|putrāṇāṃ sarveṣām abhavat tadā.
34.15 kṛt'|âbhisamayāḥ sarve suvarṇa|vikṛta|dhvajāḥ
rakt'|âmbara|dharāḥ sarve sarve rakta|vibhūṣaṇāḥ
sarve rakta|patākāś ca sarve vai hema|mālinaḥ
candan'|âguru|digdh'|âṅgāḥ sragviṇaḥ sūkṣma|vāsasaḥ
sahitāḥ paryadhāvanta Kārṣṇiṃ prati yuyutsavaḥ.
teṣāṃ daśa|sahasrāṇi babhūvur dṛḍha|dhanvinām
pautraṃ tava puras|kṛtya lakṣmaṇaṃ priya|darśanam
anyonya|sama|duḥkhās te anyonya|sama|sāhasāḥ
anyonya|spardhamānāś ca anyonyasya hite ratāḥ.
Duryodhanas tu, rāj'|êndra, sainya|madhye vyavasthitaḥ
Karṇa|Duḥśāsana|Kṛpair vṛto rājā mahā|rathaiḥ
34.20 deva|rāj'|ôpamaḥ śrīmāñ śveta|cchattr'|âbhisaṃvṛtaḥ
cāmara|vyajan'|âkṣepair udayann iva bhās|karaḥ.
pramukhe tasya sainyasya Droṇo 'vasthita|nāyakaḥ
Sindhu|rājas tath" âtiṣṭhac chrīmān Merur iv' âcalaḥ.
Sindhu|rājasya pārśva|sthā Aśvatthāma|puro|gamāḥ
sutās tava mahā|rāja triṃśat tri|daśa|saṃnibhāḥ.
Gāndhāra|rājaḥ Kitavaḥ Śalyo Bhūriśravās tathā
pārśvataḥ Sindhu|rājasya vyarājanta mahā|rathāḥ.

tataḥ pravavṛte yuddhaṃ tumulaṃ loma|harṣaṇam
tāvakānāṃ pareṣāṃ ca mṛtyuṃ kṛtvā nivartanam.

O majesty, the Teacher drew the troops into the shape
of the wheel and the godlike kings stood arrayed within it.
Each Káurava prince resplendent as the sun had his place as
a spoke in that wheel. Their numbers were vast. Their stan- 34.15
dards all interlocked were picked out in gold, their apparel
was bright and bright their finery and fluttering flags, and
bright their chains of gold. Their arms and legs were sprinkled with aloe and sandal, and they wore garlands around
their necks and cloaks of the finest fabric and all of them
rushed as one to do battle with Karshni. Your handsome
and fortunate son had the loyalty of ten thousand warriors
who raised their stout bows to him and all of them shared
the same grievances and the same determination and jostled
with one another to show their commitment to the common cause. Flanked by his great fighters Karna, Duhshásana
and Kripa, Duryódhana stood among his troops my king
like the very equal of the lord of the gods, immaculate in 34.20
the circle of shade his white parasol cast. The plumes on
his horses' heads quivered as they rode. On he came like
the rising sun. Meanwhile at the very head of the host rode
its trusted commander Drona, and behind him the Sindhu
king noble as Mount Meru. At the king's side were Ashvattháman and thirty of your sons, great as the everlasting
gods. Then came three mighty warriors, blazing at Sindhu's
side: Shalya and Bhuri·shravas and Shákuni, gambler king
of the Gandháras.

And so friend met foe once more in the ghastly crash of battle. Only with death would they rest.

SAMJAYA uvāca.

35.1 TAD ANĪKAM AN|ādhṛṣyaṃ Bhāradvājena pālitaṃ
Pārthāḥ samabhyavartanta Bhīmasena|puro|gamāḥ
Sātyakiś Cekitānaś ca Dhṛṣṭadyumnaś ca Pārṣataḥ
Kuntibhojaś ca vikrānto Drupadaś ca mahā|rathaḥ
Ārjuniḥ Kṣatradharmā ca Bṛhatkṣatraś ca vīryavān
Cedi|po Dhṛṣṭaketuś ca Mādrī|putrau Ghaṭotkacaḥ
Yudhāmanyuś ca vikrāntaḥ Śikhaṇḍī c' â|parājitaḥ
Uttamaujāś ca dur|dharṣo Virāṭaś ca mahā|rathaḥ
35.5 Draupadeyāś ca saṃrabdhāḥ Śaiśupāliś ca vīryavān
Kekayāś ca mahā|vīryāḥ Sṛñjayāś ca sahasraśaḥ.
ete c' ânye ca sa|gaṇāḥ kṛt'|âstrā yuddha|dur|madāḥ
samabhyadhāvan sahasā Bhāradvājaṃ yuyutsavaḥ.
samīpe vartamānāṃs tān Bhāradvājo 'pi vīryavān
a|sambhrāntaḥ śar'|âughena mahatā samavārayat.
mah"|âughāḥ salilasy' êva girim āsādya durbhidam
Droṇaṃ te n' âbhyavartanta velām iva jal'|āśayāḥ.
pīḍyamānāḥ śarai, rājan, Droṇa|cāpa|viniḥsṛtaiḥ
na śekuḥ pramukhe sthātuṃ Bhāradvājasya Pāṇḍavāḥ.
35.10 tad adbhutam apaśyāma Droṇasya bhujayor balam
yad enaṃ n' âbhyavartanta Pāñcālāḥ Sṛñjayaiḥ saha.
tam āyāntam abhikruddhaṃ
Droṇaṃ dṛṣṭvā Yudhiṣṭhiraḥ
bahudhā cintayām āsa
Droṇasya prativāraṇam.
a|śakyaṃ tu tam anyena Droṇaṃ matvā Yudhiṣṭhiraḥ
a|viṣahyaṃ guruṃ bhāraṃ Saubhadre samavāsṛjat
Vāsudevād an|avaraṃ Phalgunāc c' â|mit'|âujasam
abravīt para|vīra|ghnam Abhimanyum idaṃ vacaḥ.

SÁNJAYA spoke.

FOUR OF THE SONS of Pritha rode out towards the unassailable line of men protected by Bharad·vaja's son. Bhima·sena came first, then Sátyaki and Chekitána and Dhrishta·dyumna grandson of Príshata, then the bold chieftain of the Kuntis, the champion Drúpada, and Abhimányu and Kshatra·dharman and valiant Brihat·kshatra, then Dhrishta·ketu prince of the Chedis and the twin sons of Madri and Ghatótkacha and bold Yudha·manyu and triumphant Shikhándin, and dauntless Uttamáujas and the great Viráta. After them rode the five fiery children of Dráupadi and Shishu·pala's fearless son, and then the mighty Kékayas and Srínjayas in their thousands. Still others guarded each by his own plunged forward in the delirium of war to slake his thirst for blood. But mighty Drona stood calm before them, and with a great burst of arrows he drove them back. Like a vast mass of water dammed by solid rock or like the ocean rolling against the coast those warriors broke against Drona. My king, the Pándavas could not even get close to him as their blood was let by the arrows he scattered from his bow. It was a wonder to behold. With but the might of his two arms Drona kept at bay Panchála and Srínjaya alike.

35.1

35.5

35.10

Yudhi·shthira looked upon Drona's furious work and thought desperately about how he might be overcome. Deciding that there was no one who could defeat him, the king nonetheless chose to place this impossible burden upon the shoulders of Abhimányu son of Subhádra, bane of foes and Vasudéva's equal and a warrior as hymned for his brilliance as his father. These were the words the king spoke.

«etya no n' Ârjuno garhed yathā, tāta, tathā kuru
cakra|vyūhasya na vayaṃ vidmo bhedaṃ kathaṃ cana
35.15 tvaṃ v" Ârjuno vā Kṛṣṇo vā bhindyāt Pradyumna eva vā
cakra|vyūhaṃ mahā|bāho pañcamo n' ôpapadyate.
Abhimanyo varaṃ, tāta, yācatāṃ dātum arhasi
pitṝṇāṃ mātulānāṃ ca sainyānāṃ c' âiva sarvaśaḥ.
Dhanaṃjayo hi nas tāta garhayed etya saṃyugāt
kṣipram astraṃ samādāya Droṇ'|ânīkaṃ viśātaya.»

ABHIMANYUR uvāca.

Droṇasya dṛḍham atyugram anīka|pravaraṃ yudhi
pitṝṇāṃ jayam ākāṅkṣann avagāhe 'vilambitam.
upadiṣṭo hi me pitrā yogo 'nīka|viśātane
n' ôtsahe tu vinirgantum ahaṃ kasyāṃ cid āpadi.

YUDHIṢṬHIRA uvāca.

35.20 bhindhy anīkaṃ yudhāṃ śreṣṭha
dvāraṃ saṃjanayasva naḥ
vayaṃ tv" ânugamiṣyāmo
yena tvaṃ, tāta, yāsyasi.
Dhanaṃjaya|samaṃ yuddhe tvāṃ vayaṃ, tāta, saṃyuge
praṇidhāy' ânuyāsyāmo rakṣantaḥ sarvato|mukhāḥ.

"My son. You must do as I say or on his return we will face Árjuna's reproach. I can see no way at all to breach the Káurava wheel. Only you or Árjuna or Krishna or mighty 35.15
Pradyúmna but no fifth beside you could stand a chance in this task. My dear child Abhimányu. You have to do what I say since it is not just I who ask it of you but all of us, every one of your fathers and uncles and every warrior who fights in this army. If you do not then my son when Dhanan·jaya makes his way back I will be the one with whom he finds fault. Do not hesitate. Draw a sharp arrow from your quiver and slice apart what Drona has put together."

ABHIMÁNYU spoke.

Victory for my fathers is all I desire. It may be sheer and forbidding yet without waiting I will break through the wall of Drona's troops and plunge beyond it. My father has taught me the secret art for destroying the array of the wheel. But I fear that if something should go wrong then I will be unable to escape.

YUDHI·SHTHIRA spoke.

Break through this wall and force open a door for us 35.20
and we will follow in your wake, my son. You are a warrior beyond compare, Dhanan·jaya's equal. We will be close behind you, my child, and in your train we will protect you from any and every quarter.

BHĪMA uvāca.

aham tv" ânugamiṣyāmi Dhṛṣṭadyumno 'tha Sātyakiḥ
Pāñcālāḥ Kekayā Matsyās tathā sarve Prabhadrakāḥ.
sakṛd bhinnaṃ tvayā vyūhaṃ tatra tatra vayaṃ punaḥ
vayaṃ pradhvaṃsayiṣyāmo nighnamānā varān varān.

ABHIMANYUR uvāca.

aham etat pravekṣyāmi Droṇ'|ânīkaṃ dur|āsadam
pataṃ|ga iva saṃkruddho jvalitaṃ jāta|vedasam.
35.25 tat karm' âdya kariṣyāmi hitaṃ yad vaṃśayor dvayoḥ
mātulasya ca yat prītiṃ kariṣyāmi pituś ca me.
śiśun" âikena saṃgrāme kālyamānāni saṃghaśaḥ
drakṣyanti sarva|bhūtāni dviṣat|sainyāni vai mayā.
n' âhaṃ Pārthena jātaḥ syāṃ na ca jātaḥ Subhadrayā
yadi me saṃyuge kaś cij jīvito n' âdya mucyate.
yadi n' âika|rathen' âhaṃ samagraṃ kṣatra|maṇḍalaṃ
na karomy aṣṭadhā yuddhe na bhavāmy Arjun'|ātma|jaḥ.

YUDHIṢṬHIRA uvāca.

evaṃ te bhāṣamāṇasya balaṃ Saubhadra vardhatām
yas tvam utsahase bhettuṃ Droṇ'|ânīkaṃ dur|āsadaṃ
35.30 rakṣitaṃ puruṣa|vyāghrair mah"|êṣv|āsair mahā|balaiḥ
sādhya|Rudra|Marut|kalpair Vasv|Agny|Āditya|vikramaiḥ.

SAṂJAYA uvāca.

tasya tad vacanaṃ śrutvā sa yantāram acodayat.

BHIMA spoke.

I will be at your heels, and Dhrishta·dyumna, Sátyaki and all the Panchálas, and the Kékayas, Matsyas and the Prabhádrakas. As soon as you have broken their column it will be our turn—it will be for us to smash and destroy their champions as we choose.

spoke.

Then I will hurl myself at Drona's impenetrable array like a moth on a mad flight into the flickering depths of the fire. I will do what is right for both courses of my blood and in 35.25
so doing bring happiness to my father and my uncle alike. Today everyone will watch as the horde of our enemies is driven back before a lone young man: before me. I am no child of Partha, no child of Subhádra unless any that breathe who cross my path are today cut free from this world. Alone upon my chariot I will carve this dense circle of warriors into eight pieces or I declare that I am not the son of Árjuna.

YUDHI·SHTHIRA spoke.

O son of Subhádra may these words make you ever stronger as you go to your trying task. The enemy array shaped by Drona is defended by great tigers, mighty bow- 35.30
men who are like the gods of the tempest and the gods of the wind and the sky, and whose courage is akin to the courage of the Adítyas or of the Vasus or of Agni.

SÁNJAYA spoke.

Abhimányu heard these words from the king. Then he called out to his charioteer.

«Sumitr', âśvān raṇe kṣipraṃ Droṇ'|ânīkāya codaya.»

SAMJAYA uvāca.

36.1 SAUBHADRAS TU vacaḥ śrutvā Dharma|rājasya dhīmataḥ
acodayata yantāraṃ Droṇ'|ânīkāya, Bhārata.
tena saṃcodyamānas tu yāhi yāh' îti sārathiḥ
pratyuvāca tato, rājann, Abhimanyum idaṃ vacaḥ.
«ati|bhāro 'yam āyuṣmann
āhitas tvayi Pāṇḍavaiḥ
sampradhārya kṣamaṃ buddhyā
tatas tvaṃ yoddhum arhasi.
ācāryo hi kṛtī Droṇaḥ param'|âstre kṛta|śramaḥ
atyanta|sukha|saṃvṛddhas tvaṃ c' â|yuddha|viśāradaḥ.»
36.5 tato 'bhimanyuḥ prahasan sārathiṃ vākyam abravīt.
«sārathe, ko nv ayaṃ Droṇaḥ samagraṃ kṣatram eva vā?
Airāvata|gataṃ Śakraṃ sah'|âmara|gaṇair aham
yodhayeyaṃ raṇa|mukhe na me kṣatre 'dya vismayaḥ.
na mam' âitad dviṣat|sainyaṃ kalām arhati ṣoḍaśīm.
api viśva|jitaṃ Viṣṇuṃ mātulaṃ prāpya, sūta|ja,
pitaraṃ c' Ârjunaṃ yuddhe na bhīr mām upayāsyati.»
tato 'bhimanyus tāṃ vācaṃ kadarthī|kṛtya sāratheḥ
yāh' îty ev' âbravīd enaṃ Droṇ'|ânīkāya māciram.
36.10 tataḥ saṃcodayām āsa hayān asya tri|hāyanān
n' âtihṛṣṭa|manāḥ sūto hema|bhāṇḍa|paricchadān.

"Drive the horses into battle, Sumítra. We are bound for Drona's army."

SÁNJAYA spoke.

O BHÁRATA. SAUBHÁDRA heard the command he had been given by the wise and righteous king. He ordered his driver to make for the vanguard of Drona's host. But when he heard Abhimányu's order Sumítra spoke to his master. O majesty, this is what he said. 36.1

"The Pándavas have placed a heavy burden on your shoulders. Think carefully upon it before you see fit to ride into battle. Drona is your teacher. He is a wise man and he has labored long and hard to learn the highest arts of combat. But your upbringing knew no affliction. You lack his experience in war."

Abhimányu smiled then. This was his reply to Sumítra. 36.5

"Tell me, half-caste. Who is this Drona of whom you speak? Does his power know no bounds? Were Indra to climb upon Airávata and lead the whole throng of the deathless powers against me I would stand to face him and fight my ground. Let there be no cause for surprise at what I can do. This troop of fiends before us is not worthy of the tips of my thumbs.

Horseman's son.* Know this. Were I to meet in war Vishnu my uncle whom none can overcome or come face to face with Árjuna my father, still I would not be afraid."

So Abhimányu spurned his driver's admonition and ordered him again to make all haste for Drona and his men.
With little joy in his heart Sumítra urged on the steeds. Be- 36.10
neath harnesses tooled in gold their strong legs churned as

te preṣitāḥ Sumitreṇa Droṇ'|ânīkāya vājinaḥ
Droṇam abhyadravan rājan mahā|vega|parākramāḥ.
tam udīkṣya tath" āyāntaṃ sarve Droṇa|puro|gamāḥ
abhyavartanta Kauravyāḥ Pāṇḍavāś ca tam anvayuḥ.
sa karṇikāra|pravar'|ôcchrita|dhvajaḥ
suvarṇa|varm" Ārjunir Arjunād varaḥ
yuyutsayā Droṇa|mukhān mahā|rathān
samāsadat siṃha|śiśur yathā dvipān.
te viśantaṃ mudā yuktāḥ samprahāraṃ pracakrire
āsīd Gāṅga iv' āvarto muhūrtam udadhāv iva.
36.15 śūrāṇāṃ yudhyamānānāṃ nighnatām itar'|êtaram
saṃgrāmas tumulo rājan prāvartata su|dāruṇaḥ.
pravartamāne saṃgrāme tasminn ati|bhayaṃ|kare
Droṇasya miṣato vyūhaṃ bhittvā prāviśad Ārjuniḥ.
taṃ praviṣṭaṃ vinighnantaṃ śatru|madhye mahā|balaṃ
hasty|aśva|ratha|patty|aughāḥ parivavrur udāyudhāḥ.
nānā|vāditra|nirghoṣaiḥ kṣveḍit'|āsphoṭa|garjitaiḥ
huṃ|kāraiḥ siṃha|nādaiś ca tiṣṭha tiṣṭh' êti nisvanaiḥ
ghorair halahalā|śabdair mā gās tiṣṭh' âihi mām iti
asāv aham amutr' êti pravadanto muhur muhuḥ
36.20 bṛṃhitaiḥ śiñjitair hāsaiḥ khura|nemi|svanair api
saṃnādayanto vasu|dhām abhidudruvur Ārjunim.
teṣām āpatatāṃ vīraḥ
śīghram pūrvam atho dṛḍham

he set those three-year-old horses to a gallop towards Drona's line. On at Drona they flew. Drona looked up from the midst of the Káuravas as one by one they all turned to face Abhimányu riding out with the rest of the Pándavas at his heels.

Clad in golden armor and with his pennant trailing from a flagpole tall and resplendent as a flowering tree, Árjuna's son was the image and equal of his father. He fell in full frenzy upon the mighty fighters of Drona like a lion cub falling on a herd of elephants. And as he plunged towards them excitement inflamed them and they lurched forward to meet his approach. At the moment they came together it
was like the Ganges pouring into the ocean, and with horror 36.15
and noise the struggle between the two armies of warring clans began o king yet again. Indeed the dread confrontation was barely underway when before Drona's very gaze Árjuni crashed through his front line and split it in two. He drove his way into the heart of the horde while all about him were knotted elephants and horses and chariots and soldiers with swords held high. And all of them rushed at Árjuna's son.

As they rolled and galloped towards him, the earth resounded beneath wheel and hoof with the rising peal of bells and laughter, and voices calling across space as one told another where he was, to come closer, to stay and fight, voices that merged with rude ululations and the cacophony
of challenge and counter-challenge and a great animal groan 36.20
and hum swelling with the wail of a thousand clarions and screams and cries and bellows. They piled in upon him, but it was that swiftbowed hero who struck his brothers first, and he did so quickly and hard. He knew their weaknesses

kṣipr'|âstro nyavadhīd bhrātṝn
marma|jño marma|bhedibhiḥ.
te hanyamānā vi|vaśā nānā|liṅgaiḥ śitaiḥ śaraiḥ
abhipetus tam ev' ājau śalabhā iva pāvakam.
tatas teṣāṃ śarīraiś ca śarīr'|âvayavaiś ca saḥ
saṃtastāra kṣitiṃ kṣipraṃ kuśair vedim iv' âdhvare.
baddha|godh"|âṅguli|trāṇān sa|śar'|âsana|sāyakān
s'|âsi|carm'|âṅkuś'|âbhīśūn sa|tomara|paraśvadhān
36.25 sa|gad"|âyo|guḍa|prāsān sa'|rṣṭi|tomara|paṭṭiśān
sa|bhiṇḍi|pāla|parighān sa|śakti|vara|kampanān
sa|pratoda|mahā|śaṅkhān sa|kuntān sa|kaca|grahān
sa|mudgara|kṣepaṇīyān sa|pāśa|parigh'|ôpalān
sa|keyūr'|âṅgadān bāhūn hṛdya|gandh'|ânulepanān
saṃcicched' Ārjunis tūrṇaṃ tvadīyānāṃ sahasraśaḥ.
taiḥ sphuradbhir mahā|rāja śuśubhe bhūḥ su|lohitaiḥ
pañc'|âsyaiḥ panna|gaiś chinnair Garuḍen' êva māriṣa.
su|nās"|ānana|keś'|ântair a|vraṇaiś cāru|kuṇḍalaiḥ
saṃdaṣṭ'|âuṣṭha|puṭaiḥ krodhāt kṣaradbhiḥ śoṇitaṃ bahu
36.30 cāru|srañ|mukuṭ'|ôṣṇīṣair maṇi|ratna|virājitaiḥ
vi|nāla|nalin'|ākārair divā|kara|śaśi|prabhaiḥ
hita|priyaṃ|vadaiḥ kāle bahubhiḥ puṇya|gandhibhiḥ
dviṣac|chirobhiḥ pṛthivīm avatastāra Phālguniḥ.

and there he drove his brutal attack, pinning them beneath his sharp and numberless arrows. They fell powerless upon him in that violence like moths to a flame. Their bodies and the limbs of which those bodies were built Abhimányu scattered over the soil like so many blades of grass strewn across an altar for olden rites. First it was the arms that he cut cruelly away, arms strapped in armguards with plectrums on the thumbs of their hands, hands that held arrows and the bows from which they flew, hands that held bridles and hooks and shields and swords, that held javelins and 36.25
maces and spears, morningstars and bludgeons and blades and pikes and tridents, slings and studded clubs, hammers and darts, hands that held whips and great conches and staves and claws and mallets and shot and chains and rods and stones, hands at the ends of arms bound in bracelets and torcs and perfumed in jasmine. They were cut down trembling around him like the fiveheaded serpents that Gáruda slew. And the earth shone with their vermilion blood.

Then came their heads. The Red Star Fighter's son strewed the earth with the oilscented heads of his foes, from whose mouths delicate words once fell, whose countenances were 36.30
bright as the sun and moon or lotuses plucked from their stalks, so many all wrapped in turbans or framed in crowns or fine garlands or lustered in gemstones or jewels but now pulsing with blood, some with their eyelids and lips dashed by his angry hand but some with their noses still proud and their features and locks of hair still pristine and with the finest of earrings still in their ears.

gandharva|nagar'|ākārān vidhivat kalpitān rathān
v'|īṣā|mukhān citra|veṇūn nyasta|daṇḍaka|bandhurān
vi|jaṅgha|kūbarāṃs tatra vi|nemi|daśanān api
vi|cakr'|ôpaskar'|ôpasthān bhagn'|ôpakaraṇān api
prapātit'|ôpastaraṇān hata|yodhān sahasraśaḥ
śarair viśakalī|kurvan dikṣu sarvāsv adṛśyata.

36.35 punar dvipān dvip'|ārohān vaijayanty aṅkuśa|dhvajān
tūṇān varmāṇy atho kakṣyā graiveyāṃś ca sa|kambalān
ghaṇṭāḥ śuṇḍān viṣāṇ'|âgrān jara|mālāḥ pad'|ânu|gān
śarair niśita|dhār'|âgraiḥ śātravāṇām aśātayat.
Vanāyu|jān pārvatīyān Kāmbojān atha Bāhlikān
sthira|vāladhi|karṇ'|âkṣāñ javanān sādhu|vāhinaḥ
ārūḍhān śikṣitair yodhaiḥ śakty|ṛṣṭi|prāsa|yodhibhiḥ
vidhvasta|cāru|mukuṭān viprakīrṇa|prakīrṇakān
nirasta|jihvā|nayanān niṣkīrṇ'|ântra|yakṛd|ghanān
hat'|ārohāṃ chinna|ghaṇṭān kravy'|âda|gaṇa|modanān
36.40 nikṛtta|varma|kavacāñ śakṛn|mūtr'|âsṛg|āplutān
nipātayann aśva|varāṃs tāvakān sa vyarocata.

All across the field you could see him as he went carving into splinters with his arrows every chariot that he found. Bedizened from scripture like the cities of heaven, the planks of those cars were pulled from their brightbannered prows, handles and curlicues wrenched from their stocks and shanks and housings tugged away, spokes punched out of wheels if the wheels still remained, and shafts and ornaments gone and paraphernalia crushed and the warriors they once carried all dead.

With arrows sharpened at tip and edge he threw down 36.35
elephants and the men that rode them and pennants and poles, hooks and quivers and armor, girdles and chains and blankets and bells. He lopped off their trunks and tusks and the dried garlands they wore and killed the men that came after them on foot. And he killed their horses, your horses, those fleet and welltrained steeds strong in tail ear and eye and bred in Bahlíka and Kambója and in the mountains and in Vanáyu, horses that had carried skilled warriors who had fought with spear and javelin and bow, horses streaming now with shit piss and blood, plate armor and harnesses ripped from dead carcasses become no more than bounty for carrioneaters, their riders dead and the bells that once hung
from them dashed in, piles of organs and entrails unraveled 36.40
from guts, and tongues and eyes pulled from sockets, silk torn in ribbons and the plumes of their headgear like molted feathers across the ground.

eko Viṣṇur iv' â|cintyaḥ kṛtvā prāk karma duṣ|karaṃ
tathā nirmathitaṃ tena try|aṅgaṃ tava balaṃ mahat
vyabhinat sa padāty|oghāṃs tvadīyān eva sarvaśaḥ.
evam ekena tāṃ senāṃ Saubhadreṇa śitaiḥ śaraiḥ
bhṛśaṃ viprahatāṃ dṛṣṭvā Skanden' êv' âsurīṃ camūm
tvadīyās tava putrāś ca vīkṣamāṇā diśo daśa
saṃśuṣk'|āsyāś calan|netrāḥ prasvinnā roma|harṣiṇāḥ
palāyana|kṛt'|ôtsāhā nir|utsāhā dviṣaj|jaye
gotra|nāmabhir anyonyaṃ krandanto jīvit'|âiṣiṇaḥ
36.45 hatān putrān pitṝn bhrātṝn suhṛt|sambandhi|bāndhavān
prātiṣṭhanta samutsṛjya tvarayanto haya|dvipān.

SAMJAYA uvāca.

37.1 TĀṂ PRABHAGNĀṂ camūṃ dṛṣṭvā
Saubhadreṇ' â|mit'|âujasā
Duryodhano bhṛśaṃ kruddhaḥ
svayaṃ Saubhadram abhyayāt.
tato rājānam āvṛttaṃ Saubhadraṃ prati saṃyuge
dṛṣṭvā Droṇo 'bravīd yodhān paryāpluta|nar'|âdhipān.
«pur" Âbhimanyur lakṣaṃ naḥ paśyatāṃ hanti vīryavān
tam ādravata mā bhaiṣṭa kṣipraṃ rakṣata Kauravam.»
tataḥ kṛta|jñā balinaḥ su|hṛdo jita|kāśinaḥ
trāsyamānā bhayād vīraṃ parivavrus tav' ātma|jam.
37.5 Droṇo Drauṇiḥ Kṛpaḥ Karṇaḥ Kṛtavarmā ca Saubalaḥ
Bṛhadbalo Madra|rājo Bhūrir Bhūriśravāḥ Śalaḥ

All this wrought by one boy. It would have seemed near impossible but like Vishnu who surpasses our mortal thoughts he had ruined chariots, riders, soldiers, every stratum of your great army. The whole mass of your infantry had been blasted before him. With his sharp shafts the son of Subhádra had singlehandedly crushed an army as if he were Skanda taming the demon horde. Your sons looked about them and wherever they turned their heads it was devastation that they beheld. Their mouths were dry, their eyes danced, sweat broke out on their brows and they felt their hair stand on end. All of their remaining strength they saved for their flight and then they had no more. The day belonged to their enemy. Names were on their sorrowing
tongues for it was life that they sought but dead sons, fathers 36.45
and brothers, friends and kin by blood and law to whom they bade farewell, before they spurred on their horses and elephants and made good their escape.

SÁNJAYA spoke.

DURYÓDHANA WATCHED his army collapsing beneath 37.1
Saubhádra's measureless might and his temper could not bear the sight. He rode out towards him.

Drona saw the king making for Saubhádra and addressed the lords who were fighting at his side.

"Keep Duryódhana safe lest Abhimányu snatches his prize from before our very eyes. Be quick, and be brave."

They knew their duty, and despite their fear drew in
around your bold son to show their mettle. There were Dro- 37.5
na and Ashvattháman, Kripa, Karna, Krita·varman, Sáubala, Brihad·bala and the Madra king, Bhuri, Bhuri·shravas,

Pauravo Vṛṣasenaś ca visṛjantaḥ śitāñ śarān
Saubhadraṃ śara|varṣeṇa mahatā samavākiran.
sammohayitvā tam atha Duryodhanam a|mocayan,
āsyād grāsam iv' ākṣiptaṃ mamṛṣe n' Ârjun'|ātma|jaḥ.
tāñ śar'|âugheṇa mahatā s'|âśva|sūtān mahā|rathān
vimukhī|kṛtya Saubhadraḥ siṃha|nādam ath' ânadat.
tasya nādaṃ tataḥ śrutvā siṃhasy' êv' āmiṣ'|âiṣiṇaḥ
n' âmṛṣyanta su|saṃrabdhāḥ punar Droṇa|mukhā rathāḥ.
37.10 ta enaṃ koṣṭhakī|kṛtya ratha|vaṃśena, māriṣa,
vyasṛjann iṣu|jālāni nānā|liṅgāni saṃghaśaḥ.
tāny antar|ikṣe ciccheda pautras tava śitaiḥ śaraiḥ
tāṃś c' âiva prativivyādha tad adbhutam iv' âbhavat.
tatas te kopitās tena śarair āśī|viṣ'|ôpamaiḥ
parivavrur jighāṃsantaḥ Saubhadram a|palāyinam.
samudram iva paryastaṃ tvadīyaṃ tad bal'|ârṇavam
dadhār' âiko "rjunir bāṇair vel" êva Bharata'|rṣabha.
śūrāṇāṃ yudhyamānānāṃ nighnatām itar'|êtaram
Abhimanyoḥ pareṣāṃ ca n' āsīt kaś cit parāṅ|mukhaḥ.
37.15 tasmiṃs tu ghore saṃgrāme vartamāne bhayaṃ|kare
Duḥsaho navabhir bāṇair Abhimanyum avidhyata
Duḥśāsano dvādaśabhiḥ Kṛpaḥ Śāradvatas tribhiḥ
Droṇas tu sapta|daśabhiḥ śarair āśī|viṣ'|ôpamaiḥ
Viviṃśatis tu saptatyā Kṛtavarmā ca saptabhiḥ
Bṛhadbalas tath" âṣṭābhir Aśvatthāmā ca saptabhiḥ
Bhūriśravās tribhir bāṇair Madr'|ēśaḥ ṣaḍbhir āśu|gaiḥ
dvābhyāṃ śarābhyāṃ Śakunis tribhir Duryodhano nṛ|paḥ.

Shala, Páurava and Vrisha·sena, and loosing whetted shafts they showered Saubhádra in a great deluge of arrows that halted his advance and forced him to let Duryódhana go. For Árjuna's son, it was as if a morsel of food had been struck from his mouth and he could not endure it. With a vast mass of arrows he took off the heads of warriors and drivers and horses and roared a lion's roar as he did. It was the roar of a lion in sight of its prey and, filling the ears of Drona and his warriors it drove them wild once again.

O father they surrounded him with a thicket of cars and 37.10
together they wove a haze of arrows above his head. Using his own sharp shafts your grandson cut their arrows from the sky and with miraculous skill struck back at them. Now mad with anger and baying for his blood Drona's men covered Subhádra's defenseless child in arrows deadly as vipers. O bull of the Bharatas, as your warriors surged in a tide towards him, Árjuni was the shore that kept them back with only his reeds. They did not hesitate but jostling with one another fought forward to reach him and the battle around him grew bloodier and more fierce.

Dúhsaha struck Abhimányu with nine of his arrows, 37.15
Duhshásana found him with a dozen and Kripa son of Sharádvat struck him with three. Seventeen shafts deadly as snakes flew at him from Drona, seventy from Vivínshati and seven from Krita·varman, and three arrows came from Bhuri·shravas and six rushed from the Madra king, while Shákuni struck him twice and King Duryódhana thrice. But o majesty he seemed to dance as with three shafts flying true from his bow then three again fiery Abhimányu

sa tu tān prativivyādha tribhis tribhir a|jihma|gaiḥ
nṛtyann iva, mahā|rāja, cāpa|hastaḥ pratāpavān.
37.20 tato 'bhimanyuḥ saṃkruddhas tāpyamānas tav' ātma|jaiḥ
vidarśayan vai su|mahac chikṣ"|âbhyāsa|kṛtam balaṃ.
Garuḍ'|ânila|raṃhobhir yantur vākya|karair hayaiḥ
dāntair Aśmaka|dāyādaṃ tvaramāṇam avārayat.
vivyādha daśabhir bāṇais tiṣṭha tiṣṭh' êti c' âbravīt.
tasy' Âbhimanyur daśabhir hayān sūtaṃ dhvajaṃ śaraiḥ
bāhū dhanuḥ śiraś c' ōrvyāṃ smayamāno nyapātayat.
tatas tasmin hate vīre Saubhadreṇ' Âśmak'|ēśvare
saṃcacāla balaṃ sarvaṃ palāyana|parāyaṇam.
37.25 tataḥ Karṇaḥ Kṛpo Droṇo Drauṇir Gāndhāra|rāṭ Śalaḥ
Śalyo Bhūriśravāḥ Krāthaḥ Somadatto Viviṃśatiḥ
Vṛṣasenaḥ Suṣeṇaś ca Kuṇḍabhedī Pratardanaḥ
Vṛndārako Lalitthaś ca Prabāhur Dīrghalocanaḥ
Duryodhanaś ca saṃkruddhaḥ śara|varṣair avākiran.
so 'tividdho mah"|êṣv|āsair Abhimanyur a|jihma|gaiḥ
śaram ādatta Karṇāya varma|kāy'|âvabhedinam.
tasya bhittvā tanu|trāṇaṃ dehaṃ nirbhidya c' āśu|gaḥ
prāviśad dharaṇīṃ vegād valmīkam iva panna|gaḥ.
sa ten' âtiprahāreṇa vyathito vihvalann iva
saṃcacāla raṇe Karṇaḥ kṣiti|kampe yath" âcalaḥ.
37.30 ath' ânyair niśitair bāṇaiḥ Suṣeṇaṃ Dīrghalocanam
Kuṇḍabhedim ca saṃkruddhas tribhis trīn avadhīd balī.
Karṇas taṃ pañca|viṃśatyā nārācānāṃ samarpayat
Aśvatthāmā ca viṃśatyā Kṛtavarmā ca saptabhiḥ.

struck back. He flared hot with anger from your sons' at- 37.20
tacks and revealed then his extraordinary strength so honed
by discipline and skill.

Driving horses that were mild, faithful to the hand that
guided them and swift as the wind from Gáruda's wings,
he rode to meet the heir of Áshmaka as he raced towards
him. Striking Abhimányu with ten of his arrows the prince
called at him to stand and fight. Abhimányu smiled. Ten
arrows flew from his bow and first his foe's steeds, driver
and standard and then bow, hands and head went tumbling
down to the ground. He had been a great lord of his land
but when Saubhádra slew him his fellow soldiers shook
in doubt and fear. And the rain of arrows poured down 37.25
again from Karna, Kripa, Drona, Drauni, the Gandhára
king and Shala, from Shalya, Bhuri·shravas, Kratha, So-
ma·datta, Vivínshati, Vrisha·sena, Sushéna, Kunda·bhedin
and Pratárdana, Vrindáraka, Lalíttha, Prabáhu, Dirgha·ló-
chana and Duryódhana, now berserk with rage. Abhimányu suffered terribly beneath the arrows flying from their
mighty bows but notching a single shaft of his own crafted
to cut through armor and bone he aimed at Karna and sent
it tearing through the warrior's mail and body, and from
the force of its flight it flew on and bored into the ground
like a snake into a burrow. Struck by that shuddering blow,
Karna staggered in his car like a mountain shaken by an
earthquake. Sighting Sushéna, Dirgha·lóchana and Kun- 37.30
da·bhedin, Abhimányu sent with crazed force three sharp
arrows at the three of them before Karna struck him once
more with twenty-five iron shafts, Ashvattháman hit him
with twenty, and Krita·varman with seven.

sa śar'|ârdita|sarv'|âṅgaḥ kruddhaḥ Śakr'|ātma|j'|ātma|jaḥ
vicaran dadṛśe sainyaiḥ pāśa|hasta iv' ântakaḥ.
Śalyaṃ ca śara|varṣeṇa samīpa|stham avākirat
udakrośan mahā|bāhus tava sainyāni bhīṣayan.
tataḥ sa viddho 'stra|vidā marma|bhidbhir a|jihma|gaiḥ
Śalyo rājan rath'|ôpasthe niṣasāda mumoha ca.
37.35 taṃ hi dṛṣṭvā tathā viddhaṃ Saubhadreṇa yaśasvinā
samprādravac camūḥ sarvā Bhāradvājasya paśyataḥ.
taṃ samprekṣya mahā|bāhuṃ rukma|puṅkhaiḥ samāvṛtaṃ
tvadīyāḥ prapalāyante mṛgāḥ siṃh'|ârditā iva.
sa tu raṇa|yaśas" âbhipūjyamānaḥ
pitṛ|sura|cāraṇa|siddha|yakṣa|saṃghaiḥ
avani|tala|gataiś ca bhūta|saṃghair
ativibabhau huta|bhug yath" ājya|siktaḥ.

DHṚTARĀṢṬRA uvāca.

38.1 TATHĀ PRAMATHAMĀNAṂ taṃ mah"|êṣv|āsān a|jihma|gaiḥ
Ārjuniṃ māmakāḥ sarve ke tv enaṃ samavārayan.

SAṂJAYA uvāca.

sṛṇu rājan kumārasya raṇe vikrīḍitaṃ mahat
bibhitsato rath'|ânīkaṃ Bhāradvājena rakṣitam.
Madr'|ēśaṃ sāditaṃ dṛṣṭvā Saubhadreṇ' āśu|gai raṇe
Śalyād avarajaḥ kruddhaḥ kiran bāṇān samabhyayāt.
tasy' Ārjuniḥ śiro|grīvaṃ pāṇi|pādaṃ dhanur hayān
chattraṃ dhvajaṃ niyantāraṃ tri|veṇuṃ talpam eva ca
38.5 cakraṃ yugaṃ ca tūṇīraṃ hy anukarṣaṃ ca sāyakaiḥ

His limbs were now all needled with arrows and the son of the son of Indra rode madly through the army's lines like Death, noose in hand.* He came past Shalya and raising his great arms sprayed him in arrows, screaming out his hatred for the army around him, and his marrowpiercing shafts flew true from his masterly hands and struck Shalya, who
sank in a daze o king to the seat of his car. Drona's battalion 37.35
saw Shalya overcome by the energy of Saubhádra and they began to crumble. Their commander was powerless to halt them. The sight of one of their champions pinned in bright shafts drove them away in terror like deer before a lion. Abhimányu's splendor blazed in that battle. The heavenly host of forefathers and gods, of seers saints and spirits, all sang out his praises. The ghosts that walk the earth joined their chorus. And Abhimányu flared ever higher, like a thirsty fire given a drink of oil.

DHRITA·RASHTRA spoke.

DID ANY OF MY soldiers stand firm before Árjuna's son 38.1
as he tore through the rows of warriors with his trueflying shafts?

SÁNJAYA spoke.

Listen o king to how as he strove to breach it the youth sported as if at play with the array that Bharadvája had shaped. When the younger brother of Shalya saw the king of the Madras stilled by the quick shafts of Saubhádra he went at him in a rage, scattering darts before him as he rode. But arrows from Árjuni's light fingers cut away his foe's head from his neck, cut to pieces his hands and his feet, his horses and bow and parasol, oriflamme, driver, chariot, and then

patākām cakra|goptārau sarv'|ôpakaraṇāni ca
laghu|hastaḥ praciccheda dadṛśe taṃ na kaś cana.
sa papāta kṣitau kṣīṇaḥ praviddh'|ābharaṇ'|âmbaraḥ.
Vāyun" êva mahāṃś caityaḥ sambhagno '|mita|tejasā
anugās tasya vitrastāḥ prādravan sarvato diśam.
Ārjuneḥ karma tad dṛṣṭvā sampraṇeduḥ samantataḥ
nādena sarva|bhūtāni sādhu sādhv iti Bhārata.
Śalya|bhrātary ath' ārugṇe bahuśas tasya sainikāḥ
kul'|âdhivāsa|nāmāni śrāvayanto 'rjun'|ātma|jam.
38.10 abhyadhāvanta saṃkruddhā vividh'|āyudha|pāṇayaḥ
rathair aśvair gajaiś c' ânye padbhiś c' ânye bal'|ôtkaṭāḥ.
bāṇa|śabdena mahatā khura|nemi|svanena ca
huṃ|kāraiḥ kṣveḍit'|ôtkruṣṭaiḥ siṃha|nādaiḥ sa|garjitaiḥ
jyā|talatra|svanair anye garjanto 'rjuna|nandanam
bruvantaś ca «na no jīvan mokṣyase jīvitād» iti.

tāṃs tathā bruvato dṛṣṭvā Saubhadraḥ prahasann iva
yo yo 'smai prāharat pūrvaṃ taṃ taṃ vivyādha patribhiḥ.
saṃdarśayiṣyann astrāṇi vicitrāṇi laghūni ca
Ārjuniḥ samare śūro mṛdu|pūrvam ayudhyata.
38.15 Vāsudevād upāttaṃ yad astraṃ yac ca Dhanañjayāt
adarśayata tat Kārṣṇiḥ Kṛṣṇābhyām a|viśeṣavat.
dūram asya guruṃ bhāraṃ sādhvasaṃ ca punaḥ punaḥ
saṃdadhad visṛjaṃś c' êṣūn nir|viśeṣam adṛśyata.

the seat from the car's housing, its wheels, yoke, quivers and 38.5
axle, its banner pole and wheelguards and every bolt and shaft that remained. And he did it all in a blur that no eye could follow. Trailing chains and tattered rags the broken form of Shalya's brother fell to earth like a tall sacred tree cracked by the immense force of the wind god himself, and his terrified train scattered in every direction. From every soul on his side a roar went at Árjuni's feat. O Bhárata they cried out in praise to see Shalya's brother brought down, and they chanted at Abhimányu in glee the names of his fathers and forefathers.

But others were filled with anger. Weapons glittering in 38.10
their hands, some came on chariot, horse and elephant, some on foot. Bloodlust crazed them all. Above the deafening clatter of arrows and the thunder of hooves and wheels, and bellows rolling through the gathering din and lions' roars and the trumpeting of elephants, and above the snap of bowstring against armguard, still others screamed out their warning to the youth who was Árjuna's joy: "You will not escape us with your life!"

Saubhádra looked back at them when he heard their threat. A smile played across his lips. Any who came upon him he instantly struck aside with his quarrels. His skill so dazzling and swift was clear to us all that day as the son of Árjuna battled with a strength tempered by a curious kind
of mildness. Karshni unveiled tricks learned from Vasudéva 38.15
and from Dhanan·jaya and each time it was as if both of the Dark Ones fought by his side. Once more he made light of his grave burden and its dangers and as he sent his arrows high they blended into a single mass before which hung

cāpa|maṇḍalam ev' âsya visphurad dikṣv adṛśyata
su|dīptasya śarat|kāle Savitur maṇḍalaṃ yathā.
jyā|śabdaḥ śuśruve tasya tala|śabdaś ca dāruṇaḥ
mah"|âśani|mucaḥ kāle payo|dasy' êva nisvanaḥ.
hrīmān a|marṣī Saubhadro māna|kṛt priya|darśanaḥ
saṃmimānayiṣur vīrān iṣv|astraiś c' âpy ayudhyata.
38.20 mṛdur bhūtvā, mahā|rāja, dāruṇaḥ samapadyata
varṣ'|âbhyatīto bhagavāñ śarad' îva divā|karaḥ.
śarān vicitrān bahuśo rukma|puṅkhāñ śilā|śitān
mumoca śataśaḥ kruddho gabhastīn iva bhās|karaḥ.
kṣuraprair vatsa|dantaiś ca vipāṭhaiś ca mahā|yaśāḥ
nārācair ardha|candr'|ābhair bhallair añjalikair api
avākirad rath'|ânīkaṃ Bhāradvājasya paśyataḥ
tatas tat sainyam abhavad vimukhaṃ śara|pīḍitam.

DHṚTARĀṢṬRA uvāca.

39.1 DVAIDHĪ|BHAVATI me cittaṃ hriyā tuṣṭyā ca, Saṃjaya,
mama putrasya yat sainyaṃ Saubhadraḥ samavārayat.
vistareṇ' âiva me śaṃsa sarvaṃ, Gāvalgaṇe, punaḥ
vikrīḍitaṃ kumārasya Skandasy' êv' âsuraiḥ saha.

SAṂJAYA uvāca.

hanta, te sampravakṣyāmi vimardam ati|dāruṇam
ekasya ca bahūnāṃ ca yath" āsīt tumulo raṇaḥ.
Abhimanyuḥ kṛt'|ôtsāhaḥ kṛt'|ôtsāhān ariṃ|damān
ratha|stho rathinaḥ sarvāṃs tāvakān abhyavarṣayat.
39.5 Droṇaṃ Karṇaṃ Kṛpaṃ Śalyaṃ

the circle of his bow, shimmering in the skies above like the brightburning disk of the autumnal sun. The thrum of his bowstring and the eerie whisper of his hands were like the tremors of a dusk raincloud alive with lightning. Modest and mild and generous as he was, the handsome Saubhádra strove at first to honor his enemies with the arrows and blows he sent at them. But as he fought on, from 38.20
calm to fearsomeness he turned, my king, as the holy sun at the turning of the year burgeons through the rain. Like rays of the sun, arrows bright and golden and whetted to a gleam flew from his bow in their hundreds. Wrath rose within him. Biting and barbed were the spearlike shafts and splinters curved like halfmoons and iron bolts and darts that Abhimányu scattered upon the facing line, while Bharad·vaja's son looked helplessly on. And beneath this torture of arrows the faces of his enemies fell.

DHRITA·RASHTRA spoke.

O SÁNJAYA. YOU TELL me of Saubhádra's eclipse of the 39.1
army of my son and shame and pleasure vie in my heart. Describe everything to me. Spare nothing, Gaválgani. I want to hear how the boy played with us as once Skanda played with the demons.

SÁNJAYA spoke.

Then I shall describe to you a bloody contest of one against many and spare no detail of the violent struggle that ensued. Supreme was Abhimányu's courage and supreme the courage of those who sought to tame him. From his bow came a rain that fell on all the chariots manned by
all the warriors in your son's army. Down upon Drona, 39.5

Drauṇiṃ bhojaṃ Bṛhadbalam
Duryodhanaṃ Saumadattiṃ
Śakuniṃ ca mahā|balam
nānā|nṛ|pān nṛ|pa|sutān sainyāni vividhāni ca
alāta|cakravat sarvān tvaramāṇaḥ samarpayat.
nighnann a|mitrān Saubhadraḥ param'|âstraḥ pratāpavān
adarśayata tejasvī dikṣu sarvāsu, Bhārata.
tad dṛṣṭvā caritaṃ tasya Saubhadrasy' â|mit'|âujasaḥ
samakampanta sainyāni tvadīyāni punaḥ punaḥ.
ath' âbravīn mahā|prājño Bhāradvājaḥ pratāpavān
harṣeṇ' ôtphulla|nayanaḥ Kṛpam ābhāṣya sa|tvaram
39.10 ghaṭṭayann iva marmāṇi putrasya tava, Bhārata,
Abhimanyuṃ raṇe dṛṣṭvā tadā raṇa|viśāradam.
«eṣa gacchati Saubhadraḥ Pārthānām agrato yuvā
nandayan su|hṛdaḥ sarvān rājānaṃ ca Yudhiṣṭhiram
Nakulaṃ Sahadevaṃ ca
Bhīmasenaṃ ca Pāṇḍavam
bandhūn sambandhinaś c' ânyān
madhya|sthān su|hṛdas tathā.
n' âsya yuddhe samaṃ manye
kaṃ cid anyaṃ dhanur|dharam
icchan hanyād imāṃ senāṃ
kim artham api n' êcchati.»
Droṇasya prīti|saṃyuktaṃ śrutvā vākyaṃ tav' ātma|jaḥ
Ārjuniṃ prati saṃkruddho Droṇaṃ dṛṣṭvā smayann iva.
39.15 atha Duryodhanaḥ Karṇam abravīd Bāhlikaṃ nṛ|pam
Duḥsāsanaṃ Madra|rājaṃ tāṃs tāṃś c' ânyān mahā|rathān.

upon Karna, Kripa and Shalya, upon Ashvattháman and Lord Brihad·bala, upon Duryódhana and Saumadátti and mighty Shákuni, upon all the many kings and sons of kings and soldiers of every rank he came wheeling like a ring of burning coals. With weapons not of this world in his hands Saubhádra slew any who came against him and we saw his splendor as he blazed across the skies. O Bhárata. How your soldiers shook and trembled at the sight of Saubhádra's awesome course. Bharad·vaja's wise and brilliant son called
out to nimble Kripa, his eyes wide with wonder at the sight 39.10
of the mastery Abhimányu was displaying, and he spoke words that seemed, o Bhárata, to crush the very bones in Duryódhana's body.

"Look at this tender child born to Subhádra who fights in the van of the Parthas, and see what joy he brings to his family, to King Yudhi·shthira and Nákula, Saha·deva and Bhima·sena son of Pandu, and all his kin and allies and friends. None who bear the bow could be said to be his equal. If he wished it he could annihilate this force. And we might ask why he seems minded otherwise."

Drona's words betrayed him. Your son heard the affection for Abhimányu in his voice and anger rose up within him.
He looked at Drona with a mocking smile then spoke to 39.15
them all, to Karna, King Bahlíka, Duhshásana, the king of the Madras and the other heroes who were there.

«sarva|mūrdh'|âvasiktānām ācāryo brahma|vittamaḥ
Arjunasya sutaṃ mūḍho n' âyaṃ hantum ih' êcchati.
na hy asya samare mucyed antako 'py ātatāyinaḥ
kim aṅga punar ev' ânyo martyaḥ satyaṃ bravīmi vaḥ.
Arjunasya sutaṃ tv eṣa śiṣyatvād abhirakṣati
śiṣyāḥ putrāś ca dayitās tad apatyaṃ ca dharmiṇām.
saṃrakṣyamāṇo Droṇena manyate vīryam ātmanaḥ
ātma|sambhāvito mūḍhas taṃ pramathnīta mā ciram.»
39.20 evam uktās tu te rājñā Sātvatī|putram abhyayuḥ
saṃrabdhās taṃ jighāṃsanto Bhāradvājasya paśyataḥ.
Duḥśāsanas tu tac chrutvā Duryodhana|vacas tadā
abravīt Kuru|śārdūlo Duryodhanam idaṃ vacaḥ.
«aham enaṃ haniṣyāmi mahā|rāja bravīmi te
miṣatāṃ Pāṇḍu|putrāṇāṃ Pāñcālānāṃ ca paśyatām.
grasiṣyāmy adya Saubhadraṃ yathā Rāhur divā|karam»
utkruśya c' âbravīd vākyaṃ Kuru|rājam idaṃ punaḥ.
«śrutvā Kṛṣṇau mayā grastaṃ Saubhadram ati|māninau
gamiṣyataḥ preta|lokaṃ jīva|lokān na saṃśayaḥ.
tau ca śrutvā mṛtau vyaktaṃ Pāṇḍoḥ kṣetr'|ôdbhavāḥ sutāḥ
ek'|âhnā sa|su|hṛd|vargāḥ klaibyādd hāsyanti jīvitam.
39.25 tasmād asmin hate śatrau hatāḥ sarve '|hitās tava
śivena dhyāhi mā rājann eṣa hanmi ripuṃ tava.»

"Behold the teacher of the whole warrior caste, this wise and holy sage. He has gone into a swoon over Árjuna's child and does not seek his death. If the Destroyer himself stepped out here today and drew his bow upon him, even he could not bear Drona back to his kingdom. And what of a mere mortal? The truth is that Drona is protecting the son of Árjuna because he was his pupil, because disciples and their children and those beloved to them are all as good as kin as far as the virtuous are concerned. It is Drona who protects him yet Abhimányu dreams that it is his own prowess that he has to thank for his survival. He is just a fool in thrall to his delusion. There is no time to waste. He must be crushed."

Inspired by what Duryódhana had said, his warriors rode 39.20
out once more for Abhimányu, the boy's death in their hearts. All the while Bharad·vaja merely looked on. Then the tiger of the Kurus Duhshásana spoke these words to his brother.

"I say to you my king that I will kill Abhimányu, and the Pándavas and Panchálas will stand about blinking as I do. I will swallow up Saubhádra like Rahu swallowed the sun." This he baldly stated, then after a pause he began to speak once more to the Kuru sovereign. "Have no doubt. When the proud Dark Ones hear that I have devoured Saubhádra they will both leave the world of the living, bound for the world of the dead. Mark my words. When they hear that the Krishnas are dead the sons sprung from Pandu's soil* will in but a single day give up their craven lives, as will all their kin and kind. With the death of but one of their number 39.25

evam uktvā nadan, rājan, putro Duḥśāsanas tava
Saubhadram abhyayāt kruddhaḥ śara|varṣair avākiran.
tam ati|kruddham āyāntaṃ tava putram ariṃ|damaḥ
Abhimanyuḥ śarais tīkṣṇaiḥ ṣaḍ|viṃśatyā samarpayat.
Duḥśāsanas tu saṃkruddhaḥ prabhinna iva kuñjaraḥ
ayodhayata Saubhadram Abhimanyuś ca taṃ raṇe.
tau maṇḍalāni citrāṇi rathābhyāṃ savya|dakṣiṇam
caramāṇāv ayudhyetāṃ ratha|śikṣā|viśāradau.
39.30 atha paṇava|mṛdaṃga|dundubhīnāṃ
kṛkara|mahānaka|bheri|jharjharāṇām
ninadam ati|bhṛśaṃ narāḥ pracakrur
lavaṇa|jal'|ôdbhava|siṃha|nāda|miśram.

SAṂJAYA uvāca.

40.1 ŚARA|VIKṢATA|GĀTRAS tu praty|a|mitram avasthitam
Abhimanyuḥ smayan dhīmān Duḥśāsanam ath' âbravīt.
«diṣṭyā paśyāmi saṃgrāme māninaṃ śūram āgatam
niṣṭhuraṃ tyakta|dharmāṇam ākrośana|parāyaṇam.
yat sabhāyāṃ tvayā rājño Dhṛtarāṣṭrasya śṛṇvataḥ
kopitaḥ paruṣair vākyair Dharma|rājo Yudhiṣṭhiraḥ
jay'|ônmattena Bhīmaś ca bahv|a|baddhaṃ prabhāṣatā
akṣa|kūṭaṃ samāśritya Saubalasy' ātmano balam
40.5 tat tvay" êdam anuprāptaṃ prakopād vai mah"|ātmanām
para|vitt'|âpahārasya krodhasy' â|praśamasya ca
lobhasya jñāna|nāśasya drohasy' âty|āhitasya ca
pitṝṇāṃ mama rājyasya haraṇasy' ôgra|dhanvinām

all of your enemies will fall. So wish me well o majesty. I go
to slay your foe."

My king, when he had said these words your son Duhshásana rushed at Saubhádra roaring with anger and unleashed
a torrent of arrows as he went. But at his frenzied approach
the burner of foes Abhimányu struck back with six and
twenty of his own keen shafts. Like a furious and wounded
elephant Duhshásana came at Saubhádra and Abhimányu at
him. They both had great skill in riding and they wheeled
right and left, leaving spiraling tracks in their wake. On 39.30
they fought, while from the men around them there arose a
mighty cacophony of drums of war, of tamp and crash and
clatter and rumble, the noise mingling with roars such as
are heard of beasts and of the briny sea.

SÁNJAYA spoke.

ARROWS IN HIS ARMS and legs, Abhimányu stood and 40.1
faced his foe and smiled. The words he spoke were well
chosen.

"Behold. A hero upon the field at last. A proud one,
too. With rude speech and derelict morals and insults on
his tongue. Hail to him. For those vile boasts you made
and the twisted insults that in your drunken triumph and
before the ears of your lord Dhrita·rashtra you spoke that
day in the hall, and so insulted the good King Yudhi·shthira
and his brother Bhima, and for the theft of what belongs 40.5
to another, and for your lawless passions and your dizzy
greed and treachery and violence and because you stole the
kingdom from the dark archers who are my fathers, come o
fool from behind the trick of the light that Sáubala calls his

sadyaś c' ôgram a|dharmasya phalam prāpnuhi, dur|mate,
śāsit" âsmy adya te bāṇaiḥ sarva|sainyasya paśyataḥ.
ady' âham an|ṛṇas tasya kopasya bhavitā raṇe
a|marṣitāyāḥ Kṛṣṇāyāḥ kāṅkṣitasya ca me pituḥ.
adya Kauravya Bhīmasya bhavit" âsmy an|ṛṇo yudhi
na hi me mokṣyase jīvan yadi n' ôtsṛjase raṇam.»
40.10 evam uktvā mahā|bāhur bāṇaṃ Duḥśāsan'|ântakam
saṃdadhe para|vīra|ghnaḥ kāl'|âgny|anila|varcasam.
tasy' ôras tūrṇam āsādya jatru|deśe vibhidya tam
jagāma saha puṅkhena valmīkam iva panna|gaḥ.
ath' âinaṃ pañca|viṃśatyā punar eva samārpayat.
śarair asi|sama|sparṣair ākarṇa|sama|coditaiḥ
sa gāḍha|viddho vyathito rath'|ôpastha upāviśat
Duḥśāsano, mahā|rāja, kaśmalaṃ c' āviśan mahat.
sārathis tvaramāṇas tu Duḥśāsanam a|cetanam
raṇa|madhyād apovāha Saubhadra|śara|pīḍitam.
40.15 Pāṇḍavā Draupadeyāś ca Virāṭaś ca samīkṣya taṃ
Pāñcālāḥ Kekayāś c' âiva siṃha|nādam ath' ānadan.
vāditrāṇi ca sarvāṇi nānā|liṅgāni sarvaśaḥ
prāvādayanta saṃhṛṣṭāḥ Pāṇḍūnāṃ tatra sainikāḥ.
apaśyan smayamānāś ca Saubhadrasya viceṣṭitam
atyanta|vairiṇaṃ dṛptaṃ dṛṣṭvā śatruṃ parājitam.
Dharma|Māruta|Śakrāṇām Aśvinoḥ pratimās tathā
dhārayanto dhvaj'|âgreṣu Draupadeyā mahā|rathāḥ

army and reap now the terrible reward for your crime, as it is one you have earned by the fury you have kindled in mighty souls. With my arrows I will punish you this day before the eyes of all your comrades and in exacting vengeance for your crime I will lift the polluting fury that dwells in Krishná's pained heart and make good my father's wish.* This day o son of Kuru I will do my duty to Bhima with the swing of my sword. You may surrender. For otherwise you will not escape the coming battle alive."

Thus spoke the mighty scourge of foes and he let fly a 40.10
single arrow destined for Duhshásana's heart deadly as the wind from the fire of time. It sank deep into Duhshásana's chest all the way to the nock like a snake into the earth, and lodged beneath his collarbone. Back went Abhimányu's bowstring to his ear and then five and twenty more sharp as swords took to the air and each one hit its mark. Pierced to the quick, Duhshásana reeled and fell to the floor of his car. A great shadow fell upon your son, my king, but as he slipped into darkness under the bite of Saubhádra's arrows his helmsman quickly bore him from the fray.

Then up came a wild cry from the Pándavas and Dráu- 40.15
padi's sons and from Viráta and the Panchálas and Kékayas, for they saw what Abhimányu had done. They were elated at Saubhádra's feat and the Pándava horde blew into their horns in concert all across the battlefield. Joyously they watched as Saubhádra cast down the vaunting malice and pride of their enemy. Bearing above them the faces of Dharma and Vayu, of Indra and the Ashvins, the mighty Draupadéyas came on with their morale renewed, and with them

Sātyakiś Cekitānaś ca Dhṛṣṭadyumna|Śikhaṇḍinau
Kekayā Dhṛṣṭaketuś ca Matsya|Pāñcāla|Sṛñjayāḥ
40.20 Pāṇḍavāś ca mudā yuktā Yudhiṣṭhira|puro|gamāḥ
abhyavartanta sahitā Droṇ'|ânīkaṃ bibhitsavaḥ.
tato 'bhavan mahad yuddhaṃ tvadīyānāṃ paraiḥ saha
jayam ākāṅkṣamāṇānāṃ śūrāṇām a|nivartinām.

tathā tu vartamāne vai saṃgrāme 'ti|bhayaṃ|kare.
Duryodhano, mahā|rāja, Rādheyam idam abravīt.

«paśya Duḥśāsanaṃ vīram Abhimanyu|vaśaṃ gatam
pratapantam iv' Ādityaṃ nighnantaṃ śātravān raṇe.
atha c' âite su|saṃrabdhāḥ siṃhā iva bal'|ôtkaṭāḥ
Saubhadram udyatās trātum abhyadhāvanta Pāṇḍavāḥ.»

40.25 tataḥ Karṇaḥ śarais tīkṣṇair Abhimanyuṃ dur|āsadam
abhyavarṣata saṃkruddhaḥ putrasya hita|kṛt tava.
tasya c' ânucarāṃs tīkṣṇair vivyādha param'|êṣubhiḥ
avajñā|pūrvakaṃ śūraḥ Saubhadrasya raṇ'|âjire.
Abhimanyus tu Rādheyaṃ tri|saptatyā śilī|mukhaiḥ
avidhyat tvarito rājan Droṇaṃ prepsur mahā|manāḥ.
taṃ tadā n' âśakat kaś cid Droṇād vārayituṃ rathī
ārujantaṃ ratha|vrātān vajra|hast'|ātma|j'|ātma|jam.
tataḥ Karṇo jaya|prepsur mānī sarva|dhanuṣmatām
Saubhadraṃ śataśo 'vidhyad uttam'|âstrāṇi darśayan.

40.30 so 'strair astra|vidāṃ śreṣṭho Rāma|śiṣyaḥ pratāpavān
samare śatru|dur|dharṣam Abhimanyum apīḍayat.
sa tathā pīḍyamānas tu Rādheyen' âstra|vṛṣṭibhiḥ
samare 'mara|saṃkāśaḥ Saubhadro na vyaṣīryata.

came Sátyaki and Chekitána and Dhrishta·dyumna and Shikhándin, the Kékayas and Dhrishta·ketu, the Matsyas, Panchálas and Srínjayas and Pándavas, all as one behind Yu- 40.20
dhi·shthira, all desperate to destroy Drona's array. But your son too wanted victory. And his warriors fought without turning.

O majesty. As the battle between the two sides grew more gruesome about him, Duryódhana turned to speak to Karna.

"Duhshásana was like a blazing sun cutting through our enemies but see how Abhimányu has brought him low. And the Pándavas are wild as lions in their frenzy. They follow on to protect the boy from harm."

Fury was in Karna, and ever devoted to your son's weal 40.25
he sent forth a shower of sharp arrows at the inviolable Abhimányu. With shafts wellhoned and finely wrought the hero struck with contempt at Saubhádra's guard, but proud Abhimányu was undeterred and sent back at Radha's son three and seventy stonetipped darts as he made swiftly for Drona, and from Drona o majesty there were none who could keep him as son of the son of the wielder of the thunderbolt he tore on through the knots of men. But Karna whom all knowers of the bow revere wanted blood, and with spectacular skill pinned Saubhádra beneath a hundred of his shafts.

The best of bowmen who had been Rama's disciple had 40.30
fire in him then. Abhimányu's other enemies could not reach him, but Karna pressed hard upon him in that battle. Yet Saubhádra did not fade from the fight despite the pain of the rain of arrows sent by Radha's son and like a deathless

tataḥ śilā|śitais tīkṣṇair bhallair ānata|parvabhiḥ
chittvā dhanūṃṣi śūrāṇām Ārjuniḥ Karṇam ārdayat.
dhanur|maṇḍala|nirmuktaiḥ śarair āśī|viṣ'|ôpamaiḥ
sa|cchattra|dhvaja|yantāraṃ s'|âśvam āśu smayann iva
Karṇaḥ pañc' âsya cikṣepa bāṇān saṃnata|parvaṇaḥ
a|sambhrāntaś ca tān sarvān agṛhṇāt Phālgun'|ātma|jaḥ.
40.35 tato muhūrtāt Karṇasya bāṇen' âikena vīryavān
sa|dhvajaṃ kārmukaṃ vīraś chittvā bhūmāv apātayat.
tataḥ kṛcchra|gataṃ Karṇaṃ dṛṣṭvā Karṇād an|antaraḥ
Saubhadram abhyayāt tūrṇaṃ dṛḍham āyamya kārmukaṃ.
tata uccukruśuḥ Pārthās teṣāṃ c' ânucarā janāḥ
vāditrāṇi ca saṃjaghnuḥ Saubhadraṃ c' âpi tuṣṭuvuḥ.

SAMJAYA uvāca.

41.1 SO 'NUGARJAN dhanuṣ|pāṇir jyāṃ vikarṣan punaḥ punaḥ
tayor mah"|ātmanos tūrṇaṃ rath'|ântaram avāpatat.
so 'vidhyad daśabhir bāṇair Abhimanyuṃ dur|āsadam
sa|cchattra|dhvaja|yantāraṃ s'|âśvam āśu smayann iva.
pitṛ|paitāmahaṃ karma kurvāṇam ati|mānuṣam
dṛṣṭv' ârditaṃ śaraiḥ Kārṣṇiṃ tvadīyā hṛṣit" âbhavan.
tasy' Âbhimanyur āyamya smayann ekena patriṇā
śiraḥ pracyāvayām āsa tad rathāt prāpatad bhuvi.

god he stood his ground. The smooth shafts of his iron darts bit with their stonesharp tips through the bows of those around him as he made to fight back against Karna. Karna simply smiled. Plummeting down from the curve of his bow, arrows deadly as cobras fell on Abhimányu's driver, parasol, standard and horses, but the son of the Warrior of the Red Stars fought on unbending and deflected them all.
In but a moment and with a single shaft the great fighter 40.35
split Karna's bow and standard and brought them spinning down to earth. Karna began to struggle. Bow in hand his younger brother saw his plight and wheeled to face indomitable Abhimányu, while around him the cry went up above a thunder of drums as the Parthas and the men at their side all cheered on Subhádra's child.

SÁNJAYA spoke.

KARNA'S BROTHER raised his bow and called out to Abhi- 41.1
mányu and drew back his bowstring and rode right in between the chariots of the two great warriors with a smile on his face. Ten shafts came quickly upon peerless Abhimányu and fell across his horses, driver, standard and parasol. After the prodigies he had wrought in his father's name, the sight of Karshni harrowed beneath that attack lifted for a moment your sons' spirits. But his countenance still light, Abhimányu raised his bow and with a single arrow clove away his foe's head from his body and sent it tumbling down to the ground.

41.5 karṇikāram iv' ôddhūtaṃ vātena mathitaṃ nagāt
bhrātaraṃ nihataṃ dṛṣṭvā, rājan, Karṇo vyathāṃ yayau.
vimukhī|kṛtya Karṇaṃ tu Saubhadraḥ kaṅka|patribhiḥ
anyān api mah"|êṣv|āsāṃs tūrṇam ev' âbhidudruve.
tatas tad vitataṃ sainyaṃ hasty|aśva|ratha|pattimat
kruddho 'bhimanyur abhinnat tigma|tejā mahā|yaśā.
Karṇas tu bahubhir bāṇair ardyamāno 'bhimanyunā
apāyāj javanair aśvais tato 'nīkam abhidyata.
śalabhair iva c' ākāśe dhārābhir iva c' āvṛte
Abhimanyoḥ śarai rājan na prājñāyata kiṃ cana.
41.10 tāvakānāṃ tu yodhānāṃ vadhyatāṃ niśitaiḥ śaraiḥ
anyatra Saindhavād, rājan, na sma kaś cid atiṣṭhata.
Saubhadras tu tataḥ śaṅkhaṃ pradhmāpya puruṣa'|rṣabhaḥ
śīghram abhyapatat senāṃ Bhāratīṃ Bharata'|rṣabha.
madhyaṃ Bhārata|sainyānām Ārjuniḥ paryavartata
ratha|nāg'|âśva|manu|jān ardayan niśitaiḥ śaraiḥ,
sampraviśy' âkarod bhūmiṃ kabandha|gaṇa|saṃkulām.
Saubhadra|cāpa|prabhavair nikṛttāḥ param'|êṣubhiḥ
svān ev' âbhimukhān ghnantaḥ prādravañ jīvit'|ârthinaḥ.
te ghorā raudra|karmāṇo vi|pāṭhā bahavaḥ śitāḥ
nighnanto ratha|nāg'|âśvāñ jagmur āśu vasuṃ|dharām.
41.15 s'|āyudhāḥ s'|âṅguli|trāṇāḥ sa|gadāḥ s'|âṅga|dā raṇe
dṛśyante bāhavaś chinnā hem'|ābharaṇa|bhūṣitāḥ.
śarāś cāpāni khaḍgāś ca śarīrāṇi śirāṃsi ca
sa|kuṇḍalāni sragvīṇi bhūmāv āsan sahasraśaḥ.

O majesty. When Karna saw his brother cut down like a 41.5
bayur tree plucked by the wind and cast from a mountain
peak, how his heart welled with pain. Karna faltered and
Saubhádra did not wait and loosing shafts fletched in vulture feathers he rushed at the next row of warriors. Gloried
in fire, Abhimányu began to break apart the warp of elephants and horses and men with the force of his wrath and
splendor. Even Karna slid away with his swift steeds beneath
the crush of arrows he sent at them, and the vanguard then
was broken.

Majesty, as Abhimányu's arrows flew it was like the air
had been filled with locusts or rain and nothing could be
made out. Cut down by those sharp shafts not a single 41.10
of your fighters o king stood his ground except for the
son of Sindhu. O bull of the Bharatas as he blew into his
conch Árjuni bull in the world of men flew in a blur at
the army of your kin and whirled on deep into the heart of
the Bhárata horde. Through chariots and through elephants
and through horses and through men he plunged, and he
studded all he found in biting darts and piled up the limbless
dead upon the earth. Transfixed by the fine shafts born
of Saubhádra's bow his victims blundered over their own
companions as they ran in desperation to save their lives.
Awful and honed and deadly were the spearlike shafts that
tore through chariots and elephants and horses and then
thudded to rest in the bounteous earth. Among the swords, 41.15
the thumbrings, platemail and torcs that lay strewn across
the plain there glittered apparel and ornaments of gold.
Arrows and bows and swords and the trunks and heads of
the dead came to rest in their hundreds upon the earth, still

s'|ôpaskarair adhiṣṭhānair īṣā|daṇḍaiś ca bandhuraiḥ
akṣair vimathitaiś cakrair bhagnaiś ca bahudhā yugaiḥ
śakti|cāp'|âsibhiś c' âiva patitaiś ca mahā|dhvajaiḥ
carma|cāpa|śaraiś c' âiva vyapakīrṇaiḥ samantataḥ
nihataiḥ kṣatriyair aśvair vāraṇaiś ca, viśāṃ pate,
a|gamya|kalpā pṛthivī kṣaṇen' āsīt su|dāruṇā.

41.20 vadhyatāṃ rāja|putrāṇāṃ krandatām itar'|êtaram
prādur āsīn mahā|śabdo bhīrūṇāṃ bhaya|vardhanaḥ.
sa śabdo Bharata|śreṣṭha diśaḥ sarvā vyanādayat
Saubhadraś c' ādravat senāṃ nighnann aśva|ratha|dvipān.
kakṣam agnir iv' ôtsṛṣṭo nirdahaṃs tarasā ripūn
madhye Bhārata|sainyānām Ārjuniḥ pratyadṛśyata.
vicarantaṃ diśaḥ sarvāḥ pradiśaś c' âpi Bhārata
taṃ tadā n' ânupaśyāmaḥ sainyena ca rajasā vṛtaḥ
ādadānaṃ gaj'|âśvānāṃ nṛṇāṃ c' āyūṃṣi, Bhārata.
kṣaṇena bhūyo paśyāmi sūryaṃ madhyaṃ|dine yathā
Abhimanyuṃ, mahā|rāja, pratapantaṃ dviṣad|gaṇān.

41.25 sa Vāsava|samaḥ saṃkhye Vāsavasy' ātma|j'|ātma|jaḥ
Abhimanyur, mahā|rāja, sainya|madhye vyarocata.

bedecked in earrings and woven wreaths. The ribs of the chariots, their seats and curved handles and crushed axles and buckled wheels and a thousand yokes, and bows and arrows and spears and fallen standards and armor, and more bows and more arrows were scattered as far as the eye could see and o lord of men the earth lost beneath this maze of dead warriors and horses and all their paraphernalia was a passing vision awful to behold.

O best of the Bharatas, as the sons of kings died and cried 41.20
out to one another a grim chorus gathered to fill the whole world in a rumble that struck terror into our trembling hearts. And on Saubhádra rode on his spree through horse and car and man and on and on he raged through his foes like a fire billowing through a forest of dead trees, on to the very center of this gathering of the Bharatas. For a moment we saw him, but in seconds as he wheeled through every point in the compass and then each in between, the fog of the battle closed around him and we could see him no more. For a moment I glimpsed him once again risen like the midday sun as he stole away the breath from the throats
of the creatures that moved about him. Son of the son of 41.25
Indra, Indra he became. That day in the heat of the fray Abhimányu blazed, and hot were the fires in which his haters burned.

DHṚTARĀṢṬRA uvāca.

42.1 BĀLAM ATYANTA|sukhinaṃ sva|bāhu|bala|darpitam
yuddheṣu kuśalaṃ vīraṃ kula|putraṃ tanu|tyajam
gāhamānam anīkāni sad|aśvais taṃ tri|hāyanaiḥ
api Yaudhiṣṭhirāt sainyāt kaś cid anvapatad balī.

SAṂJAYA uvāca.

Yudhiṣṭhiro Bhīmasenaḥ Śikhaṇḍī Sātyakir Yamau
Dhṛṣṭadyumno Virāṭaś ca Drupadaś ca sa|Kaikayaḥ
Dhṛṣṭaketuś ca saṃrabdho Matsyāś c' ânvapatan raṇe
ten' âiva tu pathā yantāraḥ pitaro mātulaiḥ saha.
42.5 abhyadravan parīpsanto vyūḍh'|ânīkāḥ prahāriṇaḥ
tān dṛṣṭvā dravataḥ śūrān tvadīyā vimukh" âbhavan.
tatas tad vimukhaṃ dṛṣṭvā tava sūnor mahad balam
jāmātā tava tejasvī saṃstambhayiṣur ādravat.
Saindhavasya mahā|rāja putro rājā Jayadrathaḥ
sa putra|gṛddhinaḥ Pārthān saha|sainyān avārayat.
ugra|dhanvā mah"|êṣv|āso divyam astram udīrayan
Vārddhakṣatrir upāsedhat pravaṇād iva kuñjarān.

DHRITA·RASHTRA spoke.

THOUGH BUT A BOY he was of noble stock and already 42.1
an adept in the arts of war. I can imagine him exultant and dizzy with the strength of his own two arms, casting aside all fear for his life and plunging on through the lines of men, behind fine horses who young like he had passed but three summers on this earth. Which of Yudhi·shthira's men followed after the brave child?

SÁNJAYA spoke.

Their champions were close behind him. Yudhi·shthira, Bhima·sena, Shikhándin, Sátyaki and the twins, Dhrishta·dyumna and Viráta, Drúpada and the Kaikéyas and fierce Dhrishta·ketu, his fathers and his uncles and their drivers
all racing together at his heels to defend him. Your children 42.5
watched them approach and their hearts sank. But one man saw Duryódhana's great army losing its spirit and he rushed forward to restore it. That man o majesty was your son-in-law Jayad·ratha, the fiery prince of Sindhu. As the Parthas and their men rode to protect their scion it was the great and deadly archer Jayad·ratha who raised his celestial bow and drove them off as he might elephants from a fragile grove.

DHṚTARĀṢṬRA uvāca.

atilbhāram ahaṃ manye Saindhave, Saṃjay', āhitam
yad ekaḥ Pāṇḍavān kruddhān putra|prepsūn avārayat.
42.10 aty|adbhutam idaṃ manye balaṃ śauryaṃ ca Saindhave
tasya prabrūhi me vīryaṃ karma c' âgryaṃ mah"|ātmanaḥ.
kiṃ dattaṃ hutam iṣṭaṃ vā su|taptam atha vā tapaḥ
Sindhurājo hi yen' âikaḥ kruddhān Pārthān avārayat?

SAMJAYA uvāca.

Draupadī|haraṇe yat tad Bhīmasenena nirjitaḥ
mānāt sa taptavān rājā var'|ârthī su|mahat tapaḥ.
indriyāṇ' îndriy'|ārthebhyaḥ priyebhyaḥ saṃnivartya saḥ
kṣut|pipāsā|tapa|sahaḥ kṛśo dhamani|saṃtataḥ.
devam ārādhayac Charvaṃ gṛṇan brahma sanātanam
bhakt'|ānukampī bhagavāṃs tasya cakre tato dayām.
42.15 svapn'|ânte 'py atha c' âiv' āha Haraḥ Sindhu|pateḥ sutam.
«varaṃ vṛṇīṣva prīto 'smi, Jayadratha, kim icchasi?»
evam uktas tu Śarveṇa Sindhu|rājo Jayadrathaḥ
uvāca praṇato Rudraṃ prāñjalir niyat'|ātmavān.
«Pāṇḍaveyān ahaṃ saṃkhye bhīma|vīrya|parākramān
vārayeyaṃ rathen' âikaḥ samastān» iti Bhārata.

DHRITA·RASHTRA spoke.

O Sánjaya. Jayad·ratha took a great burden upon himself when he went alone against the Pándavas' love and wrath. Such an act of might and daring defies belief. Tell me of 42.10
this strong fighter and of the valor of his great act. What was the gift or sacrifice or rite or fierce austerity that meant the son of Sindhu could stand alone against the rage of the Parthas?

SÁNJAYA spoke.

Humiliated by Bhima·sena during Dráupadi's abduction, it was out of wounded pride and in search of a blessing that the king had burned in meditation. He closed his senses to all the sweet things of the world until, as he wasted away in the flames of hunger and thirst, the veins of his body became like cords beneath his skin. Intoning praises he came before the God Who Kills With Arrows. The great deity was pleased with the king's devotion and took pity on him. At the very end of his dream the Sindhu king heard 42.15
the Destroyer's voice.

"O Jayad·ratha. Name what it is you seek and I will grant it to you."

Jayad·ratha prince of Sindhu heard the God Who Kills With Arrows and raising his hands in reverence he bowed low and spoke with due humility to the fearsome being. And this o Bhárata is what he said.

"When the Pandus mass against me, may it be that I can stand alone on my chariot and withstand their awful bravery and might."

evam uktas tu dev'|ēśo Jayadratham ath' âbravīt.
«dadāmi te varaṃ, saumya, vinā Pārthaṃ Dhanaṃjayam.
vārayiṣyasi saṃgrāme caturaḥ Pāṇḍu|nandanān.»
evam astv iti dev'|ēśam uktv" âbudhyata pārthivaḥ.
42.20 sa tena vara|dānena divyen' âstra|balena ca
ekaḥ saṃdhārayām āsa Pāṇḍavānām anīkinīm.
tasya jyā|tala|ghoṣeṇa kṣatriyān bhayam āviśat
parāṃs tu tava sainyasya harṣaḥ paramako 'bhavat.
dṛṣṭvā tu kṣatriyā bhāraṃ Saindhave sarvam arpitam
utkruśy' âbhyadravan rājan yena Yaudhiṣṭhiraṃ balam.

SAṂJAYA uvāca.

43.1 YAN MĀṂ PṚCCHASI, rāj'|êndra, Sindhu|rājasya vikramam
śṛṇu tat sarvam ākhyāsye yathā Pāṇḍūn ayodhayat.
tam ūhur vājino vaśyāḥ Saindhavāḥ sādhu|vāhinaḥ
vikurvāṇā bṛhanto 'śvāḥ śvasan'|ôpama|raṃhasaḥ.
gandharva|nagar'|ākāraṃ vidhivat kalpitaṃ ratham
tasy' âbhyaśobhayat ketur vārāho rājato mahān.
śveta|cchattra|patākābhiś cāmara|vyajanena ca
sa babhau rāja|liṅgais tais Tārā|patir iv' âmbare.
43.5 muktā|vajra|maṇi|svarṇair bhūṣitaṃ tad ayas|mayam
varūthaṃ vibabhau tasya jyotirbhiḥ kham iv' âvṛtam.
sa visphārya mahac cāpaṃ kirann iṣu|gaṇān bahūn
tat khaṇḍaṃ pūrayām āsa yad vyadārayad Ārjuniḥ.

The lord of the gods addressed Jayad·ratha in reply.

"My worthy son, I will give you what you ask. And so I say that you will withstand in battle four of Pandu's children. Only Dhanan·jaya son of Pritha will pass you by."

The lord of the gods finished speaking and the king woke up. And so it was that armed with a gift from the gods and 42.20
with the force of the weapons of heaven he stood all alone before the Pándava horde. The sigh of his bowstring brought fear among our foe's troops and excitement among our own. The warriors watched Jayad·ratha shoulder his great burden and whooping as they went they rushed o majesty at Yudhi·shthira's front line.

SÁNJAYA spoke.

DIVINE KING. You asked to hear of the courage of the 43.1
Sindhu lord. Listen now and I will tell you one by one of his exploits against the Pandus.

Fleet and surefooted and mild of temper were the strong Sindhu steeds that with the force of the rushing wind whirled him on. His chariot was decked by design like a city of the skies and the great banner of the silver boar danced bright above his head. White was the column of his standard and white his parasol, and with his fan in one hand he shone in his majestic trappings like the moon shining in the firmament. Studded in pearls and crystal and in gemstones 43.5
and gold, his iron shield sparkled like a sky covered in stars. Jayad·ratha drew back his great bow and with a dense flight of arrows closed the wound in the host that Árjuni had opened.

sa Sātyakiṃ tribhir bāṇair aṣṭabhiś ca Vṛkodaram
Dhṛṣṭadyumnaṃ tathā ṣaṣṭyā Virāṭaṃ daśabhiḥ śaraiḥ
Drupadaṃ pañcabhis tīkṣṇair saptabhiś ca Śikhaṇḍinam
Kaikeyān pañca|viṃśatyā Draupadeyāṃs tribhis tribhiḥ
Yudhiṣṭhiraṃ ca saptatyā tataḥ śeṣān apānudat
iṣu|jālena mahatā tad adbhutam iv' âbhavat.
43.10 ath' âsya sita|pītena bhallen' ādiśya kārmukaṃ
ciccheda prahasan rājan Dharma|putraḥ pratāpavān.
akṣṇor nimeṣa|mātreṇa
so 'nyad ādāya kārmukam
vivyādha daśabhiḥ Pārthaṃ
tāṃś c' âiv' ânyāṃs tribhis tribhiḥ.
tasya tal lāghavaṃ jñātvā Bhīmo bhallais tribhiḥ punaḥ
dhanur dhvajaṃ ca chattraṃ ca kṣitau kṣipram apātayat.
so 'nyad ādāya balavān sajjaṃ kṛtvā ca kārmukam
Bhīmasy' âpātayat ketuṃ dhanur aśvāṃś ca, māriṣa.
sa hat'|âśvād avaplutya chinna|dhanvā rath'|ôttamāt
Sātyaker āpluto yānaṃ giry|agram iva kesarī.
43.15 tatas tvadīyāḥ saṃhṛṣṭāḥ sādhu sādhv iti cukruśuḥ
Sindhu|rājasya tat karma prekṣy' â|śraddheyam adbhutam.
saṃkruddhān Pāṇḍavān eko yad dadhār' âstra|tejasā
tat tasya karma bhūtāni sarvāṇy ev' âbhyapūjayan.
Saubhadreṇa hataiḥ pūrvaṃ s'|ôttar'|āyodhibhir dvipaiḥ
Pāṇḍūnāṃ darśitaḥ panthāḥ Saindhavena nivāritaḥ.

Three shafts struck Sátyaki and eight struck Vrikódara, then sixty found Dhrishta·dyumna and ten Viráta. Five sharp points bit into Drúpada, seven into Shikhándin, five and twenty pierced the Kaikéyas, the sons of Dráupadi he struck with three then three again, and at Yudhi·shthira he sent a full seventy. Their other companions he drove back with the broad stream flowing from his bow, and what we saw before our eyes was no less than a prodigy. Then, my 43.10
lord, the brilliant son of Dharma struck back and with a mocking smile aimed a pale yellow shaft at his enemy's bow and letting fly split it in two. In the winking of an eye Jayad·ratha swept up another and struck Pritha's son ten times before sending three then three again at his brother. Bhima saw how quick he was and with three arrows of his own, my king, he knocked Jayad·ratha's new bow to the earth and sliced through his pole and parasol. But the hardy fighter took up yet another and strung it and with it felled the steeds of Bhima, struck the bow from his hands and his pennant from its housing. Abandoning his broken bow, Bhima leapt up from his dead horses and his toppled car and like a lion bounding for a rock landed full in the chariot that held Sátyaki. All the same, the glory was the Sindhu's.

Your soldiers watched and cheered in praise for we were 43.15
all in awe of what he had done. With nothing more than the brilliance of his bow one man had for a moment stemmed the wrath of the Pándava horde. Saubhádra had quickly brought down elephants and their high riders and carved a path through their carcasses, but the Sindhu king had forced it shut. They all struggled, Pándavas and Kékayas and Panchálas and Matsyas, but none of them could withstand

yatamānās tu te vīrā Matsya|Pāñcāla|Kekayāḥ
Pāṇḍavāś c' ânvapadyanta pratiśekur na Saindhavam.
yo yo hi yatate bhettuṃ Droṇ'|ânīkaṃ tav' âhitaḥ
taṃ tam eva varaṃ prāpya Saindhavaḥ pratyavārayat.

SAṂJAYA uvāca.

44.1 SAINDHAVENA niruddheṣu jaya|gṛddhiṣu Pāṇḍuṣu
su|ghoram abhavad yuddhaṃ tvadīyānāṃ paraiḥ saha.
praviśy' âth' Ārjuniḥ senāṃ satya|saṃdho durāsadaḥ
vyakṣobhayata tejasvī makaraḥ sāgaraṃ yathā.
taṃ tathā śara|varṣeṇa kṣobhayantam ariṃ|damam
yathā|pradhānaṃ Saubhadram abhyayur nara|sattamāḥ.
teṣāṃ tasya ca saṃmardo dāruṇaḥ samapadyata
sṛjatāṃ śara|varṣāṇi prasaktam a|mit'|âujasām.
44.5 ratha|vrajena saṃruddhas tair a|mitrais tath" Ārjuniḥ
Vṛṣasenasya yantāraṃ hatvā ciccheda kārmukam.
tasya vivyādha balavāñ śarair aśvān a|jihma|gaiḥ
vātāyamānair atha tair aśvair apahṛto raṇāt.
ten' ântareṇ' Âbhimanyor yant" âpāsārayad ratham
ratha|vrajās tato hṛṣṭāḥ sādhu sādhv iti cukruśuḥ.
taṃ siṃham iva saṃkruddhaṃ pramathnantaṃ śarair arīn
ārād āyāntam abhyetya Vasātīyo 'bhyayād drutam.
so 'bhimanyuṃ śaraiḥ ṣaṣṭyā rukma|puṅkhair avākirat,
abravīc ca «na me jīvañ jīvato yudhi mokṣyase.»

him. One by one the enemy strove to widen the breach in Drona's line and blessed by the gods Jayad·ratha drove them off, one by one.

SÁNJAYA spoke.

DESPERATE TO triumph though they were, the Pandus 44.1
were held back by the Sindhu king. The battle between the two sides raged fiercely. Árjuna's son had been true to his word and he plunged splendored and unassailable into the Kuru swell and it pitched about him as if it hid a beast of the deep. But as the arrows of their fierce tormentor rained down and churned through their ranks footsoldier to king the mighty Kurus came back against him. Where they
clashed the chaos became ever more awful. Archers let loose 44.5
arrows in floods and a ring of hostile chariots hemmed him about, but with level yet measureless brilliance Árjuni felled the driver of Vrisha·sena's car then cut in two the warrior's bow and sent arrows straight into his horses' hides. The two steeds that went like the wind bore him from the battlefield, and Abhimányu's driver let them go for they saw how they were weakened. The more was Abhimányu's glory and the warriors who watched his mercy cried out their praise, but arrows flying he tore on through his enemies baleful as a lion with barely a pause. As Abhimányu arced through their ranks Vasatíya was next to swing into his track and charge.

Sixty brightfletched arrows he scattered upon Abhimányu and he called out to him the while.

"Only one of us will escape this battle alive!"

44.10 tam ayas|maya|varmāṇam iṣuṇā dūra|pātinā
vivyādha hṛdi Saubhadraḥ sa papāta vy|asuḥ kṣitau.
Vasātīyaṃ hataṃ dṛṣṭvā kruddhāḥ kṣatriya|puṃ|gavāḥ
parivavrus tadā rājaṃs tava pautraṃ jighāṃsavaḥ.
visphārayantaś cāpāni nānā|rūpāṇy an|ekaśaḥ
tad yuddham abhavad raudraṃ Saubhadrasy' âribhiḥ saha.
teṣāṃ śarān s'|êṣv|asanāñ śarīrāṇi śirāṃsi ca
sa|kuṇḍalāni sragvīṇi kruddhaś ciccheda Phālguniḥ.
sa|khaḍgāḥ s'|âṅguli|trāṇāḥ sa|paṭṭiśa|paraśvadhāḥ
adṛśyanta bhujāś chinnā hem'|ābharaṇa|bhūṣitāḥ.
44.15 sragbhir ābharaṇair vastraiḥ patitaiś ca mahā|dhvajaiḥ
varmabhiś carmabhir hārair mukuṭaiś chattra|cāmaraiḥ
apaskarair adhiṣṭhānair īṣā|daṇḍaka|bandhuraiḥ
akṣair vimathitaiś cakrair bhagnaiś ca bahudhā yugaiḥ
anukarṣaiḥ patākābhis tathā sārathi|vājibhiḥ
rathaiś ca bhagnair nāgaiś ca hataiḥ kīrṇ" âbhavan mahī.
nihataiḥ kṣatriyaiḥ śūrair nānā|jana|pad'|ēśvaraiḥ
jaya|gṛddhair vṛtā bhūmir dāruṇā samapadyata.
diśo vicaratas tasya sarvāś ca pradiśas tathā
raṇe 'bhimanyoḥ kruddhasya rūpam antar|adhīyata.
44.20 kāñcanaṃ yad yad asy' āsīd varma c' ābharaṇāni ca
dhanuṣaś ca śarāṇāṃ ca tad apaśyāma kevalam.
taṃ tadā n' āśakat kaś cic cakṣurbhyām abhivīkṣitum
ādadānaṃ śarair yodhān madhye sūryam iva sthitam.

And so it was that with a farflying shaft Abhimányu 44.10
breached the iron about Vasatíya's chest, and pierced to his heart his victim fell lifeless upon the earth. At the sight of his death, anger coursed through his taurine companions and all about they drew their myriad bows as they descended upon your grandson, my king, baying for his life. Now the battle between Saubhádra and his foes took on an aspect yet darker. Abhimányu's blood was up. He shattered bows and arrows and bodies and severed heads still dangling rings and flowers. Arms clasped in golden circlets we saw lopped from shoulders, and hands whose beringed fingers were still wrapped tight around sword and
spear and axe. All about were garlands and bracelets and 44.15
raiment and fallen poles, armor and shields, pendants and diadems, parasols and chowries and pieces of chariot, and slats and rails and shafts and crowns and staves. The earth was thick with them, with twisted bars and broken wheels, yokes in their hundreds and pennants and axletrees, all lying alongside drivers and steeds, the ribs of chariots, the bodies of elephants. How savage the land looked burdened in the dead. There they lay, warriors and heroes of legend, lords and footsoldiers from every tribe of the world all of whom had once hungered for dominion. And whirling at their heart and across every quarter of the sky went the violent
form of Abhimányu. All that we could see was his armor 44.20
of gold and his chains and his bow and his arrows. Him we could not glimpse as he went snatching warriors from our midst. Our eyes were blind before the sun that burned among us.

SAMJAYA uvāca.

45.1 ĀDADĀNAS TU śūrāṇām āyūṃṣy abhavad Ārjuniḥ
antakaḥ sarva|bhūtānāṃ prāṇān kāla iv' āgate.
sa Śakra iva vikrāntaḥ Śakra|sūnoḥ suto balī
Abhimanyus tad" ânīkaṃ loḍayan bahv aśobhata.
praviśy' âiva tu rāj'|êndra kṣatriy'|Êndr'|ântak'|ôpamaḥ
satya|śravasam ādatta vyāghro mṛgam iv' ôlbaṇaḥ.
satya|śravasi c' ākṣipte tvaramāṇā mahā|rathāḥ
pragṛhya vipulaṃ śastram Abhimanyum upādravan.
45.5 «ahaṃ pūrvam ahaṃ pūrvam» iti kṣatriya|puṃ|gavāḥ
spardhamānāḥ samājagmur jighāṃsanto 'rjun'|ātma|jam.
kṣatriyāṇām anīkāni pradrutāny abhidhāvatām
jagrāha timir āsādya kṣudra|matsyān iv' ârṇave.
ye ke cana gatās tasya samīpam a|palāyinaḥ
na te pratinyavartanta samudrād iva sindhavaḥ.
mahā|grāha|gṛhīt" êva vāta|vega|bhay'|ârditā
samakampata sā senā vibhraṣṭā naur iv' ârṇave.
atha Rukmaratho nāma Madr'|ēśvara|suto balī
trastām āśvāsayan senām a|trasto vākyam abravīt.
45.10 «alaṃ trāsena vaḥ, śūrā. n' âiṣa kaś cin mayi sthite
aham enaṃ grahīṣyāmi jīva|grāhaṃ na saṃśayaḥ.»

SÁNJAYA spoke.

ÁRJUNA'S SON snatched away the lives of those warriors 45.1
as Death stills the breath of all creatures when the end of days is at hand. His prowess matched Indra for he was the child of Indra's son. O how he shone as he roiled the army that surrounded him and roamed through those ranks of mighty champions as if come to bear off their souls. He leapt that day upon his everlasting fame and caught it like a lone tiger catching a deer. And with such glory about him, other warrior bulls swept up tempered swords and rushed to
be the first to meet him in battle. They thronged around the 45.5
son of Árjuna and each strove with the other to be the one to claim victory against him. But as they poured towards him in droves, as if he were a whale in the foaming sea he caught them streaming into his jaws and devoured them like minnows. None who came close were safe and as rivers melt into the ocean forever none of them returned. The army trembled in his leviathan's bite and before the dismal threat of his tempests, a ship lost on the spume.

But there was one who tried to rally the Kurus then. Rukma·ratha* by name, he was the son of the lord of the Madras, and he spoke to his army valiant and unafraid.

"Heroes! Enough with this weakness. This one is no 45.10
match for me. Banish your doubt for I will take Abhimányu and I will take him alive."

evam uktvā tu Saubhadram abhidudrāva vīryavān
su|kalpiten' ôhyamānaḥ syandanena virājatā.
so 'bhimanyuṃ tribhir bāṇair bhittvā vakṣasy ath' ânadat
tribhiś ca dakṣiṇe bāhau savye ca niśitais tribhiḥ.
sa tasy' êṣv|asanaṃ chittvā Phālguniḥ savya|dakṣiṇau
bhujau śiraś ca sv|akṣi|bhru kṣitau kṣipram apātayat.
Dṛṣṭvā Rukmarathaṃ rugṇaṃ putraṃ Śalyasya māninam
jīva|grāhaṃ jighṛkṣantaṃ Saubhadreṇa yaśasvinā.
45.15 saṃgrāma|dur|madā, rājan, rāja|putrāḥ prahāriṇaḥ
vayasyāḥ Śalya|putrasya suvarṇa|vikṛta|dhvajāḥ
tāla|mātrāṇi cāpāni vikarṣanto mahā|rathāḥ
Ārjuniṃ śara|varṣeṇa samantāt paryavārayan.
śūraiḥ śikṣā|bal'|ôpetais taruṇair aty|a|marṣaṇaiḥ
dṛṣṭv" âikaṃ samare śūraṃ Saubhadram a|parājitam.
chādyamānaṃ śara|vrātair hṛṣṭo Duryodhano 'bhavat
Vaivasvatasya bhavanaṃ gatam hy enam amanyata.
suvarṇa|puṅkhair iṣubhir nānā|liṅgaiḥ su|taijanaiḥ
a|dṛśyam Ārjuniṃ cakrur nimeṣāt te nṛ|p'|ātma|jāḥ.
45.20 sa|sūt'|âśva|dhvajaṃ tasya syandanaṃ taṃ ca, māriṣa,
ācitaṃ samapaśyāma śvā|vidhaṃ śalalair iva.
sa gāḍha|viddhaḥ kruddhas tu tottrair gaja iv' ârditaḥ
gāndharvam astram āyacchad ratha|māyāṃ ca Bhārata.
Arjunena tapas taptvā gandharvebhyo yad āhṛtam
Tumburu|pramukhebhyo vai ten' âmohayat' â|hitān.

Speaking thus he came bravely at his foe, borne in a chariot all decked and aglitter. He roared as with three arrows he speared Abhimányu's chest, with three his right arm and with three sharp shafts his left. But Phálguni was quick and he broke Rukma·ratha's bow in two and then sliced off both his arms and cut clean away his finebrowed head. Down it fell to the earth. Rukma·ratha son of Shalya had been slain at Saubhádra's celebrated hand and his boast that he would capture his enemy alive had proved hubris. O 45.15
majesty, with their brilliant banners seething in the wind above their heads, the warcrazed fighters who were sons of kings and friends of Shalya's heir looked down upon his body as it lay on the ground.

Back went those warriors' bows tall as palms and they buried Árjuni beneath a welter of arrows. The sight of bold Saubhádra lone and unconquered at the heart of the fray enwoven now in the mesh of darts cast with skill and strength by those young and hotheaded princes filled Duryódhana with excitement. He dreamt indeed that Abhimányu was bound at last for the solar lodge. For as the princes loosed their bows in but the winking of an eye Árjuni was lost behind a screen of reeds filigreed in gold. Banner, driver and 45.20
car all disappeared along with the boy himself as a porcupine disappears behind its quills. But those spines were like goads driven into an elephant's hide, and pierced to the quick his fury flared. Then it was o Bhárata that he drew forth the weapon that came from the spirits of heaven: magic he wove about his chariot. Árjuna had burned in the flames of meditation and been gifted this weapon by Túmburu and his kind, and now Abhimányu unleashed its turmoil upon his

ekadhā śatadhā, rājan, dṛśyate sma sahasradhā
alāta|cakravat saṃkhye kṣipram astrāṇi darśayan.
ratha|cary"|âstra|māyābhir mohayitvā paraṃ|tapaḥ
bibheda śatadhā, rājañ, śarīrāṇi mahī|kṣitām.

45.25 prāṇāḥ prāṇa|bhṛtāṃ saṃkhye preṣitā niśitaiḥ śaraiḥ,
rājan, prāpur amuṃ lokaṃ śarīrāṇy avaniṃ yayuḥ.
dhanūṃṣy aśvān niyantṝṃś ca
dhvajān bāhūṃś ca s'|âṅga|dān
śirāṃsi ca śitair bhallais
teṣāṃ ciccheda Phālguniḥ.
cūt'|ārāmo yathā bhagnaḥ pañca|varṣa|phal'|ôpagaḥ
rāja|putra|śataṃ tadvat Saubhadreṇ' âpatadd hatam.
kruddh'|āśī|viṣa|saṃkāśān su|kumārān sukh'|ôcitān
ekena nihatān dṛṣṭvā bhīto Duryodhano 'bhavat.
rathinaḥ kuñjarān aśvān padātīṃś c' âpi majjataḥ
dṛṣṭvā Duryodhanaḥ kṣipram upāyāt tam amarṣitaḥ.

45.30 tayoḥ kṣaṇam iv' āpūrṇaḥ saṃgrāmaḥ samapadyata
ath' âbhavat te vimukhaḥ putraḥ śara|śat'|ârditaḥ.

DHṚTARĀṢṬRA uvāca.

46.1 YATHĀ VADASI ME, sūta, ekasya bahubhiḥ saha
saṃgrāmaṃ tumulaṃ ghoraṃ jayaṃ c' âiva mah"|ātmanaḥ
a|śraddheyam iv' āścaryaṃ Saubhadrasy' âtha vikramam
kiṃ tu n' âtyadbhutaṃ teṣāṃ yeṣāṃ dharmo vyapāśrayaḥ.

tormentors. Light were his fingers and out fanned his attack and like a circle of embers it seemed that one became a hundred and a hundred became a thousand. Burner of foes he bewildered them with attacks of sorcery along his wheeling path, before in their hundreds he cut down dead the lords of this earth.

O my king. In that reckoning he forced with whetted 45.25
shafts the very breath from the lungs of the living. Their spirits passed to the world yonder and their bodies went to the soil. Before Phálguni's biting iron fell bows and horses beyond number, drivers and banners in a cascade speckled in gold. A hundred sons of kings fell dead at Saubhádra's hand. It was as though a mango grove bowed by the fruit of five summers had suddenly been razed to the ground. Once they had lived in palaces but now these youths vehement as vipers lay dead at the feet of a solitary fighter. And now it was terror that came upon Duryódhana, as his gaze fell upon warriors, elephants, horses, soldiers, all laid open to the marrow.

Unable to bear what he saw he drew up quickly before
the boy, but their battle seemed to last only a moment. 45.30
Your son's spirit ebbed away beneath the force of a hundred blows.

DHRITA·RASHTRA spoke.

HORSEMAN. AS YOU tell me your tale of this fierce and 46.1
terrible struggle between lonely Saubhádra and his many foes, it is this solitary child whose unbeaten courage seems to me most a thing of wonder. Yet such bravery is perhaps less of a prodigy when found in those who cleave to their

Duryodhane tu vimukhe rāja|putra|śate hate
Saubhadre pratipattiṃ kāṃ pratyapadyanta māmakāḥ?

SAMJAYA uvāca.

saṃśuṣk'|āsyāś calan|netrāḥ prasvinnā loma|harṣiṇaḥ
palāyana|kṛt'|ôtsāhā nir|utsāhā dviṣaj|jaye.
46.5 hatān bhrātṝn pitṝn putrān suhṛt|sambandhi|bāndhavān
utsṛjy' ôtsṛjya saṃjagmus tvarayanto haya|dvipān.
tān prabhagnāṃs tathā dṛṣṭvā Droṇo Drauṇir Bṛhadbalaḥ
Kṛpo Duryodhanaḥ Karṇaḥ Kṛtavarm" âtha Saubalaḥ
abhyadhāvan su|saṃkruddhāḥ Saubhadram a|parājitam
te 'pi pautreṇa te rājan prāyaśo vimukhī|kṛtāḥ.
ekas tu sukha|saṃvṛddho bālyād darpāc ca nir|bhayaḥ
iṣv|astra|vin mahā|tejā Lakṣmaṇo "rjunim abhyayāt.
tam anvag ev' âsya pitā putra|gṛddhī nyavartata
anu Duryodhanaṃ c' ânye nyavartanta mahā|rathāḥ.
46.10 taṃ te 'bhiṣiṣicur bāṇair meghā girim iv' âmbubhiḥ
sa ca tān pramamāth' âiko viṣvag vāto yath" âmbu|dān.
pautraṃ tava ca dur|dharṣaṃ Lakṣmaṇaṃ priya|darśanam
pituḥ samīpe tiṣṭhantaṃ śūram udyata|kārmukam
atyanta|sukha|saṃvṛddhaṃ dhan'|ēśvara|sut'|ôpamam
āsasāda raṇe Kārṣṇir matto mattam iva dvipam.
Lakṣmaṇena tu saṃgamya Saubhadraḥ para|vīra|hā
śaraiḥ su|niśitais tīkṣṇair bāhvor urasi c' ârpitaḥ.
saṃkruddho vai mahā|bāhur daṇḍ'|āhata iv' ôra|gaḥ
pautras tava, mahā|rāja, tava pautram abhāṣata.

duty in the world. Duryódhana was downcast and princes lay dead in their hundreds. How did my men find the spirit to rally against Subhádra's son?

SÁNJAYA spoke.

It was the enemy's day. Disheveled and drenched in sweat,
with faces drawn and eyes reeling, your men's only remaining strength was born of the will to run. From their hands 46.5
had slipped brothers, fathers and sons, friends, family and
loved ones, and now they spurred on their steeds to wherever
it was they were bound themselves. O majesty, as the ranks
caved in about them the group of Drona and Ashvatthäman,
Brihad·bala, Kripa, Duryódhana, Karna, Krita·varman and
Sáubala made a last crazed dash for the unbowed son of Subhádra. But the youth drove them back one by one. There
was one fearless soul who from inexperience or arrogance
bred in the plush palace of his youth came close to Árjuni,
and that was the splendored acolyte of the arrow Lákshmana. His father turned back as he passed, anxious for his son,
and then other warriors followed Duryódhana and fell in
behind him. They all sprinkled arrows upon Abhimányu 46.10
like drops from rainclouds on a mountain peak, but as if he
were a whirling wind he tore on alone through their darkening sky. Your grandson Lákshmana was a fighter fierce
at arms and fair of visage and he stood beside his father a
true warrior, his bow raised to the sky. The wealth in which
he had been born would have been no vaster had he been
the child of Kubéra, yet on the battlefield he ran wild as an
elephant. In a madness the Dark One's son descended upon
him and they clashed. Lákshmana's sharp and biting shafts

46.15 «su|dṛṣṭaḥ kriyatāṃ loko hy amuṃ lokaṃ gamiṣyasi
paśyatāṃ bāndhavānāṃ tvāṃ nayāmi Yama|sādanam.»
evam uktvā tato bhallaṃ Saubhadraḥ para|vīra|hā
udbabarha mahā|bāhur nirmukt'|ôra|ga|saṃnibham.
sa tasya bhuja|nirmukto Lakṣmaṇasya su|darśanam
su|nasaṃ su|bhru|keś'|ântaṃ śiro 'hārṣīt sa|kuṇḍalam.
Lakṣmaṇaṃ nihataṃ dṛṣṭvā hā h" êty uccukruśur janāḥ
tato Duryodhanaḥ kruddhaḥ priye putre nipātite
«hat' âinam!» iti cukrośa kṣatriyān kṣatriya'|rṣabhaḥ.
tato Droṇaḥ Kṛpaḥ Karṇo Droṇa|putro Bṛhadbalaḥ
Kṛtavarmā ca Hārdikyaḥ ṣaḍ rathāḥ paryavārayan.
46.20 sa tān viddhvā śitair bāṇair vimukhī|kṛtya c' Ārjuniḥ
vegen' âbhyapatat kruddhaḥ Saindhavasya mahad balam.
āvavrus tasya panthānaṃ gaj'|ânīkena daṃśitāḥ
Kaliṅgāś ca Niṣādāś ca Krātha|putraś ca vīryavān
tat prasaktam iv' âtyarthaṃ yuddham āsīd, viśāṃ pate.
tatas tat kuñjar'|ânīkaṃ vyadhamad dhṛṣṭam Ārjuniḥ
yathā vāyur nitya|gatir jala|dān śataśo 'mbare.
tataḥ Krāthaḥ śara|vrātair Ārjuniṃ samavārayat
ath' êtare saṃnivṛttāḥ punar Droṇa|mukhā rathāḥ
param'|âstrāṇi tanvānāḥ Saubhadram abhidudruvuḥ.
tān nivāry' Ārjunir bāṇaiḥ Krātha|putram ath' ârdayat

cut into the arms and chest of Subhádra's vengeful son. Like
a snake struck by a stick the mighty warrior reared up in
anger, and one child of your wide clan addressed the other.
"Feast your eyes upon this world, for you are bound for 46.15
one beyond it. Your fathers and brothers will watch now as
I lead you away to where Yama dwells."

Such were Abhimányu's words, and from his quiver came
an iron arrow like a snake shedding its skin which he notched
and then loosed from his hand and which flew and hewed
off the head of Lákshmana so fine of feature in nose and
brow, its earrings and locks of hair so fair. Lákshmana's death
brought a shocked cry from the mass of men. When he saw
his dear son felled, wrath filled Duryódhana. "Kill him!"
screamed the bull to his herd. About Abhimányu came the
six chariots of Drona and Kripa, Karna and Drona's son,
and Brihad·bala and Krita·varman born to Hrídika. But 46.20
with sharp shafts Árjuna's son struck them once again and
forced them back before he fell with hotheaded violence
upon Sáindhava's broad host. The valiant son of King Kratha drew up a wall of elephants ridden by mailed Kalíngas
and Nishádas and cut off his path with their bulk. The battle
grew yet more monstrous my lord. Like a tireless wind in a
sky of a hundred clouds the son of Árjuna blew through that
bold column of beasts and although Kratha's son covered
Árjuni in sheets of arrows and the other warriors headed by
Drona came rushing in about him and spread above him
their high darts, he beat them all back with his own and
then struck hard at the child of Kratha. The taste for blood
quickened in him and with an edgeless swarm of arrows he 46.25
sheared off the boy's head from his shoulders still wearing

śar'|âugheṇ' â|prameyeṇa tvaramāṇo jighāṃsayā.
46.25 sa|dhanur|bāṇa|keyūrau bāhū sa|mukuṭaṃ śiraḥ
chattraṃ dhvajaṃ niyantāram aśvāṃś c' âsya nyapātayat.
kula|śīla|śruta|balaiḥ kīrtyā c' âstra|balena ca
yukte tasmin hate vīrāḥ prāyaśo vimukh" âbhavan.

DHṚTARĀṢṬRA uvāca.

47.1 TATHĀ PRAVIṢṬAṂ taruṇaṃ Saubhadram a|parājitam
kul'|ânurūpaṃ kurvāṇaṃ saṃgrāmeṣv a|palāyinam
ājāneyaiḥ su|balibhir yuktam aśvais tri|hāyanaiḥ
plavamānam iv' ākāśe ke śūrāḥ paryavārayan?

SAMJAYA uvāca.

Abhimanyuḥ praviśy' âiva tāvakān niśitaiḥ śaraiḥ
akarot pārthivān sarvān vimukhān Pāṇḍu|nandanaḥ.
taṃ tu Droṇaḥ Kṛpaḥ Karṇo Drauṇiś ca sa|Bṛhadbalaḥ
Kṛtavarmā ca Hārdikyaḥ ṣaḍ rathāḥ paryavārayan.
47.5 dṛṣṭvā tu Saindhave bhāram ati|mātraṃ samāhitam
sainyaṃ tava mahā|rāja Yudhiṣṭhiram upādravat.
Saubhadram itare vīram abhyavarṣañ śar'|âmbubhiḥ
tāla|mātrāṇi cāpāni vikarṣanto mahā|balāḥ.
tāṃs tu sarvān mah"|êṣv|āsān sarva|vidyāsu niṣṭhitān
vyaṣṭambhayad raṇe bāṇaiḥ Saubhadraḥ para|vīra|hā.
Droṇaṃ pañcāśat" âviddhyad viṃśatyā ca Bṛhadbalam
aśītyā Kṛtavarmāṇaṃ Kṛpaṃ ṣaṣṭyā śilī|mukhaiḥ.
rukma|puṅkhair mahā|vegair ākarṇa|sama|coditaiḥ
avidhyad daśabhir bāṇair Aśvatthāmānam Ārjuniḥ.

its crown and his bangled arms from his trunk and then down came quiver and bow, parasol and pole, and finally steeds and driver.

Neither might nor study nor virtue nor nobility nor glory nor the force of a bow could save the prince from his death. And what sorrow came among the warriors at his fall.

DHRITA·RASHTRA spoke.

So YOUNG SAUBHÁDRA stood deep in the throng, unslain 47.1
and unretreating. The very image of his father. Riding behind his powerful three-year-old nobleblood steeds it must have seemed as if he soared through the sky. Could any of those heroes bring him down?

SÁNJAYA spoke.

Deep into the multitudes of your army Abhimányu joy of the Pandus drove his sharp arrows and all the lords he encountered he sent into retreat. But six chariots pressed in about him, atop them Drona, Kripa, Karna, Drauni, Bri-
had·bala and Krita·varman son of Hrídika. My king, most 47.5
of your men had seen Sáindhava shoulder his burdensome task and had ridden out for Yudhi·shthira. But these six champions had stayed with him, and now they drew back their bows tall as palms and rained arrowed waters down upon the head of brave and brazen Saubhádra. All of them were masters of all their art and yet the arrows that came back from Abhimányu's deadly fingers pinned each of them where he stood. Fifty stone tips struck Drona and twenty Brihad·bala, eighty stuck Krita·varman and sixty found Kripa. Back flew Árjuni's hand to his ear and up surged those
golden arrows. Ten more of them bit into Ashvatthâman. All 47.10

47.10 sa Karṇaṃ karṇinā karṇe pītena niśitena ca
Phālgunir dviṣatāṃ madhye vivyādha param'|êṣuṇā.
pātayitvā Kṛpasy' âśvāṃs tath" ôbhau pārṣṇi|sārathī
ath' âinaṃ daśabhir bāṇaiḥ pratyavidhyat stan'|ântare.
tato Vṛndārakaṃ vīraṃ Kurūṇāṃ kīrti|vardhanam
putrāṇāṃ tava vīrāṇāṃ paśyatām avadhīd balī.

taṃ Drauṇiḥ pañca|viṃśatyā kṣudrakāṇāṃ samarpayat
varaṃ varam a|mitrāṇām ārujantam a|bhītavat.
sa tu bāṇaiḥ śitais tūrṇaṃ pratyavidhyata, māriṣa,
paśyatāṃ Dhārtarāṣṭrāṇām Aśvatthāmānam Ārjuniḥ.
47.15 ṣaṣṭyā śarāṇāṃ taṃ Drauṇis tiryag|dhāraiḥ su|tejanaiḥ
ugrair n' âkampayad viddhvā Mainākam iva parvatam.
sa tu Drauṇir dvi|saptatyā hema|puṅkhair a|jihma|gaiḥ
pratyavidhyan mahā|tejā balavān apakāriṇam.
tasmin Droṇo bāṇa|śataṃ putra|gṛddhī nyapātayat
Aśvatthāmā tath" âṣṭau ca parīpsan pitaraṃ raṇe
Karṇo dvā|viṃśatiṃ bhallān Kṛtavarmā catur|daśa
Bṛhadbalas tu pañcāśat Kṛpaḥ Śāradvato daśa.
tāṃs tān pratyavadhīt sarvān daśabhir daśabhiḥ śaraiḥ,
taṃ Kosalānām adhipaḥ karṇin" âtāḍayadd hṛdi.

47.20 sa tasy' âśvān dhvajaṃ cāpaṃ sūtaṃ c' âpātayat kṣitau
atha Kosala|rājas tu vi|rathaḥ khaḍga|carma|dhṛt
iyeṣa Phālguneḥ kāyāc chiro hartuṃ sa|kuṇḍalam.
sa Kosalānāṃ bhartāraṃ rāja|putraṃ Bṛhadbalam
hṛdi vivyādha bāṇena sa bhinna|hṛdayo 'patat.
babhañja ca sahasrāṇi daśa rājñāṃ mah"|ātmanāṃ

about Abhimányu stood his foes. Yet right through Karna's ear he sent a single perfect sharp and yellowhued arrow and then he brought down Kripa's horse and both his flankriders and struck the brahmin himself right in the chest with ten more of his darts. The mighty champion of the Kurus Vrindáraka, who had brought us such fame, strong Abhimányu crushed next before the very eyes of his brothers.

As Árjuni harrowed his enemies with a careless caprice it was Ashvatthámán who sent at him a volley of five and twenty slender darts, but my king the boy's whetted shafts
struck him back without a moment passing. Drauni took 47.15
arrows beveled both sides to fine and deadly points and shot sixty straight at his foe. Yet when they struck Abhimányu he did not falter, and remained still as Mount Maindruka. With two and seventy trueflying shafts borne on fletchings flecked in gold, strong and splendored Drauni struck at his adversary, then on Abhimányu's head rained a hundred more arrows from Drona's bow as he strove to protect his progeny, and son answering father, Ashvatthámán fired another eighty presaging two and twenty broad shafts from Karna and from Krita·varman fourteen, fifty from Brihad·bala and ten more from Kripa son of Sharádvat. Yet each of their arrows Árjuni matched with ten.

The chief of the Kósalas was next to strike him in the chest 47.20
but Abhimányu knocked to the earth his whole panoply of horses, pennant, parasol and driver. Out of the wreckage climbed the prince holding sword and shield, desperate to strike his enemy's goldberinged head from his neck, but it was Prince Brihad·bala the ward of the Kósalas whom Phálguni turned to and struck in the heart. Pierced to the quick

sṛjatām a|śivā vācaḥ khaḍga|kārmuka|dhāriṇām.
tathā Bṛhadbalaṃ hatvā Saubhadro vyacarad raṇe
vyaṣṭambhayan mah"|êṣv|āso yodhāṃs tava śar'|âmbubhiḥ.

SAMJAYA uvāca.

48.1 SA KARṆAṂ KARṆINĀ karṇe punar vivyādha Phālguniḥ
śaraiḥ pañcāśatā c' âinam avidhyat kopayan bhṛśam.
prativivyādha Rādheyas tāvadbhir atha taṃ punaḥ
śarair ācita|sarv'|âṅgo bahv aśobhata, Bhārata.
Karṇaṃ c' âpy akarot kruddho rudhir'|ôtpīḍa|vāhinam
Karṇo 'pi vibabhau śūraḥ śaraiś chinno 'sṛg|āplutaḥ.
tau tathā śara|citr'|âṅgau rudhireṇa samukṣitau
babhūvatur mah"|ātmānau puṣpitāv iva kiṃśukau.
48.5 atha Karṇasya sacivān ṣaṭ śūrāṃś citra|yodhinaḥ
s'|âśva|sūta|dhvaja|rathān Saubhadro nijaghāna ha.
tath" êtarān mah"|êṣv|āsān daśabhir daśabhiḥ śaraiḥ
pratyavidhyad a|sambhrāntas tad adbhutam iv' âbhavat.
Māgadhasya punaḥ putraṃ hatvā ṣaḍbhir a|jihma|gaiḥ
s'|âśvaṃ sa|sūtaṃ taruṇam Aśvaketum apātayat.
Mārttikāvatakaṃ bhojaṃ tataḥ kuñjara|ketanam
kṣurapreṇa samunmathya nanāda visṛjañ śarān.

he fell. A full ten thousand of those great kings with curses on their tongues and bows and swords in their hands Abhimányu had now killed. With Brihad·bala dead, Saubhádra circled the field and halted your warriors and archers where they stood. Down fell his arrows like drops of rain.

SÁNJAYA spoke.

ANGER FLASHED AGAIN in the son of the Red Star Fighter 48.1
and he sent another single arrow like a ring straight through Karna's ear and then a full volley of fifty more. O Bhárata, back came Karna's counterattack shaft for shaft and Abhimányu's limbs bristled thick with stalks. In wrath still he dug from Karna channels of gore. Cut by his arrowheads mighty Karna glistened and fought on bathed in blood. The bodies of those two fabled warriors were livid with wounds and spotted in scarlet and together they looked like
twin flames-of-the-forest in bloom. Six brave and dazzling 48.5
fighters allied to Karna were the next victims of Subhádra's son and he crushed them away along with their horses, drivers, pennants and cars, and then with arrows in braces of ten he struck down yet more. All the while his aim was immaculate. With six trueflying shafts he finished Ashva·ketu prince of Mágadha, bringing down the youth along with his driver and all his steeds, and then a razorsharp shaft from his bow tore beneath the oriflamme of the elephant into the lord of the people called the Marttikávatakas. And Abhimányu roared as his arrows flew.

tasya Dauḥśāsanir viddhvā caturbhiś caturo hayān
sūtam ekena vivyādha daśabhiś c' Ârjun'|ātma|jam.
48.10 tato Dauḥśāsanim Kārṣṇir viddhvā saptabhir āśu|gaiḥ
saṃrambhād rakta|nayano vākyam uccair ath' âbravīt.
«pitā tav' āhavaṃ tyaktvā gataḥ kāpuruṣo yathā.
diṣṭyā tvam api jānīṣe yoddhuṃ na tv adya mokṣyase.»
etāvad uktvā vacanaṃ karmāra|parimārjitam
nārācaṃ visasarj' âsmai taṃ Drauṇis tribhir ācchinat.
tasy' Ārjunir dhvajaṃ chittvā Śalyaṃ tribhir atāḍayat
taṃ Śalyo navabhir bāṇair gārdhra|patrair atāḍayat.
hṛdya|sambhrāntavad rājaṃs tad adbhutam iv' âbhavat.
tasy' Ārjunir dhvajaṃ chittvā
hatv" ôbhau ca pārṣṇi|sārathī
taṃ vivyādh' āyasaiḥ ṣaḍbhiḥ
so 'pakrāmad rath'|ântaram,
48.15 Śatruṃjayaṃ Candraketuṃ Meghavegaṃ Suvarcasam
Sūryabhāsaṃ ca pañc' âitān hatvā vivyādha Saubalam,
taṃ Saubalas tribhir viddhvā Duryodhanam ath' âbravīt.
«sarva enaṃ pramathnīmaḥ pur" âik'|âikaṃ hinasti naḥ
vadh'|ôpāyaṃ cintyatāṃ vai, nṛ|pa, Droṇa|Kṛp'|ādibhiḥ.»
ath' âbravīt punar Droṇaṃ Karṇo Vaikartano raṇe.
«purā sarvān pramathnāti brūhy asya vadham āśu naḥ.»

Duhshásana's son fired back at Árjuna's heir, four arrows for four horses, one for his driver and ten for the boy himself.
Karshni's eyes flashed red with anger and firing seven shafts 48.10
he cast out these words. "Your father ran like a coward from the battlefield. You have my praise, for you at least can fight. But today you will not escape with your life." As he spoke, he loosed at his enemy an arrow of iron polished by the blacksmith's cloth, but with three of his own Drona's son cut it out of the air. Three more arrows Abhimányu shot at Shalya and they cut his banner from its pole. Shalya let fly nine of his vulturefeathered arrows in return. But what came next my king was a true wonder to behold. It was as if Árjuna's son came loose in his own heart.

With Shalya's banner down Abhimányu killed both his flankriders, and pierced by six metal shafts Shalya himself
finally leapt away for another car. Abhimányu's next victims 48.15
were five. He struck Shatrun·jaya, Chandra·ketu, Megha·vega, Suvárchas and Surya·bhasa. And then he found Súbala's son with his arrows, who in answer fired back a volley of three and then turned to Duryódhana to speak.

"Let us move in for the kill together my lord before he slays us one by one. Drona and Kripa and the others must think of some way to stop him."

At the heart of the fray, Karna progeny of the sun shouted across to Drona.

"For too long now Abhimányu has been grinding us away to nothing. Speak, Drona! How can we beat him?"

tato Droṇo mah"|êṣvāsaḥ sarvāṃs tān pratyabhāṣata.
«asti v" âsy' ântaraṃ kiṃ cit kumārasy' âtha paśyati?
anv apy asy' ântaraṃ hy adya carataḥ sarvato diśam?
śīghratāṃ nara|siṃhasya Pāṇḍaveyasya paśyata.
48.20 dhanur|maṇḍalam ev' âsya ratha|mārgeṣu dṛśyate
saṃdadhānasya viśikhāñ śīghraṃ c' âiva vimuñcataḥ.
ārujann iva me prāṇān mohayann api sāyakaiḥ
praharṣayati mā bhūyaḥ Saubhadraḥ para|vīra|hā.
ati mā nandayaty eṣa Saubhadro vicaran raṇe
antaraṃ yasya saṃrabdhā na paśyanti mahā|rathāḥ.
asyato laghu|hastasya diśaḥ sarvā mah"|êṣubhiḥ
na viśeṣaṃ prapaśyāmi raṇe Gāṇḍīva|dhanvanaḥ.»
atha Karṇaḥ punar Droṇam āh' Ārjuni|śar'|ârditaḥ.
«sthātavyam iti tiṣṭhāmi pīḍyamāno 'bhimanyunā.
48.25 tejasvinaḥ kumārasya śarāḥ parama|dāruṇāḥ
kṣiṇvanti hṛdayaṃ me 'dya ghorāḥ pāvaka|tejasaḥ.»
tam ācāryo 'bravīt Karṇaṃ śanakaiḥ prahasann iva.
«a|bhedyam asya kavacaṃ yuvā c' āśu|parākramaḥ.
upadiṣṭā mayā asya pituḥ kavaca|dhāraṇā
tām eṣa nikhilāṃ vetti dhruvaṃ para|puraṃ|jayaḥ.
śakyaṃ tv asya dhanuś chettuṃ jyāṃ ca bāṇaiḥ samāhitaiḥ
abhīśavo hayāś c' âiva tath" ôbhau pārṣṇi|sārathī.
etat kuru mah"|êṣvāsa Rādheya yadi śakyate
ath' âinaṃ vimukhī|kṛtya paścāt praharaṇaṃ kuru.

And the great archer Drona addressed his reply to them all.

"Do any here see a flaw in this young prince? Do you even see a chink in the sky that he has not darkened as he races about us? Behold the force of life in this lion cub born
to the Pándavas. From the courses of our chariots we can see 48.20
only the shape of his bow for as soon as the groove of one of his arrows touches its string it is gone. As he sets his missiles in flight he snatches the very breath from my throat. I wish that the slayer of foes the son of Subhádra would terrorize us no more just as I wish that his heart would fade as he flies through the fray. But his great vehemence overwhelms all of us, all of these warriors, none of whom for the work of his nimble fingers can see through to the horizon any more. His onslaught I can compare only to the work of one other: he who bears the bow named Gandíva."

Ailing beneath Abhimányu's attack, Karna spoke again. "I stand my ground only because my will tells me I must,
but this youth's fierce arrows are whittling away my resolve. 48.25
In them burns a fire born of his bright fury."

A slight smile appeared on the teacher's lips and his words came slowly. "Abhimányu is young. His hand is quick, his armor inviolable. I am the one who taught the father of this destroyer of cities how to protect himself, and he has passed on every nuance of those lessons to his son. Yet if your aim is true you can destroy his bow, sever its string, strike his horses and their harnesses and riders. O son of Radha your talents as an archer are supreme. Do this if you can and he
is distracted by your onslaught strike the fatal blow. With 48.30
a bow in his hand he can be beaten neither by god nor by

48.30 sa|dhanuṣko na śakyo 'yam api jetuṃ sur'|âsuraiḥ
vi|rathaṃ vi|dhanuṣkaṃ ca kuruṣv' âinaṃ yad' îcchasi.»
tad ācārya|vacaḥ śrutvā Karṇo Vaikartanas tvaran
asyato laghu|hastasya pṛṣatkair dhanur ācchinat.
aśvān asy' âvadhīd Bhojo Gautamaḥ pārṣṇi|sārathī
śeṣās tu cchinna|dhanvānaṃ śara|varṣair avākiran.
tvaramāṇās tvarā|kāle vi|rathaṃ ṣaṇ mahā|rathāḥ
śara|varṣair a|karuṇā bālam ekam avākiran.
sa cchinna|dhanvā vi|rathaḥ sva|dharmam anupālayan
khaḍga|carma|dharaḥ śrīmān utpapāta vihāyasā.
48.35 mārgaiḥ sa kaiśik'|ādyaiś ca lāghavena balena ca
Ārjunir vyacarad vyomni bhṛśaṃ vai pakṣi|rāḍ iva.
mayy eva nipataty eṣa s'|âsir ity ūrdhva|dṛṣṭayaḥ
vivyadhus taṃ mah"|êṣvāsāḥ samare chidra|darśinaḥ.
tasya Droṇo 'cchinan muṣṭau khaḍgaṃ maṇi|maya|tsarum
kṣurapreṇa mahā|tejās tvaramāṇaḥ sa|patna|jit.
Rādheyo niśitair bāṇair vyadhamac carma c' ôttamam,
vy|asi|carm'|êṣu|pūrṇ'|âṅgaḥ so 'ntar|ikṣāt punaḥ kṣitim
āsthitaś cakram udyamya Droṇaṃ kruddho 'bhyadhāvata.
sa cakra|reṇ'|ûjjvala|śobhit'|âṅgo
babhāv atīv' ônnata|cakra|pāṇiḥ
raṇe 'bhimanyuḥ kṣaṇam āsa raudraḥ
sa Vāsudev'|ânukṛtiṃ prakurvan.
48.40 sruta|rudhira|kṛt'|âika|rāga|vaktro
bhru|kuṭi|puṭā|kuṭilo 'ti|siṃha|nādaḥ
prabhur a|mita|balo raṇe 'bhimanyur
nṛ|pa|vara|madhya|gato virājate sma.

demon. If it is your will to win, deny him his bow and deny him his chariot."

Hearing his teacher's words Karna born of the sun sent without pause a flock of arrows at the bow that Abhimányu plucked in his quickfingered hands while the Bhoja Gáutama cut down his steeds and their flankriders. Abhimányu's bow broke in his grasp, and the other warriors poured upon him arrows in sheets. Those archers were fast and merciless and in an instant he was without his chariot, a lone child in a storm of scattered shafts, bow broken and car lost but still true to who he was for then he rose again, brandishing his sword and shield, flying up and cutting across the sky
and every grace and all might and speed were his, the son 48.35
of Árjuna there in the vast air like the king of the birds. Looking up from the battle each of the six saw him and each thought that it would be upon him that Abhimányu's sword would fall. They glimpsed their only chance and struck. Bane of his enemies the mighty Drona broke with a forged arrow the boy's sword, leaving its gemstudded hilt still in his hand, and then with sharp shafts Radha's son shattered his fine shield. Without sword and without shield down came Abhimányu once more to earth. His body was full of arrows. Getting to his feet he swept up a chariot wheel and ran at Drona in a fury, his body all alight in its spirals of dust, and with the wheel in his hands raised above his head for just a moment Abhimányu was a fierce image
for Vasudéva himself, his mouth a pure stream flowing red, 48.40
agog with lion's howls, his brows and eyes all twisted up. In the midst of that gathering of kings his might was in that instant without parallel. And there he shone, magnificent.

SAMJAYA uvāca.

49.1 VIṢṆOḤ SVASUR nanda|karaḥ sa Viṣṇv|āyudha|bhūṣitaḥ
rarāj' âtirathaḥ saṃkhye Janārdana iv' âparaḥ.
Mārut'|ôddhūta|keś'|ântam udyat'|āri|var'|āyudham
vapuḥ samīkṣya pṛthv"|īśā duḥ|samīkṣyaṃ surair api
tac cakraṃ bhṛśam udvignāḥ saṃcicchidur an|ekadhā
mahā|rathas tataḥ Kārṣṇiḥ saṃjagrāha mahā|gadām.
vi|dhanuḥ|syandan'|âsis tair vi|cakraś c'|âribhiḥ kṛtaḥ
Abhimanyur mahā|bāhur Aśvatthāmānam ārdayat.
49.5 sa gadām udyatāṃ dṛṣṭvā jvalantīm aśanīm iva
apākrāmad rath'|ôpasthād vikramāṃs trīn nara'|rṣabhaḥ.
tasy' âśvān gadayā hatvā tath" ôbhau pārṣṇi|sārathī
śar'|ācit'|âṅgaḥ Saubhadraḥ śvāvidvat pratyadṛśyata.
tataḥ Subala|dāy'|ādaṃ Kālikeyam apothayat
jaghāna c' âsy' ânucarān Gāndhārān sapta|saptatiṃ.
punar Brahmavaśātīyān jaghāna rathino daśa
Kekayānāṃ rathān sapta hatvā ca daśa kuñjarān.
Dauḥśāsani|rathaṃ s'|âśvaṃ gadayā samapothayat.
tato Dauḥśāsaniḥ kruddho gadām udyamya, māriṣa,
abhidudrāva Saubhadraṃ tiṣṭha tiṣṭh' êti c' âbravīt.
49.10 tāv udyata|gadau vīrāv anyonya|vadha|kāṅkṣiṇau
bhrātṛvyau samprajahrāte pur" êva Tryambak'|Ândhakau.
tāv anyonyaṃ gad'|âgrābhyām āhatya patitau kṣitau
Indra|dhvajāv iv' ôtsṛṣṭau raṇa|madhye paraṃ|tapau.
Dauḥśāsanir ath' ôtthāya Kurūṇāṃ kīrti|vardhanaḥ

SÁNJAYA spoke.

STARRED IN THE weapons of Vishnu the joy of Vishnu's 49.1
sister stood resplendent on the plain. Like the stirrer of
men's hearts he had no peer. His hair fluttered in the wind
and in his upraised hand was the weapon he had won from
his foe. The kings beheld that apparition beyond even the
ken of the gods and starting in fear they smashed the wheel
clean from his fingers. Now Abhimányu had lost his bow,
his sword, and the wheelrim that had been knocked from
his hands. Yet the Dark One's child was a great warrior and
he lifted in his strong arms a huge mace and lunged with it
at Ashvatthámán. Mighty Ashvatthámán saw Abhimányu's 49.5
club high above him like a fork of lightning and with three
skips leapt from the seat of his chariot, and as he did, the
son of Subhádra quilled in arrows like a porcupine crushed
Ashvatthámán's horses and both his drivers beneath his club.
He thrust aside Kalikéya the son of Súbala and wiped out
seventy of his Gandhára followers. Ten of the Brahma·va-
shatíyas were the next to fall and then seven Kékaya cars and
ten of their elephants and swinging his club he hammered
apart the steeds and chariot of Duhshásana's son.

Hot with anger Dauhshásani picked up a club of his own
and flew at Saubhádra, my lord, screaming for him to stand
and fight. The two fierce warriors each baying for the other's 49.10
blood swung their maces high and crashed together like Try·
ámbaka and Ándhaka of old, and trading blow for blow they
knocked one another to the ground, two murderous foes
like banners of Indra cast down in the midst of the fray. But
to the glory of the Kurus it was Dauhshásani who was first
to rise, and he brought down his mace on Saubhádra's head

uttiṣṭhamānaṃ Saubhadraṃ gadayā mūrdhny atāḍayat.
gadā|vegena mahatā vyāyāmena ca mohitaḥ
vicetā nyapatad bhūmau Saubhadraḥ para|vīra|hā.
evaṃ vinihato, rājann, eko bahubhir āhave.
49.15 kṣobhayitvā camūṃ sarvāṃ nalinīm iva kuñjaraḥ
aśobhata hato vīro vyādhair vana|gajo yathā.
taṃ tathā patitaṃ śūraṃ tāvakāḥ paryavārayan
dāvaṃ dagdhvā yathā śāntaṃ pāvakaṃ śiśir'|âtyaye
vimṛdya taru|śṛṅgāṇi saṃnivṛttam iv' ânilam
astaṃ gatam iv' Ādityaṃ taptvā Bhārata|vāhinīm
upaplutaṃ yathā somaṃ saṃśuṣkam iva sāgaram
pūrṇa|candr'|ābha|vadanaṃ kāka|pakṣa|vṛt'|ākṣikam.
taṃ bhūmau patitaṃ dṛṣṭvā tāvakās te mahā|rathāḥ
mudā paramayā yuktāś cukruśuḥ siṃhavan muhuḥ.
49.20 āsīt paramako harṣas tāvakānāṃ viśāṃ pate
itareṣāṃ tu vīrāṇāṃ netrebhyaḥ prāpataj jalam.
antar|ikṣe ca bhūtāni prākrośante viśāṃ pate
dṛṣṭvā nipatitaṃ śūraṃ cyutaṃ candram iv' âmbarāt.
Droṇa|Karṇa|mukhaiḥ ṣaḍbhir Dhārtarāṣṭrair mahā|rathaiḥ
eko 'yaṃ nihataḥ śete n' âiṣa dharmo mato hi naḥ.
tasmiṃs tu nihate vīre bahv aśobhata medinī
dyaur yathā pūrṇa|candreṇa nakṣatra|gaṇa|mālinī.
rukma|puṅkhaiś ca sampūrṇā rudhir'|âugha|pariplutā
uttam'|âṅgaiś ca śūrāṇāṃ bhrājamānaiḥ sa|kuṇḍalaiḥ

as the boy tottered to his feet. He reeled beneath the force of the blow, and then at last the deadly son of Subhádra toppled to the ground. He breathed no more.

O my king. So it was that one died at the hands of many. One warrior who had trampled our whole army as if it were 49.15
just a lotus beneath his feet but now lay in the splendor of death, a wild elephant killed by his hunters. Your soldiers stood in a circle around him where he fell. He was like a mild blaze set at the end of the cold months that had now burned and burned until it was out, a wind that had bent low the branches at the tops of the trees and now was still, a sun that in the passing day had scorched the river of the Bharatas and had now descended. He was like *soma* lost from the cup, like an ocean dried to dust. His face glowed like the full moon, his eyes hidden behind dark locks of hair. Your warriors looked upon him, and as they looked they roared with joy, thrilled and delirious at the scene.

My lord, we celebrated as tears fell from the eyes of our 49.20
foes. In the sky above creatures cried out at the sight of that warrior lying on the earth like the moon fallen from the firmament. Six of the fighters from Dhrita·rashtra's horde, and Drona and Karna chief among them, had cut this lone body to the ground in what I would name a sin. Yet how beautiful the rich earth was as it cradled that dead hero. It was like a night sky at full moon etched in constellations. Heaps of arrowshafts inlaid with gold, the perfect limbs of the dead still clasped by glittering bracelets, the rainbow 49.25
colors of cloths and flags, the tattered shreds of chowries and livery and all the raiment of battle festooned every inch of the earth. It was awash with blood. Strewn with the dazzling

49.25 vicitraiś ca paristomaiḥ patākābhiś ca saṃvṛtā
cāmaraiś ca kuthābhiś ca praviddhaiś c' âmbar'|ôttamaiḥ
tath" âśva|nara|nāgānām alaṃ|kāraiś ca su|prabhaiḥ
khaḍgaiḥ su|niśitaiḥ pītair nirmuktair bhuja|gair iva
cāpaiś ca vi|śikhaiś chinnaiḥ śakty|ṛṣṭi|prāsa|kampanaiḥ
vividhair āyudhaiś c' ânyaiḥ saṃvṛtā bhūr aśobhata
vājibhiś c' âpi nir|jīvaiḥ śvasadbhiḥ śoṇit'|ôkṣitaiḥ
s'|ārohair viṣamā bhūmiḥ Saubhadreṇa nipātitaiḥ
s'|âṅkuśaiḥ sa|mahā|mātraiḥ sa|varm'|āyudha|ketubhiḥ
parvatair iva vidhvastair viśikh'|ônmathitair gajaiḥ
49.30 pṛthivyām anukīrṇaiś ca vy|aśva|sārathi|yodhibhiḥ
hradair iva prakṣubhitair hata|nāgai rath'|ôttamaiḥ
padāti|saṃghaiś ca hatair vividh'|āyudha|bhūṣaṇaiḥ
bhīrūṇāṃ trāsa|jananī ghora|rūp" âbhavan mahī.
taṃ dṛṣṭvā patitaṃ bhūmau candr'|ârka|sa|dṛśa|dyutim
tāvakānāṃ parā prītiḥ Pāṇḍūnāṃ c' âbhavad vyathā.
Abhimanyau hate, rājañ, śiśuke '|prāpta|yauvane
samprādravac camūḥ sarvā Dharma|rājasya paśyataḥ.
dīryamāṇaṃ balaṃ dṛṣṭvā Saubhadre vinipātite
Ajātaśatrus tān vīrān idaṃ vacanam abravīt.
49.35 «svargam eṣa gataḥ śūro yo hato na parāṅ|mukhaḥ.
saṃstambhayata mā bhaiṣṭa vijeṣyāmo raṇe ripūn.»

embroideries that once covered horse, man and elephant, and by swords whose lethal edges had drunk deep as if by snakes that had sloughed their skins, by bows and broken arrows and daggers, spears, javelins, maces and weapons too numerous to count, the surface of the earth shone. Steeds lay drenched red as they sighed their last and fell silent and the earth itself was a jumble of riders, of Saubhádra's victims, of iron hooks and drivers, vestments, blades, poles and elephants like broken crags pierced all over with
arrows. Wellmade chariots had been scattered all across the 49.30
earth, empty now of warriors and drivers, bereft of steeds, upturned in rippling lakes that held dead elephants and the corpses of soldiers in piles with all their daggers and adornments. It was a vision of horror and it struck fear into timid hearts.

The Pandus looked upon the broken figure of Abhimányu who had once been bright as the sun and moon and they were struck down with sorrow. Still only a boy and dead before his prime. But to your side, my king, how sweet a sight was his corpse.

The whole army of the Pándavas rushed to the feet of the righteous king. The matchless Yudhi·shthira looked upon them and saw how his men suffered at the youth's death and said to them the following words.

"Here is a hero bound for heaven. He was one that would 49.35
die rather than run. Take heart, do not be downcast. We will win this war and overcome our traitors."

ity evaṃ sa mahā|tejā duḥkhitebhyo mahā|dyutiḥ
Dharma|rājo yudhāṃ śreṣṭho bruvan duḥkham apānudat.
yuddhe hy āśī|viṣ'|ākārān rāja|putrān raṇe ripūn
pūrvaṃ nihatya saṃgrāme paścād Ārjunir anvayāt.
hatvā daśa|sahasrāṇi Kausalyaṃ ca mahā|ratham
Kṛṣṇ'|Ârjuna|samaḥ Kārṣṇiḥ Śakra|sadma|gato dhruvam.
rath'|âśva|nara|mātaṅgān vinihatya sahasraśaḥ
a|vitṛptaḥ sa saṃgrāmād a|śocyaḥ puṇya|karma|kṛt
gataḥ puṇya|kṛtāl̃ lokān bhāsvarān puṇya|nirjitān.

SAṂJAYA uvāca.

50.1 VAYAṂ TU PRAVARAṂ hatvā teṣāṃ taiḥ śara|pīḍitāḥ
niveśāy' âbhyupāyāmaḥ sāy'|âhne rudhir'|ôkṣitāḥ.
nirīkṣamāṇās tu vayaṃ pare c' āyodhanaṃ śanaiḥ
apayātā, mahā|rāja, glāniṃ prāptā vi|cetasaḥ.
tato niśāyā divasasya c' â|śivaḥ
śivā|rutaḥ saṃdhir avartat' âdbhutaḥ
kuśe|śay'|āpīḍa|nibhe divā|kare
vilambamāne 'stam upetya parvatam.
var'|âsi|śakty|ṛṣṭi|varūtha|carmaṇāṃ
vibhūṣaṇānāṃ ca samākṣipan prabhāḥ
divaṃ ca bhūmiṃ ca samānayann iva
priyāṃ tanuṃ bhānur upaiti pāvakam.

Speaking thus the mighty and splendored king and best of warriors shone a light into their dark despair, and his words drove away their anguish.

So it was that in the ecstasy of battle and the tumult of men Abhimányu fought and killed the serpent princes who were his foes and then passed on. The great lord of Kósala and ten thousand of his men fell before the dark child and equal of the Krishnas before he took the hard road to Indra's home. Thousands of cars and horses and elephants and men all fell before him, and while he departed this earthly confusion insatiate he is not to be mourned. What he did was holy and when he departed he left for the shining lands, lands found only by the pure in deed and soul.

SÁNJAYA spoke.

WE HAD KILLED THEIR champion but still we felt the 50.1
wounds where his arrows had struck us and we returned to camp at the end of the day soaked in blood. My king, as we made our way back weak with exhaustion, we all gazed out across the battlefield insensate and wordless into a dusk alive with strangeness, an uneasy time disjointed from night and day, all full of the cries of jackals. The sun sank down slowly behind the mountains of the west like a lotus crushed in a hand. Its rays struck against the wondrous swords, lances, spears and shields, against the suits of armor and the finery of the dead, and heaven melted into earth where the delicate and gorgeous flame in the sky blazed at the horizon.

50.5 mah"|âbhra|kūṭ'|âcala|śṛṅga|saṃnibhair
dvipair an|ekair iva vajra|pātitaiḥ
sa|vaijayanty|aṅkuśa|varma|yantṛbhir
nipātitair naṣṭa|gatiś citā kṣitiḥ.
hat'|ēśvaraiś cūrṇita|patty|upaskarair
hat'|âśva|sūtair vi|patāka|ketubhiḥ
mahā|rathair bhūḥ śuśubhe vicūrṇitaiḥ
purair iv' â|mitra|hatair, nar'|âdhipa.
rath'|âśva|vṛndaiḥ saha sādibhir hataiḥ
praviddha|bhāṇḍ'|ābharaṇaiḥ pṛthag|vidhaiḥ
nirasta|jihvā|daśan'|ântra|locanair
dharā babhau ghora|virūpa|darśanā.
praviddha|varm'|ābharaṇ'|âmbar'|āyudhā
vipanna|hasty|aśva|rath'|ânugā narāḥ
mah"|ârha|śayy"|āstaraṇ'|ôcitās tadā
kṣitāv a|nāthā iva śerate hatāḥ.
atīva hṛṣṭāḥ śva|sṛgāla|vāyasā
bakāḥ su|parṇāś ca vṛkās tarakṣavaḥ
vayāṃsy asṛk|pāny atha rakṣasāṃ gaṇāḥ
piśāca|saṃghāś ca su|dāruṇā raṇe.
50.10 tvaco vinirbhidya piban vasām asṛk
tath" âiva majjāḥ piśitāni c' âśnuvan
vapāṃ vilumpanti hasanti gānti ca
prakarṣamāṇāḥ kuṇapāny an|ekaśaḥ.
śarīra|saṃghāṭa|vahā asṛg|jalā
rath'|ôḍupā kuñjara|śaila|saṅkaṭā

Among flags, hooks and the corpses of drivers fallen from 50.5
their backs a hundred elephants lay dead like cloudcapped peaks of mountains struck down by lightning. They were heaped so high that the paths of the earth were lost beneath them. My lord, the bodies of kings, the crushed limbs of their soldiers and the tattered garments they had worn, the dead drivers and horses and their lost banners and pennants and the trunks of mutilated heroes lay resplendent across the ground. So immense was the slaughter it was as if city upon city had been slain by raiders. Thick with clusters of cars and dead horses and riders, jeweled with dazzling fabrics and ornaments and the torn-out tongues and teeth and bowels and eyes of the dead, the earth bore an appalling bounty of men whose swords, armor, bracelets and clothes had been ripped from them, their followers and chariots and horses and elephants scattered in every direction. Once they had lain on the plush cushions and couches of kings but now they slept on the ground like the kinless dead.

Then came dogs and jackals, crows, herons, vultures, wolves, hyenas and other beasts of prey all bristling with pleasure. Drinkers of blood and hosts of goblins and a
throng of ghosts filled the place with horrors. Peeling back 50.10
the skins from corpses, they drank up the blood and fat and sank their teeth into flesh and marrow. They twisted out intestines and cackled and sang, dragging body after body behind them. A river flowed from the mighty dead that night and it was as treacherous and as terrifying as the Váitarani itself. Its weeds were the glinting banks of swords growing in the flesh that was its mud and its pebbles were the heads of the dead. On its surface chariots bobbed like rafts along

manuṣya|śīrṣ'|ôpala|māṃsa|kardamā
praviddha|nānā|vidha|śastra|mālinī.
mahā|bhayā Vaitaraṇ" îva dus|tarā
pravartitā yodha|varais tadā nadī
uvāha madhyena raṇ'|âjire bhṛśaṃ
bhay'|âvahā jīva|mṛta|pravāhinī.
pibanti c' âśnanti ca yatra dur|dṛśāḥ
piśāca|saṃghās tu nadanti bhairavāḥ
su|nanditāḥ prāṇa|bhṛtāṃ bhayaṃ|karāḥ
samāna|bhakṣāḥ śva|sṛgāla|pakṣiṇaḥ.
tathā tad āyodhanam ugra|darśanaṃ
niśā|mukhe pitṛ|pati|rāṣṭra|saṃnibham
nirīkṣamāṇāḥ śanakair jahur narāḥ
samutthit'|ānṛtta|kabandha|saṃkulam.
50.15 apeta|vidhvasta|mah"|ârha|bhūṣaṇaṃ
nipātitaṃ Śakra|samaṃ mahā|ratham
raṇe 'bhimanyuṃ dadṛśus tadā janā
vyapoḍha|havyaṃ sadas' îva pāvakam.

SAṂJAYA uvāca.

51.1 TASMIṂS TU NIHATE vīre Saubhadre ratha|yūtha|pe
vimukta|ratha|saṃnāhāḥ sarve nikṣipta|kārmukāḥ.
upopaviṣṭā rājānaṃ parivārya Yudhiṣṭhiram
tad eva duḥkhaṃ dhyāyantaḥ Saubhadra|gata|mānasāḥ.
tato Yudhiṣṭhiro rājā vilalāpa su|duḥkhitaḥ.
«Abhimanyau hate vīre bhātṛ|putre mahā|rathe
Droṇ'|ânīkam a|sambādhaṃ mama priya|cikīrṣayā
bhittvā vyūhaṃ praviṣṭo 'sau go|madhyam iva kesarī.
51.5 yasya śūrā mah"|êṣv|āsāḥ pratyanīka|gatā raṇe

rocky straits formed by dead elephants, and in its waters of blood sank bodies like vessels of clay. Its rough currents plunged through the whole of the battlefield, swirling with the living and the dead. Its freight was fear itself. The place where we had fought was now awful to behold, packed with ghosts foul and fell that howled and gulped and chewed as all around them flocked hounds, jackals and winged things consuming all that they could in a frenzy that chilled the hearts of those who still drew breath. In the early night it was as if Death's kingdom had risen before our eyes. The living stole away as quietly as they could as around them headless bodies rose up and danced.

And still men looked upon that supreme warrior, all his great and worthy decorations now stripped and ruined, Abhimányu, Indra's equal, lying dead, like a pyre without offerings at the edge of sacrificial ground. 50.15

SÁNJAYA spoke.

THE GREAT WARD of warriors Saubhádra was dead. His companions all descended from their chariots and took off their armor and cast down their fashioned bows. Then they came around their king Yudhi·shthira and sat before him. Each of them was deep in sorrow, his thoughts fixed on Subhádra's son. King Yudhi·shthira spoke to them, and his words were choked with sadness. 51.1

"Abhimányu is dead. Brave and strong son of my brother. So fervently did he want to help me, and he did: Drona's array has been broken. He plunged into its depths and destroyed it from within like a lion let loose among cattle.
He shattered its ranks and drove back its archers nimble 51.5

prabhagnā vinivartante kṛt'|âstrā yuddha|dur|madāḥ.
atyanta|śatrur asmākaṃ yena Duḥśāsanaḥ śaraiḥ
kṣipraṃ hy abhimukhaḥ saṃkye vi|saṃjño vimukhī|kṛtaḥ.
sa tīrtvā dus|taraṃ vīro Droṇ'|ânīkam mah"|ârṇavam
prāpya Dauḥśāsaniṃ Kārṣṇir yāto Vaivasvata|kṣayam.
kathaṃ drakṣyāmi Kaunteyaṃ Saubhadre nihate 'rjunam
Subhadrāṃ vā mahā|bhāgāṃ priyaṃ putram a|paśyatīm?
kiṃ svid vayam apet'|ârtham a|śliṣṭam a|samañjasam
tāv ubhau prativakṣyāmo Hṛṣīkeśa|Dhanaṃjayau?
51.10 aham eva Subhadrāyāḥ Keśav'|Ârjunayor api
priya|kāmo jay'|ākāṅkṣī kṛtavān idam a|priyam.
na lubdho budhyate doṣān mohāl lobhaḥ pravartate
madhu|lipsur hi n' â|paśyaṃ prapātam aham īdṛśaṃ.
yo hi bhojye puras|kāryo yāneṣu śayaneṣu ca
bhūṣaṇeṣu ca so 'smābhir bālo yudhi puras|kṛtaḥ.
kathaṃ hi bālas taruṇo yuddhānām a|viśāradaḥ
sad|aśva iva sambādhe vi|ṣame kṣemam arhati.
aho 'dya vayam apy enaṃ mahīm anuśayīmahi
Bībhatsoḥ kopa|dīptasya dagdhāḥ kṛpaṇa|cakṣuṣā.
51.15 a|lubdho matimān hrīmān kṣamāvān rūpavān balī
vapuṣmān māna|kṛd vīraḥ priyaḥ satya|parāyaṇaḥ
yasya ślāghanti vibudhāḥ karmāṇy ūrjita|karmaṇaḥ
Nivātakavacāñ jaghne Kālakeyāṃś ca vīryavān
Mahendra|śatravo yena Hiraṇyapura|vāsinaḥ
akṣṇor nimeṣa|mātreṇa Paulomāḥ sa|gaṇā hatāḥ

and wild though they are. His quick arrows left our sworn enemy Duhshásana lost and confused at the head of his column. He boldly crossed the fathomless sea that was Drona's seething array to reach Duhshásana's own child before at last he departed for the broken harbor of the sun.

Abhimányu is dead. How will I look Árjuna son of Kunti in the eye? Or the flawless Subhádra when she comes looking for her dear son? Will I lie to Hrishi·kesha and Dhanan·jaya? Will I speak evasively? With crooked words?
I wanted to bring Subhádra joy, I so dearly hoped to seal 51.10
victory for Késhava and for Árjuna. Yet it is I who have caused this calamity. A desperate fool does not wake from his delusions, for his desire is born of his folly. I yearned, I wanted what was sweet, and I did not foresee how things would end.

What were his due? Love and sleep, the pleasures of the road, jewelers' work. Yet I placed a mere boy at the head of my army. How could I have done such a thing? A young child with no experience of fighting, a foal in a pack of rude stallions. He should have been protected. O but I too should lie down upon the earth at his side before the flames
leap from his father's burning eyes and consume me. How 51.15
my brother will hate me for this. He is no fool. A man of peace and wisdom, of intent and strength and goodness, a hero, someone who is beloved of and cares for others, a man whose highest goal is truth. Sages tell of his deeds for he does things that are beyond the reach of normal men. He it was who crushed beneath his might the Niváta·kávachas and Kalakéyas, he who came in the winking of an eye to smash the golden city and the foes of great Indra led by

parebhyo' py a|bhay'|ârthibhyo yo dadāty a|bhayaṃ vibhuḥ
tasy' âsmābhir na śakitas trātum ady' ātma|jo bhayāt.
bhayaṃ tu su|mahat prāptaṃ
Dhārtarāṣṭraṃ mahad balam
Pārthaḥ putra|vadhāt kruddhaḥ
Kauravāñ śoṣayiṣyati.
51.20 kṣudraḥ kṣudra|sahāyaś ca sva|pakṣa|kṣayam āturaḥ
vyaktaṃ Duryodhano dṛṣṭvā śocan hāsyati jīvitam.
na me jayaḥ prīti|karo na rājyaṃ
na c' âmaratvaṃ na suraiḥ sa|lokatā
imaṃ samīkṣy' â|prativīrya|pauruṣaṃ
nipātitaṃ deva|var'|ātma|j'|ātma|jam.»

SAMJAYA uvāca.

52.1 ATH' ÂINAṂ VILAPANTAṂ taṃ
Kuntī|putraṃ Yudhiṣṭhiram
Kṛṣṇadvaipāyanas tatra
ājagāma mahān ṛṣiḥ.
arcayitvā yathā|nyāyam upaviṣṭaṃ Yudhiṣṭhiraḥ
abravīc choka|saṃtapto bhrātuḥ putra|vadhena saḥ.
«a|dharma|yuktair bahubhiḥ parivārya mahā|rathaiḥ
yudhyamāno mah"|êṣv|āsaiḥ Saubhadro nihato raṇe.
bālaś c' â|bāla|buddhiś ca Saubhadraḥ para|vīra|hā
an|upāyena saṃgrāme yudhyamāno viśeṣataḥ
52.5 may" âpy uktaḥ sa saṃgrāme ‹dvāraṃ saṃjanayasva naḥ›
praviṣṭe 'bhyantare tasmin Saindhavena nivāritāḥ.
nanu nāma samaṃ yuddham eṣṭavyaṃ yuddha|jīvibhiḥ
idaṃ c' âiv' â|samaṃ yuddham īdṛśaṃ yat kṛtaṃ paraiḥ.

Pulóman who dwelt therein. Such is his generosity that he is merciful even to his foes if it is for mercy that they ask. Yet today I could not even save his son.

The destruction that Dhrita·rashtra's great army has brought upon itself will be terrible. The Káuravas will be burnt away to nothing by the fury that the death of his boy will light inside Partha. Petty tyrant in his petty court, 51.20
Duryódhana will witness the annihilation of his friends and he will give up his life I am sure in a bonfire of sickness and of sorrow. But be it victory or the throne, immortality or the realms of the gods, nothing could bring me joy again. For I have seen life bursting and without limits suddenly stoppered up. I have seen none other than the son of the son of the greatest of gods struck down before me, dead."

SÁNJAYA spoke.

AND SO YUDHI·SHTHIRA son of Kuntí mourned. Then the 52.1
great sage Krishna Dvaipáyana came before him.* When he arrived Yudhi·shthira paid him due reverence and spoke to him, still burning with grief at the death of his brother's son.

"Abhimányu is dead. His killers were a circle of strong and wicked warriors from among the mighty Kuru bowmen against whom he fought. He may have been a boy but he had a man's heart. He fought alone and without concern for his own safety, burning his foes from his path. 'Open a way 52.5
through the vanguard for us,' I told him. And on he went, deep among them, but alas our own pursuit of him was hindered by the Sindhu king. His killers fought a crooked battle against him, one that none who live by war could call

ten' âsmi bhṛśa|saṃtaptaḥ śoka|bāṣpa|samākulaḥ
śamaṃ n' âiv' âdhigacchāmi cintayānaḥ punaḥ punaḥ.»

SAMJAYA uvāca.

tam tathā vilapantaṃ vai śoka|vyākula|mānasam
uvāca bhagavān Vyāso Yudhiṣṭhiram idaṃ vacaḥ.

VYĀSA uvāca.

Yudhiṣṭhira, mahā|prājña, sarva|śāstra|viśārada,
vyasaneṣu na muhyanti tvādṛśā, Bharata'|rṣabha.
52.10 svargeṣu gataḥ śūraḥ śatrūn hatvā bahūn raṇe
a|bāla|sa|dṛśaṃ karma kṛtvā vai puruṣ'|ôttamaḥ.
an|atikramaṇīyo vai vidhir eṣa Yudhiṣṭhira
deva|dānava|gandharvān mṛtyur harati, Bhārata.

YUDHIṢṬHIRA uvāca.

ime vai pṛthivī|pālāḥ śerate pṛthivī|tale
nihatāḥ pṛtanā|madhye mṛta|saṃjñā mahā|balāḥ.
nāg'|âyuta|balāś c' ânye vāyu|vega|balās tathā
ta ete nihatāḥ saṃkhye tulya|rūpā narair narāḥ.
n' âiṣāṃ paśyāmi hantāraṃ prāṇināṃ saṃyuge kva cit
vikrameṇ' ôpapannā hi tejo|bala|samanvitāḥ.
52.15 jetavyam iti c' ânyonyaṃ nityaṃ yeṣāṃ hṛdi sthitam
atha c' ême hatāḥ prājñāḥ śerate vigat'|âyuṣaḥ.
mṛtā iti ca śabdo 'yaṃ vartate ca tato 'rthavat
ime mṛtā mahī|pālāḥ prāyaśo bhīma|vikramāḥ.

evenhanded. It burns me without end to think of it. I am full of grief, full of tears. Again and again I return to it and I can find no peace."

SÁNJAYA spoke.

Holy Vyasa addressed Yudhi·shthira as he sorrowed, his heart aching in grief. These were the words that he said.

VYASA spoke.

O Yudhi·shthira. Deep is your wisdom and you have studied hard the sacred books. O bull of the Bharatas, men like you do not fade in the face of calamity. A hero slays 52.10
foe upon foe in war and then goes to dwell in the wards of heaven. Saubhádra achieved things beyond his years. He was a man indeed and one of the best there have been. But Yudhi·shthira, Death is ordained and it will not be transgressed. Hear me Bhárata. Death visits even demon and spirit and god.

YUDHI·SHTHIRA spoke.

In life kings rule the earth and at life's end when war is done they make their bed upon it. So are these mighty ones acquainted with death. Some have the strength of a hundred elephants and some the power of the winds yet when they die in battle they are men and nothing but men. Nowhere do I see any still standing if he once took the breath of another: these are fighters of main and splendor and written in the heart of each for all time is the will to overcome his other. When their lives have left them and 52.15
they sleep in death then at last they come to know this thing. Death is a word that gets its meaning from this, from the demise of the bold lords of the earth. Heroes though

niś|ceṣṭā nir|abhīmānāḥ śūrāḥ śatru|vaśaṃ|gatāḥ
rāja|putrāś ca saṃrabdhā Vaiśvānara|mukhaṃ gatāḥ.
atra me saṃśayaḥ prāptaḥ: kutaḥ saṃjñā mṛtā iti?
kasya mṛtyuḥ? kuto mṛtyuḥ? kathaṃ saṃharate prajāḥ?
haraty amara|saṃkāśa tan me brūhi pitā|maha.

SAṂJAYA uvāca.

taṃ tathā paripṛcchantaṃ Kuntī|putraṃ Yudhiṣṭhiram
āśvāsanam idaṃ vākyam uvāca bhagavān ṛṣiḥ.

VYĀSA uvāca.

52.20 atr' âpy udāharant' îmam itihāsaṃ purātanam
Akampanasya kathitaṃ Nāradena purā, nṛ|pa.
sa c' âpi rājā rāj'|êndra putra|vyasanam uttamaṃ
a|prasahyatamaṃ loke prāptavān iti me matiḥ.
tad ahaṃ sampravakṣyāmi Mṛtyoḥ prabhavam uttamam
tatas tvaṃ mokṣyase duḥkhāt sneha|bandhana|saṃśrayāt.
purā vṛttam idaṃ, tāta,
śṛṇu kīrtayato mama
dhanyam ākhyānam āyuṣyaṃ
śoka|ghnaṃ puṣṭi|vardhanam.
pavitram ari|saṃgha|ghnaṃ maṅgalānāṃ ca maṅgalaṃ
yath" âiva ved'|âdhyayanam upākhyānam idaṃ tathā.
52.25 śravaṇīyaṃ mahā|rāja prātar nityaṃ nṛ|p'|ôttamaiḥ
putrān āyuṣmato rājyam īhamānaiḥ śriyaṃ tathā.

they are in the end these fiery sons of kings die powerless and without pride, and broken by the will of an opponent each sets out for the place of Vaishvánara and his kin. But I wonder to myself. From where does our sense of death arise? From what or from where does Death herself come? Why does she* steal away the living? For steal she does. Tell me o great and godlike father.

SÁNJAYA spoke.

Thus did Yudhi·shthira son of Kuntí put his question to the holy sage, and gentle were the words with which Vyasa replied.

VYASA spoke.

There is an ancient tale told about this question, my king, 52.20
one that Nárada told to Akámpana in olden times. It is said that this king too suffered that most terrible loss that any can suffer—the death of his child. I will tell you now of the very origin of Death. When you have heard me you will be free of the pain that comes the love that binds you to it. Listen closely my son to this old story for it is rich in wisdom and it will banish your misery and return you to life. I say that it will not only cleanse your soul, it will drive down those who want to harm you. It is the highest bliss for in profundity this tale matches any to be found in the
Vedas. O majesty a king who cares for the longevity of his 52.25
sons and for his kingdom and wealth would do well to hear this story when he wakes for every day that he lives.

purā kṛta|yuge tāta āsīd rājā hy Akampanaḥ,
sa śatru|vaśam āpanno madhye saṃgrāma|mūrdhani.
tasya putro Harir nāma Nārāyaṇa|samo bale
śrīmān kṛt'|âstro medhāvī yudhi Śakr'|ôpamo balī.
sa śatrubhiḥ parivṛto bahudhā raṇa|mūrdhani
vyasyan bāṇa|sahasrāṇi yodheṣu ca gajeṣu ca.
sa karma duṣ|karaṃ kṛtvā saṃgrāme śatru|tāpanaḥ
śatrubhir nihataḥ saṃkhye pṛtanāyāṃ, Yudhiṣṭhira.
52.30 sa rājā preta|kṛtyāni tasya kṛtvā śuc" ânvitaḥ
śocann ahani rātrau ca n' âlabhat sukham ātmanaḥ.
tasya śokaṃ viditvā tu putra|vyasana|sambhavam
ath' ājagāma deva'|rṣir Nārado 'sya samīpataḥ.
sa tu rājā mahā|bhāgo dṛṣṭvā deva'|rṣi|sattamam
pūjayitvā yathā|nyāyaṃ kathām akathayat tadā.
tasya sarvaṃ samācaṣṭa yathā vṛttaṃ, nar'|ēśvara,
śatrubhir vijayaṃ saṃkhye putrasya ca vadhaṃ tathā.
«mama putro, mahā|vīrya, Indra|Viṣṇu|sama|dyutiḥ
śatrubhir bahubhiḥ saṃkhye parākramya hato balī.
52.35 ka eṣa mṛtyur, bhagavan, kiṃ|vīrya|bala|pauruṣaḥ?
etad icchāmi tattvena śrotuṃ matimatāṃ vara.»

Many years ago, during the era before our own, there was a king by the name of Akámpana. He was fighting a war and he had suffered defeat at his enemy's hands. He had a handsome son named Hari who was strong as Naráyana. A skilled fighter with a strategist's mind, his bravery bore compare to Indra's. During the king's defeat his son was hemmed in by his foe at the very center of the fray. He sent up from among the warriors and elephants around him a last, huge volley of arrows. O Yudhi·shthira despite this daring deed and fearsome though the prince was, that day was to be one when his opponents would slay him.

His griefstricken father performed his son's last rites. By 52.30
day and by night he mourned the boy's loss and clung ceaselessly to his despair. And the divine seer Nárada heard of the misery that his son's death had bred in him and he went to visit the king. When the vaunted king received his guest he bowed down to him as was right and then told him all that had happened. No detail did he leave out, but he recounted to the sage both his enemy's victory and the story of the death of his child.

"O mighty one. My son was as glorious as Indra and Vishnu. And as he fought with courage and strength against his adversaries he was struck down in battle by a horde of
them. Tell me o holiness: who is this Death? Does he* have 52.35
the courage or the strength or the mettle of a man? You are the wisest seer who lives. I want to hear the truth."

tasya tad vacanaṃ śrutvā Nārado vara|daḥ prabhuḥ
ākhyānam idam ācaṣṭa putra|śok'|âpahaṃ mahat.

NĀRADA uvāca.

śṛṇu, rājan mahā|bāho, ākhyānaṃ bahu|vistaram
yathā vṛttaṃ śrutaṃ c' âiva may" âpi vasu|dh"|âdhipa.
prajāḥ sṛṣṭvā tadā Brahmā ādi|sarge pitā|mahaḥ
a|saṃhṛtaṃ mahā|tejā dṛṣṭvā jagad idaṃ prabhuḥ.
tasya cintā samutpannā saṃhāraṃ prati, pārthiva,
cintayan na hy asau veda saṃhāraṃ, vasu|dh"|âdhipa.
52.40 tasya roṣān mahā|rāja khebhyo 'gnir udatiṣṭhata
tena sarvā diśo vyāptāḥ s'|ântar|deśā didhakṣatā.
tato divaṃ bhuvaṃ khaṃ ca jvālā|mālā|samākulaṃ
car'|â|caraṃ jagat sarvaṃ dadāha bhagavān prabhuḥ.
tato hatāni bhūtāni carāṇi sthāvarāṇi ca
mahatā krodha|vegena trāsayann iva vīryavān.

tato Rudro jaṭī Sthāṇur niśā|cara|patir Haraḥ
jagāma śaraṇaṃ devaṃ Brahmāṇaṃ Parameṣṭhinam.
tasminn āpatite Sthāṇau prajānāṃ hita|kāmyayā
abravīt paramo devo jvalann iva mahā|muniḥ.
52.45 «kiṃ kurma kāmaṃ kām'|ârha kāmāj jāto 'si putraka?
kariṣyāmi priyaṃ sarvaṃ brūhi Sthāṇo yad icchasi.»

Nárada was generous and learned. He heard the king's plea and he told this great story to release him from the longing he felt for his departed son.

NÁRADA spoke.

Mighty lord listen now to this recondite tale. You will hear it as I once heard it told to me o king of this bounteous earth. At the beginning of things, when the great father Brahma had made the creatures, he looked in his splendor upon the world over which he ruled. O majesty, anxiety took root in him about its burgeoning because he could not see how it would end. A fire born of anger rose up from 52.40
the spaces of his body and my king every quarter of the world was engulfed in its blaze. Sky and earth and air were all garlanded in dancing flame. The high and holy Lord ignited all in the world that moved and all that was still and destroying every object in this changing universe with the great force of his fury the mighty Brahma sent terror quaking through the quick and the dead.

Then the Still One* with twisted hair, the lord of the nightwalkers, the ghastly destroyer, came to the abode of Brahma Paraméshthin. He feared for the survival of living things. He cast himself down at Brahma's feet. From out of his fires the supreme god and great ascetic addressed his child.

"Son born of desire what would you have me do? All that 52.45
you wish will be yours. I will do whatever you want, so tell me now o Still One what it is you came here for."

STHĀṆUR uvāca.

53.1 PRAJĀ|SARGA|NIMITTAM hi kṛto yatnas tvayā, vibho,
tvayā sṛṣṭāś ca vṛddhāś ca bhūta|grāmāḥ pṛthag|vidhāḥ.
tās tav' êha punaḥ krodhāt prajā dahyanti sarvaśaḥ
tā dṛṣṭvā mama kāruṇyaṃ prasīda bhagavan prabho.

BRAHM" ôvāca.

saṃhartuṃ na ca me kāma etad evaṃ bhaved iti
pṛthivyā hita|kāmaṃ tu tato māṃ manyur āviśat.
iyaṃ hi māṃ sadā devī bhār'|ārtā samacūcudat
saṃhār'|ârthaṃ Mahādeva bhāreṇ' âbhihatā satī.
53.5 tato 'haṃ n' âdhigacchāmi tapye bahu|vidhaṃ tadā
saṃhāram a|prameyasya tato māṃ manyur āviśat.

RUDRA uvāca.

saṃhār'|ârthaṃ prasīdasva mā ruṣo vasu|dh"|âdhipa
mā prajāḥ sthāvarāś c' âiva jaṅgamāś ca vyanīnaśaḥ.
tava prasādād bhagavann idaṃ vartet tridhā jagat
an|āgatam atītaṃ ca yac ca samprati vartate.
bhagāvan krodha|saṃdīptaḥ krodhād agnim avāsṛjat
sa dahaty aśma|kūṭāni drumāṃś ca saritas tathā.
palvalāni ca sarvāṇi sarve c' âiva tṛṇ'|ôlapāḥ
sthāvaraṃ jaṅgamaṃ c' âiva niḥ|śeṣaṃ kurute jagat.
53.10 tad etad bhasmasād bhūtaṃ jagat sthāvara|jaṅgamam
prasīda bhagavan sa tvaṃ roṣo na syād varo mama.
sarve hi sṛṣṭā naṣyanti tava deva kathaṃ cana

THE STILL ONE spoke.

O EXALTED ONE. The work of the creation of living things 53.1
was yours and by you the diverse creatures of the spheres are born and grow old. But now all across the world these same beings burn in the pyre of your rage. To watch them suffer brings pity to my heart. O great and venerable sire, I implore you that you overcome your fury.

BRAHMA spoke.

No lust to destroy brought this to pass. Rage possesses me because I fear for the survival of the earth. The goddess is pained by her burden and it is she who drives me to seek the destruction of my creatures. She is too kind o Maha·de-
va and she suffers terribly for it. But I can find no way of 53.5
destroying this manifold and measureless cosmos, and this is why such fury burns within me.

RUDRA spoke.

Be at peace for the sake of the flowery sphere that calls you master. Put an end to your fury, lest you destroy all that you have created, all that moves and all that is still, as only by your grace my lord can this triple world survive for in you is what is yet to come, what is past, and what is now upon us. Your rage burns and fire sparks forth from its heat and this fire consumes rocks, hills, trees, rivers. All the sweet pools and all the shrublands and all the meadows and every
plant and creature perish from it. Everything is turning to 53.10
ash. Find peace, my lord. My wish is simply that your fury could be at an end. Your entire creation o celestial one is almost destroyed and before it is too late your splendor must be eclipsed and you must somehow cool your temper for

tasmān nivartatāṃ tejas tvayy ev' êha pralīyatām.
tat paśya deva su|bhṛśaṃ prajānāṃ hita|kāmyayā
yath" ême prāṇinaḥ sarve nivarteraṃs tathā kuru.
a|bhāvaṃ n' êha gaccheyur utsanna|jananāḥ prajāḥ
ādi|deva niyukto 'smi tvayā lokeṣu loka|kṛt.
mā vinaśyej jagan|nātha jagat sthāvara|jaṅgamam
prasād'|âbhimukhaṃ devaṃ tasmād evaṃ bravīmy aham.

NĀRADA uvāca.

53.15 śrutvā hi vacanaṃ devaḥ prajānāṃ hita|kāraṇe
tejaḥ saṃdhārayām āsa punar ev' ântar|ātmani.
tato 'gnim upasaṃhṛtya bhagavāl̃ loka|sat|kṛtaḥ
pravṛttiṃ ca nivṛttiṃ ca kalpayām āsa vai prabhuḥ.
upasaṃharatas tasya tam agniṃ roṣa|jaṃ tadā
prādur babhūva viśvebhyo gobhyo nārī mah"|ātmanaḥ
kṛṣṇā raktā tathā piṅga|rakta|jihv'|āsya|locanā
kuṇḍalābhyāṃ ca, rāj'|êndra, taptābhyāṃ tapta|bhūṣaṇā.
sā niḥsṛtya tathā khebhyo dakṣiṇāṃ diśam āśritā
smayamānā ca s" âvekṣya devau viśv'|ēśvarāv ubhau.
53.20 tām āhūya tadā devo lok'|ādi|nidhan'|ēśvaraḥ,
«mṛtyo» iti «mahī|pāla jahi c' êmāḥ prajā» iti.
«tvaṃ hi saṃhāra|buddhy" âtha prādur|bhūtā ruṣo mama
tasmāt saṃhara sarvās tvaṃ prajāḥ sa|jaḍa|paṇḍitāḥ.
mama tvaṃ hi niyogena tataḥ śreyo hy avāpsyasi.»

you alone can do so. O heavenly one, behold what you have done and for the survival of your children waste no time. Act before all life is erased. If you do not then all future generations will pass from this world into oblivion hand in hand with their ancestors.

O god of the beginning. In these worlds I am yours to command, for it is you who made them. Avert the catastrophe of this still and swaying world, this world over which you rule.

NÁRADA spoke.

The god heard Maha·deva's plea and for the sake of living 53.15
things stowed his splendor once more within himself. As he buried that fire, the revered and holy lord of the world made clear for the first time what it is to act and what it is to withdraw. Majesty, once he had stilled the flames born of his wrath, from his eyes and ears there stepped a woman deep of soul who was dark and red and whose eyes and face and tongue were of a tawny hue and who was decked in burnt things and wore upon her wrists two blackened bracelets. Emerging from the gaps in his body the woman moved around to his right and with a smile looked across
at the two gods of all that is. Then he who marked out the 53.20
world arraigned her thus.

"O Death. You are the earth's guardian. Destroy these creatures. You were born of my rage to bring about the end of things. Gather in all these beings from idiot to sage and know that only good can come to you for it will be my command that you obey."

evam uktā tu sā tena Mṛtyuḥ kamala|locanā
dadhyau c' âtyartham a|balā praruroda ca su|svaram
pāṇibhyāṃ pratijagrāha tāny aśrūṇi pitā|mahaḥ
sarva|bhūta|hit'|ârthāya tāṃ c' âpy anunayat tadā.

NĀRADA uvāca.

54.1 VINĪYA DUḤKHAM a|balā ātmany eva Prajā|patim
uvāca prāñjalir bhūtvā lat" êv' āvarjitā punaḥ.

MṚTYUR uvāca.

tvayā sṛṣṭā kathaṃ nārī īdṛśī vadatāṃ vara
krūraṃ karm' âhitaṃ kuryāṃ tad eva kim u jānatī.
bibhemy aham a|dharmādd hi prasīda bhagavan prabho
priyān putrān vayasyāṃś ca bhrātṝn mātṝḥ pitṝn patīn.
upadhyāsyanti me deva mṛteṣv ebhyo bibhemy aham
kṛpaṇānāṃ hi rudatāṃ ye patanty aśru|bindavaḥ.
54.5 tebhyo 'haṃ bhagavan bhītā śaraṇaṃ tv" âham āgatā
Yamasya bhavanaṃ deva gaccheyaṃ na sur'|ôttama.
kāyena vinay'|ôpetā mūrdhn" ôdagra|nakhena ca
etad icchāmy ahaṃ kāmaṃ tvatto loka|pitā|maha.
iccheyaṃ tvat|prasādādd hi tapas taptuṃ praj"|ēśvara.
pradiś' êmaṃ varaṃ deva tvaṃ mahyaṃ bhagavan prabho.
tvayā hy uktā gamiṣyāmi Dhenuk'|āśramam uttamam
tatra tapsye tapas tīvraṃ tav' âiv' ārādhane ratā.
na hi śakṣyāmi, dev'|ēśa, prāṇān prāṇa|bhṛtāṃ priyān

She of the rose eyes heard the god's words. But as she reflected in her heart upon them she began to weep, and her weeping was gentle and plangent. In turn the great father who cares for all the beings of the world comforted her, and in his hands caught her falling tears.

NÁRADA spoke.

SOMEHOW THE GENTLE lady forced her sorrow down into 54.1
her heart and then, with her hands raised reverentially like slender branches above her head, she spoke to the lord of beings.

DEATH spoke.

O lord. I would know how a woman such as myself who is born of you could perform so dire a task as this in full knowledge of what it is she does. Take pity on me great lord of heaven: I fear that it is wrong. I fear the teardrops falling from the eyes of those who weep in sorrow for the memories of their beloved sons and babies and brothers and mothers and fathers and husbands. I fear what they will say about me
among mortals. My lord I ask for your asylum. O greatest 54.5
of the celestial gods I do not want to set foot in the house of Yama. As my very form is made of your kindness then by the tips of these fingers that I reach out to you now I beg you o generous father of the world, grant me but one wish. O mighty and illustrious ruler of all things, by your grace and your covenant I ask you for a gift most reverend: that I may do penance. If you give me leave I will take myself to Dhénuka's high retreat and there I will burn in the keen heat of meditation and devote myself to your adoration. O

hartuṃ vilapamānānām a|dharmād abhirakṣa mām.

BRAHM" ôvāca.

54.10 Mṛtyo saṃkalpit" âsi tvaṃ prajā|saṃhāra|hetunā,
gaccha saṃhara sarvās tvaṃ prajā mā te vicāraṇā.
bhavitā tv etad evaṃ hi n' âitaj jātv anyathā bhavet,
bhavatv a|ninditā loke kuruṣva vacanaṃ mama.

NĀRADA uvāca.

evam ukt" âbhavat prītā prāñjalir bhagavan|mukhī
saṃhāre n' âkarod buddhiṃ prajānāṃ hita|kāmyayā.
tūṣṇīm āsīt tadā devaḥ prajānām īśvar'|ēśvaraḥ
prasādaṃ c' āgamat kṣipram ātmany eva pitā|mahaḥ.
smayamānaś ca lok'|ēśo lokān sarvān avekṣya ca
lokās tv āsan yathā|pūrvaṃ dṛṣṭās ten' âpamanyunā.
54.15 nivṛtta|roṣe tasmiṃs tu bhagavaty a|parājite
sā kany" âpi jagām' âtha samīpāt tasya dhīmataḥ.
apasṛty' â|pratiśrutya prajā|saṃharaṇaṃ tadā,
tvaramāṇā ca, rāj'|êndra, Mṛtyur Dhenukam abhyagāt.
sā tatra paramaṃ tīvraṃ cacāra vratam uttamam
sā tadā hy eka|pādena tasthau padmāni ṣo|ḍaśa.
pañca c' âbdāni kāruṇyāt prajānām tu hit'|âiṣiṇī
indriyāṇ' îndriy'|ârthebhyaḥ priyebhyaḥ saṃnivartya sā.
tatas tv ekena pādena punar anyāni sapta vai
tasthau padmāni ṣaṭ c' âiva sapta c' âikaṃ ca pārthiva.
54.20 tataḥ padm'|âyutaṃ c' âiva mṛgaiḥ saha cacāra sā
punar gatvā tato Nandāṃ puṇyāṃ śīt'|âmal'|ôdakām.

lord of the gods. I cannot steal the dear breath from the throats of these wretched creatures. Save me from this evil.

BRAHMA spoke.

As Death you were born to end the lives of things. Go 54.10
and gather in all that breathes. Do not hesitate, for this is ordained and it cannot be revoked. No censure will fall on you among men. But you must do as I have told you.

NÁRADA spoke.

Death bowed at holy Brahma's command and raised her hands in honor before her. Her compassion for the living meant that she could not resolve the conflict within her. All the same, the heavenly and supernal god and father of beings felt well pleased and was content now in his very soul. He looked gladly upon the realms of his dominion and they lay beneath his untroubled eyes restored to their state before the
fire came. Now that the supreme one's wrath had abated, 54.15
the girl slipped away from his wise audience without any promise to follow through her destroyer's course.

O majesty, Death hastened to reach Dhénuka. There she undertook the most exalted and most severe of oaths. To begin she stood upon but a single foot for the course of sixteen aeons. Such was her compassion and concern for the creatures that for five aeons more she closed herself away from the delights and pleasures of the senses. Balanced on a single foot she spent the passage of seven and then six more aeons. And then another aeon passed with her standing so.
O regent of the earth she then went among the wild beasts 54.20
as the epochs turned and turned until at last she reached the cold and spirituous waters of holy Nanda. Seven hundred

apsu varṣa|sahasrāṇi sapta c' âikaṃ ca s" ânayat
dhārayitvā tu niyamaṃ Nandāyāṃ vīta|kalmaṣā.
sā pūrvaṃ Kauśikīṃ puṇyāṃ jāgāma niyame dhṛtā
tatra vāyu|jal'|āhārā cacāra niyamaṃ punaḥ.
pañca|gaṅgāsu sā puṇye kanyā Vetasakeṣu ca
tapo|viśeṣair bahubhiḥ karśayad deham ātmanaḥ.
tato gatvā tu sā Gaṅgāṃ mahā|Meruṃ ca kevalam
tasthau c' âśm" êva niś|ceṣṭā prāṇ'|āyāma|parāyaṇā.
54.25 punar Himavato mūrdhni yatra devāḥ pur" âyajan
tatr' âṅguṣṭhena sā tasthau nikharvaṃ paramā śubhā.
puṣkareṣv atha Gokarṇe Naimiṣe Malaye tathā
apākarṣat svakaṃ dehaṃ niyamair manasaḥ priyaiḥ.

an|anya|devatā nityaṃ dṛḍha|bhaktā pitā|mahe
tasthau pitā|mahaṃ c' âiva toṣayām āsa dharmataḥ.
tatas tām abravīt prīto lokānāṃ prabhavo 'vyayaḥ
saumyena manasā rājan prītaḥ prīta|manās tadā.

«Mṛtyo, kim idam atyantaṃ tapāṃsi caras' îti ha?»
tato 'bravīt punar Mṛtyur bhagavantaṃ pitā|maham.
54.30 «n' âhaṃ hanyāṃ prajā deva sva|sthāś c' ākrośatīs tathā
etad icchāmi sarv'|ēśa tvatto varam ahaṃ prabho.
a|dharma|bhaya|bhīt" âsmi tato 'haṃ tapa āsthitā
bhītāyās tu mahā|bhāga prayacch' â|bhayam a|vyaya.
ārtā c' ân|āgasī nārī yācāmi bhava me gatiḥ.»

years she passed in those pools, then a century more. At Nanda she followed her vows in purity and did not falter even once. Bent upon her observances she went next to the ancient precincts of the river Káushiki and she pursued her strictures further, living only on wind and rain. At the five rivers in the country of the Vétasakas the young girl continued her devotions and dragged her body through transports of pain untold and unreckoned. Then from the Ganges she sought the high and lonely peak of Meru, and there she stood still as stone, closed into the discipline of the
breath. So high and pure she was. On snowy Hímavat where 54.25
the gods perform their rites she propped herself for years beyond number upon only the tip of her thumb. Among the flowers of Go·karna and in Náimisha and Málaya she wore down her body with the vows to which she had bound her soul.

Her devotion to the great father and to him alone was adamantine and eternal, and the great father was justly pleased to see her so. The beloved and boundless source of all things spoke to her then with a mild temper and gentle countenance for o majesty he was truly moved.

"Tell me o Death. Why do you scorch yourself like this in penance without end?"

And Death replied to the holy father.

"O heavenly one. I will not kill creatures who live in 54.30
peace with one another and for that you have condemned me. High lord of all that is, I ask you to grant me this single wish. I am so afraid of the sin that you demand and that is why I drive myself through this penance. O illustrious and infinite majesty, set me free from my terror. I am a sinless

tām abravīt tato devo bhūta|bhavya|bhaviṣya|vit.

«a|dharmo n' âsti te Mṛtyo saṃharantyā imāḥ prajāḥ
mayā c' ôktaṃ mṛṣā bhadre bhavitā na kathaṃ cana
tasmāt saṃhara kalyāṇi prajāḥ sarvāś catur|vidhāḥ
dharmaḥ sanātanaś ca tvāṃ sarvathā pāvayiṣyati.
54.35 loka|pālo Yamaś c' âiva sahāyā vyādhayaś ca te
ahaṃ ca vibudhāś c' âiva punar dāsyāmi te varam
yathā tvam enasā muktā vi|rajāḥ khyātim eṣyasi.»

s" âivam uktā mahā|rāja kṛt'|âñjalir idaṃ vibhum
punar ev' âbravīd vākyaṃ prasādya śirasā tadā.

«yady evam etat kartavyaṃ mayā na syād vinā, prabho,
tav' ājñā mūrdhni me nyastā yat te vakṣyāmi tac chṛṇu.
lobhaḥ krodho 'bhyasūy" ērṣyā droho mohaś ca dehinām
a|hrīś c' ânyonya|paruṣā dehaṃ bhindyuḥ pṛthag|vidhāḥ.»

BRAHM" ôvāca.

tathā bhaviṣyate Mṛtyo sādhu saṃhara vai prajāḥ,
a|dharmas te na bhavitā n' âpadhyāsyāmy ahaṃ, śubhe.
54.40 yāny aśru|bindūni kare mam' āsate
te vyādhayaḥ prāṇinām ātma|jātāḥ
te mārayiṣyanti narān gat'|âsūn
n' â|dharmas te bhavitā mā sma bhaiṣīḥ.
n' â|dharmas te bhavitā prāṇināṃ vai

woman and in despair I beg that you allow me to remain so."

He who knows time past and present and time to come then spoke thus to Death.

"Your destruction of these beings could in no way be a sin. Fair one, I have commanded you and may it not be in vain. Destroy every member of the four species of created thing and rightness will be at your side everywhere and for
all time. The world's guardian Yama will be with you and 54.35
the plagues* will be with you. And I and the wise will make you a gift. As you perform this task without smear or sin so will you make your fame among us."

Death heard his words o majesty. She raised her hands in reverence and replied to the king with her eyes downcast.

"O lord. If it is I who must do this then may it never be done without me. Because you have bestowed upon my head this task I have something to ask you to hear. May it be that greed and rage, malice and envy, falseness and folly and hubris and recrimination in all their forms come from within man and be the things that destroy him."

BRAHMA spoke.

It will be so. Now o Death go and destroy the creatures, as is fit. There will be no sin in it and I will not revile you,
fair one. The teardrops that I have caught in my hands will 54.40
become the plagues of things that live and will be born from within them. They will be the ones who take life from the dying and do not be afraid for the violence will not be yours to perform nor will any living things do you harm. You will become order incarnate, order's queen. For through your

tvaṃ vai dharmas tvaṃ hi dharmasya c' ēśā
dharmyā bhūtvā dharma|nityā dharitrī
tasmāt prāṇān sarvath" êmān niyaccha.
sarveṣāṃ vai prāṇināṃ kāma|roṣau
saṃtyajya tvaṃ saṃharasv' êha jīvān
evaṃ dharmas tvāṃ bhaviṣyaty an|anto
mithyā|vṛttān mārayiṣyaty a|dharmaḥ.
ten' ātmānaṃ pāvayasv' ātmanā tvaṃ
pāpe "tmānaṃ majjayiṣyanty a|satyāt
tasmāt kāmaṃ roṣam apy āgataṃ tvaṃ
saṃtyajy' âtaḥ saṃharasv' êha jīvān.

NĀRADA uvāca.

sā vai bhītā Mṛtyu|saṃjñ"|ôpadeśāc
chāpād bhītā «bāḍham» ity abravīt tam.
sā ca prāṇaṃ prāṇinām anta|kāle
kāma|krodhau tyajya haraty a|saktā.
54.45 Mṛtyus teṣāṃ vyādhayas tat|prasūtā
vyādhī rogo rujyate yena jantuḥ
sarveṣāṃ vai prāṇināṃ prāyaṇ'|ânte
tasmāc chokaṃ mā kṛthā niṣ|phalaṃ tvam.
sarve devāḥ prāṇibhiḥ prāyaṇ'|ânte
gatvā vṛttā saṃnivṛttās tath" âiva.
evaṃ sarve prāṇinas tatra gatvā
vṛttā devā martyavad, rāja|siṃha.
vāyur bhīmo bhīma|nādo mah"|âujā
bhettā dehān prāṇināṃ sarva|go 'sau
no vā vṛttiṃ n' âiva vṛttaṃ kadā cit
prāpnoty ugro 'n|anta|tejo|viśiṣṭaḥ.

justice order will dwell within you and you will uphold it. Go now and through the whole world still the breath of the living. Set aside any love or passion you feel towards living things and go abroad to gather in their lives for in doing so you will yourself become concord unending. Wrongdoing will bring death upon those whose acts twist from what is right. So immerse yourself in their evil and falsehood and in doing so render yourself pure. Any love or fury that has taken root in you tear out, then go into the world and gather in the lives you find.

NÁRADA spoke.

Afraid of Brahma's curse and afraid that in her very name was stamped the nature of her calling, at last the young woman succumbed. Love and anger were in her but she set them aside. Now when the time comes she takes the breath from the lungs of the living and she does so without
passion. Death comes as the plagues that are born within 54.45
us, and the suffering brought on by affliction is by nature dispelled when the time for the living thing to breathe comes to an end. So release your grief, for it is fruitless. Death is an event even in the lives of gods who pass away as men do when their time is done. Thus it is for all living things. O lion in the world of men, gods are in this no different from mortals. Death is a strong wind that howls in mighty gusts across everything and she smashes apart what things she finds. Her violence is without end and her terrible course is plotted through how we choose to live and what it is we do.

sarve devā martya|saṃjñā|viśiṣṭās
tasmāt putraṃ mā śuco, rāja|siṃha.
svargaṃ prāpto modate tvat|tanū|jo
nityaṃ ramyān vīra|lokān avāpya.
tyaktvā duḥkhaṃ saṃgataḥ puṇya|kṛdbhir
eṣā mṛtyur deva|diṣṭā prajānām
prāpte kāle saṃharantī yathāvat
svayaṃ kṛtā prāṇa|harā prajānām.
54.50 ātmānaṃ vai prāṇino ghnanti sarve
n' âinaṃ Mṛtyur daṇḍa|pāṇir hinasti.
tasmān mṛtān n' ânuśocanti dhīrā
satyaṃ jñātvā niścayaṃ brahma|sṛṣṭam
itthaṃ sṛṣṭiṃ daiva|kḷptāṃ viditvā
putrān naṣṭāc chokam āśu tyajasva.

VYĀSA uvāca.

etac chrutv" ârthavad vākyaṃ Nāradena prakāśitam
uvāc' Âkampano rājā sakhāyaṃ Nāradaṃ tathā.
«vyapeta|śokaḥ prīto 'smi, bhagavann ṛṣi|sattama
śrutv" êtihāsaṃ tvattas tu kṛt'|ârtho 'smy abhivādaye.»
tath" ôkto Nāradas tena rājñā ṛṣi|var'|ôttamaḥ
jagāma nandanaṃ śīghraṃ deva'|rṣir a|mit'|ātmavān.
puṇyaṃ yaśasyaṃ svargyaṃ ca dhanyam āyuṣyam eva ca
asy' êtihāsasya sadā śravaṇaṃ śrāvaṇaṃ tathā.
54.55 etad artha|padaṃ śrutvā tadā rājā Yudhiṣṭhira
kṣatra|dharmaṃ ca vijñāya śūrāṇāṃ ca parāṃ gatim.
samprāpto 'sau mahā|vīryaḥ svarga|lokaṃ mahā|rathaḥ
Abhimanyuḥ parān hatvā pramukhe sarva|dhanvinām.
yudhyamāno mah"|êṣv|āso hataḥ so 'bhimukho raṇe
asinā gadayā śaktyā dhanuṣā ca mahā|rathaḥ.

Lion among kings. Every god is acquainted with Death. Do not feel sorrow for your son. His are the pleasures of heaven and the everlasting delights of the realms of heroes. He has cast off sorrow and rests now in the company of the saints. For Death among mortals is ordained by the highest god. And while she gathers us in each by our turn when our time comes, as must the one whose charge is the breath of things, yet do all things in the end bring ruin
upon themselves. It is not Death with his staff* who slays 54.50
us. Thus the wise do not mourn the dead, as they have understood the nature of Brahma's creation. Understand that the universe was shaped by a power above you and for not one more moment feel the pain of departed children.

VYASA spoke.

Nárada had finished his profound tale and it was the turn of King Akámpana to speak to his friend.

"O high and holy sage, my grief has left me. I have heard your tale and I understand its meaning. I thank you for it."

When the great sage heard the king's words he was pleased deep in his divine and limitless soul.

The words of this holy tale are celebrated as the stuff of
heaven and of wealth and of life. Hear them. King Akám- 54.55
pana grasped their meaning o Yudhi·shthira and with it he came to understand the tasks of a warrior and the lofty path of the hero. In the midst of the archer horde the mighty and valiant Abhimányu cast down his enemies and rose up to heaven. Wielder of arrow and sword in the thick of combat, he fought as he died: by sword and by club and by spear and by bow. Soma's son has shed this mortal dust and returned

virajāḥ Soma|sūnuḥ sa punas tatra pralīyate
tasmāt parāṃ dhṛtiṃ kṛtvā bhrātṛbhiḥ saha, Pāṇḍava,
a|pramattaḥ su|saṃnaddhaḥ śīghraṃ yoddhum upākrama.

to whence he came. So make firm your resolve, o son of Pandu, cast away your delirium, buckle on your armor and go forth with your four brothers to fight.

NOTES

Bold *references are to the English text;* ***bold italic*** *references are to the Sanskrit text. An asterisk (*) in the body of the text marks the word or passage being annotated.*

1.1 Bhishma began his life as heir to Kuru·kshetra, but in order that his father could marry Sátyavati he revoked his right to accession and became a celibate ascetic, thereby ensuring that he would have no future children of his own who might later have designs on the throne. He becomes the epic's great renunciate, and hence his appellation, an exoteric compound meaning "he whose vows are of the gods."

1.1 **Shikhándin** is born Amba, princess of Kashi, and is abducted by Bhishma along with her two sisters as brides for Vichítra·virya, Sátyavati's second son. Discovering that Amba is betrothed to another king, Bhishma decides to release her, but the king refuses to take her back. Amba becomes a renunciate. She later appeals to Rudra that she may be reborn as a man to take her revenge on Bhishma. He grants her wish, and it is as the male Shikhándin that she joins the Pándava army and so becomes instrumental in the brahmin's fall. Cf. note to 7.22.

1.4 ***Kauravya*** here is ambiguous, but probably refers to Duryódhana.

1.6 Translating ***ātman*** is not a simple matter, as the literal meaning, "self" or "soul," is often redundant in Sanskrit. The reader will notice that its presence in the English translation is selective.

1.12 There is a whole array of words in the epic connoting different kinds of rulership. I use the terms "king" and "**chieftain**" more or less interchangeably.

1.21 When Bhishma is brought down at the end of Book Six, he makes a final and unsuccessful attempt to persuade Duryódhana to make peace with the Pándavas.

1.25 Although I have followed one convention in calling an *asura* a **demon**, the Christian connotations of the English term can be misleading. A folk etymology proposes *a-sura*, "un-god," as the origin of the word: gods and demons in the Vedic tradition are defined principally through their mutual antagonism.

1.32 Before Kunti marries Pandu she spends some time in the service of the seer Durvásas, who in return for her devotion gives to her a spell by means of which she can have a son by any god she chooses. With her first attempt she invokes the sun god Surya, and the product of their union is Karna. But she is shocked and disturbed by what she has done, and casts the boy into a river. The charioteer Ádhiratha and his wife Radha rescue and adopt the abandoned child. Karna's identity as the elder brother of the five Pándavas remains hidden from almost all the characters in the epic, including Karna himself, until Bhishma reveals the secret to him at the end of Book Six. When he hears that he is Kunti's son, Karna feels that he has already cast in his lot with Duryódhana, and decides not to reveal his true identity.

1.34 Literally "man-bull" and thus "**bull in the herd of men**," unfolding with a certain liberty the metaphorical "herd" from the more succinct form of the Sanskrit compound. Other compounds with related meanings I treat similarly.

1.35 Literally "the lords of the gods, of the depths, of wealth and of the dead:" in Vedic cosmology Indra, Váruna, Kubéra and Yama.

1.39 Discussing tactics just before battle commences, Bhishma belittles Karna's abilities in public, infuriating the great ally of the Káuravas to such an extent that he vows not to fight as long as Bhishma is alive. He criticizes what he perceives with some justification as Bhishma's partiality towards the Pándava cause and urges Duryódhana to cast the commander out as a negative influence on the army's morale. But when Bhishma is finally defeated in Book Six, Karna is moved by his plight, and during a conversation between them Bhishma reveals that his insult was intended to discourage Karna from fighting, as he was well aware of the warrior's capabilities and sought to protect the Pándavas from their full force. Bhishma then urges Karna to return to the battle, and the two of them are reconciled in the closing chapters of the book.

2.30 Bhima·sena is known for his enormous appetite, and hence his moniker. Although not as derogatory as it might sound, this particular designation is used to refer to Bhima·sena more often by the Káuravas than by the Pándavas.

2.32 **Yama** is a *loka/pāla*, a "guardian of the world," and while closely associated with the deity Dharma, his principal identity is as the god of death. Precisely where Yama's abode is to be found is difficult to say. Originally Yama is the guardian of the fore-fathers dwelling in heaven, but later he descends to rule a kind of underworld similar to the Hades of ancient Greece. Dead heroes have several destinations, and are at other times said to be bound for *svarga*, "heaven," the wider residence of the celestials; indeed, Karna has earlier spoken of Bhishma's journey post-mortem to *svarga* (1.38).

3.14 **Gandíva** is the name of Árjuna's bow. Its etymology is obscure, perhaps suggesting the horn of the rhinoceros, or "diamond-joints." I choose to leave it untranslated.

4.10 As a youth, Karna arrives one day in the royal city of Hástina·pura while the Pándavas and Káuravas are showing off their newly acquired martial skills in what begins as a friendly competition. Karna puts himself forward and matches Drona's best student Árjuna trick for trick. Árjuna berates Karna for intruding on the occasion, and the brahmin Kripa questions whether Karna's lineage permits him to compete with the highborn Pándava. At this point in the narrative Karna is unaware of his royal parentage, and in response to Kripa's inquiry he can only hang his head in shame. Duryódhana spots his chance and defends Karna against the abuse coming from Kripa and Árjuna. He and Karna become friends, and in the end Duryódhana gives him the kingdom of Anga. In the light of Bhishma's revelation to Karna at the end of the previous book (cf. note to 1.39), Bhishma's words here have a particular resonance, of which only he and Karna are aware.

5.9 Apart from being the hero's name, a *karṇa* is an "ear," but also, perhaps by resemblance, a "**rudder**." It is upon this meaning that Duryódhana puns here in his appeal to Karna.

6.5 The deity known as Rudra in the Vedas and Shiva in later systems is at a transitional phase in the 'Maha·bhárata,' where he goes by several different names, ***Kāpālin*** being one of them. The **Rudras** are a class of storm deities under his command.

6.6 Although in the main I translate the term ***dharma***, here it occurs in a list with other deities and seems to refer to the god rather than the abstract noun, although the distinction within Sanskrit is always elided.

7.1 The central brahmin characters of the 'Maha·bhárata'—Bhishma, Drona and Kripa—are not just priests, nor do they remain bookishly aloof from the political universe. They are in fact instructors and deadly practitioners within the sphere of activity that properly belongs to the kshatriya, the member of the royal or warrior caste. Indeed, their involvement in the cut and thrust of the power struggle becomes a source of unease and resentment for many of the epic's kshatriya characters.

7.4 Drona's emphasis here sheds some light on his motives for fighting with the Káuravas: his archenemy **Drúpada** is an ally of the Pándavas. Friends in childhood, the kshatriya Drúpada rejects Drona in later life when the brahmin comes to visit him. After Drona is engaged by Bhishma as instructor to the Pándavas, he sends them on a raid to storm Drúpada's palace and imprison him. Drona taunts him a little when he is in his cage, and then releases him and offers him back a piece of his kingdom. The animosity between the two men is perpetuated in their children: Drúpada's son Dhrishta·dyumna is born out a sacrificial fire when the king prays for an avenger, and Drona accurately prophesies his own death at Dhrishta·dyumna's hand. Later it will be Drona's son Ashvattháman who kills Dhrishta·dyumna during the nocturnal massacre of Book Ten.

7.11 It is common in the 'Maha·bhárata' for the name of a people and the name of its chieftain to be identical. So "the Kalíngas" designates a particular group, while "**Kalínga**" means one of their number, most likely their king (as here).

7.22 Though he agrees to Duryódhana's request that he take up the generalship of the Káurava forces, Bhishma has been mentor to both the Káuravas and the Pándavas, and he retains an affection towards the latter. In fact he goes so far as to explain to the Pándavas how they will be able to kill him despite his seeming invincibility. The contradictions of Bhishma's position are also present for Drona, and they provide a rich vein of narrative tension during his term as commander.

7.29 **Sudárshana** is the name both of Krishna's discus and of one of Dhrita·rashtra's sons.

8.2 Drona is conceived in vitro when his father, the seer Bharad·vaja, catches a glimpse of the nymph Ghritáchi nude, and ejaculates into a trough.

9.6 Although I translate ***daivaṃ*** as "**fate**," it designates something quite nebulous which emanates "from the gods," and which acts upon human life without predetermining it. Indeed, the adverb *daivavat* can mean simply "by chance."

9.29 What Dhrita·rashtra literally says is "the four Vedas and their limbs, and the fifth Veda of legends." The four principal Vedas are the 'Rig Veda,' the 'Yajur Veda,' the 'Sama Veda' and the 'Athárva Veda.' These are the oldest Sanskrit texts and they contain detailed descriptions of myths, rituals, prayers and spells; their "limbs" are associated texts of exegesis, grammar and astronomy. It is not clear what Dhrita·rashtra exactly means by "legends," but the epic poems and Puránas were later accorded the collective status of "fifth Veda."

10.73 In a cast of characters with protean identities, Krishna is particularly elusive, and the vexed question of his nature as god and man has been a subject of debate for the better part of three millennia. Born the son of a cowherd, as Dhrita·rashtra has already told us, he is something of an arriviste among the company of the Pándavas. He is a chieftain of the Vrishni people, whose territory borders on the tract of land over which the Pándavas are briefly granted dominion in an earlier part of the epic, and his first appearance in the narrative is as their ally. But he plays a delicate diplomatic game, and after stating his initial intention to remain neutral in the war, he subsequently becomes Árjuna's charioteer, promising that he will not himself raise arms during the conflict. The main players in the epic's drama are all incarnations of gods or demons, but only Krishna, as Vishnu's avatar on earth, delivers so grand a sermon as the 'Bhágavad Gita.' Although the words of the 'Gita' have attracted the most attention, his behaviour in the rest of the war is equally interesting for the light it sheds on his role within the epic as a whole.

11.21 The word ***hut'|âśana*** is one of the many terms in Sanskrit for "fire," into which sacrificial offerings are cast during many of the religious rituals of ancient India. The event to which Dhrita·rashtra here refers occurs at the end of the first book of the epic.

11.24 During the gambling match when Yudhi·shthira stakes Dráupadi and loses her to the Káuravas, Duhshásana drags her into the assembly hall by her hair and then sets about stripping her in front of her husbands. But her undergarments keep magically restoring themselves as he tries to tear them away. It is this **miracle** to which Dhrita·rashtra refers.

11.30 The compound *vṛṣṇi|vīreṇa* could simply mean "by the Vrishni hero [Krishna]," but *vṛṣṇi* also means simply "strong" or "powerful," and, by extension, "**ram**." I try here to capture these multiple meanings in my choice of translation.

11.47 In the middle of a densely-worded speech Dhrita·rashtra introduces this very obscure homily. It might be that he is referring to some kind of ritual correspondence between **grass** and **lightning** derived from the magical significations of Vedic religion. He is playing somehow on the double meaning of ***pakva*** as both "cooked" and "ripe for death." I take him to mean that grass seems harmless, but fire transforms it into a destructive force, and that the weak can easily be finished off. Whatever its precise meaning, and to introduce another metaphor, Dhrita·rashtra is referring to the "butterfly effect" that his loyalties have had: the disastrous repercussions of a critical choice made in the past.

12.12 Drona says that Yudhi·shthira has reached "enemylessness," ***a/jāta/śatrutā***, playing on the king's other name Ajáta·shatru, literally "he whose conqueror has not yet been born."

12.28 The adjective ***phalguna*** means "red," while *Phālguna* is a derivative from the noun *Phalgunī*, which is the name of a twin-star constellation in ancient Indian astronomy. Both *Phalguna* and *Phālguna* are names for Árjuna. In calling him the **Red Star Fighter** I have tried to combine the resonances of both these words. Abhimányu is quite frequently identified as *Phālguni*, "son of the Red Star Fighter."

14.64 Literally "the son of Krishna," Krishna in this case being Árjuna. Cf. Introduction, note 1.

14.82 The stone rather than the organ: **cat's eye** is a kind of chalcedony or quartz, occurring naturally in various compositions and colors.

16.21 A **wheelguard** is a sort of attendant charged with the task of protecting the wheels of a royal chariot from attack.

17.11 The Tri·gartas have so far played only a minor role in the 'Maha·bhárata.' Earlier in the epic, their principalities are attacked on separate occasions by Nákula and by his brother Árjuna, which may explain their virulent animosity towards the Pándavas.

17.39 From this point on, the Tri·gartas and those who have taken their vow with them become known as ***saṃśaptaka***s, warriors who have "sworn together" to conquer their enemies or die.

19.19 Cf. Introduction, note 1.

20.19 The periodic condition of "musth" to which elephant bulls are subject is still not fully understood, although it is linked to reproduction. For months at a time, the elephant produces up to sixty times its usual levels of testosterone and becomes wildly aggressive and impossible to control; a symptom of an elephant being in musth is the production of an oily fluid from the temporal glands, in Sanskrit ***mada***, a term with no single-word English equivalent.

21.4 Here and elsewhere I try to make up for the poverty of words in English in comparison with the embarrassment of riches that Sanskrit enjoys when describing pachyderms.

21.7 The front axle of a chariot has a *pārṣṇi* at each end, and the outer horses of the team are yoked to them. A ***pārṣṇi/sārathi*** is responsible for controlling one of these horses.

23.34 One of the many lost secrets of Vedic religion, ***soma*** was some kind of plant of critical importance in the performance of its rituals. The plant was pressed and its juice extracted to be used as an offering to the gods and as a beverage of the priests, probably hallucinogenic in effect.

23.61 The word ***kalāya*** can refer to a species of panic grass, but it seems to have a range of references. I return to its etymology, which is suggestive of some genus of dark bloom.

23.84 Sánjaya now moves from their horses to the adornments of the Pándava cars. The Sanskrit word ***dhvaja*** refers primarily to the wooden pole at the back of a chariot, but can also refer what one of these carries: carvings, statues, flags and whatever good-luck charms or trinkets a warrior wanted to take into battle with him. (My thanks to Dániel Balogh for his suggestions to me about a chariot's dashboard furniture.)

24.13 **Vídura** is the younger half-brother of Pandu and Dhrita·rashtra, the son by Krishna Dvaipáyana of a servant girl. When Duryódhana is born, Vídura immediately sees the danger that he will pose to the dynasty, and he advises Dhrita·rashtra to abandon the child. Dhrita·rashta refuses to do so. At the dicing match Vídura again predicts that the outcome of the conflict will be a devastating war, and accuses Dhrita·rashtra of doing nothing to avert the crisis.

25.62 **Ghatótkacha** is Bhima·sena's half-man half-*rákshasa* son. A *rákshasa* is a demonic creature, a kind of imp or goblin associated with the night and capable of various supernatural tricks.

26.53 An astonishingly rich term in Sanskrit, it is hard to capture the subtlety of the compound ***Vaivasvata/kṣayam*** in translation. *Vaivasvata* means "of the Bright One," i.e., the **sun**, and is largely used as a patronymic for Yama, king of the dead, yet here as elsewhere the rest of the verse is illuminated in the word's glimmer. The Sanskrit *kṣaya* means, from separate roots, both "abode" and "decay."

30.24 This **Jyotíshka** appears only in the Calcutta edition of the text, and I have retained it mainly for its eccentricity. It is clearly related somehow to the word *jyotis*, "light, sky, heaven."

36.8 In the chariot warfare of the 'Maha·bhárata' a **horseman** is a driver: the term ***sūta*** describes a caste in the same way as do "kshatriya" and "brahmin" and one inferior in status to both. In referring baldly to Sumítra's birth, Abhimányu puts him in his place for the insubordination of suggesting that he reconsider Yudhi·shthira's demands. As it turns out, Sumítra's hesitancy will be revealed as having been quite justified.

37.34 The **noose** is an accoutrement of Yama, much like the grim reaper's scythe. His noose is not a symbol for hanging, but is rather used by the god to "bind" the soul after its extraction from the physical body of the deceased.

39.24 Sanskrit ***kṣetra*** means "land" or "domain," but also "wife" or even "womb." A few lines earlier Duhshásana referred to the Pándavas as "sons of Pandu," but now he draws sardonic attention to their unorthodox parenthood and hints at their illegitimacy by describing them as born of the "**soil**" rather than the "seed" of Pandu.

40.9 Abhimányu is here referring to what could be Duhshásana's most scandalous crime against the Pándavas (cf. note to 11.24).

During the incident, Bhima·sena vows to kill Duhshásana and drink his blood, and this is why Abhimányu mentions Bhima·sena in particular.

45.9 This **Rukma·ratha** is Shalya' son, not Drona.

52.2 One of the epic's many Krishnas, **Krishna Dvaipáyana**, also called Vyasa, is the premarital son of Sátyavati by the seer Paráshara. Initially his mother abandons her baby on the island (*dvīpa*) of his birth, but later she calls upon him to impregnate her second son's widows and provide the land of the Kurus with heirs. The widows give birth to Pandu and Dhrita·rashtra. Vyasa is also named as the mythical composer of the epic itself, and it is his student Vaishampáyana who recites it for the first time. Otherwise Vyasa takes a relatively low-key, omniscient position in the narrative, appearing at its reflective moments to offer guidance to the main characters and leaving his stepbrother Bhishma to perform a more grandfatherly role towards them.

52.19 Yudhi·shthira's personification of **Death** leads Vyasa to describe a figure set apart from Yama, who strictly speaking is the ruler of the kingdom of the dead rather than "death" itself. The word for "death" in Sanskrit can be either masculine or feminine in gender, and it is this duality on which Vyasa plays in the story he is about to tell. In English, grammar forces us to decide when to treat *mṛtyu* as an abstract noun and when as a personification, a distinction which Sanskrit can leave obscure.

52.35 Akámpana uses the masculine form of the pronoun to refer to **Death**, unlike Yudhi·shthira, whose choice of words is not so committed.

52.43 One of Rudra-Śiva's names. The god is said to remain motionless as a tree trunk during his austerities.

54.36 Brahma at last makes explicit the distinction between the female Death and the male deity **Yama**, here mentioned as a *loka/pāla*, a guardian of the world and its ordering principles.

54.50 Although the predicate ***daṇḍa/pāṇir*** could be masculine or feminine, Vyasa has not mentioned a "staff" in relation to the female **Death** until he speaks these lines, while the *daṇḍa* is part of the classical iconography of Yama. I take it that Vyasa here slips back to the conventional figuration of Yama as Death to round off his tale. Either way, what is preserved in the Sanskrit and lost in the English is the subtlety and proximity of the distinctions that his myth has drawn.

PROPER NAMES AND EPITHETS

ÁBHIBHU Ruler of Kashi.

ABHIMÁNYU Son of Árjuna and Subhádra. Also known as Árjuni, Karshni, Phálguni, Saubhádra.

ABHÍRA A people.

ÁCHALA Brother-in-law of Dhrita·rashtra and brother of Shákuni.

ÁCHYUTA Name for many characters in the epic, including Bala·rama and Yudhi·shthira, but principally designating Krishna.

ÁDITI One of the daughters of Daksha and the mother of the *adítya*s.

ADÍTYA Metronymic for a son of Áditi. The *adítya*s are the seven gods of the firmament.

AGÁVAHA A Vrishni warrior.

AGNI God of fire.

AIRÁVATA Elephant ridden by Indra into battle.

AJÁTA·SHATRU Yudhi·shthira.

AKÁMPANA A legendary king in a story told by Vyasa.

ALÁMBUSHA A demon allied with the Kurus and slain by Ghatótkacha.

AMBÁSHTHA A people and their king, allied to the Káuravas.

ÁMBIKA Mother of Dhrita·rashtra.

ANADHRÍSHTI A king allied to the Pándavas.

ÁNDHAKA A demon killed by Rudra.

ANDHRA A people conquered by Karna.

ANGA A people and their king, allied to the Káuravas.

ÁNGADA A son of Dhrita·rashtra.

ÁNGIRAS Born from Brahma's mouth, a divine seer named as the composer of hymns, laws and a treatise on astronomy.

ANIRÚDDHA Son of Pradyúmna and grandson of Krishna.

ANUVÍNDA A prince of Avánti, allied to the Káuravas. Brother of Vinda.

ÁRJUNA Third of the five Pándava brothers, son of Pandu and Kuntí.

Also known as Dhanan·jaya, Pándava, Partha, Phálguna, Savya·sachin, Kirítin, Káunteya, Jishnu.

ÁRJUNI Patronymic for Abhimányu.

ARIM·ÉJAYA A Vrishni fighter.

ARTÁYANI Patronymic for Shalya.

ÁSHMAKA Name of a people and their king, allied to the Káuravas.

ASHVA·KETU Son of the Mágadha king, allied to the Káuravas.

ASHVATTHÁMAN Son of Drona and Kripi.

ASHVINS Twin gods, healers of the *deva*s. Fathers of Saha·deva and Nákula by Madri.

ÁURASAKA A people conquered by Krishna.

AVÁNTI A people and a place.

AVÁNTYA People or king of Avánti.

BAHLÍKA A people.

BALI A demon, son of Viróchana and father of Bana.

BHAGA·DATTA King of Prag·jyótisha, allied to the Káuravas.

BHARAD·VAJA An ancient seer, father of Drona and grandfather of Ashvatthámam.

BHARADVÁJA Patronymic for Drona.

BHARATA Primordial ruler of North India and ancestor of most of the characters in the 'Maha·bhárata.' Any of his descendents, and thus most of the characters of the epic, can be called a Bharata.

BHÁRATA Descendant of Bharata, hence used as often as preceding.

BHIMA Second of the five Pándava brothers, son of Pandu and Kuntí. Also known as Bhima·sena, Kauntéya, Pándava, Partha, Vrikódara.

BHIMA·SENA Bhima.

BHISHMA Son of Shántanu and Ganga, leader of the Káurava forces until his demise at the end of the book preceding 'Drona.' Also known as Apagéya, Deva·vrata and Shántanava.

BHUMIN·JAYA A Káurava warrior.

BHURI Son of Soma·datta, allied to the Káuravas.

BHUTA·KARMAN A warrior allied to the Káuravas.

BHUTA·SHARMAN A Káurava warrior.

BHURI·SHRAVAS A warrior allied to the Káuravas.

BRAHMA Creator and supreme deity.

BRAHMA PARAMÉSHTHIN Brahma.

BRAHMA·VASHATÍYA A people.

BRIHAD·BALA King of Kósala, allied to the Káuravas.

BRIHÁNTA A Kuru warrior, brother of Kshema·dhurti.

BRIHAT·KSHATRA One of the five Kaikéya brothers. Also the name of a Níshadha king.

CHAITRASÉNI Patronymic for the son of Chitra·sena, Dhrita·rashtra's grandson. Also the name of a Pándava warrior slain by Drona.

CHANDRA·KETU A Kuru warrior.

CHANDRA·SENA Son of Samúdra·sena, allied to the Káuravas.

CHANDRA·VARMAN A warrior allied to the Káuravas.

CHARU·DESHNA Son of Krishna and Rúkmini.

CHEDI A people.

CHEKITÁNA A Vrishni warrior allied to the Pándavas.

CHITRA A warrior allied to the Pándavas.

CHITRA·MALYA A warrior allied to the Pándavas.

CHITRA·RATHA Name of several kings; in 'Drona' the son of Shibi.

CHITRA·SENA A son of Dhrita·rashtra.

CHITRÁYUDHA Name of a hero on the Pándava side, but also of one of Dhrita·rashtra's sons.

DÁNAVA A child of Danu, and so a member of a class of beings opposed to the *devas*.

DANDA·DHARA A Pándava warrior.

DANDA·KETU A prince allied to the Pándavas, mentioned only in 'Drona.'

DÁRADA A people.

DASHÁRHA A people; used as a name for Krishna, a chief of the Dashárhas.

DASHÉRAKA A people.

DAUHSHÁSANI Patronymic for Duhshásana's son, killer of Abhimányu.

DEVA·DATTA Árjuna's conch.

DÉVAKI Daughter of Devaka, wife of Vasu·deva and mother of Krishna.

DEVA·VRATA Bhishma.

DHANAN·JAYA Árjuna.

DHARMA A god, and Yudhi·shthira's father.

DHARMA·RAJA Yudhi·shthira.

DHÉNUKA A devotional site.

DHRISHTA·DYUMNA Son of the Panchála king Drúpada, born from a sacrificial fire. Brother of Dráupadi and general of the Pándava army.

DHRISHTA·KETU A Chedi prince allied to the Pándavas.

DHRITA·RASHTRA Blind king of the Kurus. Son of Krishna Dvaipáyanaand Ámbika. Father of Duryódhana and a hundred other children.

DIRGHA·LÓCHANA A Káurava warrior.

DRAUNI Patronymic for Ashvatthámán.

DRÁUPADI Daughter of Drúpada and wife of the five Pándava brothers. Also known as Krishná. She has five sons: Prativíndhya, Suta·soma, Shruta·kirti, Shatáníka and Shruta·sena.

DRAUPADÉYA Metronymic for one of the above.

DRONA Son of Bharad·vaja, husband of Kripi and father of Ashvattháman. Also known as Bharádvaja, and Rukma·ratha. Drona is the teacher of the sons of Pandu and Dhrita·rashtra, and general of the Káurava forces during the course of 'Drona.'

DRÚPADA King of the Panchálas and father of Dhrishta·dyumna. Sworn enemy of Drona.

Dúhsaha A son of Dhrita·rashtra.

Duhshásana A son of Dhrita·rashtra.

Dúrjaya A son of Dhrita·rashtra.

Durmárshana A son of Dhrita·rashtra.

Dúrmukha A son of Dhrita·rashtra.

Duryódhana Eldest son of Dhrita·rashtra and Gandhári. Also known as Suyódhana and Dhartaráshtra.

Gada A Vrishni warrior and Krishna's younger brother.

Gandhára A people ruled by Shákuni.

Gandhári Wife of Dhrita·rashtra and mother of Duryódhana and a hundred other children.

Gandíva Árjuna's bow.

Ganga The Ganges river, goddess and mother of Bhishma.

Gáruda Bird god.

Gáutama Patronymic for Kripa, grandson of Gótama. Also the name of a Bhoja warrior.

Gaválgana Father of Sánjaya.

Gaválgani Patronymic for Sánjaya.

Ghatótkacha Semidemonic son of Bhima and Hidímba.

Giri·vraja Capital of the Mágadhas.

Go·karna A holy site.

Go·pala A people.

Go·vinda Krishna.

Haidímba Metronymic for Ghatótkacha.

Hari Son of Akámpana.

Hástina·pura Capital of the Kurus on the river Ganges.

Hema·varna Son of Rochamána, allied to the Pándavas.

Himálaya Mountain and god.

HIRANYÁKSHA A demon.

HRÍDIKA Father of Krita·varman.

HRISHI·KESHA Krishna.

INDRA King of the gods. Also known as Mághavan, Shakra, Vásava.

JÁHNAVI Ganga, the daughter of Jahnu.

JAMAD·AGNI A seer, father of Párashu·rama.

JAMBHA A demon slain by Indra.

JAMBU A mythical river.

JANAM·ÉJAYA Son of Paríkshit. At his sacrifice Vaishampáyana recites the 'Maha·bhárata' for the first time.

JANÁRDANA Krishna.

JARA·SANDHA King of the Mágadhas, allied to the Káuravas.

JAYAD·RATHA King of the Sindhus, allied to the Káuravas.

JHALLIN A Vrishni warrior.

JISHNU Árjuna.

JYOTÍSHKA The "light weapon" used by Árjuna against Prag·jyótisha.

KAIKÉYA One of the five brothers who rule the Kékaya people and are allied to the Pándavas. Sometimes Vinda or Anuvínda, Kékaya kings of Avánti allied to the Káuravas.

KAILÁSA A mountain and abode of Kubéra.

KALAKÉYA A tribe of demons.

KALIKÉYA A Kuru warrior, son of Súbala.

KALÍNGA A people and their king.

KAMBÓJA A people and their king, who is also known as Sudákshina.

KANSA Son of Ugra·sena and King of Máthura.

KAPÁLIN Rudra-Shiva.

KARA·KARSHA A warrior allied to the Kurus.

KARNA Son of Surya (the sun) and Kuntí. Adopted by the charioteer

Ádhiratha and his wife Radha. Also known as Radhéya and Suta·putra.

KARSHNI Patronymic for Abhimányu, "son of Krishna," i.e., Árjuna.

KARÚSHA A people.

KASHI A people, a place and its king (cf. Varánasi).

KASHMÍRAKA A people, obviously connected to present Kashmir.

KÁURAVA Descendant of Kuru. Often refers to Dhrita·rashtra's sons and their followers, although the Pándavas are also sometimes called Káuravas.

KAURÁVYA As above.

KÁUSHIKI A river.

KÉKAYA A people, some of whom (under the leadership of five brothers) are allied to the Pándavas, and some to the Kauravas.

KÉSHAVA Krishna.

KIRÁTA A people.

KIRÍTIN Árjuna.

KRITIN Father of Ruchi·parvan.

KÓSALA A people.

KRATHA A Kuru king.

KRIPA Son of Sharádvat, grandson of Gótama and brother of Kripi. Allied to the Káuravas.

KRISHNA Son of Vasu·deva and Dévaki, identified with Vishnu/Naráyana. Also known as Áchyuta, Go·vinda, Hrishi·kesha, Janárdana, Késhava, Vasudéva, Mádhava, Shauri, Pundarikáksha. The "two Krishnas" are Krishna and Árjuna.

KRISHNÁ Dráupadi.

KRISHNA DVAIPÁYANA Son of Sátyavati and the seer Paráshara. Father of Dhrita·rashtra, Pandu and Vídura. Also known as Vyasa.

KRITA·VARMAN A Vrishni prince and son of Hrídika, allied to the Káuravas.

KSHATRAN·JAYA A son of Dhrishta·dyumna.

KSHATRA·DEVA A son of Dhrishta·dyumna.

KSHATRA·DHARMAN A son of Dhrishta·dyumna, slain by Drona.

KSHEMA·DHURTI Brother of Brihánta, allied to the Káuravas.

KSHEMA·SHARMAN A Káurava warrior.

KUBÉRA Originally the chief of the spirits of darkness, and in later theology the god of riches.

KUMÁRA Name of Yudhi·shthira's wheelguard.

KUNDA·BHEDIN Son of Dhrita·rashtra.

KUNTI A people, but more also and more importantly the wife of Pandu. Mother of the Pándavas and Karna. Also known as Pritha.

KUNTI·BHOJA Adoptive father of Kuntí, allied to the Pándavas. Also called Púrujit.

KURU Ancestor of the Bháratas. The Kurus are the descendants of Kuru and include both the Káuravas and the Pándavas, although the name largely refers to Dhrita·rashtra's sons and their followers.

LÁKSHMANA A son of Duryódhana.

LALÍTTHA A people linked to the Tri·gartas.

MÁDHAVA A people, and used to refer variously to Krishna, Sátyaki and Krita·varman.

MADRA/MÁDRAKA A people.

MADRI Second wife of Pandu. Princess of the Madras, sister of Shalya and mother of the twins Nákula and Saha·deva by the two Ashvin gods.

MÁGADHA A people.

MÁGHAVAN Indra.

MAHA·DEVA Rudra-Shiva.

MAINÁKA A mountain.

MÁLADA A people.

MÁLAVA A people and its king.

MÁLAYA A mountain.

MÁNDARA A mountain used as a staff by the gods to churn the ocean.

MÁNIMAT A king allied to the Pándavas.

MARUTS Storm gods, followers of Indra.

MARTTIKÁVATAKA A people and a country.

MATSYA A people, mostly allied to the Pándavas, and their king.

MAVÉLLAKA A people linked to the Tri·gartas.

MEGHA·VEGA A Kuru warrior.

MÉKALA A people conquered by Karna.

MERU Mountain at the center of the cosmos.

MURU A demon slain by Krishna.

NÁGNAJIT A king overthrown by Karna.

NÍSHATHA A Vrishni ruler, son of Bala·rama.

NÁIMISHA A sacred forest.

NÁKULA One of the Pándava brothers (twin of Saha·deva).

NÁKULI Patronymic for Shatáníka, Nákula's son.

NANDA A river.

NARA Primordial Man, often considered a god and paired with Naráyana. Identified with Árjuna.

NÁRADA A divine seer.

NÁRAKA A demon, son of the Earth.

NARÁYANA The god Vishnu, often linked with Nara. Identified with Krishna. At the same time the name of a people.

NILA King of Mahíshmati slain by Ashvattháman.

NISHÁDA A people and their king.

NÍSHADHA A people allied to the Káuravas.

NIVÁTA·KÁVACHAS A tribe of demons destroyed by Árjuna.

PANCHAJÁNYA Conch carried by Krishna, obtained from the demon Pancha·jana.

PANCHA·JANA Demon slain by Krishna.

PANCHÁLA A people allied to the Pándavas. The king of the Panchálas is Drúpada. Sworn enemies of Drona.

PÁNDAVA A son of Pandu, so Yudhi·shthira, Bhima, Árjuna, Nákula or Saha·deva. The "Pándavas" as a whole are the sons of Pandu, their relatives and their followers.

PANDU Son of Krishna Dvaipáyana, half brother of Dhrita·rashtra and Vídura and "father" of the Pándavas. In the plural it refers to the Pándava army as a whole.

PANDYA A people and their king.

PÁRASHU·RAMA Son of Jamad·agni and Rénuka, and a hero of legend who once wiped out the warrior caste.

PÁRSHATA Patronymic for Dhrishta·dyumna and Drúpada.

PARTHA Son of Pritha, so Yudhi·shthira, Bhima·sena or Árjuna. Also refers to the followers of the sons of Pritha.

PATÁCCHARA·HANTRI A warrior allied to the Pándavas.

PAUNDRA A people.

PÁURAVA Descendant of Puru. Name of a people and king.

PHÁLGUNA Árjuna.

PHÁLGUNI Patronymic for Abhimányu.

PISHÁCHA Generally a class of demonic beings, but in the 'Maha·bhárata' also the name of a people.

PITHA A demon slain by Krishna.

PRABÁHU A Kuru warrior.

PRABHÁDRAKA A warrior from a certain division of the Panchálas.

PRADYÚMNA Son of Krishna and Rúkmini.

PRALÁMBA A demon slain by Krishna.

PRÁSTHALA A principality ruled by Sushárman, one of the Tri·gartas.

PRATÁRDANA A Kuru warrior.

PRATIVÍNDHYA One of the Draupadéyas.

PRÍSHATA Father of Drúpada, grandfather of Dhrishta·dyumna.

PRITHA Kuntí.

PRITHU A Vrishni prince.

PULÁSTYA One of the sons of Brahma, from whom Ghatótkacha received his bow.

PULÓMAN A demon.

PUNDARIKÁKSHA The Lotus Eyed One, namely, Krishna.

PÚRUJIT A Kunti chieftain.

PÚSHKARA Name of a collocation of holy sites.

RADHA Adoptive mother of Karna.

RAJA·PURA A city of the Kambójas.

RAMA Párashu·rama.

RATHA·SENA A warrior allied to the Pándavas, mentioned only once in the entire epic.

RÁVANA A king of the demons.

RIKSHA·DEVA Son of Shikhándin.

ROCHAMÁNA A Pándava warrior.

RÓHINI A goddess, daughter of Daksha and wife of the moon.

RUDRA The fierce deity later known as Shiva. Also called Maha·deva, Sharva, Sthanu, Try·ámbaka, Kapálin.

RUCHI·PARVAN A Pándava warrior.

RÚKMINI Wife of Krishna.

SAHA·DEVA One of the Pándava brothers, twin brother of Nákula.

SÁINDHAVA Principally Jayad·ratha, King of the Sindhus, but also his father Vriddha·kshatra.

SAMBA Son of Krishna and Jámbavati.

SAMÍKA A Vrishni warrior.

SAMÚDRA·SENA Father of Chandra·sena, allied to the Káuravas.

SÁNJAYA Son of Gaválgana and charioteer of Dhrita·rashtra, to whom he narrates the events of the great battle.

SÁRANA A Vrishni warrior, son of Vasu·deva.

SÁRAYU A river.

SATYA·DHARMAN One of the Tri·garta princes.

SATYA·DHRITI A Pándava warrior.

SÁTVATA Name of a tribe of the Yádavas, and used in the singular of Krita·varman and Sátyaki.

SATYA·KARMAN One of the Tri·garta princes.

SÁTYAKI Patronymic for Yuyudhána, a Vrishni king allied to the Pándavas. Satya·ratha one of the Tri·garta princes.

SATYA·VRATA One of the Tri·garta princes.

SATYA·DHARMAN One of the Tri·garta princes.

SATYÉSHU One of the Tri·garta princes.

SÁUBALA Patronymic for Shákuni.

SAUBHÁDRA Metronymic for Abhimányu.

SAUMADÁTTI Patronymic for Bhuri·shravas, son of Soma·datta.

SAUVÍRA A people associated with the Sindhus.

SAVYA·SACHIN Árjuna.

SENA·BINDU A Panchála fighter killed by Drona, and also a man fighting on the Káurava side.

SHAINÉYA Patronymic for Sátyaki, grandson of Shini.

SHAKA A people.

SHÁKUNA A people.

SHÁKUNI Son of the Gandhára king Súbala and father of Ulúka.

SHALA Son of Soma·datta, and brother of Bhuri and Bhuri·shravas. Allied to the Káuravas.

SHALVA A people and their king.

SHALYA King of the Madras, brother of Madri. Also known as Artáyani.

SHÁMBARA A demon slain by Indra.

SHÁNTANU Father of Bhishma.

SHARÁDVAT Father of Kripa.

SHARÁDVATA Patronymic for Kripa.

SHARVA Rudra-Shiva.

SHATÁNÍKA Son of Nákula and Dráupadi.

SHATRUN·JAYA A son of Dhrita·rashtra.

SHAURI Patronymic for Krishna.

SHIKHÁNDIN Son (originally daughter) of Drúpada. Allied to the Pándavas and pivotal in Árjuna's victory over Bhishma.

SHINI Father of Sátyaka and grandfather of Sátyaki.

SHURA·SENA A people.

SHRÉNIMAT A Pándava warrior.

SHRUTA·KARMAN Son of Saha·deva and Dráupadi.

SHRUTA·KIRTI Son of Árjuna and Dráupadi.

SÍNHALA A people.

SINHA·SENA A warrior allied to the Pándavas.

SKANDA A protean deity, son of Shiva or Agni in the Veda and god of war.

SOMA·DATTA Father of Bhuri·shravas, allied to the Káuravas.

SRÍNJAYA A people often grouped with the Panchálas.

STHANU Rudra-Shiva.

SUBÁHU One of Dhrita·rashtra's sons, and also a Tri·garta warrior.

SÚBALA Father of Shákuni.

SUBHÁDRA Mother of Abhimányu.

SUDÁKSHINA King of the Kambójas, allied to the Káuravas.

SUDÁMAN A Pándava warrior.

SUDÁRSHANA A son of Dhrita·rashtra. Also the name of Krishna's discus.

SÚDHANUS A Tri·garta warrior.

SUDHÁNVAN A Panchála king.

SUDHÁRMAN A Tri·garta warrior.

SUKSHÁTRA Son of the Kósala king.

SUMÍTRA Abhimányu's charioteer.

SUNÁMAN Brother of Kansa.

SÚRATHA A Tri·garta warrior.

SURYA·BHASA A Kuru warrior.

SUSHÁRMAN King of the Tri·gartas.

SUSHÉNA A warrior allied to the Káuravas.

SUTA·PUTRA "Driver's son," largely used to refer to Karna, but said of various charioteers in the epic.

SUTA·SOMA One of the Draupadéyas.

SUVÁRCHAS Two warriors, one of whom fights for the Káuravas, the other for the Pándavas.

SUYÓDHANA Duryódhana.

TRI·GARTA A people and the five brothers who are their chieftains.

TRY·ÁMBAKA The Three Eyed God, namely Rudra-Shiva.

TUNDIKÉRA A people and their king.

TVASHTRI A magical attack named after the armorer of the gods.

UCCHAIH·SHRAVAS Name of a celestial horse.

UDAYÉNDU A city of the Kurus, where Suta·soma was born.

ÚLMUKA A Vrishni warrior.

ÚSHANAS An ancient seer.

UTTAMÁUJAS A Panchála warrior allied to the Pándavas. Brother of Yudha·manyu.

ÚTKALA A people conquered by Karna.

VANÁYU A people and a place.

VAIKÁRTANA Patronymic for Karna, son of the sun.

VAISHAMPÁYANA Disciple of Krishna Dvaipáyana . Recites the 'Maha·bhárata' at Janam·éjaya's snake sacrifice.

VÁISHNAVA A magical attack wielded by different characters in the epic.

VAISHVÁNARA Agni.

VÁITARANI The river running through the realm of the dead.

VARANÁVATA A city.

VARÁNASI A city in the country of the Kashis, now known by the same name.

VARDDHAKSHÉMI Patronymic for Anadhríshti.

VARSHNÉYA Principally Krishna, though designating any of Vrishni stock.

VÁRUNA One of the greatest of the Vedic gods.

VASATÍYA A people and their king.

VÁSAVA Indra.

VASÍSHTHA A divine seer, son of the god Váruna.

VASU One of a group of Vedic gods.

VASU·DANA A warrior on the Pándava side.

VASU·DEVA Father of Krishna.

VASUDÉVA Patronymic for Krishna.

VATA·DHANA A people conquered by Krishna and Árjuna.

VAYÁVYA The "weapon of Vayu" wielded by Árjuna in 'Drona.'

VÉTASAKA A people in whose country Death performs her austerities.

VIDÉHA A people.

VIDÚRA A place known for its metals and gemstones.

VÍDURA Half brother of Dhrita·rashtra and Pandu.

VIDU·RATHA A prince of the Vrishnis.

VÍJAYA Normally a name for Árjuna, but in 'Drona' also a son of Dhrita·rashtra.

VIKÁRNA A son of Dhrita·rashtra.

VINDA Brother of Anuvínda and prince of Avánti, allied to the Káuravas.

VIPÁTA Karna's younger brother.

VÍPRITHU A Vrishni ruler.

VIRÁTA The king of the Matsyas.

VIRÓCHANA A demon.

VISHNU One of the major gods in the Hindu pantheon, incarnated in Krishna.

VIVÁSVAT Father of Yama.

VIVÍNSHATI A son of Dhrita·rashtra.

VRIKÓDARA Bhima.

VRIDDHA·KSHATRA King of the Sindhus and father of Jayad·ratha.

VRIDDHA·KSHEMA Ancestor of Anadhríshti.

VRIKA A Pándava warrior.

VRINDÁRAKA A son of Dhrita·rashtra.

VRÍSHAKA A Gandhára prince, brother-in-law of Dhrita·rashtra.

VISHVAK·SENA Krishna.

VRISHA·SENA A son of Karna.

VRISHNI A Yádava people connected with the Ándhakas and the Bhojas. Krishna, Sátyaki and Krita·varman are Vrishnis.

VRITRA A demon slain by Indra.

VYAGHRA·DATTA A warrior allied to the Pándavas.

VYASA A seer, supposed to have compiled the 'Maha·bhárata.'

YÁDAVA A people descended from Yadu and linked with the Vrishnis.

YAJNYA·SENA Drúpada.

YAJNYASÉNI Patronymic for Shikhándin and Dhrishta·dyumna.

YAMA God of the dead, son of Vivásvat.

YÁMUNA A river, the present Jamna.

YAUDHÉYA A people.

YÁVANA A people whom scholars have connected with the ancient Greeks.

YUDHA·MANYU A Panchála warrior allied to the Pándavas. Brother of Uttamáujas.

YUDHI·SHTHIRA Eldest of the Pándava brothers. Also known as Ajáta·shatru, Dharma·raja, Partha, Pándava, Kauntéya.

YUGAN·DHARA A Pándava warrior slain by Drona.

YUYUDHÁNA Pándava warrior also known as Sátyaki.

YUYÚTSU Son of Dhrita·rashtra and a woman of the merchant caste. Allied to the Pándavas.

INDEX

Sanskrit words are given in the English alphabetical order, according to the accented CSL pronuncuation aid. They are followed by the conventional diacritics in brackets.

Permitted finals:

k	ṭ	t	p	ṅ	n	m	(*Except* āḥ/aḥ) ḥ/r	āḥ	aḥ	*Initial letters:*
k	ṭ	t	p	ṅ	n	ṃ	ḥ	āḥ	aḥ	k/kh
g	ḍ	d	b	ṅ	n	ṃ	r	ā	o	g/gh
k	ṭ	c	p	ṅ	ṃś	ṃ	ś	āś	aś	c/ch
g	ḍ	j	b	ṅ	ñ	ṃ	r	ā	o	j/jh
k	ṭ	ṭ	p	ṅ	ṃṣ	ṃ	ṣ	āṣ	aṣ	ṭ/ṭh
g	ḍ	ḍ	b	ṅ	ṇ	ṃ	r	ā	o	ḍ/ḍh
k	ṭ	t	p	ṅ	ṃs	ṃ	s	ās	as	t/th
g	ḍ	d	b	ṅ	n	ṃ	r	ā	o	d/dh
k	ṭ	t	p	ṅ	n	ṃ	ḥ	ā	aḥ	p/ph
g	ḍ	d	b	ṅ	n	ṃ	r	ā	o	b/bh
ṅ	ṇ	n	m	ṅ	n	ṃ	r	ā	o	*nasals* (n/m)
g	ḍ	d	b	ṅ	n	ṃ	r	ā	o	y/v
g	ḍ	d	b	ṅ	n	ṃ	*zero*[1]	ā	o	r
g	ḍ	l	b	ṅ	l̃[2]	ṃ	r	ā	o	l
k	ṭ	c ch	p	ṅ	ñ ś/ch	ṃ	ḥ	āḥ	aḥ	ś
k	ṭ	t	p	ṅ	n	ṃ	ḥ	āḥ	aḥ	ṣ/s
gg h	ḍḍ h	dd h	bb h	ṅ	n	ṃ	r	ā	o	h
g	ḍ	d	b	ṅ/ṅṅ[3]	n/nn[3]	m	r	ā	a[4]	*vowels*
k	ṭ	t	p	ṅ	n	m	ḥ	āḥ	āḥ	*zero*

[1]ḥ or r disappears, and if a/i/u precedes, this lengthens to ā/ī/ū. [2]e.g. tān+lokān=tāl̃ lokān.
[3]The doubling occurs if the preceding vowel is short. [4]Except: aḥ+a=o '.